THE ART OF ILLUMINATED MANUSCRIPTS

ILLUSTRATED SACRED WRITINGS

BEING

A SERIES OF ILLUSTRATIONS

OF

THE ANCIENT VERSIONS OF THE BIBLE,

COPIED FROM

Illuminated Manuscripts,

EXECUTED BETWEEN THE FOURTH AND SIXTEENTH CENTURIES.

BY J. O. WESTWOOD, F.L.S.,

HONORARY AND CORRESPONDING MEMBER OF THE HISTORICAL, PHYSIOGRAPHICAL, PHILOMATIC, AND OTHER SOCIETIES OF PARIS, MOSCOW, LUND, LILLE, QUEBEC, BOSTON (U. S.) ETC.

ARCH CAPE PRESS
NEW YORK

Originally published under the title
Palæographia Sacra Pictoria
by William Smith, Fleet Street, London, 1843-5

This 1988 edition published by Arch Cape Press, a division of dilithium Press, Ltd.,
distributed by Crown Publishers, Inc., 225 Park Avenue South,
New York, New York 10003.

ISBN 0-517-66296-5

Printed and bound in Hong Kong

hgfedcba

PREFACE.

THE object of the present volume is to lay before the public a series of Illustrations of Ancient Art as varied in their style as could conveniently be obtained consistent with the desire, at the same time entertained, of rendering the work interesting by confining it to a single subject—of all others the most important—namely, the historical investigation of the Sacred Text of the Bible through the darkness of the middle ages.

The great truths of our holy religion are, in fact, so entirely dependent upon the purity of the received versions, and these equally so upon the genuineness and date of manuscripts, that in this respect alone the present volume may claim some degree of interest, forming, as it does, a kind of new Edition of the Vindiciæ Canonicarum Scripturarum of Blanchini, now more than a hundred years old, with this difference, namely, that the learned Father's object was to prove the correctness of the text of the Latin Vulgate, the version used by the Church to which he belonged ; whereas mine has been to show that in all ages versions of the Scriptures have been made into the mother tongue of almost every nation.

It is scarcely necessary to enter at any length into the question of the great value of illuminated manuscripts as affording a knowledge of the arts of design, ornamental and pictorial, at the period when executed. In Italy, it is true, the paintings of Herculaneum and Pompeii, and those of many of the catacombs, together with the frescoes and the mosaics of many of the most ancient churches still exist, exclusive of sculptures; but in Cisalpine countries we have but manuscripts and carved stones to tell the tale of ancient art, and even the latter of these resources are fast disappearing, although worthy of being preserved with almost religious care, evidencing, as they do in so many instances, the early state of religion in our land. On the other hand, the vast stores of manuscripts contained in our public and private collections, of the ornaments and drawings of which no fac-similes have yet been published, afford abundant materials to the artist in search of illustrations of the arts of composition, ornamental design, and illumination, through a period of nearly a thousand years, namely, from the 6th or 7th to the 16th or 17th centuries. With such invaluable materials, I have been able to offer a much more complete series of illustrations of ancient art, as practised in these islands, than had before been published ; and have thereby clearly established the fact of the existence of a native school of religion and art in our sister island, by a series of fac-similes from Irish MSS., executed between the 7th and 10th centuries, although the existence of such documents had been denied, not only by Astle and other palæographers, but also by the latest Irish historians. The collation of many of these MSS. has also furnished additional (although unlooked for) evidence that the ancient church in these islands was independent of Rome, and that it corresponded, on the contrary, with the Eastern churches.

The works published in this country illustrative of the various styles of art employed in manuscripts, are but few in number. Astle's excellent volume on the " Origin and Progress of Writing," now nearly fifty years old, is, as its title imparts, more expressly devoted to the various styles of writing ; and in this respect the 31 plates, with which it is illustrated, form an invaluable series of authorities, especially such as are devoted to the productions of our own country. The " Illuminated Ornaments" of Shaw are, on the other hand, especially confined to ornamental designs and patterns, as exhibited in MSS. from the 13th to the 16th centuries; whilst the various works of Strutt, and part of the first volume of the " Bibliographical Decameron " of Dibdin, and Shaw's " Dresses and Decorations," contain many engravings of miniatures from illuminated MSS.

On the Continent, D'Agincourt[1] has also furnished us with an elaborate series of materials upon this branch of the subject ; but his selections are almost entirely devoted to Greek and Roman art, and are also uncoloured. Many of the plates of Willemin's fine work,[2] and some of those of that of Du Sommerard,[3] are also especially devoted to the illustration of art exhibited in MSS. from the 9th to the 15th centuries ; nor must the excellent Treatise of Langlois[4] be forgotten.   None of these works, however, from their nature and objects, afford a combined idea of the style of writing (or palæography), ornamental writing (or caligraphy), ornamental details, exclusive of the writing (or illumination) and miniatures of MSS.   It is in the superb works of Silvestre and Champollion,[5] and the Comte Bastard, that we find such a combination of objects brought before the public in the highest possible style of art.

The object of the present volume is therefore to follow, at a very humble distance, the plan of these last-mentioned works, endeavouring, by a more extended illustration of our national palæographic monuments, than their materials could possibly furnish, to give a national character to the book ; which indeed was the more indispensable, because the style of art in these islands, from the seventh to the eleventh century, was infinitely more elaborate than that of any other existing, or, indeed, of any subsequent school ; and which, having been carried by the Anglo-Saxon missionaries to the Continent, became the origin of the styles employed in the finest MSS. executed abroad in those ages ; and even until the revival of art, in the thirteenth and fourteenth centuries.

With this object in view, I determined, in order not to extend the work beyond a moderate limit, to confine my researches to Theological, and indeed, for the most part, to MSS. of the Sacred Scriptures themselves, which, with very few exceptions, comprise a more important series of monuments of early art than those devoted to other subjects ; and which the sacred nature of the subject, and the devotion of our ancestors, have caused not only to be the most elegantly ornamented, but also the most carefully preserved.   The widely-extended inquiries made at the present day into the early history, antiquities, and writings of the Church, had likewise some weight in determining this selection ; whilst the MSS. of the more important versions and translations of the Scriptures into the different languages of Europe and Asia previous to the sixteenth century, would afford an interesting series of specimens of the arts of design, ornamental illumination, and caligraphy, as practised at various periods by the different nations for which these versions were made.

In illustrating the means by which a knowledge of the Divine Truths was, from age to age, imparted to the ancient nations of the world in their own tongues (of which great privilege the gift of tongues by the Holy Spirit, on the day of Pentecost, was but another mighty exemplification), it will be convenient to adopt the following classification of the versions of the Holy Scriptures :—

§ A.—Those written in the Original Languages of Scripture.

§ B.—Oriental Versions of the Scriptures.

§ C.—Western Versions ; divided into—

a. Those which are esteemed ancient, made either from the Greek, or Anti-Hieronymian Latin Versions.

b. Those of a more recent date made from the Vulgate, but antecedent to the invention of Printing.

§ A.—The HEBREW text of the Old Testament, as the earliest revelation of Divine Truth, of course takes the foremost place in our series.   The Samaritan version of the Pentateuch, written in the original Hebrew characters in use before the Captivity, affords a wonderful confirmation of the history of the Books of Moses ; as it is not to be supposed that the Samaritans would have adopted and translated the books of the Jews, unless

[1] Histoire de l'Art pas les Monuments, 6 vols. fol.

[2] Monuments Français inédits, pour servir à l'Histoire des Arts.

[3] Les Arts au Moyen Age.

[4] Essai sur la Caligraphie.   Rouen, 1841.

[5] Palæographie Universelle, 4 vols., comprising 300 plates, imperial folio; the price, unbound, being 70 guineas.

[6] Miniatures et Ornemens des Manuscrits.—Published at so enormous a price, that I believe there are not more than two copies in this country.

they had been received prior to the separation and enmity of the two people; the period, at the latest, of the return from the Captivity. The purity of the Hebrew text is thus confirmed; although the Jews, during the Captivity, relinquished their old mode of writing and adopted that of the Chaldees.

The GREEK text of the New Testament is now almost universally admitted to be the original language in which that portion of the Bible was written (the Greek Septuagint version of the Old Testament having been made two or three hundred years previously). The existing manuscripts of the Greek Scriptures have been classified by modern critics according to recensions or families; the most simple and approved of which is that of Professor Scholz, who considers that all the variations which exist in these MSS. are resolvable into their having been transcribed from Constantinopolitan or Alexandrian exemplars. The former he considers to have been, from the earliest times, the most strict and faithful recension. It was that which was principally used in the liturgical offices of the East, and its fidelity is argued from the exact uniformity of all the MSS. which can be traced historically to Constantinople, where the imperial power and patriarchal jurisdiction were so long centred. It is also consistent with the careful discipline of the Constantinopolitan Church, and with the exact quotations of the Greek fathers. On the other hand, the Alexandrian copies have been written with a considerable degree of carelessness, and do not appear to have been intended, even in the country where written, for reading in public service. The former of these recensions has been adopted in the Syriac, Mœso-Gothic and Sclavonic versions, and forms the basis of our modern text; whilst the latter was followed in several Latin, Coptic, and Ethiopic translations.[1]

§ B.—The command given by our Saviour to his disciples to go into all the nations and preach the Gospel to every creature, constitutes the great and leading feature of the Christian, as distinguished from the Jewish dispensation. In obedience to the commands of their Divine Master, his disciples and their followers passed into the countries adjacent to the Holy Land, translating the Scriptures into the language of each, so that "every creature"—"might be taught of God."

These ancient versions, which were thus executed in the East, are the following :—

1st. The SYRIAC, of which there are several dialects or revisions; namely, the *Peschito*, or Literal Version; the *Philoxinian* Version; the *Karkaphensian* Version; and the *Syro-Estrangelo* and *Palæstino-Syriac* Versions.

2nd. The EGYPTIAN, of which there are also several dialects; namely, the Coptic, Sahidic, Ammonian, and Bashmouric Versions.

3rd. The ETHIOPIC Version.

4th. The ARABIC Version.

5th. The ARMENIAN Version.

6th. The PERSIAN Version, mentioned by Chrysostom and Theodoret; but of which it does not appear that there are any fragments now extant,[2] and of which, therefore, no fac-simile is given in this work.

§ C.—It was, however, in the countries west of the Holy Land, and especially in imperial Rome, that a mightier revolution was to be effected by the introduction of the Gospel; and to which, in fact, the Christianity of Europe is almost entirely to be attributed.

a. We possess, indeed, ample proof that, almost at the earliest period of Christianity, translations of the Scriptures were made from the Greek into,

1st. The LATIN language; and that, in fact, they had become so numerous, before the time of St. Jerome, that it became requisite that a revision of them should be made with the original Greek, which was

---

[1] The reader will find an excellent view of the different systems of recensions of Greek manuscripts in the 2nd vol. of Horne's Introduction.

[2] There are, however, more modern versions of the Persian Scriptures (see Horne, ii. p. 233), especially of the Pentateuch executed about the 9th century, and of the Gospels, a MS. of which latter belonging to Dr. Pococke, dated 1314, supplied the Persian text in Walton's Polyglot.

effected by that learned Father of the Church; and which has ever since been, with several slight revisions, the text of the Scriptures adopted by the Romish Church. These more ancient Latin Versions are termed the OLD ITALIC or ANTE-HIERONYMIAN, and the corrected Version of St. Jerome that of the VULGATE.

At a very early period likewise, translations were made from the Greek or Ante-Hieronymian Versions into the following Western languages:—

2nd. The SCLAVONIAN, which has subsequently become the version of the Græco-Russian Church.

3rd. The MŒSO-GOTHIC Version of Ulphilas.

4th. The THEOTISC Version of ancient Germany; and

5th. The ANGLO-SAXON Version.

All of which, from their origin, necessarily possess a far higher importance in Biblical criticism than,

b. the following more recent versions, which were for the most part founded upon the Latin Vulgate; and which are, I believe, the whole of those which were executed previous to the invention of printing[1] (which event necessarily forms a terminus to our work). These are—

1st. The EARLY ENGLISH Version.

2nd. The EARLY FRENCH Version.

3rd. The EARLY GERMAN Version.

4th. The ICELANDIC Version.

5th. The HUNGARIAN Version.

6th. The BOHEMIAN Version.

7th. The ITALIAN Version.

———

The nature of the materials, as well as the palæographical peculiarities of ancient MSS. must now shortly engage our attention.

The materials of which books have been composed have been extremely varied, in various nations and in different periods of civilisation. Plates of lead, brass[2], and copper; bricks, stone[3], wood, and waxen tablets[4], were anciently employed for this purpose; and ivory was also used, according to Pomponius, for the laws of the Decemvirs. Chaucer also records its use for tablets, as at the present time :—

> " His fellow had a staffe tipped with horne,
> A pair of tables all of iverie,
> And a pointell polished fetouslie,
> And wrote alway the names . . ."—CHAUCER's *Sompner's Tale.*

At a later period the bark of trees (liber) formed the chief material in the composition of books, thence named *libri;* and this material is still employed in many parts of the East. Leaves also, especially of the palm-tree, were also employed; as in the Sybil leaves, described by Virgil:—

> " Fata canit *foliis*que notas et nomina mandat
> Quæcunque in *foliis* descripsit carmina virgo."—*Æneid.* lib. iii.

[1] See Preface, by the translators of King James's Bible; Marsh, History of Translations of the Scriptures, 8vo, London, 1812; Thompson and Orme, Historical Sketch of the Translations of the Scriptures, Perth, 1815, 8vo; Le Long, Bibliotheca Sacra, Paris, 2 vols. fol. 1723; Dr. Adam Clarke and J. B. B. Clarke, A concise View of the Succession of Sacred Literature, from the Invention of Alphabetic Characters to 1445, London, 1831-32, 2 vols. 8vo; Townley, Illustrations of Biblical Literature, London 1821, 3 vols. 8vo.

[2] The twelve tables graven on brass among the Romans; the two tables of brass written before the birth of Christ, discovered at Heraclea in 1722, and published by Mazochius in 1758; and the seven Eugubian tables,—may be cited as instances of this usage.

[3] Thus the Decalogue was written on two tables of stone; and Herodotus mentions a letter sent by Themistocles to the Ionians (lib. vii. cap. 22), which was written on plates of stone (ενταμνων εντοισι λιθοισι γραμματα).

[4] " Dextra tenet ferrum [*i. e.* stylum] vacuam tenet altera ceram ; Incipit et dubitat scribit damnatque tabellas," &c. (OVID *Metam.*)

The materials of books were afterwards derived from the Egyptian plant Papyrus, which, owing to its flexibility, was rolled up into a scroll [1], which was termed by the Romans *volumen*; whilst, as more durable and convenient, leather made from the skins of sheep and goats was also employed from the most early ages, as affirmed by Herodotus and Diodorus; and this was succeeded by the use of parchment and vellum, on which European MSS. were chiefly written, until the invention of paper. The finest and whitest vellum is generally indicative of great age in a MS. MSS. also written upon purple vellum are of great age and excessive rarity, having been evidently executed for the use of princes.

The origin of letters, the invention of the alphabet, the notation of language, the relative claims of ancient nations to the invention of letters, and the various classifications of language proposed by philologists, are intricate questions, into which, although more or less connected with the purely palæographic portion of this work, I do not consider it necessary to enter in this Preface, further than to observe that, with the exception of our Chaldaic or square Hebrew, Syriac, Ethiopic, and Arabic fac-similes (the letters of which may be traced to the ancient Hebrew or Samaritan alphabet and thence to the Phœnician), the various kinds of writing exhibited in our plates may be referred either to the Greek or Latin alphabets as their source (which latter, indeed, was also derived from the Greek).

The most ancient MSS. in Greek and Roman letters, as well as their immediate derivatives, are written in large and fine rounded characters, which have been termed UNCIALS, and of which fine examples may be seen in the plates of purple Greek MSS., Coptic MSS. (sp. 5), Græco-Latin MSS. (sp. 1, 2, and 4), the Gospels of St. Augustine, and Mœsogothic Gospels.

Manuscripts written in large square CAPITALS, similar to the fine letters employed upon coins, &c., are of extreme rarity, the finest known specimen being the fragment of Virgil in the collection of M. Pithou, engraved by Mabillon, and in the "Traité de Diplomatique." Such capitals we find more ordinarily employed for the headings of books and particular passages, as may be seen in our third plate of Gospels of Mac Durnan, the first plate from the Book of Kells, the Bibles of Alchuine and Charles the Bald, and the Coronation Gospels of the Anglo-Saxon kings.

A narrower kind of capitals, more negligently written, and with the tops and bottoms of the letters oblique, termed RUSTIC CAPITALS, was of more ordinary occurrence in ancient MSS., as well as in inscriptions; this being, in fact, the principal kind of writing discovered on the walls of Herculaneum, &c. MSS. entirely written in this character, are, however, of extreme rarity; examples exist in Vatican and Florence Virgils, the Prudentius of the Bibliothèque du Roi, and several pages, of which a facsimile is given in the plate of the Psalter of St. Augustine, which is the only specimen in this country. This kind of capitals was, however, of more common usage for the headings of chapters, &c.; as in the legend over the head of the Evangelist, in the plate from the Gospels of St. Augustine, and that over the miniature of the judgment of our first parents, in the plate from the Bible of Alchuine. These characters were thus partially employed even until the tenth or eleventh century, as in the specimen No. 6, in the plate of the Anglo-Saxon Books of Moses.

It is not to be supposed however, that these fine and large characters were employed in ordinary use. A running hand or CURSIVE *alphabet* was also practised, and this, when more slowly and carefully written, became what is termed the MINUSCULE alphabet; the chief difference between them being, that the former, on account of the celerity with which it was executed required the letters to be conjoined, whilst in the latter the letters were more usually written separate.[2] Our plate of the Greek Gospels will afford a good example of the later

---

[1] Papyrus (whence our name paper) became a principal article of commerce, both in Europe and Asia, it having been in use in Egypt (as Pliny asserts, lib. xiii. c. 11 & 13) three centuries before the reign of Alexander. This material was especially in use for charters and other diplomatic acts, many of which are still in existence. It was used for epistolary correspondence in Italy in the time of Charlemagne, and by the popes even in the 11th and 12th centuries. Specimens of early Greek and Coptic Papyri are given in the plates of this work.

[2] Casley's idea that minuscule letters were not invented before the 7th century is entirely fallacious.

Greek minuscule, whilst the finest specimens of Latin minuscule letters are found in the MSS. of the Caroline period, and which having suffered the degradation of the modern Gothic style during the 13th, 14th, and 15th centuries, were again renovated in the 16th; as may be seen in the plates from the Soanean Clovio, and the Prayer Book of King Sigismund.

Of the advantages to be obtained from a knowledge of the particular forms which have been given to the different letters at various periods, and by the scribes of various countries, there cannot, I conceive, be any reasonable doubt. To assert with Maffei, Ottley, &c., that nothing is more fallacious than the idea of being able to determine the ages of MSS. and ancient inscriptions from the particular forms of their characters, and that the existence of various national styles of writing is a mere fanciful suggestion,—are opinions perfectly untenable, and at variance with the truth of all palæographical science. An extreme case (but one which has been strenuously maintained at great length by Mr. Ottley, in the 26th volume of the Archæologia,) will be sufficient to prove the futility of the former of these assertions; this author having wasted great labour in endeavouring to prove that a MS. in the British Musuem, written in the renovated Caroline minuscule characters, was executed in the third or fourth century! As well might he have asserted that a MS. written in the modern Gothic letters was of the time of Charlemagne. As to the national characteristics of ancient writing, a simple inspection of a varied series of MS. such as are given in the elaborate plates of the Benedictines, or even in those of this work, will be sufficient to disprove the assertion of their non-existence. To affirm that the Anglo-Saxon, Lombardic, Caroline, and Visigothic styles of writing are not nationally characteristic, because, all are derived from the old Latin mode of writing, is not more contrary to the truth than to say that the German and English languages are not nationally distinct, because both are sprung from the same root.

The knowledge of these national characteristics in the style of writing, and the various modifications which have been introduced by time in each country, constitute the science of Palæography, first placed on a solid foundation by Mabillon[1], subsequently illustrated by Montfaucon[2], Baringius[3], Blanchini[4], Trombelli[5], the Benedictines Toustain and Tessin[6], Maffei[7], the Abbot Von Bessel[8], Walther[9], Hickes[10], Casley[11], Astle[12], Kopp[13], Wailly[14]; and lastly, Messrs. Silvestre and Champollion.

Our attention must now be directed to a concise notice of the various manners in which MSS. have been from time to time ornamented. We shall treat this branch of the subject by noticing,

    1st, The different modes by which the writing, that is, the letters themselves, were ornamented.

    2nd, The miniatures with which the text was illustrated; and,

    3rd, The ornamental borders, &c. with which MSS. were decorated.

    1st, The simplest mode in which an attempt at ornament was introduced into the most ancient MSS., consisted in the employment of different coloured inks, especially red, vermilion, cinnabar, or purple, and which was employed for writing the first two or three lines of each book, or even the first word—as may be seen in the plates of the Gospels and Psalter of St. Augustine, which are almost the oldest MSS. illustrated in this work. Subsequently the same coloured ink was employed for particular words and passages; sometimes for the heading of chapters (whence the term rubric), sometimes still more generally, as in the

---

[1] The chief work of this author is 'De Re Diplomatica,' libri vi.—1681. 2nd edition, greatly enlarged. Paris, 1709, fol.

[2] Palæographia Græca, fol. Paris, 1708. Ejusd. Diarium Italicum. Paris, 1702.

[3] Clavis Diplomatica. Hanover, 1737.

[4] Vindiciæ Canonicarum Scripturarum, &c. Romæ, 1740. fol. Ejusd. Evangel. quadruplex, 4 vols. fol. 1749.

[5] Arte di conoscere l'eta de codici, 1778.

[6] Nouveau Traité de Diplomatique, 6 vols. 4to, 1784.

[7] Istoria Diplomatica, Mantua, 1727. Ejusd. Verona Illustrata, Verona, 173.

[8] Chronicon Gottwicense, 2 vols. fol. 1732.

[9] Lexicon Diplomaticum, fol. Gotting. 1747.

[10] Linguarum veterum septentrionalium Thesaurus, 3 vols. fol. 1705.

[11] Catalogue of the King's MSS., 1734, 4to, with 16 plates.

[12] On the Origin of writing, 4to.

[13] Bilder und Schriften der Vorzeit, 1819. Ejusd. Palæo-Critica, 1817.

[14] Paléographie, 2 vols. fol. with plates, forming portion of the "Documents inédits de France," recently published.

In addition to which, the illustrated catalogues of the chief Continental MS. libraries contain much valuable information.

Anglo-Saxon Psalter at Cambridge, in which the Anglo-Saxon version throughout is written in red ink, and a MSS. in the Harleian Library (No. 2795) containing a Latin copy of the Gospels entirely written in red ink, in Caroline minuscule letters. In the oldest MSS. executed in this country, the red, and other colours. have been mixed up with some thick kind of varnish, which has rendered them almost imperishable [1]. Other coloured inks were also employed during the middle ages, especially blue and green; in addition to which, some of the most sumptuous MSS. are written, either partially or entirely, with gold and silver ink. The Golden Gospels in the Harleian library, and in the Bibliothèque du Roi, both written in fine uncials, and another copy of the Gospels in the former library, (No. 2797), in minuscule characters, are written throughout with golden ink.

Another mode of ornamenting the letters consisted in forming the initial letters of chapters (capitula, whence such letters are termed *capitals*), the first letter in a page, the first line, or title of a book, or even all the letters in the first page of a larger size than the text of the volume, and which were either plainly formed, or executed with a greater or less share of ornamental detail. The earliest MSS. present us with plain capitals, of a size somewhat larger than the text. (See the plates of early Greek and Græco-Latin MSS.)

But in the sixth and seventh centuries we meet with instances in which they are still larger (one or two inches high), and somewhat more ornamented in their design and diversified in their colours, in MSS. written in Italy; as in the Vatican Virgil, written in the large square capitals of the sixth century, the Theodosian Code at Munich of the sixth century, and the Morals of St, Gregory at Munich of the seventh or eighth century,—all figured by Silvestre. Another very early instance is given in our Plate of the Gospels of St. Augustine. It is, however, in Irish and Anglo-Saxon MSS. written between the end of the seventh and tenth centuries, that we find the most extraordinary instances of these enlarged and ornamented capitals, several of which are represented in our Plates. The delicacy and decision of the work in these gigantic letters, sometimes nearly a foot in height, are incredible; and the inventive skill displayed in the complicated flourishes. in which are generally intermixed the heads of strange lacertine animals [2], is both so singularly ingenious and elegant, that they far surpass in neatness, precision, and delicacy, all that is to be found in the ancient MSS. executed by Continental artists; and as it is well known that missionaries from these countries carried their religion and arts to many parts of the Continent, it is not unreasonable to assert that many of the splendid capital letters of the Caroline period were executed in imitation of the style of our earlier codices. In some of the finest Franco-Gallic MSS. however, we perceive a distinct style of ornaments introduced into these gigantic letters, evidently borrowed from the purer forms of classic art, consisting of elegant foliage, and other arabesque patterns; such indeed as occur in the remains of Herculaneum, and on the walls of the catacombs of the early Christians in Italy.

In fine Lombardic MSS. of the eighth to the twelfth centuries, we find the large capital letters blazoned with patches of different colours.

The earliest and finest MSS. executed in England and Ireland, are not ornamented with gold; but in the Caroline MSS. we find it abundantly used. Our MSS. also have the capitals almost invariably decorated with marginal rows of red dots, and the smaller ones with the open spaces daubed with various colours (as in the

---

[1] For want of some such varnish mixed with their colouring, the miniatures of early Greek MSS. are greatly—often entirely, defaced.

[2] The Benedictines favour us with the following amusing notion:—
" Les ornemens des lettres grises Anglo-Saxonnes semblent n'être le fruit que d'imaginations atroces et mélancoliques. Jamais d'idées riantes, tout se ressent de la dureté du climat. Lorsque la génie ne manque pas absolument, un fond de rudesse et de barbarie caractérise d'autant mieux les MSS. et les lettres historiées qu'on a plus affecté de les embellir."!!! (N. Tr. de Dipl. 2. 122.) Dr. O'Conor, in his

Epist. nuncup., has another idea as to the origin of the peculiarities of the Irish capitals scarcely less amusing.

Setting aside the idea that the constant introduction of these lacertine animals was the mere result of the caprice of the artist, it may be suggested that the worship of the ophidian reptiles, of which the Egyptian Euphrates was the founder, circ. A.D. 180, and which was combated by Sts. Irenæus and Epiphanius, might possibly have had some influence in the matter.

second plate of the Gospels of MacDurnan). The latter practice was also much in vogue on the Continent. Another equally common fashion was, to conjoin the capital letters of the heading of books, often almost unintelligibly. (See especially our plate of the Visigothic Apocalypse.) At a later period figures were introduced into these large capital letters, illustrating the text, of which an early instance occurs in the plate copied from the Bible of Alchuine. More decided instances might indeed be adduced, as for instance, the initial of the Psalm Exultate Deo, in some MSS. has the open spaces filled with figures, engaged in playing on various instruments; and the initial B of the Book of Psalms often contains in its open spaces, drawings, illustrating the life of the Psalmist, of which a splendid specimen is given by Langlois.

In many instances, indeed, the letters were formed of strangely contorted figures of animals [1], birds, &c. When human figures are thus employed, the capitals are termed anthromorphic; if animals, they are zoomorphic; if bird, ornithoid; if fish, ichthyomorphic; if serpents, ophiomorphic, and if plants or leaves are introduced, they receive the name of anthophylloid. A singular, and very extensive series of such capitals, is given by the Benedictines in their Vol. II., plate 19 [2]. Many curious specimens will also be found in the plates of this work.

It would, indeed, be an endless task to describe the peculiar modes in which these letters were ornamented, as they varied with the caprice or taste of the illuminator; but it may be mentioned, that in the eleventh and following centuries, these large capitals were generally painted of a light-blue, green, or red colour, and were often ornamented by a profusion of foliage and branches, interlacing each other in elegant but extremely intricate and curious circles; and that in the fourteenth century, long and often elegant scroll-like patterns were added to the letters, forming marginal ornaments to the page, often drawn with the pen alone, but displaying great freedom and taste.

During the fourteenth and fifteenth centuries, these capitals, although much reduced in size, were most elaborately painted in opaque colours, the open spaces of the letters filled in with foliage or flowers touched with opaque and especially white paint, with wonderful effect.

2nd. There is abundance of evidence to prove, that from the earliest period manuscripts have been ornamented with miniature paintings illustrating the text.

The splendid papyri of the Egyptians which have survived to our times, show that in eastern Africa the practice prevailed of painting the subjects of their works, and various Roman authors attest the same thing. Thus Pliny mentions (Hist. Nat. lib. xxv., c. 2) that certain physicians painted, in their works, the plants which they had described; and the same author (lib. xxxv. c. 2) describes the praises which Cicero, in his treatise entitled " *Atticus*," gives to Varro, who had introduced into his works not only the names, but also the effigies of more than 700 illustrious persons. Seneca also (De Tranquill. Anim. ix.) speaks of books ornamented *cum imaginibus*. Martial (Epigr. 186), says,

> " Quam brevis immensum cepit membrana Maronem,
> Ipsius vultus prima tabella gerit."

And Fabricius (Bibl. Lat. cura Ernesti, i. p. 125) gives the title of a work on miniature painting, by Varro, entitled " *Hebdomadum, sive de imaginibus libri.*"

The earliest MSS. with miniatures (and they are among the oldest which have survived to our times) simply contain small square drawings let into the text, without any ornamental adjuncts. The Imperial Library at Vienna possesses three of these invaluable relics : namely, a ROMAN CALENDAR, described by Lambecius, and

---

[1] The finest instance of this mode of treatment which I have met with is in the Gospels of Louis le Debonnaire in the Bibliothèque du Roi, in which each gospel commences with a large letter, formed of the respective Evangelical symbolical animal. The Gospels of Bishop Leofric, in the Bodleian Library, also contain some very curious capitals of this kind.

[2] Numerous other instances from Greek and Latin MSS. are cited by the Benedictines (N. Tr. de Dipl. ii. 117—120).

considered by Schwarz [1] as "*egregium vetustatis monumentum atque pulcherrimum Bibl. Vindobon. cimelium,*" containing allegorical figures of the Months, eight in number, each about eight inches high, finely draped and exquisitely drawn, and which are supposed to have been executed during the reign of Constantine, the son of Constantine the Great: the famous purple Greek CODEX GENESEOS, with forty-eight miniatures, and the DIOSCORIDES, written for the empress Juliana Anicia at the beginning of the sixth century, and ornamented with her own portrait and numerous miniatures and drawings of plants, whereof Lambecius gave a series of fac-similes, in nine folio copper plates.

The Vatican possesses part of a VIRGIL [2] profusely ornamented with miniatures, possibly not later than the time of Constantine the Great; whereof copies have been published by D'Agincourt and others, and of which there is a fac-simile among the Lansdowne MSS. in the British Museum, executed by Bartoli. Another MS. of VIRGIL was until lately [3] also in the Vatican library, which is ascribed to the fourth or fifth century by most authors, being written in large fine rustic capitals; but which D'Agincourt, on account of the rudeness of the drawings, places in the twelfth or thirteenth. [4]

The Ambrosian Library at Milan contains a MS. of part of the ILIAD, of very remote date, with miniatures, which I believe, however, have not yet been published, although long announced by Professor Maio. (Dibdin, Bibl. Dec. I. p. xlii.)

The famous Syriac Book of the Gospels in the library of Florence, contains many drawings, also executed in the sixth century, and which is described in the article on Syriac MSS.

The libraries of our own country can boast of some relics of not later date than any of the above: namely, the Codex Cottonianus Geneseos, probably of the fourth century; and the Gospels of St. Augustine, with its miniatures, most probably of the sixth (both illustrated in this work); and the Golden Greek Canons (Brit. Mus. MS. Add., No. 5111), elaborately illustrated by Mr. Shaw, and also referred by Sir F. Madden, to the sixth century.

In most of these MSS. the drawings are not destitute of some of the pure classical taste of former ages; but in Continental MSS. of the two or three succeeding centuries, we find a great decrease in energy of expression and elegance of design: indeed but very few illuminated MSS. can be pointed out as having been certainly executed between the sixth and ninth centuries, at the commencement of which latter period the genius of the great Charlemagne instilled fresh vigour both into literature and the fine arts. In the few, however, which remain to us, a certain influence of the antique art may be traced, although greatly decreasing in purity.

In our own country, notwithstanding the extraordinary skill manifested in the ornamenting of MSS., the art of miniature painting had fallen during the seventh and eighth centuries to its lowest ebb; it is, indeed, impossible to imagine anything more childish than the miniatures contained in the splendid Hibernian and Anglo-Saxon MSS. of this period. Neither can it be said to have materially improved between the eighth and eleventh centuries, the drawing of the human figure being rude, and the extremities singularly and awkwardly attenuated, and the draperies fluttering in all directions.

The miniatures, indeed, of the splendid Caroline Bibles exhibit a strong influence of Byzantine art; and the engravings of D'Agincourt fully prove that the Greek artists during this period had not fallen so low as their brethren of Western Europe. Our own libraries are, unfortunately, lamentably deficient in illuminated Greek MSS. of this period; the Evangelistiaria (which are the chief ornamented MSS. which we possess), repeating with dull monotony the figures of the Evangelists seated writing, stiff and lifeless in expression. The

---

[1] De ornamentis Librorum veter. 1756, 4to. p. 38.

[2] The miniatures of the Vatican Terence, described by Dibdin (Bibl. Decam. i. p. 40), and others as contemporary with those of the Virgil, are of the 9th century; the Vatican MS., 3226, of the 5th century, having been confounded by De la Rue, &c., with No. 3868 of the 9th.

[3] It is stated by Langlois and D'Agincourt, that this MS. has been restored to the Bibliothèque du Roi.

[4] Perhaps it would be impossible to give a greater proof of the effects produced by almost blindly following out a favourite theory, than is to be found in this supposition of D'Agincourt, which is only equalled by the idea of Mr. Ottley, that the Aratus with miniatures in the British Museum is of the 2nd or 3rd century.

Bibliothèque du Roi possesses two noble Greek MSS. of the ninth and tenth centuries[1], in which we trace many traditions of classic art. In one a female figure of Night clad in a black robe, and a veil sprinkled with stars, and holding a reversed flambeau, is highly allegorical; nor is the Journey of the Israelites through the desert, protected by the cloud and pillar of fire, less so. In a fine series of Greek drawings in the Vatican (figured by D'Agincourt), there are many similar traditions of ancient art: as, for instance, the city of Gabaon represented as a female full of anxiety; and in a Latin MS. of the ninth century, in the Bibl. du Roi, the river Jordan is typified by two figures holding vases, one bearing the letters IOR, and the other DAN, from which a flood of water is discharged. (See also the Baptism of Christ, in the Benedictional of St. Ethelwold.)

But if the miniatures of Western Europe in these and the one or two succeeding centuries be deficient in artistic skill, they amply compensate us by the invaluable materials which they furnish of the architecture, costume, armour, amusements, ceremonies, &c., of the people at the different periods when executed, because it appears to have been almost the invariable custom to represent the various persons, &c., in the costume of the period. Thus in the Anglo-Saxon copies of the drawings of the MSS. of Aratus above referred to, and engraved in Mr. Ottley's Memoir, we find that the Anglo-Saxon artist had completely given an Anglo-Saxon character to his Continental originals; and thus at a later period we see (in our plate of early French MSS.) the soldiers of King Herod in helmets furnished with the nasal, and the weeping mothers of Judea clad in the fashions of the twelfth century; whilst the Church of Laodicea is transformed into a Moorish temple in our plate from the Visigothic Apocalypse.

For nearly two centuries previous to the Conquest, most of the miniatures executed in this country were drawn in coloured outlines, often with considerable freedom, although but little skill was evinced in the design, and of which specimens are given in several of our Anglo-Saxon plates[2]; but in the twelfth century a totally different style was introduced (possibly brought from the East, where it had long prevailed), namely, employing very rich but opaque colours for the figures, drawn with heavy black outlines with solid, highly burnished gold, backgrounds. Possibly two of the finest examples of this style, are the Bestiarium of the Ashmolean Museum at Oxford, and the Psalter of St. Louis in the library of the Arsenal at Paris. This style remained in vogue until the second half of the thirteenth century, in which we begin to perceive an evident improvement, both in the design and execution of the miniatures of MSS., and correcter perspective in the backgrounds.

During the long reign of King Henry III. in England, who was fond of the arts, painting gradually improved, as may be easily conceived from the following singular and interesting entry in the Close Rolls of the thirty-sixth year of his reign:—" Mandatum est Radulpho de Dungun *custodi librorum regis*, quod magistro Willielmo *pictori regis* habere faciat colores ad depingendum parvam garderobam reginæ et emendendum picturam magnæ cameræ regis et cameræ reginæ."

During the fourteenth century the miniatures of Western Europe strongly exhibit the influence of Gothic architecture, in the lively flowing motions of the figures and drapery, and the more natural expression of the features; the outlines being but slightly traced with the pen, the surfaces painted with water-colours, but only with slight indications of the shadows. Towards the end of this century we find a beautiful effect produced by the backgrounds of the miniatures being elaborately tesselated in minute patches of gold and contrasted colours, with delicate geometrical patterns formed of paler opaque lines.

---

[1] These two MSS. are cited by Waagen, to disprove Mr. Ottley's idea, that the MS. of Aratus, in the Harleian Library, is of the 2nd or 3rd century, the miniatures in these Greek MSS. being much nearer to the paintings of Pompeii than those of the Aratus MS.

[2] Other instances may be seen in a series of little sketches, of the occupations of each month, in an Anglo-Saxon calendar in the Cottonian Library, of which Shaw has given excellent fac-similes (Dresses and Decorations, vol. i.), and in a small Psalter of the 10th century, also in the Cottonian Library (Titus, D. xxvii.), a fac-simile from which is given by Dibdin, which was executed at Hyde Abbey or Newminster, which was celebrated for the beauty of its MSS., amongst which may be mentioned the incomparable Benedictional of St. Ethelwold, belonging to the Duke of Devonshire, and fully illustrated (but not in colours) in the 24th volume of the Archæologia, which from the splendour of its execution forms almost an isolated exception to the general characteristics of the later Anglo-Saxon MSS.

The zeal with which the fine arts were cultivated in the monasteries during the thirteenth, fourteenth, and fifteenth centuries—of which our finest churches offer such magnificent examples—is also fully proved by the immense number of illuminated devotional works which have come down to our times. Missals, Breviaries, Hours, Lectionaria, Benedictionals, Pontificalia, and Choral books of immense size (which are still used in some of the cathedrals abroad), occur in every collection, more or less decorated with the monkish painter's art. " Oui, certes," exclaims Langlois, " c'est en robe noire, la tête couverte de *cucullus*, et ceinte de la couronne monacale, que dans les Gaules " [he might have added, throughout the civilised world], " la science est descendue des dernierès époques romaines jusqu'à nos jours." In addition to these kinds of works, romances, legends, and chronicles, formed the standard of lighter reading; and these we accordingly also find brilliantly illuminated, and very frequently adorned with a frontispiece, in which the author is represented presenting his work to the monarch or other patron for whom it was intended.

It is chiefly in MSS. executed at this period by French or Flemish artists, that we find the great perfection of the art; as those executed in Italy, with a few exceptions, still retained much of the dry narrowless style of the later Greek school; in which, with unmeaning figures, a curious effect was produced by the greenish tone of the shades of the flesh tints. The historical circumstances of this period may possibly have contributed to the almost constant employment of Flemish and French artists by the English. The city of Bruges was, indeed, especially celebrated for its illuminators; and it was here that John Van Eyck practised the art of miniature painting.

The revival of art by Cimabue, Giotto, &c., indeed, materially influenced the taste and style of the miniature painters of MSS., as it was a common circumstance that they also practised the art of designing the larger productions of the pencil, as was indeed the case with Giotto, Simone Nenni, Pietro Perugino, Lucas van Leyden, Julio Clovio, &c., by whom, in the fifteenth and sixteenth centuries, the art of illumination was brought to its highest state of excellence, when it was eclipsed by the printing press. Still for a considerable period the illuminator's art was called into use to fill up the blanks left in the early printed books, in order that they might have as much the appearance of manuscripts as possible; but after the middle of the sixteenth century the art was almost laid aside, or only taken up for some very particular object. Perhaps the latest illuminated MS. executed on the Continent is the immense Graduale preserved at Rouen, the wonder of all beholders, and the work of the monk D'Eaubonne, whose entire life (in the seventeenth century) was devoted to its completion. The capitals in this MS. are of very large size, painted to represent the most beautiful marbles, and ornamented with natural flowers, and the miniatures would not have been unworthy of Julio Clovio himself; whilst in our own country a volume of moral sentences, ornamented with " grace, beauty, and delightful caprice," and selected by Sir Nicolas Bacon for the Lady Lumley (Brit. Mus. MSS. Reg. 17, A. xxiii.), and the fine Lectionarium of Cardinal Wolsey, still preserved at Christ Church College, Oxford, are amongst the latest specimens of the illuminator's skill.[1]

In addition to the various catalogues of the chief MSS. libraries at home and abroad, the works of Montfauçon,[2] Strutt,[3] Dibdin,[4] Willemin,[5] D'Agincourt,[6] Du Sommerard,[7] Shaw,[8] Langlois,[9] Didron,[10] Silvestre

---

[1] A fac-simile from the latter MS. will be found in our " Illuminated Illustrations of the Bible," which, both in the design and colouring of the original, reminds us strongly of the subsequent school of Rubens.

[2] Monumens de la Monarchie Française, 1755, 5 vols., fol.

[3] Regal and Ecclesiastical Antiquities of England, 1773, 1793, and 1842, (edited by J. R. Planche). Ejusd. Manners and Customs of the Inhabitants of England, 3 vols., 4to., 1774-6. Dresses and Habits of the People of England, 2 vols. 4to., 1796-9. Sports and Pastimes, 1801, 4to.

[4] Bibliographical Decameron, vol. i. ; and Bibliogr. and Antiquarian Tour in France, &c., 3 vols. 8vo.

[5] Monumens Français inédits pour servir à l'Histoire des Arts. Paris, 2 vols. fol.

[6] Histoire de l'Art par les Monuments. 6 vols. fol.

[7] Les Arts au Moyen Age.

[8] Illuminated Ornaments, copied from MSS. of the Middle Ages, with an Introduction by Sir F. Madden. 1 vol. small folio.—Ejusd. Dresses and Decorations of the Middle Ages, 2 vols., London, 1843.

[9] Essai sur la Caligraphie des Manuscrits du Moyen Age. Rouen, 1841.

[10] Iconographie Chrétienne, Histoire de Dieu, 4to., Paris, 1843.

and Champollion,[1] Humphreys,[2] Denon and Duval,[3] Maitland,[4] the Count Bastard, and our own Illuminated Illustrations of the Bible above referred to, as well as various Memoirs published in the volumes of the Archæologia, and a series of short papers in the Penny Magazine for 1839,—are worthy of examination in connexion with the subject before us. A work on the subject by Waagen has also been announced.

3rd. The merely ornamental accessories of Manuscripts will not detain our attention long. In the earliest MSS. we find some slight attempt at ornament at the end of the different portions of a work, consisting of crosses or small scrolls in different coloured inks ; as may be seen in the Codex Alexandrinus at the British Museum. The finest early MSS. of the Gospels were also ornamented with ornamental columns of an architectural character, inclosing the Eusebian Canons ; and upon which, in Anglo-Saxon and Caroline MSS., vast labour was bestowed. Perhaps the earliest instance of this custom appears in the beautiful golden Greek Canons, figured by Shaw; and in the famous Syriac Gospels of the 6th century, the ornaments of which latter appear indeed to have been the originals of many which are found in the early Anglo-Saxon and Irish MSS., and which certainly have no prototype in the classical ornaments of Italy during the few centuries succeeding the commencement of the Christian era. It is also not a little curious to find the same style of interlaced ribands in Egyptian[5] and Ethiopic MSS. Our plate of the Gospels of St. Augustine, of the 6th century, offers a valuable illustration of the state of art in Italy during that period, and shows that the pure arabesque of the finest period of Roman art was not entirely lost.

Early Greek MSS. of the Scriptures are generally ornamented with beautiful headings at the commencement of each book, running across the top of the page, (a style adopted subsequently in Armenian and Sclavonic MSS.,) the lateral margins of the pages being rarely adorned with arabesques or ornamental borders. In the early illuminated Anglo-Saxon and Irish MSS. we find borders extending entirely or partially round the page ; the former generally broken into small portions, each consisting of a different pattern, and the latter mostly formed to represent some gigantic animal, with the head at the top of the page, and the legs and feet at the bottom : instances of which may be seen in our plates, from the Gospels of Mac Durnan and the Psalter of Ricemarchus. A few of the very finest have a page entirely covered with elaborate tessellations opposite the commencement of each Gospel, of which we find no similiar instances in Continental MSS. At a later period a very splendid style of ornamental border was introduced by the Anglo-Saxon artists, of which the Continental MSS. offer no instance, and of which a specimen is given in the plate of the Gospels of King Canute.

In the fine MSS. of the Caroline school, we find the pages and columns sometimes entirely surrounded with narrow borders, in which foliage of all kinds is represented in opaque colours. (See the plate from the Evangelistiarium of Charlemagne.)

At a still later period, (12th, 13th, and 14th centuries,) the borders of MSS. were ornamented by long scroll-like patterns, springing from the illuminated capitals; often consisting of red and blue lines, drawn with the pen, or broader, more ornamental, and enriched with colours and gold, and in which grotesques of all kinds were introduced with a more or less lavish hand.

During the 14th and 15th centuries, MSS. were generally ornamented with distinct borders, in which blue and golden Gothic architectural foliage were introduced, with natural flowers, and the open spaces adorned with little golden radiated stars ; amongst which, at the foot or sides of the page, were generally emblazoned the arms of the person for whom the volume was written, with the same kind of architectural foliage at the sides, and which is maintained to the present time by heraldic painters.

[1] Palæographie Universelle, 4 vols. large fol., Paris.

[2] Illuminated Illustrations of Froissart, 2 vols. 8vo.—Ejusd. The Illuminated Books of the Middle Ages, fol., in parts.

[3] Monumens des Arts du Dessin chez les Peuples tant anciens que modernes rec. par Denon, et décrites par A. Duval, Paris, 1839, 4 vols. fol.

[4] A series of Papers on Sacred Art, published in the Brit. Mag. 1842. See also the Bibliothèque Protypographique, ou Librairies des Fils du Roi Jean, Charles V., Jean de Berri, Philippe de Bourgogne et les siens. 4to. Paris, 1830.

[5] In a little work on Egypt recently published by C. Knight, there are engravings of torques precisely similar to those found in Ireland.

Many of these borders in the 15th century have the backgrounds of gold, which, however, became at length a very slight wash ; with flowers, buds, and insects, painted with great regard to nature, and appearing raised by shades thrown beneath them.

These peculiarities are more especially evident in English, French, and Flemish MSS. ; whereas, during the 15th and 16th centuries, different styles of ornament were employed in the margins of MSS., consisting in many cases of arabesques in a purely classical style, and decorated with miniatures, representations of gems, and marbles, &c., often executed in a marvellously beautiful manner. Complicated scroll-work patterns, enriched with coloured grounds, and with little white dots and golden stars, characterize the borders of many Italian MSS. of the 14th and 15th centuries.

ERRATA.

GRÆCO-LATIN MS. Page 5, line 29, *read* ολιγοστος.

— 37, — adtende.

last line, — carnis resurrectione.

GOSPELS OF MAC DURNAN. Page 11, line 43, *read* supersubstantialem, and (col. ii.) pl. 59, instead of pl. 46.

12, The letter p is occasionally misprinted in the Anglo-Saxon instead of *p*.

PSALTER OF KING ATHELSTAN. Page 2, line 18, *read* annus *incarnationis* Domini.

4, — 21, — Glā in excelsis dō et sūp trā pax.

GOSPELS OF KING CANUTE. Page 1, line 14, *read* narrationem.

CORONATION ON THE BOOK OF THE ANGLO-SAXON KINGS. Page 2, line 28, I have ascertained that this miniature belonged to the Psalter of King Henry VI. (Domit. XVII), being the illumination of the 52nd Psalm. The coats of arms are more recent.

Page 4, line 13. The long stroke alluded to is intended for the cross of the t. It is not quite correctly represented in the plate.

LOMBARDIC MSS. Page 2, line 27, *read* dixit hoc *et* uxoribus.

ANGLO-SAXON BOOKS OF MOSES. Page 4, line 34, *for* Ethitbal *read* Ethilbal.

PSALTER OF ST. AUGUSTINE. Page 5, line 13, *for* centu *read* CENTUM.

DIRECTIONS TO THE BINDER.

It is suggested that it will be most convenient to arrange the Plates of this work in accordance with the following Index, founded upon the different Versions of the Bible.

LIST OF THE MANUSCRIPTS,

WHEREOF FAC-SIMILES ARE GIVEN IN THIS WORK.

[The N°. at the end of each MS., enclosed in brackets, refers to the arrangement of the Plates given in the Directions to the Binder.]

LONDON.

British Museum.   Cottonian MSS.

Samaritan Pentateuch. Claudius, B. 8. [No. 1.]
Greek Book of Genesis, with Miniatures, Sæc. 4 ? [No. 3.]
Fragments of Purple Greek Gospels. Sæc. 4. Titus, C. xv. [No. 4.]
Latin Psalter. Galba, A. 5. Sæc. xi. ? [No. 18.]
Latin Psalter of King Athelstan, Sæc. viii. and ix. [No. 22.]
Coronation Gospels of the Anglo-Saxon Kings. Sæc. ix. Tiberius, A. 2. [No. 22.]
Latin Psalter of King Henry VI. Sæc. 15. Domitian, xvii. [No. 32.]
Anglo-Saxon Heptateuch of Ælfric. Claudius, B. iv., Sæc. xi. [No. 39.]
Latin and Anglo-Saxon Psalter of St. Augustine. Sæc. v., vii., x. Vespasian, A. i. [No. 40.]
Latin and Anglo-Saxon Psalter. Tiberius, c. vi. Sæc. 11. [No. 41.]
Latin and Anglo-Saxon Gospels of Lindisfarne. Nero, D. iv., Sæc. vii. [No. 45.]
Theotisc Gospel Harmony. Caligula, A. 7. Sæc. x. [No. 38.]
Latin and Norman French Psalter. Nero, C. 4, Sæc. xii. [No. 47.]

Royal MSS.

Codex Alexandrinus. Sæc. 5 ? [No. 3.]
Purple Latin Gospels. Sæc. viii., 1 E. vi. [No. 21.]
Latin Gospels of King Canute. Sæc. x., 1 D. 9. [No. 23.]
Prayer Book of King Henry VII. Sæc. xv. [No. 34.]
Prayer Book of King Henry VIII. Sæc. xvi. [No. 34.]
Psalter of King Henry VIII. Sæc. xvi. [No. 34.]
Latin and Anglo-Saxon Psalter. Sæc. ix., 2 B. 5. [No. 42.]
Russian Psalter. 16 B. 2. [No. 37.]

Harleian MSS.

Hebrew Old Testament. Nos. 5710, 5711. [No. 1.]
Greek Gospels. No. 1810, Sæc. xi. [No. 3.]
Greek Gospels. No. 5790, Sæc. xv. [No. 5.]
Latin Gospels of Maelbrigte. Sæc. xii. [No. 18.]
Latin Gospels. Sæc. xii. ? [No. 18.]
Sclavonian Gospels. No. 6311. [No. 37.]
Græco-Sclavonian Psalter. No. 5723. [No. 37.]

Burney MSS.

Fragments of Armenian Gospels. No. 277. [No. 9.]

Arundel MSS.

Greek Evangelistiarium. No. 547, Sæc. 10. [No. 3.]

Egerton MS.

English Wickliffe Bible. No. 618, Sæc. xv. [No. 46.]

Additional MSS.

Greek Psalter on Papyrus. Sæc. ix.? [No. 3.]
Syriac New Testament. No. 7157, Sæc. viii. [No. 6.]
Syriac Evangelistiarium. No. 7170. [No. 6.]
Syriac Biblical Glossary. No. 7183, Sæc. xii. [No. 6.]
Fragment of Coptic Gospels on Papyrus. Sæc. vi. ? [No. 7.]
Arabic Gospels. No. 11,856. [No. 8.]
Latin Bible of Alchuine. Sæc. ix. [No. 25.]
Latin (Visigothic) Apocalypse. Sæc. xii., No. 11,695. [No. 30.]
Icelandic Prayer Book. No. 503, Sæc. xv. ? [No. 49.]

Archiepiscopal Library, Lambeth.

Latin Gospels of MacDurnan. Sæc. viii. [Nos. 13, 14, 15.]
Latin and Anglo-Saxon Psalter. Sæc. x. [No. 42.]

Library of the Dean and Chapter of Westminster.

The Liber Regalis. Sæc. xiv. [No. 31.]

Library of the British and Foreign Bible Society.

Ethiopic Gospels.   [No. 7.]
   Ditto   [No. 7.]

Library of the Soanean Museum.

Latin Commentary on the Acts, illuminated by Julio Clovio. [No. 35.]

Library of the late Duke of Sussex.

Hebrew Pentateuch. [No. 1.]
Hebrew Pentateuch, in the Rashi character. [No. 1.]
Hebrew Pentateuch of Rabbi Jachiel. [No. 2.]
Armenian Gospels. Sæc. xiii. (now in Brit. Mus.) [No. 9.]
Prayer Book of King Sigismund of Poland (now in the Brit. Mus.) [No. 36.]
English New Testament. Sæc. xv. [No. 46.]
French Apocalypse. Sæc. xv. [No. 47.]
German Apocalypse. Sæc. xv. [No. 48.]
Italian Commentary on Apocalypse. Sæc. xv. [No. 50.]
Italian History of the Pentateuch. Sæc. xv. [No. 50.]

Library of the Rev. J. Tobin.

Latin Prayer Book of Mary of Burgundy. [No. 33.]

DUBLIN.

Library of Trinity College.

The Book of Kells. Sæc. vii. [No. 16, 17.]
Latin Gospels of St. Columba. Sæc. vi. ? [No. 19.]
Latin-Hibernian Liber Hymnorum. Sæc. ix. ? [No. 19.]

LIST OF THE MANUSCRIPTS WHEREOF FAC-SIMILES ARE GIVEN IN THIS WORK.

Latin Ante-Hieronymian Gospels. Sæc. vi. [No. 19.]
Archbishop Usher's Latin Gospels. Sæc. viii. ? [No. 19.]
Gospels of St. Mulling. Sæc. vii. [No. 19.]
Gospels of Dimma. Sæc. vii. [No. 19.]
Psalter of Ricemarchus. Sæc. xi. [No. 20.]

Library of Sir W. O'Doneil.

Psalter of St. Columba. Sæc. vii. ? [No. 19.]

Library of ————.

The Book of Armagh. Sæc. vii. [No. 19.]

OXFORD.

Bodleian Library.

Samaritan Pentateuch. Pococke, No. 5. [No. 1.]
Samaritan-Arabic Pentateuch. Arch, C. 2, 3128. [No. 1.]
Coptic-Arabic Gospels. Sæc. xii. [No. 7.]
Coptic Lectionarium. [No. 7.]
Græco-Latin Acts of Apostles. Sæc. v. ? No. 182. [No. 10.]
Fragments of Græco-Latin Old Testament. Sæc. viii. ? N. E. D. 2, 19. [No. 10.]
Latin Gospels of St. Augustine. Sæc. vi. Bodl. 857. [No. 11.]
Latin (Lombardic) Evangelistiarium (Douce, 176.) Sæc. x. [No. 28.]
Latin (Lombardic) Lectionarium Can. Bibl., 61. Sæc. xi. ? [No. 29.]
Latin (Lombardic) Psalter (Mr. Douce's.) Sæc. xi. ? [No. 29].
Anglo-Saxon Heptateuch of Ælfric. Sæc. xi. [No. 39.]
Paraphrase of the Pseudo-Cædmon. Sæc. xi. [No. 39.]
Latin and Anglo-Saxon Psalter. Sec. x. Junius 27. [No. 41.]
Latin and Anglo-Saxon Gospels of MacRegol (Codex Rushworthanus.) Sæc. viii. [No. 44.]
Anglo-Saxon Gospels. Hatton, No. 38. Sæc. xiii. [No. 45.]
Anglo-Saxon Gospels. N. E. F. 3, 15, Sæc. xi. [No. 45.]
Anglo-Saxon "Ormulum." Junius 1, Sæc. xii. [No. 46.]
English "Sowlehele." No. 779. Sæc. xiv. [No. 46.]
French Psalter. Sæc. xiii. (Douce Lib.) [No. 47.]
Bohemian New Testament. Sæc. xvi. [No. 49.]

CAMBRIDGE.

Public Library.

Syriac Pentateuch from Travancore. [No. 6.]
Græco-Latin Codex Bezæ. Sæc. v. ? [No. 10.]
Latin and Anglo-Saxon Psalter. F. f. 1, 23. Sæc. xi. [No. 41.]
Anglo-Saxon Gospels of Leofric. Sæc. xi. [No. 45.]

Library of Corpus Christi College.

Latin Gospels of St. Augustine. Sæc. vi., No. 286. [No. 11.]
St. Augustine on the Trinity. Sæc. xi. [No. 20.]
Anglo-Saxon Gospels of Ælfric. Sæc. xi. [No. 45.]

Library of St. John's College.

Latin Psalter. Sæc. ix. ? [No. 18.]

Library of Trinity College.

Latin, Anglo-Saxon, and Norman-French Psalter of Eadwine. [No. 43.]

LICHFIELD.

Gospels of St. Chad. Sæc. vii. [No. 12.]

STONYHURST COLLEGE.

St. Cuthbert's Gospel of St. John. Sæc. vii. [No. 11.]

PARIS.

Bibliothèque du Roi.

Latin Bible of Charles the Bald. Sæc. ix. [No. 26.]
St. Augustine on the Heptateuch. Sæc. ix. [No. 28.]
Latin and Anglo-Saxon Psalter. Sæc. xi. [No. 42.]
St. Isidore's Epistles in Latin and Theotisc. Sæc. ix. [No 38.]

Bibliothèque du Louvre.

Latin Evangelistiarium of Charlemagne. Sæc. viii. [No. 24.]

Library of the Arsenal.

Greek Psalter of Sedulius. Sæc. ix. [No. 3.]

ROUEN.

The Psalter of St. Ouen. [No. 20.]

RHEIMS.

Latin Lectionarium. [No. 30.]
Sclavonic Evangelistiarium. [No. 37.]

VIENNA.

Purple Greek Evangelistiarium. Sæc. ix. [No. 4.]
Theotisc Paraphrase of the Gospels. Sæc. ix. [No. 38.]
Hungarian Bible. Sæc. xiv. [No. 49.]

MUNICH.

Theotisc Paraphrase on the Canticles. Sæc. xi. [No. 38.]

UPSAL.

Mœsogothic Gospels of Ulphilas. Sæc. iv. ? [No. 49.]

ROME.

Sclavonian Evangelistiarium. Sæc. xi. [No. 37.]

VERONA.

Græco-Latin Psalm. Sæc. vi. [No. 10.]

Samaritan & Hebrew Mss.

Jacobus Usserius Armachanus Hibernia Primus

SAMARITAN AND HEBREW BIBLICAL MANUSCRIPTS.

THE authenticity of the books of Scripture, as the foundation of the religion both of the Jew and the Christian, is in a great measure involved in the history of its Biblical monuments.

From various passages in the Old Testament it appears that the sacred books of the Jews were *written* and deposited by the side of the Ark of the Covenant[1]. In the reign of Josiah there was indeed no other book of the law extant besides that found in the Temple by Hilkiah, from which, by his order, copies were made and distributed among the people, who carried them with them into their Captivity at Babylon.

During the Captivity, Daniel alludes to " the Law of Moses, the servant of God,[2] " and immediately after the return from Captivity we find Ezra, " a ready scribe in the law of Moses, which the Lord God of Israel had given[3] " together with Joshua and others, reading and " causing the people to understand" the law[4], by which is to be understood that they translated it out of the old Hebrew, in which it was at first written, into the Chaldee, which had then become the common language of the people. It is indeed a tradition universally adopted by Jews and Christians, that, about fifty years after the Temple was rebuilt, Ezra, assisted by the great synagogue, settled the Canon of the Old Testament. This genuine collection of the sacred text was placed in the Temple, the compositions of Ezra himself, Nehemiah, and Malachi, the last of the prophets, being subsequently added. " It cannot now be ascertained whether Ezra's copy of the Scriptures was destroyed by Antiochus Epiphanes, when he pillaged the Temple, nor is it material, since we know that Judas Maccabeus repaired the temple, and replaced everything requisite for the performance of Divine Worship[5], which included a correct, if not Ezra's own, copy of the Scriptures[6]. This copy, whether Ezra's or not, remained in the Temple till Jerusalem was taken by Titus, and it was then carried in triumph to Rome and laid up with the purple vail in the royal palace of Vespasian."

Numerous passages in the New Testament, Josephus, &c., proving the fact of the collection of the Old Testament Scriptures into a single volume—many quotations from them in the New Testament; and the specification of the books by Origen, who enumerates twenty-two (in which he coincides with Josephus[8])—all sufficiently attest that the canon of the Old Testament was settled at the commencement of the Christian era.

The genuineness of the Hebrew text was preserved after the destruction of Jerusalem by the sedulous care of learned academies, which flourished at Tiberias, Babylon, and other places, from the first to the twelfth century. The date of the Masorah is generally fixed about the fifth century. This work consisted of such a minute enumeration of the sections, verses, words, and letters of the Old Testament, that although there have been discovered upwards of 800 discrepancies between the Eastern and Western Recensions, they all relate with one single exception to the vowel points. The dispersion of the Jews over the face of the earth, and the discovery of the Sacred Volume in the most distant parts (as amongst the black Jews in the interior of India)[9] agreeing with those of the West of Europe, is another proof of their having preserved the original text in great purity, although evidently descended through very different channels. The Hexapla of Origen, the Jerusalem Talmud (circ. 280), the Septuagint Greek version, made about 300 years before the time of our Saviour, and the discovery of a Samaritan version of the Pentateuch written in the characters in use among the Jews before the Babylonian Captivity, are also the strongest evidences of the existence and truth of the Old Testament Scriptures.

The opinion that the Jews during the Captivity adopted the Babylonian or square Chaldaic characters, and allowed their own old characters to fall into disuse, is confirmed by coins, struck before the Captivity, and even before the Revolt of the Ten Tribes, the letters engraved upon them being the same with the modern

---

[1] See especially Deuteronomy, xxxi. 9, 24, 26, which in our Bibles is rendered *in the side of the* Ark.
[2] Daniel ix. 2, 11, 13.   [3] Ezra vii. 6.
[4] Nehemiah viii. 1—18.   [5] 1 Macc. iv. 36—59.
[6] Bishop Tomline's Elements of Theology, vol. i, p. 11.
[7] Josephus, lib. vii., c. 3, § 11.

[8] " We have not myriads of books which differ from each other, but only twenty-two books which comprehend the history of all past time, and are justly believed to be divine, and of these five are the books of Moses," &c.—*Josephus.*
[9] See Mr. Yeates's Collation of an Indian Copy of the Pentateuch.

1

Samaritan, with some slight variations in form [1]. And as there has been no friendly intercourse between the Jews and Samaritans since the Babylonish Captivity, there can be no doubt that the Pentateuch (which is the only portion of the Old Testament which the Samaritans regarded as inspired) is at the present time precisely in the same condition as it was nearly three thousand years ago. The existence of the Samaritan Pentateuch was known to Eusebius, Jerome, and some other of the early Fathers, but it afterwards fell into oblivion for nearly a thousand years, until at length its existence began to be questioned. The honour of its re-introduction was reserved for the celebrated antiquarian scholar, Archbishop Usher, who obtained six copies from the East, and from his autograph in one of them the fac-simile in my plate numbered 3. has been made. According to Dr. Kennicott (Dissertations prefixed to the Vetus Testamentum Hebraicum), only 17 MSS. of the Samaritan Pentateuch are known to be extant, and of which six are preserved in the Bodleian Library, at Oxford, and one in the Cottonian Library.

The specimen in my plate, No. 1, is copied from the Bodleian MS. (Pococke, No. 5), which consists of 124 leaves, measuring $3\frac{1}{2}$ by 3 inches in size, a page containing 42 lines. The specimen represents the first line of the book of Exodus which is also the case in Nos. 2 and 4.

The second specimen is copied from one of the MSS. obtained by Archbishop Usher, and is also now preserved in the Bodleian Library, (No. 139, Arch. C. 2, 3128). It consists of 253 leaves, measures $12\frac{1}{2}$ by 10 inches (a page containing 37 lines of plain writing), and contains a parallel Arabic version written in Samaritan characters. It is stated to have been written in the thirteenth century.

The fac-simile, No. 4, is copied from the Cottonian MS. Claudius, B. 8, which is likewise one of those procured by Archbishop Usher. It consists of 254 pages of vellum, in excellent preservation. It is of the quarto size, and was written in 1362. A fac-simile from a very similar MS. is given by Silvestre.

The total number of Chaldaic Hebrew MSS. collated by Dr. Kennicott is about 630; and the number collated by De Rossi is 479. The former of these writers states that almost all the Hebrew MSS. of the Old Testament, at present known to be extant, were written between the years 1000 and 1457; he, as well as Bishop Walton, inferring that all the manuscripts written before the years 700 or 800 were destroyed by some decree of the Jewish senate, on account of the many differences from the copies then declared genuine. De Rossi's Codex, No. 634, appears to be the oldest known MS., being assigned to the eighth century; some parts also of his No. 503 are assigned to the ninth or tenth; and the Bodleian Library possesses another MS. in two parts, also assigned by Dr. Kennicott to the tenth. My specimens, 5, 6, and 7, are apparently of the fifteenth century.

No. 5 is from a finely-written Pentateuch in the library of his late R.H. the Duke of Sussex, measuring 13 inches by 9, and having 27 lines in each page, written in an Italian hand, very similar to the Hebrew types used by Ab Conak, at Mantua. The first letters of each book is large, and gilt on a square of blue, lilac, or green, or written in coloured ink in an ornamented square, with the sides and upper and lower margin illuminated in arabesques in the Italian style, in opaque colours, with patches and radiated spots of gold.

No. 6 is from another Pentateuch in the same library, accompanied by the five Megilloth and Haptorah, measuring $7\frac{3}{4}$ inches by $5\frac{1}{2}$, written in the Oriental Rabbinical character called Rashi, with points, and containing the Masorah in the margin. The text is written in two columns, with 21 lines in each, except the title-pages of the Pentateuch, of which the first letters are in gold inclosed within a foliated space formed of lilac lines, and surrounded by an arabesque border composed of leaves, birds, &c.; one of the borders is scarlet, with a scroll of gold lines, and small green and blue leaves and flowers; another is inscribed on a blue ground, within a border of golden arabesques; and another on a golden ground, with coloured leaves, flowers, and buds. Each of these illuminations occupies the entire page, and produces a very rich effect. The shorter books are headed by a smaller illumination in the same style, one of which is copied in the Plate.

No. 7 is from a remarkably fine MS. of the Old Testament in two folio volumes, contained in the Harleian Library, Nos. 5710, 5711; the headings of all the books in which are ornamented with arabesques, often of a singular and grotesque character, but destitute of miniatures. The text is written in very fine characters; and the illuminated borders correspond with those in Italian MSS. of the period.

[1] Walton Proleg. III., p. 103—125. Carpzov and Bauer, quoted by Horne, Introd. iii., p. 3.

בראשית

בְּרֵאשִׁ֖ית בָּרָ֣א אֱלֹהִ֑ים אֵ֥ת הַשָּׁמַ֖יִם וְאֵ֥ת הָאָֽרֶץ

הַשָּׁמַ֖יִם בָּרָ֣א אֵֽ

Spanish HEBREW Pentateuch.

HEBREW PENTATEUCH OF HIS LATE ROYAL HIGHNESS THE DUKE OF SUSSEX.

EXPLANATION OF THE PLATE.

Figure 1. Commencement of the Book of Genesis; the first line in gold, greatly reduced in size; the two following lines are the Hebrew text of the first verse; and the third and fourth are the same in the Chaldaic Targum Onkelos.

Figure 2. The upper part of the illuminated heading of the book Ecclesiastes.

Figure 3. Part of the Dominical sections, written in the Rabbinical character.

Figure 4. The heading of the book of Lamentations.

Figure 5. The lower portion of the illuminated title of the book of Numbers.

THE venerable character of the Hebrew Scriptures, together with the elegance of the manuscript from whence the accompanying fac similes have been made, cannot but confer much interest upon the accompanying plate.

Without entering, on the present occasion, into the history of the Hebrew language in its origin and changes, or inquiring into the antiquity of the Hebrew characters, it will be necessary to premise that Hebrew manuscripts are divisible into three kinds :—

1st. The Samaritan, which are confined to the Pentateuch alone (all the other sacred books of the Old Testament being rejected by the Samaritans), and written in the ancient Hebrew characters, which were in use previous to the Babylonish captivity. These are of the greatest rarity.

2nd. The Chaldaic, written in the present Hebrew square characters, which were adopted during the seventy years' captivity. The Chaldaic writing has been employed by the Hebrews ever since the time of Esdras the Scribe, as appears from the Hebrew Sicles of the time of the Machabees, and great numbers of ancient monumental inscriptions. It consists of 22 letters, all of which, according to the custom of Eastern nations of suppressing the vowels, are syllables. The vowel points, to the number of 14, and 29 accent points, were afterwards added; but these are not of high antiquity, as Origen, Jerome, and the Talmud are silent respecting them.

3rd. The Rabbinical, in the rounded Hebrew characters, used by the Rabbis in their writings, as well as in their commentaries on the different sacred books, the Talmud, &c. This is either written with the letters separated, or united into a cursive hand.

In addition to these, might also be added several other kinds of writing of great antiquity, whereof the alphabets are given in the Nouv. Traité de Diplom. 1. pl. 8, Col. IV., as well as others to be found in the Cottonian MS. Titus, D 18, but that they have been entirely disused for ages.

Chaldaic Hebrew manuscripts of the Old Testament are of two kinds :—

1st. The rolled MSS. which are used in the synagogues, in writing which many minute particulars were obliged to be observed. No vowel points are introduced, the reader not being eligible until he could dispense with them; nor are any ornaments or flourished letters permitted.

2nd. The square MSS. in private use, in which the vowel points are allowed to be introduced, and the initial letters are occasionally illuminated with colours and gold; but the latter are of rare occurrence. They have generally the Targums or Chaldee paraphrases written verse by verse alternately with the text, or in parallel columns on the margin of the page; the larger Masorah being placed above and below, and the lesser Masorah between the columns, written in small letters. The writing of these manuscripts is distinguished into two kinds—the Spanish (including that of the Levant) and German; the former perfectly square, simple, and elegant; the latter crooked, intricate, and inelegant. By some writers a third kind, the Italian, is adopted, which is intermediate between these two; but it is generally united with the Spanish [1].

---

[1] Nouv. Tr. de Diplom. vol. i. p. 671; Horne, Introd. vol. ii., p. 80.

HEBREW PENTATEUCH OF HIS LATE R. H. THE DUKE OF SUSSEX.

Silvestre and Champollion[1] have given a number of specimens of Hebrew MSS. (none of which are illuminated, except in having plain golden initial letters), amongst which are the fine Bible at Bologna (of which specimens were published by Blanchini, and in the Nouv. Traité de Diplom. 1, pl. 16) ; and a fine rolled MS. of the Pentateuch lately brought from Algeria by the Duke d'Aumale. Their 4th plate comprises seven specimens from MSS. in the Bibliothèque Royale de Paris, two of which are dated 1208 and 1061 (the latter in the Italian hand, which closely approximates to the Spanish) ; a Bible of the fourteenth century, formerly belonging to Henry IV. of France ; a Pentateuch written previous to the fifteenth century, in the German character—" caractérisé par des queues très-aiguës ;" a Bible of the fourteenth century, in which " l'extrémité des montants terminés en battants de cloches annonce un type hébreu d'Espagne ;" whilst the last is a specimen of modern Hebrew, termed Cursive Rabbinical—" dont le caractère principal consiste dans l'usage d'arrondir et de pencher la plupart des traits anguleux ou droits."

The beautiful volume from which the accompanying fac similes have been taken, formed one of the gems of the library of his late R. H. the Duke of Sussex. It is described by Mr. Pettigrew[2], with the title " Pentateuchus Hebraicus et Chaldaicus, cum quinque Megilloth et Haphtaroth, MS. in Memb. sæc. XII. quarto ;" and is stated to be " unquestionably one of the most splendid Hebrew manuscripts ever executed. It consists of 360 leaves of very thin delicate white vellum, and has five entire pages of illuminations in gold and colours [all of which are given in outline by Mr. Pettigrew], and four other illuminations, each occupying half a page. The MS. is arranged in three columns," and is stated by Mr. Pettigrew to be *written in the Spanish character ;* who adds, that the beauty of the penmanship is not to be equalled, and the accuracy of the MS. is equal to the beauty of its execution. The Masorah is placed in fanciful arrangement in the margins, and between the columns. The beauty of the scription will be perceived by an inspection of the plate ; but I must observe respecting it, that, instead of according with the Spanish character, as stated by Mr. Pettigrew, it agrees in the peculiar form of its letters with those of the " Juifs d'Allemagne ou du Nord," given by the Benedictines[3], and with the specimen given in the " Palæographie Universelle," as written in the German character.

The MS. commences with an illuminated leaf, comprising, in large golden letters, the first words of the book of Genesis, surrounded by stars, and ornamented both above and below with a splendid Gothic architectural device ; the sides guarded by dragons, and with the eagle, stag, and lion rampant introduced beneath the arches in the lower compartment of the plate.

" The whole of the Pentateuch is written first in Hebrew then in Chaldee, verse by verse. Neither the chapters nor verses are numbered. The Pentateuch is divided into paraschæ (or divisions, corresponding to the portions of the Prophets read on Sabbath days), each of which commences with a larger character. After every portion, the number of letters contained in it is given. There are occasionally critical notes, written in the Rabbinical Hebrew, in the margins."

The illumination at the commencement of the book of Exodus is composed of three architectural columns, between which are displayed, on diamond-shaped shields, the rampant lion and crowned eagle with expanded wings oft repeated, with the large introductory letters in gold on an oblong shield in the centre. The illumination at the beginning of Leviticus has the introductory letters of gold in a beautiful circle, in the middle of a large circular shield, around which are displayed sixteen small round shields, each with a different animal, amongst which are the elephant bearing a castle, unicorn, and winged dragon ; the whole resting on an architectural device, the lower part of which is ornamented with dragons, of which the tails are entwined, and terminated in arabesques. The illumination of the book of Numbers is partially copied in the lower portion of the accompanying plate, the upper part being composed of three compartments, similar to the lower ones on my plate, representing a warrior with a banner, having on either side a monster with the head of a man, the wings and claws of a bird, and the tail of a dragon, terminated by the head of a beast.

I am aware how great is the difficulty of determining the age of Hebrew MSS. ; but I cannot avoid suggesting that the age given to this MS. by Mr. Pettigrew, of the twelfth century, is at least two hundred years older than it can in reality claim pretension to. This opinion, which I submit with diffidence, is founded upon the style of the architecture and armour represented in the illuminations. The architectural ornaments, as

---

[1] Palæographie Universelle, vol. i.

[2] Bibl. Sussexiana, vol. I. xiv. from which work the descriptive paragraphs quoted in the text are copied.

[3] N. Tr. de Dipl. i. pl. 8, col. 2.

shown both in the upper and lower portions of my plate, are florid Gothic, of about the middle of the fourteenth century, whereas in the twelfth the rounded Norman arch had not begun to assume a pointed character. If the MS. were in reality Spanish, and of the age assigned to it, it would afford conclusive proof of the correctness of the opinion of Sir Christopher Wren[1], that the Gothic architecture is derived from the Saracens, and that they had introduced it into Spain (an opinion which, by the bye, might be supported by the elaboration of the style in the Low Countries whilst under the power of Spain) ; but it unfortunately happens for the theory, that there are no Gothic buildings known to have been in existence during so early a period, either in the East or in Spain[2]; and even the ancient Gothic churches in Sicily (so long subject to the Arabs), are not, I believe, earlier than the thirteenth century.

The dresses and armour of the knights represented in the plate are also much later than the twelfth century, and ought, judging from the plates in Sir S. R. Meyrick's and other works on armour and ancient dresses, to be ascribed to the end of the thirteenth or beginning of the fourteenth century. It was during the first half of the latter century that plate-armour was gradually introduced.

Whether Spanish knights of the twelfth century wore armour of the kind here represented, I have been unable to discover; but in the fine Spanish MS. of the Apocalypse, in the British Museum, written A.D. 1109, the armour is quite of a different kind. The banners of these knights is of a very peculiar form, and their heraldic devices and party-coloured surcoats are worthy of notice.

The practice of wearing surcoats is supposed to have originated with the Crusaders[3]; and Sir S. R. Meyrick states that, previous to the time of King John (beginning of thirteenth century), the Italian knights wore a garment over their armour called armilausa[4], respecting which Isidorus[5] says : " Armelausa vulgo vocatur quod ante et retro divisa, atque aperta est, in armis tantum clausa, quasi armiclausa, a, littera ablata."

In the Constitution of Frederick King of Sicily (C. 96), we find the surcoat without sleeves mentioned.

The monumental effigy of William Longespee (A. D. 1224), in Salisbury Cathedral, represents him encased in mail, with the surcoat adorned with his coat of arms, which is not the case in the figure of Peter Earl of Richmond (A. D. 1248 ; Meyrick, i. 17), nor in that of De Vere, Earl of Oxford (A. D. 1280), in both which the rings of the armour are fastened on in rows in opposite directions. With the exception of the helmet, the archers and crossbow-men (A. D. 1312), represented in a MS. in the British Museum[6], are habited exactly as these knights, wearing hauberks, and chausses of gambaised work.

From the mystical and allegorical character of the Jewish writings, we may, perhaps, consider the device represented in this illumination as a representation of the soul clad in the armour of spiritual grace, prepared to defend the Word of God against the attacks of the powers of darkness. Were the manuscript a production of the twelfth century, the knights must evidently have been intended as representations of the Crusaders,—a circumstance not very likely to occur in a Jewish manuscript ; especially when we remember the relative position and feelings of these two bodies of men, so graphically described by Sir Walter Scott, in his inimitable story of " Ivanhoe."

The illumination of the Book of Deuteronomy represents a splendid building, in the Gothic style, having the first three letters in gold, of large size ; beneath which, in the middle, within an ornament formed by two equilateral triangles, interlacing each other, is the figure of an elephant, caparisoned and bearing a low castle ; with heads of various animals in the surrounding spaces.

" After the several books the final Masorah is placed. The two last leaves of the book of Numbers are arranged in two columns, one much larger than the other ; but on the recto of the last leaf the MS. is written in long lines. After Deuteronomy is a table of the portions which are read on different sabbaths, festivals, and fast days. The heads of the table are written in red, in the Hebrew character ; the others in black, in the Rabbinical character. This occupies five pages. Then follows a prayer, written in the Rabbinical character, with vowel points, used at the removal of the MS. of the Pentateuch from the ark to the reading-desk ; after which, in Rabbinical Hebrew, the prayer said by him who is nominated to read the Haphtorah. The initials of these prayers are in a larger Hebrew character, and are written in green."

[1] Wren's Parentalia, passim ; Rious's Architecture, &c.

[2] See Captain Grose's Essay, in the Preface to the Antiquities of England ; and in Essays on Gothic Architecture.

[3] Planche, Hist. Brit. Costume, p. 84.

[4] Crit. Enq. Anc. Armour, i. p. 99.

[5] Orig. lib. xix. c. 22.

[6] Royal Lib. 20, D 1 ; Meyrick, vol. i. pl. 28.

To these succeed the five rolls or Megilloth, the first word of which, ויהי is splendidly illuminated in gold and colours. Following this is the Song of Songs, with a similarly illuminated heading, whilst that of the Lamentations, which succeeds, is very characteristically written in large black letters, without any illumination (copied in the plate, spec. 4). After this succeed Ecclesiastes and Esther, with beautiful illuminated headings. The whole of this portion of the MS. is only written in Hebrew, with vowel and musical points (negenah). The Haphtorah follows, with an illumination. Every division of this part has its proper commencement in a large character. At the end of the Haphtorah is written—

חיים F. chajim

* חזק chazah

which is probably the name of the writer. On the reverse of the last leaf is written, in Rabbinical characters, the acknowledgment of the sale of the volume, from Jacob the son of Mordecai, to Jachiel the son of Uri, of which the following is a translation, including, what the lawyers term, a covenant for quiet enjoyment :—" To testify and to make it appear to Rabbi Jachiel, the son of Uri, I acknowledge that I have delivered this Pentateuch unto him, the value of which I have received in ready money from his hand into my hand, and the sale thereof is an everlasting sale. By this I confine myself to remove him from any error or dispute that might put a hindrance to this sale. Done this fourth day, the twenty-eighth of the month Ejar, A.M. 5229 (A.D. 1469). The words of Jacob, the son of Mordecai." To which the latter has affixed his monogram.

4

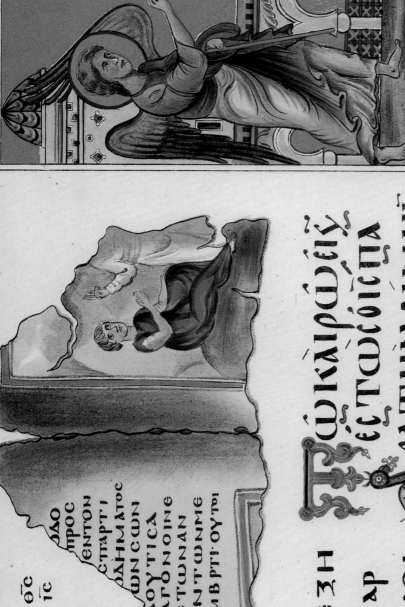

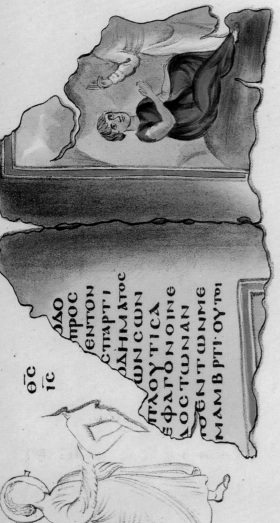

ΟС
ΙС

ΔΟ
ΠΡΟС
ΕΝΤΟΝ
СΤΑΡΤΙ
ΟΔΗΜΑΤΟС
ШΝСШΝ
ΠΛΟΥΤΙСΑ
ΕΦΑΓΟΝΟΙΝΕ
ΛΟСΤШΝΑΝ
ШΓΝΤШΝΜΕ
ΜΑΜΒΡΤΙΟΥΤΟΙ

²
CΑΛΗΜΕЗΗ
ΝΕΓΚΕΝΑΡ
ΤΟΥСΚΙΟΙ
ΝΟΝ·ψχφ

³
Τ ῶΚΑΙΡῶ ἐῖ
ἐςτῶθΘῖСΠΑ
ΡΑΤΗΝΛΙΜΝΗΝ
ΓΕΝΝΗСΑΡΕΤ

ΤΝΕΚΤΗСϹΥΝΕΛΕΞΑΝΤΑΛΕΟΝΤΑ·
ΔΙΠΛΑϹΥΟΤΟΜΟΡΤΩΔΕΝΤ·
ΕΙϹΗΛΘΕΟΝΛΔΕΠΑΝΤΕϹΟΙΧΡΟΝΤΕϹ
ΤΗϹϹΥΝ ΤΩΤΗϹ·ΚΑΙΑΛΗΓΤΕΙΧΑ

ΤΑΝΙΟΓΤΕΟΒΔΔΟΥΕΙΔΑΒΘΔΛΟΥϹϹΚΗΝΗϹ
ΕΝΓΚΟΤΕΓΤΥΚΟΥΝΚΟΙΟΙΟΓΕΝΕΙΚΟΥΤ
ΤΟΚΟΥΝΤΟΚΡΙϹΙΩΝΘΕΝΕΙΚΟΥΤΠΙΟΚ

⁵
Τ ΚΑΙ ΑΥ Κ ΙΑΓ ΓΝ Υ
ὡς δὴ ὥςπερ πολλοι, ἔως χει,
ρι σωμαων·δε αστ α---ικτπ
περι τον τιμε εφηρο φορλιε;
μορ ἐρμ ιμ τα αμ στερ·χαι

⁷
Μ ψαλτηριον· ψαλμιστω δλλ πρωτος
ἀκαριος. ἀμηρ. ος. οψεττορευοη. ερ·Βψλη.
ασεβωη. και. ερ. ολω. ἀμαρτωλω. ουκεστη.
σηλυητος· σκόττος· ετραψα.
(ετю)

EARLY GREEK MSS.

THE Septuagint translation of the Old Testament into Greek, made about 280 years before the Christian era, for the benefit of the multitude of Jews settled in Egypt, who were no longer acquainted with Biblical Hebrew (the Greek language being alone used in their ordinary intercourse), was regarded, both by the Jews and first Christians, as of the highest authority. As such it was constantly read in the synagogues and churches; was uniformly cited by the Fathers, and was the groundwork of all the translations into other languages approved by the early Christian churches.

The translation thus made proved, by God's providence, the means of keeping alive amongst the Jews the expectation of the Messiah, which would have been lost had the books in which it was foretold become a dead letter; the New Testament scriptures were also written in Greek, that being the language best understood, and spoken throughout the eastern provinces of the Roman Empire: indeed, no educated Roman was ignorant of it.

The most ancient Greek MSS. which have survived to our times are written in rounded uncial letters, without accents or separation of words, and almost destitute of ornament, if we except the paintings with which some were adorned. Of these the highest place as a Biblical MS. is assigned by most critics to the Codex Alexandrinus, now preserved in the British Museum [1]; which was sent as a present to King Charles the First by Cyrillus Lucaris, Patriarch of Constantinople, by whom it was brought from Alexandria (where it was probably written, shortly after the Council of Nice), or according to some authorities, from Mount Athos. From an Arabic inscription in the volume, it is supposed to have been written by Thecla, a noble Egyptian lady, who suffered martyrdom, but by the most celebrated Greek Biblical scholars it is referred to the 5th or 6th century. The MS. itself consists of the entire Bible, in four volumes of the quarto size; the text uniformly written, with the first three or four lines of each book in red letters; a slightly ornamented pen-and-ink line is drawn at the end of each book. A fac-simile edition of the Old Testament, in four volumes folio, was published in 1816—28, by the Rev. H. H. Baber; the New Testament having been published in 1786, by Dr. Woide. From one of the fac-similes given in the former work, the four lines under No. 3 have been copied.

The Codex Cottonianus Geneseos is considered by Biblical scholars to have been the most ancient and correct Greek Septuagint manuscript in existence; the forms of the letters being more ancient than in the famous Greek Book of Genesis in the Imperial Library of Vienna, which is generally allowed to be more than 1400 years old.[2] It was originally brought from Philippi by two Greek bishops, who presented it to King Henry VIII., whom they informed that tradition reported it to have been the identical copy which had belonged to Origen in the former half of the 3rd century. In its original state it contained 165 leaves of the quarto size, written in uncial letters, and illustrated by 250 miniatures about four inches square, which, by competent judges, were preferred as specimens of ancient art to the miniatures in the Vienna Greek Book of Genesis. Unfortunately this MS. was almost entirely destroyed by the Cottonian fire of 1731, the numerous fragments which remain, being burnt, in many cases, almost to a black mass, and all shrivelled and reduced in size. Of one of the best preserved I have been enabled, by the kindness of Sir Fred. Madden, to give a fac-simile under No. 1. A number of other specimens, which escaped the fire, are engraved in the Vetusta Monumenta of the Antiquarian Society, a few of which are now preserved in the Bristol Baptist Education Society, where I have examined them, but they were unfortunately found to be not more perfect than those in the Cottonian Library. Fortunately several collations were made of this MS. before it was so greatly injured, which have been published. From another of the fragments almost defaced, I have copied the figure of the Creator at the left hand of No. 1, which bears a striking resemblance, in its attitude, to the beautiful drawing copied in No. 5.

The specimen, No. 2, is copied from Astle's fac-simile of a page of this MS. taken before the fire happened,

---

[1] The Vatican Bible, at least in beauty of writing, will bear no comparison with this MS. Horne has given a fac-simile of the former as well as the latter.

[2] This noble MS. is written upon purple vellum, in letters of gold and silver, and is shortly described in our article upon the Purple Greek MSS.

from which it will be easy to perceive how great an alteration has been produced in its appearance. It is to be read, Σαλημ εξηνεγκεν αρτους και οινον (Gen. 14, v. 18) ; the lines in the original being eight inches long, and running across the page. The letters ΘC (from the Codex Geneseos), and IC (from the Codex Alexandrinus), show the mode in which the words God and Jesus were contracted in those MSS.

In the eighth and ninth centuries considerable variation was introduced in the form of the uncial letters, which were still however written of large size : this is especially visible in the forms of the *a*, c, ϵ, and ρ, which assumed more of a minuscule character, as in our specimen, No. 4, which is copied from a fine Evangelistiarium of the ninth or tenth century, preserved among the Arundel MSS. in the Brit. Mus., No. 574 (measuring 11½ inches by 9, and containing 328 leaves of vellum). The specimen is from the beginning of the 5th Chapter of St. Luke's Gospel—Τω καιρω εκ (εινω) εστως παρα τεν λιμνη(ν) Γεννασερετ.

This specimen, as well as No. 5, exhibits some of the ornamental initial letters which were introduced into the finer Greek MSS. after the eighth century[2]; but which never assumed the size and splendour of the initials of the Anglo-Saxon or Frankish schools. This MS. is also ornamented with full-length figures of the four Evangelists, but, as unfortunately happens with the paintings of the Byzantine school, the colours are very much rubbed off, apparently from not having been mixed up with size or gum. At the heading of each of the Gospels is a beautiful ornamental design, extending across the top of the page ; which it was the ordinary custom of the Greek artists to introduce, but which, although adopted by the Syriac and Sclavonic artists, was never practised by the illuminators of the West of Europe. These headings are generally composed of foliage and flowers, converted into arabesques of great elegance, and beautifully coloured, inclosing the title of the book.

In Greek MSS. adorned with miniatures of the Byzantine school of the middle ages, the British Museum[3] collection is by no means rich ; the manuscript, however, which has supplied our fac-simile, No. 5, is an important evidence of the state of art in the eleventh century. It is from the Harleian Gospels, No. 1810, collated by Griesbach, and which follow the Alexandrian Recension. It consists of 268 leaves, measuring 9 inches by 7 ; and contains about a score miniatures, the figures of which are in general smaller than those in my copy which represents the Annunciation (142 r), accompanied by the first verse of St. Luke's Gospel, from fo. 140 r, written in alternate lines of gold and black ink, and which is to be read (the letters in the heading being conjoined, and the last word abbreviated) :—Το κατα Λουκαν αγιον ευαγγελιον. Επειδηπερ πολλοὶ ἐπεχείρισαν ἀνατάξασθαι διήγησι περὶ τῶν πεπληροφορημένων ἐν ἡμῖν πραγματων και... The golden ground of the miniature before us, together with the Saracenic style of the architecture, are worthy of remark, as well as the purely classical style of the figures themselves, which are infinitely superior as a work of art to the drawings of the contemporary artists in our own country, France, and Germany. One of the miniatures in this MS., representing the Death of the Virgin, is precisely similar in design to the same subject in the Cottonian Norman-French Psalter, Nero, C. IV. The writing before us (No. 5), may be considered as a specimen of the minuscule Greek characters, which came into use about the tenth century, and which were afterwards almost universally employed ; as likewise of the mode in which Greek letters were conjoined in cursory writing.

The specimen, No. 6, is copied from a series of fragments of the Psalter (Ps. 10—34), written upon papyrus, preserved in the ·British Museum, purchased from Dr. Hogg, who obtained them in Egypt. The specimen before us is the heading and commencement of the 29th Psalm—ψαλμος τω δανειδ, &c. Ενεγκατε τω κ(υριο)υ, &c. From the style of the writing, this MS. is not probably more ancient than the eighth or ninth century.

The fac-simile, No. 7, is copied from a Psalter now in the library of the Arsenal, written about the beginning of the ninth century, by Sedulius, an Irish scholar, who has signed his name at the end ; copied at the foot of my plate. In this respect the MS. is of considerable interest, as affording a contrast with other Greek writings contained in Irish and Anglo-Saxon MSS., of which fac-similes are given in other articles of this work. In the original the first line is written in red letters, and the initial of the first Psalm (copied in my plate), is as usual edged with red dots. Montfaucon has given a detailed account of this curious MS. in his Pal. Gr.

[1] The Paleographia Græca of Montfaucon contains a complete illustration and investigation of the characters of Greek writing.

[2] The circumstance that the *initial* letters of the more ancient Greek and Latin MSS. were not of so much enlarged a size as to merit notice, is of itself a sufficient argument (independent of satirical exaggeration) that St. Jerome's complaint of MSS. written in large letters, is to be read, " Veteres libros . . . uncialibus " (not initialibus) "literis, *onera* magis exarata quam codices." MSS. written in letters of the size of our specimen, No. 4, and those in the plate of Purple Greek MSS. are, truly, written *burthens*.

[3] Many fine specimens, chiefly from the Vatican, are engraved by D'Agincourt. The Bibliothèque du Roi likewise possesses two or three of the ninth or tenth century, of great beauty ; and the Bodleian Library possesses several of high artistic rank, especially the Canonici MS., No. 110, and the Codex Ebnerianus of the eleventh century, unquestionably one of the most beautiful Greek MSS. in existence. It contains several drawings of great beauty, and is in a very extraordinary state of preservation.

ΤΗ Ε ΜΕΤΑΤΟΠΑϹ
Χ ΤΩ

ΤΩΚΑΙΡΩΘΚΕΙ
ΝΩ ΛΝΟϹΤΙϹ
ΕΚΤΩΝΦΑΡΙ
ϹΑΙΩΝ ΝΙΚΟ

ΔΥΝΟΜΕΘΑΤΗ
ΟΔΟΝΕΙΔΕΝΑΙ
ΛΕΓΕΙΑΥΤΩΟ
ΕΓΦΕΙΜΕΙΗΟ
ΔΟϹΚΑΙΗΑΛΗ
ΘΙΑΚΑΙΗΖΩΗ
ΟΥΔΙϹΕΡΧΕΤΑΙ
ΠΡΟϹΤΟΝ
ΕΙΜΗΔΙΕΜΟΥ
ΕΙΕΓΝΩΚΕΙΤΕ

Purple Greek MSS.

PURPLE GREEK MANUSCRIPTS.

REFERENCE TO THE PLATE.

St. John's Gospel, iii. 1, from the Vienna Evangelistiarium.   Ditto, xiv. 5, 6, 7, from the Cottonian MS., Titus, C xv.

IT was the custom of the Greeks and Romans, during the early ages of Christianity, to write their most valued productions in letters of gold and silver, and upon vellum stained with purple[1], or some analogous colour. That in these early times the sacred Scriptures should in this manner have been especially illustrated, affords the strongest proof of the high degree of respect with which they were regarded. Thus, the bishop and martyr Boniface, in his 28th Epistle, entreats the Abbess Eadburga to write the Epistles of St. Peter in letters of gold, for the greater reverence to be paid to the sacred writings, and Mabillon informs us that it was only for princes and nobles that such manuscripts were rarely written[2]; whilst in the Spicilegium of Theonas[3], we are informed that it was rather unseemly to write in this manner, unless at the particular desire of a prince.

Ovid, in his first elegy, De Tristibus, "Ad librum," l. 5, has some lines which have been supposed by some authors to prove that writing on purple materials was not uncommon in his time :—

> " Nec te purpureo velent vaccinia succo :
> Non est conveniens luctibus ille color ;
> Nec titulus minio, nec cedro charta notetur,
> Candida nec nigra cornua fronte geras[4]."

Julius Capitolanus, however, in his Life of the Emperor Maximinus the younger, more expressly states that his mother, on sending him back to his preceptor, gave him a copy of the writings of Homer, written upon purple vellum and in letters of gold. The simple style of the historian leads us to suppose that books thus written were no unheard-of novelty at the commencement of the third century of the Christian era, and the Benedictines have referred the usage to the end of the first century. St. Jerome, towards the close of the fourth century, speaks of the practice of writing books very pompously on parchment of a purple colour, in letters of gold and silver, and that entire works were written in large letters[5].

During the fifth and three following centuries the practice still continued, although it was so little known

[1] It is unquestionable that in ancient times the relative superiority of purple to other colours was greater than at present. It was frequently mentioned in connexion with the works of the Tabernacle and the dresses of the high priests, and among the heathens we know that this colour was considered peculiarly appropriate to the service of the gods ; indeed, the Babylonians and other nations used to array their gods in robes of purple. Purple was also the distinguishing mark of great dignities among several nations, and Homer intimates that it was only worn by princes, and this limitation of its use was common among other nations. See also Exodus xxxv. 35; Judges viii. 26. (Pictorial Bible, I. p. 237.)

[2] " Sed hic scribendi modus principibus et magnatibus peculiaris erat, nec tamen promiscuè ab istis usurpatus." De Re Diplomat. p. 43.

[3] Vol. xii., p. 549.

[4] The Benedictines (N. Tr. Dipl. ii. p. 99) do not consider this to imply that the interior of manuscripts, but only their covers, were stained with purple ; and by a comparison of this with the corresponding passages in Martial, lib. iii., ep. 2 ; Tibullus, lib. iii., el. 1, and Lucian, "De Philosophis mercenariis," Sir F. Madden also considers that the passage of Ovid has been misunderstood, and that the substance of the volumes was

of papyrus (charta) unstained, which was rolled up for the sake of ornament or preservation in an outer covering of parchment dyed purple or yellow. Pliny, also, is silent as to the practice in his time, so that it may be doubted whether it was then really employed. So that that " simple soul" (as Dibdin calls him) Hermannus Hugo,—who in his " Libellus de prima scribendi Origine," quoted by Kollarius, thought that purple vellum MSS. only meant books bound in vellum of that colour,—was not, after all, so worthy of ridicule as our English writer would lead us to infer; indeed, " the laugh must be on the other side of the house " when we read the suggestion of Dr. Dibdin, that little more than a tint of the purple remains, some of these manuscripts being still as dark coloured as on the day on which they were executed.

[5] " Habeant qui volunt veteres libros vel in membranis purpureis auro argentoque descriptos vel uncialibus, ut vulgo aiunt, literis, onera magis exarata quam codices ; dummodo mihi meisque permittant pauperes habere scedulas, et non tam pulchros codices quam emendatos." (Prolog. ad lib. Job.) And again, " Inficiuntur membranæ colore purpureo aurum liquescit in litteras." (Epist. ad Eustoch.)

1

in this country, that when St. Wilfred, Archbishop of York, towards the close of the seventh century, gave a copy of the Gospels thus adorned[1] to the church in that city, his biographer, Eddius, described it as a thing almost miraculous—"inauditum ante seculis nostris quoddam miraculum." Soon after this period the art appears to have fallen into disuse; and although in the reign of Charlemagne a great impulse was given to the arts, and attempts were made to re-introduce the custom of staining MSS., yet it seems generally only to have extended to a partial painting of the leaves in such places as were intended to receive the golden writing; and in the place of the bright violet, deep red, or elegant blue, a daubing of brown or very dark-coloured purple was used. This distinction has not been sufficiently attended to; and we accordingly find manuscripts of the latter class cited by several of our palæographers[2] as examples of purple-stained MSS.

Manuscripts entirely composed of leaves of purple vellum are of the greatest rarity; "sunt autem albo corvo rariores Codices istiusmodi, inprimis Græci membranacei," says Breitinger[3]; since it more frequently occurs that only certain important portions of the volume, as the titles, prefaces, or a few pages at the beginning of each Gospel, or the canon of the Mass, are written on vellum thus prepared, the remainder of the text being on white vellum.

It is further to be noticed that manuscripts written in uncial or rounded characters are far rarer than the rest, both on account of their great age and the quantity and value of the materials which would be required in their production; and, lastly, that Codices purpureo-argentei are much rarer than those entirely in golden writing, the latter material being used not only on purple but also on white vellum, whereas the silver letters would not easily be legible, except on a dark ground. Not more than six manuscript fragments of Greek Biblical MSS. on purple vellum are known to be extant[4].

From the preceding remarks the extreme value of the Codex purpureo-argenteus, from which the fac-simile in the lower part of the accompanying plate has been made, may be inferred. It is preserved amongst the Cottonian Manuscript sin the British Museum (with the mark Titus, C xv.), and comprises the following fragments from the Gospels:—

St. Matthew	Chap. XXVI., v. 57—65.
,, ...	Chap. XXVII., v. 26—34.
St. John	Chap. XIV., v. 2—10.
,, ...	Chap. XV., v. 15—22.

The sheets measure 13 inches by $10\frac{1}{2}$, and the writing is in double columns. The specimen here given contains that precious declaration of our Saviour, in which all the truths of the Gospel dispensation are concentrated:—"I am the Way, and the Truth, and the Life. No man cometh to the Father but by Me." It comprises the last line of the 5th, the whole of the 6th, and the first line of the 7th verses of the xivth chapter of St. John. The writing is in very large and massive Greek uncials; the words denoting God, Father, Jesus, Lord, Son, and Saviour, being, for dignity's sake, written in golden letters; the words ΙΗΣΟΥΣ (Jesus), ΘΕΟΣ (God), ΚΥΡΙΟΣ (Lord), &c., being contracted in the same manner as in the Alexandrian and Beza's Codices.

When we thus see a folio page of manuscript occupied with only two or three verses, we cannot wonder at the complaint of St. Jerome against these "onera magis exarata quam codices;" expressing, in other words, that great books are great evils.

Of this specimen the following is a representation in ordinary Greek characters, written as in the original, without any separation between the words, with the corresponding literal English translation:—

(ΠΩΣ)	(HOW)
ΔΥΝΟΜΕΘΑΤΕ (Ν)	AREWEABLETH (ᴇ)
ΟΔΟΝΕΙΔΕΝΑΓ'	WAYTOKNow
ΛΕΓΕΙΑΥΤΩΟΙ(ΗΣΟΥ)Σ	SAITHUNTOHIMJ(ESU)s
ΕΓΩΕΙΜΕΙΗΟ'	IAMTHEW

[1] "Quatuor Evangelia de auro purissimo in membranis depurpuratis coloratis, pro animæ suæ remedio, scribere jussit." Eddius, p. 60. And see Fleuri. Hist. Eccl. l. 39, n. 46; and Mabillon, Act. SS. sæc. IV. pl. 2, p. 552.

[2] Thus Astle (pp. 197 and 198) mentions the Harleian MSS. 2788, 2820, and 2821; and Sir F. Madden (Introd. to Shaw, Ill. Orn. Pref., p. 5) the Gospels of Athelstan (Tiber. A 2), as stained MSS., although

the purple colour is only painted on one side of the leaves, and is not seen on the other.

[3] De Antiquiss. Turic. Bibl. Græc. Psalm. libro in membr. purpur. titul. aureis ac litt. arg. exarat. 4to., 1748, p. 7, as quoted by Dibdin.

[4] Horne, Introduction, vol. ii., part 1, p. 91.

PURPLE GREEK MANUSCRIPTS.

ΔΟΣΚΑΙΗ΄Α΄ΛΗ	AYANDTHETRU
ΘΙΑ΄ΚΑΙΗ΄ΖΩΗ΄	THANDTHELIFE
ΟΥΔΙΣΕΡΧΕΤΑΙ	NOMANCOMEᴛʜ
ΠΡΟΣΤΟΝΠΡᾹ	TOTHEF(A̅T̅H̅)ᴇʀ
ΕΙΜΗΔΙΕΜΟΥ	BUTBYMᴇ
ΕΙΕΓΝΩΚΕΙΤᴇ	IFYEHADKNOWɴ

I have introduced the last two lines of the 5th and the first line of the 7th verses, to show that not only the words are broken in two at the end of the lines without any connecting marks, but that the paragraphs were also undivided into verses. They are, however, separated by *alineæ*, here appearing simply in the first letter being written rather beyond the perpendicular edge of the other lines, but scarcely larger than the other letters. The rounded E, the acutely angled first stroke of the A, the elongated Υ and P with the extremity obliquely truncate, the rounded part of the latter scarcely reaching below half the width of the lines, the acute angled M with three of its strokes thickened, and the Δ with the basal stroke elongated beyond the triangle and knobbed at each end, are peculiarities evidencing the most remote antiquity, in all of which respects it will bear comparison with the most famous codices. The colour is faded into a dingy reddish purple, which has been represented of too brown a tint in some of the impressions of the plate. The silver is greatly tarnished and turned black.

This manuscript is stated by Horne to be one of the oldest (if not the most ancient) manuscript of any part of the New Testament that is extant, and is generally acknowledged to have been executed at the end of the fourth, or, at the latest, at the beginning of the fifth, century; although Dr. Scholz refers it to the seventh or eighth. Casley, however, whose knowledge of the age of manuscripts has never been surpassed, considered that it is as old, or older, than the Codex Cottonianus Geneseos; and Mr. Baber is inclined to give it chronological precedency to any previously named MS. Dr. Dibdin[1] states that this manuscript is written in the largest Greek capitals which he had ever seen. The Bodleian Library, however, possesses a noble manuscript written in still larger but narrower characters. The Vatican Codices 351 and 1522, of which specimens are given by Blanchini, are also written in larger letters, but these are much more recent than the Cottonian MS.

The manuscript from which the upper specimen in the accompanying plate (copied from Silvestre) is taken, is a Greek Evangelistiarium in the Imperial Library of Vienna, which contains short portions of the Gospels which have been selected by the Greek Church for each of the feasts in the year, especially for those named Δεσποτικαὶ ἑορταὶ.

This volume, at the beginning of the eighteenth century, belonged to the monastery of the Augustines of St. Jean de Carbonaria, at Naples. Shortly afterwards Charles VI., Emperor of Germany, ascended the throne, and during the period that Naples was tributary to that empire, the monks presented this volume to their new sovereign. Afterwards, when the victorious armies of France ransacked Vienna, this manuscript was carried as a precious prize to Paris, where it was placed in the Royal Library, whence it was afterwards restored to Vienna.

It is a volume about 7 inches by 6 in size, with nine lines in a page, and was written at the end of the eighth century, in fine Greek uncials, both round and square, without a mixture of long-formed letters, which lessen the beauty of many manuscripts. The accents are supposed by Silvestre to be of more recent date than the text; there is no division into verses, a small Greek cross occasionally marking the stops. The fragment is part of the Gospel for Easter, from St. John, chap. iii., v. 1, which is to be read—

Τῃ Ε̄ (πιϲολὴ) μετα το Παϲ(χα)	The E(pistle) for East (er)
κ(ατα) ΙΩ(A̅N̅N̅H̅N̅)	ac(cording to)JO(HN)
ΤΩΚΑΙΡΩΕΚΕΙ	ATTHATTI
ΝΩΑΝ(Θ̅Ρ̅Ω̅Π̅)ΟΣΤΙΣ	MEACERTAINM(A)N
ΕΚΤΩΝΦΑΡΙ	OFTHEPHARI
ΣΑΙΩΝΝΙΚΟ(DHΜΟΣ)	SEESNICO(DEMUS)

I presume this to be the Evangelistiarium Kollarii 7, or Forlosia's No. 23, assigned by Horne to the ninth century. (Introd. ii., 1. p. 185.)

[1] Bibl. Decam. 1. p. lxviii.

In addition to the preceding, a slight notice of the three following will, from the extreme rarity of purple Greek manuscripts, be considered interesting :—

The Codex Argenteo-purpureus Cæsareo-Vindobonensis claims the first place : it contains a portion of the book of Genesis (chapters iii. to viii.), and part of the xxivth chapter of St. Luke's Gospel, written in Greek uncials of silver, on purple vellum, and ornamented with forty-eight drawings, which Lambecius assigns to the age of Constantine ; but by others the MS. is referred to the end of the fifth century. This Vienna manuscript has been repeatedly described in detail, and its drawings engraved by Lambecius, Nesselius, Kollarius, Montfaucon, Holmes, Astle, Horne, Dibdin, D'Agincourt, &c.

The Codex Turicensis, described by Breitinger (ut supra), is a quarto Greek manuscript of portions of the book of Psalms, consisting of 222 leaves of extremely thin purple vellum, with silver letters and golden initials, which are, however, almost illegible in many parts. A fac-simile of a portion is given in the N. Traité de Diplomat. vol. i. pl. 12. specimen 14.

The Palimpsest Codex of Isaiah, St. Matthew's Gospel, and the Orations of Gregory Nazianzen, belonging to Trinity College, Dublin, and of which the Gospel portion has been edited by Dr. Barrett[1]. The letters of the Codex Vetus were square, and much smaller than in the MS. above mentioned, but larger than those of the Alexandrian Codex, and written on vellum originally of a purple colour, apparently in the sixth century. The Codex Recens, or later writing, consists of parts of various Greek fathers, and is ascribed to the thirteenth century.

Blanchini[2] has given notices of several other Greek Manuscripts written in gold and silver letters, amongst which, he has, however, incorrectly introduced the Codex Geneseos of the Cottonian Library.

Notices of the famous Gothic manuscript of Ulphilas, written about A.D. 360, and various purple Latin MSS., written both in gold and silver letters, will find a place in other portions of this work.

---

[1] Evangelium secundum Matthæum ex Codice rescripto in Bibl. Coll. S. Trinit. juxta Dublin. 4to., 1801.

[2] Evangel. Quadruplex, vol. ii. p. 593.

Greek Gospels

GREEK GOSPELS.

DESCRIPTION OF THE PLATE.

Portrait of St. Mark, and commencement of the Gospel of St. Matthew, with ornamental heading. From Harl. MS. 5790.

THE long controversy which existed between the Greek and Romish Churches, the high, and indeed inspired character in which the Latin vulgate version of St. Jerome was regarded by the latter (although made by him from the Greek), combined with the dark and almost general ignorance of the middle ages, resulted in a total disregard of the Greek versions of the Scriptures in the west of Europe for nearly a thousand years. With the revival of literature, however, and the dissemination of knowledge by the printing-press towards the close of the fourteenth century, a spirit of inquiry was raised as to the genuineness of the existing Latin version of the Bible, in the minds of those who took part in the great religious movement which had already commenced for the reformation of the Church.

The facts, of the Septuagint version of the Old Testament having been written in Greek, and of the New Testament having been originally composed in that language, were regarded by many of these inquirers as convincing proofs that the true text of the Sacred Volume was to be found in MSS. of the Greek versions ; whilst the violent contests which had taken place between the Greek and Roman Churches rendered an agreement in the versions employed by the respective churches almost as important in sacred criticism as the agreement between the Samaritan and Hebrew versions : which so satisfactorily proves that no material alteration had been made in them during the three thousand years which had elapsed since the origin of the controversy between those two tribes.

The total number of Greek MSS. of the New Testament (whether entire or fragments only) known to have been hitherto more or less completely collated, amounts, according to the celebrated Biblical critic Scholz, to 674.

Of these MSS. the Alexandrian and Vatican Codices occupy the foremost place, as containing the entire Bible, and being of very high antiquity. The number of Greek MSS. containing the Greek version of the Old Testament in existence is not precisely known ; but Dr. Holmes collated 135 for his edition of that version ; and of these, the Cottonian Cod. Geneseos and the Cod. Cæsaræus Argenteo-purpureus, both containing miniatures, and written in fine uncial characters of very great antiquity, and the Codex Turicensis, written on purple vellum, are the most interesting in respect to the objects of this work.

The manuscripts of the New Testament, or of portions thereof, are far more numerous. The Evangelia contain the four Gospels, whilst such as contain those portions of the Gospels as were read in the service of the Church are termed Evangelistiaria, or Lectionaria. Of such as contain the New Testament, or portions thereof (not being Lectionaria), thirty-three are enumerated by Horne as written in uncial letters, amongst which the Codices,—BEZÆ, CLAROMOMONTANUS, LAUDIANUS (in the Bodleian Library, containing the Græco-Latin Acts of the Apostles) ; SAN GERMANENSIS (of the 7th century, in Græco-Latin) ; AUGIENSIS (in Trin. Coll., Cambridge, written in Græco-Latin in an Anglo-Saxon hand) ; BOERNERIANUS, at Dresden (in Græco-Latin, in an Irish hand) ; COTTONIANUS (Titus, C. xv., on purple vellum, possibly of the 4th century) ; and DUBLINENSIS, a palimpsest MS., on purple vellum, published by Dr. Barrett, are palæographically of the highest interest.

Of such as are written in minuscule or cursive characters the number is of course far greater, on account of these being much more modern in point of date. Of these Horne has given a list of 469, exclusive of 178 Evangelistiaria, and about 30 others not fully collated.

The integrity and faithfulness of the Greek text, although of such immense importance in Biblical criticism, have not prevented various transcribers from altering the Greek text to the Latin. Of this charge

1

(first raised by Erasmus, and which was by some of the earlier critics considered as the result of a united resolution adopted by both churches, and which was termed the " Fœdus cum Græcis,") the celebrated passage in 1st John, v. 7, 8, affords several instances, as it occurs in the Codices MONTFORTIANUS, at Dublin, written in the 15th century, in small cursive characters; OTTOBIANUS, in the Vatican, of the 15th century; BEROLINENSIS, also of the 15th century; NEAPOLITANUS, (being No. 173 in Scholz's Catalogue of MSS. used in the Epistles,) and the MS. at Wolfenbuttel, numbered 131 in Michaeli's list by Marsh :—in all of which the heavenly witnesses are introduced, (being translated from the Gloss added by earlier Latin transcribers of the Vulgate,) although they are wanting in all the other and infinitely more trustworthy Greek MSS.

Amongst the later Evangelia, written in minuscule Greek characters, it is impossible to find a finer example of caligraphy than is afforded by the volume from which the accompanying plate has been copied. This MS. is one of the gems of the Harleian Library in the British Museum. It is numbered 5790, and was written at Rome by one John, a priest, and completed on the 25th of April, 1478, as appears by a note on the last page of the volume. It measures 12 inches by 8, and consists of the four Gospels, each preceded by a table of sections, written in red ink. Each Gospel is preceded by a figure of its respective Evangelist (that of St. Matthew having been abstracted), and the first page of each Gospel is beautifully illuminated with an elegantly-designed heading, and a large coloured initial letter, ornamented with beautiful and delicately-drawn arabesques. The portrait of St. Mark with the Lion is copied in our plate ; St. Luke with the winged Bull is represented in the act of mending his pen, and as aged, with a long grey beard, wearing a blue and violet dress, and seated in his study, with books, candlesticks, writing-case, &c. The miniature of St. John is a charming composition ; the evangelist being represented as young and beardless, in the act of writing his Gospel, with the Eagle over his head with expanded wings.

The heading of St. Mark's Gospel consists of three small circular medallions, containing the head of Christ and two of the apostles. That of St. Luke consists of a lozenge-shaped medallion, containing a miniature of the Virgin, with the infant Jesus, encircled with a glory, represented, as the lawyers say, " en ventre sa mère," and with small circular medallions at the sides, inclosing heads of angels; and that of St. John contains a medallion of the bust of Christ, invested with the cruciferous nimbus *and cross*, and in the act of giving the benediction according to the Romish practice; at the sides are the miniatures of two angels.

In the passage copied in the plate the reversed y-like form of the v, the Γ-like form of the γ, the H-like form of the η, and the ω-form of the omega, are to be noticed.

SYRIAC MANUSCRIPTS.

THE proximity of the Holy Land to Syria, and the constant intercourse between the inhabitants, led to the early introduction of the religion of Jesus Christ into the latter country. Of this fact we have evidence in the Sacred Volume itself, one of the first Epistles addressed to the New Converts having been sent " unto the brethren which are of the Gentiles in Antioch, and Syria, and Cilicia ; "[1] and Paul and Silas going " through Syria and Cilicia confirming the churches,"[2] which must, of course, have been already established.

The ordinary language of the Jews, in the time of Jesus Christ, was the Aramæan, (so named from the extensive region of Aram), and which consisted of two dialects, the Chaldee or East Aramæan (which the Jews adopted during the Babylonian Captivity, and which was used by Christ himself in his ordinary discourse with the Jews), and the Syriac or West Aramæan,[3] which was spoken both in Syria and Mesopotamia, and which, after the captivity, became vernacular in Galilee. Hence we find numerous Syriac phrases or words introduced into the text of the New Testament, to which in general an explanation is added, as in the heart-rending exclamation of Our Saviour on the cross,[4] which the Jewish bystanders were unable to understand[5].

The Syriac language, although written in characters so unlike those of the Chaldaic, Samaritan, Arabic, and Ethiopic, differs but little from the Hebrew, and less from the Chaldaic, being like them read from right to left, but being distinguished by the vowel points, and by the admission of numerous Greek words, adopted during the reign of the Seleucidean kings in Syria[6]. The correspondence between the Syriac and Chaldee is indeed so close that if the latter be written in Syriac characters without points, it becomes Syriac, with the exception of a single inflection in the formation of the verbs[7].

The Syriac language has, however, ceased to be spoken ; being confined to the service of the Church and the books of the Syrians and Maronites, who speak Arabic, which they occasionally write in Syriac characters.

We accordingly find that the Syrians have possessed the Sacred Scriptures in their native language from a very early period ; some of the most celebrated biblical scholars[8], referring—

1.—The PESCHITO version to the first or beginning of the second century, at which time the Syrian churches flourished most, and the Christians at Edessa had a Temple erected after the model of that of Jerusalem. This version is named PESCHITO or *literal,* from its close adherence to the Hebrew text of the Old and the Greek Text of the New Testaments ; and it has been preferred by many of the most competent scholars to any of the other ancient versions, Michaelis pronouncing the latter (which agrees with the Constantinopolitan recension) to be the very best translation of the Greek Testament which he had ever read. The celebrated verse in the first Epistle of St. John (ch. v., v. 7) is wanting, as is also the story of the Woman taken in Adultery[9].

2.—The PHILOXENIAN or Syro-Philoxenian version, was made by Polycarp by direction of Philoxenus, bishop of Hierapolis, or Mabug, in Syria, about the year A.D. 508, and which was afterwards revised by Thomas of Harkel, or Heraclea, in 616. This version was first made known in Europe in 1761, by Dr. Gloucester Ridley, from three manuscripts brought from Amida in Mesopotamia. Although inferior to the Peschito, its value (having been made immediately from the Greek), is admitted by the most learned biblical scholars.

---

[1] Acts xv., v. 23.

[2] Ibid., v. 41.

[3] Adler reckons *three* dialects of the Syriac, and Champollion four.

[4] Matth. xxvii., v. 46.

[5] The introduction of such phrases has been recorded as one of the strongest intrinsic proofs of the genuineness and authenticity of the New Testament. See *Michaelis* Introduction, vol. i., p. 135. *Adler* Novi Testamenti versiones Syriacæ simplex, Philoxeniana et Hiero-solymita, 4to, Hafniæ, 1789. *Olearius* de Stylo Novi Testamenti. *Masclef* Gramm. Hebr. vol. ii., p. 114. *Michaelis* Dissertatio Philologica quâ lumina Syriaca pro illustrando Ebraismo Sacro, &c. Halæ, 1756. All quoted by Horne, Introd. pp. 29 and 31.

[6] Champollion and Silvestre.

[7] Walton Prol. cxiii., § 2, 3, 4, 5, quoted by Horne, ut supra.

[8] Bishops Walton and Lowth, Carpzov, Kennicott, Michaelis.

[9] Horne, op. cit. p. 222.

3.—The KARKAPHENSIAN version is a recension of the Peschito, executed towards the close of the tenth century, by David, a Jacobite Monk, residing in the monastery of St. Aaron, on Mount Sigara, in Mesopotamia, whence the appellation (signifying *mountain*) is derived.

4.—The SYRO-ESTRANGHELO version is a translation of Origen's Hexaplar Edition of the Greek Septuagint; which was executed in the former part of the seventh century, and corresponds exactly with the text of the Septuagint. A manuscript of this version is in the Ambrosian library at Milan, containing the latter half of the Old Testament, and which is stated by a subscription to have been copied from the exemplar corrected by Eusebius and Pamphilus from the library of Origen, which was deposited in the library of Cæsarea.

5.—The PALÆSTINO-SYRIAC Version is written in the Chaldaic dialect of Jerusalem, and is supposed to have been translated from the Greek in Palestine; a manuscript of this version, written in the eleventh century, at Antioch, is in the Vatican. Some other Syriac versions of less note are described by Masch [1].

The early manuscripts of the Syrians (previous to the year A.D. 800) were written in the character termed Estranghelo, being in general thick and massive, with the letters not joined together; it was also used for monumental inscriptions, and for titles and headings in manuscripts, as a kind of majuscule. About the year 900, however, a new character, and more cursive, convenient, and elegant, was invented by the Nestorians.

The most celebrated of all the ancient Syriac manuscripts is that of the Four Gospels, preserved in the Medici-Laurentian library at Florence, written in the year 586, by Rabula, a Scribe, in the monastery of St. John, in Zagba, a city of Mesopotamia, [2] and fully described by Assemanus [3], who published the illuminations, with which it is elegantly ornamented, in twenty-six plates, the figures in which vary from one to seven inches in height. The plates were republished by Biscionius [4]; and D'Agincourt has also given a fac-simile of one of the drawings, with details of some of the others, in the twenty-seventh plate of the division of his great work devoted to Painting. He refers it, however, to the fourth century. This is so important a manuscript in respect to the history of the arts of illumination and design in the East, that a short detail respecting it will not be out of place. The first illumination represents Christ and the twelve Apostles seated in a circle, with three lamps burning beneath a wide arch, supported by two plain columns, with foliated capitals, and with two birds at the top. The second illumination represents the Virgin and Child standing within a double arch, the columns supporting which are tessellated, and the upper arch with the several rows of zigzags, and peacocks standing at the top. The third represents Eusebius and Ammonius standing beneath a kind of tent-like canopy, supported by three columns, with undulated ornaments, two peacocks with expanded tails standing at the top. The nineteen following plates are occupied by the tables of the Eusebian Canons, arranged in columns between pillars supporting rounded arches, generally inclosed between larger and more ornamented columns supporting a large rounded arch, on the outsides of which are represented various groups of figures illustrating scriptural texts, plants and birds. In some of these plates, however, (as Plate 8) the smaller arches are of the horse-shoe character. The capitals are for the most part foliated, but in one or two they are composed of two human faces, and in a few of birds' heads. The arches, as well as the columns by which they are supported, are ornamented with chevrons, lozenges, nebules, quaterfoils, zigzags, flowers, fruit, birds, &c., many of which singularly resemble those found in the early Anglo-Saxon manuscripts, especially in the columns supporting the Eusebian Canons in the Purple Latin Gospels of the British Museum, (MS. reg. 1 E. 6) illustrated in one of the Plates of this Work. There is, however, *none of the singular interlacing of the patterns* so characteristic of the Anglo-Saxon and Irish manuscripts [5]. The twenty-third plate represents the Crucifixion of Christ and the two thieves; our Saviour being clothed in a long loose shirt, reaching from the neck to the feet, with a slit on each side for the arms, and one in front; whereas, the thieves have only a short garment

---

[1] The preceding account of the Syriac versions is abridged from Horne's Introduction, vol. ii., in the second portion of which volume (Part I., ch. i., sect. 5, § 3), will be found a list of the chief *printed* editions of the Syriac Scriptures.

[2] Sir F. Madden (Introd. to Shaw's illuminated ornaments), described a manuscript, agreeing in these particulars, as preserved in the Imperial library at Vienna; but as he refers to Biscionius, I presume it is to the Florence manuscript that he alludes.

[3] Biblioth. Med. Laurent. et Palat. Cod. MSS. Orient. fol. 1742.

[4] Cat. Hebr. MSS. in Med. Libr. 1752, fol.

[5] I mention this more particularly, because it was overlooked by the antiquarian writer Ledwich, who, from an examination of the details of this Syrian manuscript, was led to consider (Archæologia, vol. 8, p. 170) that the Anglo-Saxons received their ornamental designs from the East, as exhibited in the sacred Ciboria of the Eastern

churches, and who considered that all the columns and arches with their ornaments, represented in this manuscript, were evidently copied from Ciboria, whereas the manuscript itself bears sufficient evidence in its representations of buildings (as the tomb of Our Saviour, and some others figured at the sides of the Eusebian tables,) that the former were designed from architectural patterns, as we find the doorways of the buildings with a rounded arch at the top, supported by side columns; indeed Ledwich even asserts that in the second illumination of this manuscript, the Virgin and Child are placed under a Ciborium, supported by four pillars, but an inspection of Assemani's plate (not that of Ledwich, which quite metamorphoses the structure,) proves that the columns are architectural, and that the ornamental arch is but a fanciful design, which is easily convertible into a Gothic-ogee arch with crockets and finial!

across the middle of the body. On either side of the cross of Christ stands a soldier with the spear and sponge, and at its feet are seated three soldiers casting lots for the garments; whilst on each side of the picture stands a group of weeping disciples and females. In this drawing, the entire story is well told; and the soldier with the spear is very spiritedly designed; but the arms of the crucified figures are disproportionately long, and the heads throughout the drawings are much too small. Beneath, is represented the Resurrection from the Tomb; the angel and the two Maries standing on one side, and Christ and the same females on the other. This portion of the drawing in its style entirely betrays the impress of Byzantine art. The twenty-fourth Plate represents the Ascension; a full-length figure of Christ standing within an oval frame, supported above and at the sides by winged angels, and beneath by the four winged symbols of the Evangelists (the wings full of eyes and supporting four flaming wheels), occupies the upper part of the miniature; whilst in the centre beneath stands the Virgin Mary with uplifted hands, and on either side a group of disciples, whose attention is directed to the rising Saviour by two winged angels. The heads of Christ, the Virgin, and the angels, are encompassed with plain nimbi. The twenty-fifth miniature represents Christ disputing with the Doctors, beneath a beautifully ornamented arch; and in the twenty-sixth, the descent of the Holy Ghost like a dove, and flames of fire over the heads of the disciples, all of whom have round plain nimbi. This fine volume is written in the Estranghelo character, with the letters separate, and having somewhat the appearance of Samaritan writing.

The same library contains two other Syriac copies of the Gospels, written previous to the ninth century; one in the year 757, in which is a figure of St. Mark beneath a rounded arch, and two early Syriac Psalters.

The public library at Cambridge possesses several Syriac Manuscripts of great value, discovered by the late Rev. Dr. Buchanan, in the Syrian Churches in India. One of these is particularly valuable, having, according to Mr. Yeates[1], been written about the seventh century, and containing the Old and New Testaments in the Estranghelo character, on strong vellum, in large folio, with three columns in a page; " the words of every book are numbered, and the volume is illuminated, but not after the European manner, *the initial letters having no ornament*[2]." This peculiarity in Syriac manuscripts is worthy of remark; Sir Frederick Madden, whose great learning and official position give to his opinions so high a value, having adduced the Syriac school of art in that portion of his dissertation on Illuminated Manuscripts, in which he treats upon ornamented initials.

Syriac illuminated manuscripts are, however, of great rarity; indeed, Silvestre, in his three plates of Syriac manuscripts, has given specimens merely of black and red writing, none of which are earlier than the eleventh and thirteenth centuries. One of his specimens is written in characters very unlike the ordinary Syriac, being taken from the Book of Adam, a Sabæan manuscript, written by the Christians of St. John, in Mesopotamia, or Meredaites, so named, although their religion has nothing in common with that of Christianity; the writing and idiom are, however, both derived from the Syriac, but the form of the letters is rectangular, with the extremities recurved.

The British Museum is rich in Syriac manuscripts, of which a very careful catalogue was published in 1838. Specimens from some of the most interesting of these manuscripts are given in the accompanying Plate. The most precious of these, in a biblical point of view, is the Nestorian Codex, numbered 7157, a volume measuring $8\frac{1}{2}$ inches by 6, and consisting of 197 leaves of thin and very smooth parchment, written in the Estranghelo character, in a small and beautiful hand, with the titles and headings of the sections miniated.

It contains the New Testament, in the simple or Peschito version; and is stated, in an inscription at the end of the Epistle to the Hebrews, to have been written in the year 1079, according to the Greek computation, which corresponds with the Christian year 768, in the monastery of Beth Kuko, in the region of Adiabene. In this manuscript, all the books are divided into chapters, which are indicated in the margin; and in the Gospels, the verses are distinguished by numerals inserted in the text. The Eusebian Canons are indicated by numerals written in green colour in the text. The specimen at the foot of my Plate, numbered 8, is taken from this manuscript, being the commencement of the Acts of the Apostles (fol. 100, v.).

The illuminations on the upper part of my Plate are copied from a noble Codex Bombycinus (or, one made of silk paper), numbered 7170 (No. 26 of the Cat. Orient. MSS.), and of very large dimensions, measuring 18 inches by 14, and consisting of 265 leaves, written in double columns, in very large and thick Estranghelo characters, which are generally of black ink, but occasionally of gold, with a slender edging of red, as in the specimen marked with the number 4. It consists of lessons from the Four Evangelists, written in the simple

---

[1] By whom a collation of the Pentateuch was published. See " Christian Observer," vol. ix. p. 273, 348; and vol. xii. p. 171. Buchanan's " Christian Researches," p. 229. See also Lee, " Vetus

Testamentum Syriace; in usum Syrorum Malabarensium." London, 1823, 4to. All quoted by Horne.

[2] Horne, Intr. vol. ii. part i. p. 223.

(Peschito) version, but sometimes in the Philoxenian. The six first leaves are occupied with figures of the Evangelists, seated on ornamental seats, writing their Gospels, with the hand of God extended to each from a cloud; and a table, or index, of the lessons arranged in ornamental squares.

An inscription occurs on the 185th leaf, which may be translated, " This holy Evangeliarium was written and ornamented in the days of the holy fathers, Mar Johannes, Patriarch of the whole world, and Mar Ignatius, an Eastern Catholic: may the Lord extend their lives!" It is profusely ornamented with drawings of the chief events in the life of our Saviour, dispersed throughout the volume, sometimes occupying only a portion of one of the columns of a leaf, as is the case with the miniature in my Plate; but often extending across the entire page, and comprising a great number of figures.

The miniature in my Plate will give a tolerable idea of the style of the drawings in this fine volume. It represents the Miracle at the Pool of Bethesda. The pool itself, agitated in a most picturesque manner (although rather out of perspective) by the rod which the angel holds in his right hand; the haste with which the healed man marches off with his bed on his back; the dignified attitude of our Saviour; and the evident surprise of the Apostle (manifested by his uplifted hand), are all interestingly portrayed: whilst the characters of the architecture, and the cruciferous nimbus round the head of the Saviour, must not be overlooked. Many of the countenances throughout the Work exhibit a decidedly Eastern character, and some wear turbans. This is particularly the case in the painting representing the three kings presenting offerings to the new-born Saviour; the Virgin, reclining on the ground in an easy attitude of repose (fol. 20): whilst, in the miniature of the raising of the young man, the features of the attendants on the corpse are very Israelitish. The entry of Christ into Jerusalem is a large and singular composition. The miniatures of the betrayal of Christ by Judas to the soldiers, and that in which the Saviour is brought before the judgment-seat of Pontius Pilate, are interesting from the diversity of costume which they represent; whilst the story of Peter and the Cock crowing, is curiously delineated. The scene of the Crucifixion is also a remarkable composition (fol. 141). Christ trampling on the Gates of Death (fol. 166), is a remarkably spirited drawing, occupying the entire page; whereas, the Ascension (fol. 177), is tame, compared with that in the manuscript at Florence, described above.

The ornamental designs with which this Volume is also profusely ornamented, at the heads of the different portions, are very elegant. Two of these (represented in figures 2 and 3), have been selected as affording instances of very different style of art; No. 2 being decidedly Moorish [1], and occurring in the Alhambra, as we learn from Mr. Owen Jones's fine Work on that famed structure, whereas No. 3 (as I am informed by the same gentleman, whose long residence in Spain and Egypt rendered him so excellent an authority on such a subject) is essentially Cairesque, occurring constantly on the mosques, tombs, &c., in Cairo [2], and requiring only in its construction a flowing pencil and fanciful genius. The specimen of the Golden Writing (No. 4) is taken from the 103d leaf, being the heading of the lesson " Dominicæ Sanctæ Hosannarum in vesperis," taken from St. Matthew xxi. 1—17, and the specimen No. 5 is taken from the commencement of the lesson, " Feriæ quartæ Passionis: in Baptisterio," John v. 1—18.

The specimen at the foot of the Plate marked 7, is taken from a finely-written Codex, numbered 7183, in the British Museum, being a Glossary of Biblical and other Words, written at the beginning of the twelfth century, in the Nestorian character, the letters massive, and the margins ornamented with singular devices, one of which is here figured from the verso of the 28th leaf. There are likewise written on the margin various Greek words, in characters of a very peculiar form, quite unlike any of those collected by the Benedictines [3] in their long series of Greek letters, and more resembling those of Greek inscriptions before the Christian era. A few of these words are given on either side, at the foot of the Plate (No. 9 and 9*), which are to be read ΆΧΗΣ, ΚΕΔΡΟΣ, ΣΟΛΟΜΟΝ, ΙΥΣΑΦΑΤ, ΒΗΣΑΧΑΡ, ΟΑΜΕΟΣ.

The Harleian MS. 5512 contains a Missal in the Latin language, written in Syriac characters, having a singularly-drawn cross in the first page.

It remains to be mentioned, that the specimen (No. 6 and 6*) is taken from a Syriac Pentateuch, brought from Travancore, by the Rev. C. Buchanan, in 1806, written upon paper of a small folio size, in characters unlike those of any of the other specimens given in my Plate, or by Silvestre, or in the plate of fac-similes in the first part of the Catalogue of the Oriental MSS. in the British Museum.

---

[1] The principle of this design is very simple; requiring, however, the aid of instruments, and consisting of a series of quadrants struck from the four corners of two square areas, (placed side by side,) and interlacing together.

[2] See a design in which portions of this ornament may be traced,

taken from the tomb of Ibrahim Agi, at Cairo, in Shaw's " Cyclopædia of Ornament." [3] N. Tr. Dipl. tom. i. pl. 10 and 11.

[4] This form of the Greek letter A occurs, however, in some very early Anglo-Saxon MSS., as in the Gospels of Lindisfarne (Bibl. Cotton. Nero, D. IV.)

እስመ፡ብዙኃን፡አኀዙ፡ይ
ው፡ዋኑ፡ወይንግሩ፡▨▨▨ወይ
ምሀሩ፡ሥርዓተ፡ዜና፡ግብር፡ዘን
ሕነ፡ጠየቅናሁ፡በከም፡እይድ
ዑነ፡እልክቱ፡እሉ፡ቀደምነ፡ር

ቀደዉሁ፡ቃል፡ወእቱ፡
ወሙእቱ፡ቃል፡ኀበእ

ⲈⲚⲦⲀⲢ
ⲬⲎ ⲚⲈⲘⲤⲀ
ⲬⲘ Ⲉ ⲞⲨⲞϢⲠⲒⲤⲀ
ⲬⲒ ⲚⲀⲨ ⲬⲎⲂ Ⲇ ⲦⲈⲚ
ⲫ ̄ Ⲧ ⲞⲨⲞ ϢⲚⲈⲨ Ⲛ
Ⲛ ⲞⲨ ̄Ⲧ ⲠⲈⲠⲒ ϩⲀⲬⲒ
ⲫ ⲀⲒ ⲈⲚ ⲀⲤⲨ Ⲭ ⲚⲒ ⲤⲬⲈ ̀
Ⲉ Ⲏ ϩⲀⲦⲈⲚ ⲫ ̄Ⲧ

ⲦⲈ ⲘⲘⲞⲞⲨ ̇ ⲐⲰⲘⲀⲤ
ⲆⲈ ⲞⲨⲆⲈⲂⲞⲖ ⲄⲘⲠⲠⲘⲚⲦ
ⲤⲚⲞⲞⲨ ⲤⲠⲈ ⲦⲈⲨ ⲀⲨ
ⲘⲞⲨⲦⲈ ⲈⲢⲞϤ ⲬⲈⲆ ⲒⲆⲨ

Ⲡ ⲔⲀ ⲐⲞ Ⲗ ⲒⲔⲞⲚ Ⲧ Ⲉ ⲠⲒⲤ
Ⲧ Ⲟ Ⲗ Ⲏ ⲚⲒ Ⲱ ⲀⲚ Ⲛ Ⲉ ⲒⲤ
ⲘⲠ ⲢⲘⲈⲢ ⲈⲦ ⲠⲒⲤⲞ ⲤⲘⲞⲤ ⲞⲨ
Ⲙ Ⲁ Ⲉ Ⲛ Ⲉ Ⲧ ⲐⲘⲠ Ⲓ Ⲕ ⲞⲤⲘⲞⲤ ̇

Ethiopic & Coptic Mss.

ETHIOPIC AND COPTIC BIBLICAL MSS.

DESCRIPTION OF THE PLATE.

1. Portrait of St. Luke, and
2. Commencement of his Gospel from the Ethiopic Gospels, No. 14, in the Library of the British and Foreign Bible Society.
3. Part of ornamental heading and commencement of St. Mark's Gospel, from another MS. in the same library.
4. Drawing of the Saviour, and commencement of the Gospel of St. John, in Coptic and Arabic, from MS. of the Gospels in the Bodleian Library.
5. Part of the 20th Chapter of St. John, from Coptic Papyrus, in the British Museum.
6. Part of the Epistle of St. John, from Coptic Lectionarium in the Bodleian Library. (Hunt. 3).

OF the introduction of the Christian religion into Ethiopia we possess no distinct knowledge; but the beautiful narration connected with the Ethiopian treasurer of Queen Candace, recorded in the 8th chapter of the Acts, sufficiently proves that within 50 years from the death of our Saviour, the knowledge of His religion had penetrated into Africa, below Egypt: probably, as Dr. Whitby suggests, carried by Christianized Jews from Alexandria. It is certain, indeed, that the Ethiopic version of the Gospels agrees for the most part with the Alexandrine recension, the translation of the New Testament having been attributed to Frumentius, about the year 330. It, however, possesses some peculiar readings of considerable importance in Biblical criticism.

The Ethiopic version of the Old Testament is considered to have been made from the Septuagint, and, as is supposed, from the marks of unquestionable antiquity which it presents, as early as the fourth century. The Psalms were published at Rome in 1513 by Potken, and were subsequently reprinted by Bishop Walton in his Polyglot Bible. There are MSS. of this portion of the Scriptures in the British Museum and the British and Foreign Bible Society's library. The British Museum possesses but very few (six) Ethiopic MSS., (chiefly books of prayers,) but the latter Society has, at much pains, collected a considerable number of highly valuable Biblical MSS., and has also been at the expense of having a fonte of Ethiopic types cast from the matrices, preserved at Frankfort, of the celebrated Ethiopic traveller, Ludolphi, and which were used by the Rev. T. P. Platt in his edition of the Ethiopic Gospels, published at London in 1826, and in his work, entitled "A Catalogue of the Ethiopic Biblical Manuscripts, in the Royal Library of Paris, and in the library of the British and Foreign Bible Society; also some Account of those in the Vatican Library at Rome, with Remarks and Extracts. To which are added Specimens of Versions of the New Testament in the modern Languages of Abyssinia, and a grammatical Analysis of a Chapter in the Amharic Dialect, with fac-similes of an Ethiopic and an Amharic Manuscript." (4to, London, 1823.)

In addition to the MSS. described by Mr. Platt, the library of the British and Foreign Bible Society now possesses several other MSS. of even greater value than those contained in his list. Amongst these are the fine MS. of the Octateuch, formerly belonging to the Church Missionary Society, (upon which Professor Lee published a memoir, and of which the Rev. T. H. Horne has given an account in his Introduction, vol. ii., p. 229, and which contains a large, rude, outline likeness of St. Andrew, not destitute of expression in the features,) and also two very fine MSS. of the Gospels of the quarto size, written on vellum, one of which is preceded by prefaces, tables, &c., and is ornamented with drawings of the four Evangelists, each accompanied by his symbolical animal, but disproportionately short in their figures, each being represented as writing his Gospel, and having three long pots or glasses of ink (red and black,) standing on a small stool, and with a long knife lying on the ground in front of him. These drawings do not occupy more than half of the entire page, and are gaudily coloured with strongly-marked shades, and relieved by lights of opaque colours. Our fac-simile, No. 1, is a copy of the upper half of the portrait of St. Luke, (the others being treated in a nearly identical manner,) and No. 2 is a copy of the commencement of the Gospel of the same Evangelist; the text being read (like the Coptic and Greek) from left to right. The MS. contains no other illuminations or ornamental drawings.

No. 3 is a copy of part of the rudely executed interlaced ornamental heading, and the commencement of the Gospel of St. Mark, from another MS. on vellum, in the Library of the same Society.

The Ashmolean Library is particularly rich in Ethiopic MSS., having recently acquired the fine collection formed by the celebrated traveller, Bruce, in whose Travels (vol. ii., pp. 416 and 420) will be found an interesting account of the Ethiopic Biblical books. Messrs. Silvestre and Champollion have given several fac-similes of Ethiopic MSS., one of which (being a copy of the Gospels) is accompanied by drawings of the Evangelists in a remarkably rude style, reminding us somewhat of the early drawings of the Irish school. Another is from

1

a MS. of the Book of Enoch, presented by Bruce to Louis XV. These authors consider that the Ethiopian letters are derived from the Samaritan, notwithstanding their being read in an opposite direction.

It appears that the Christian religion was at a very early period communicated to the Egyptians, since we find that they opposed the Synod of Chalcedon, and that in the sixth century the Coptic Church was torn by the disputes of the Corruptibles and Incorruptibles.[1] Wilkinson, indeed, endeavours to prove that the Lower Egyptian version was made in the third, whilst L. Picques refers it to the fifth, and Hug has shown that it could not have been composed before the time of Hesychius, nor before the middle of the third century.

Of the Sahidic Version (or that of the dialect of Upper Egypt) a variety of fac-similes have been published by Mangarelli, in his " Ægyptiorum Codicum Reliquiæ Venetiis in Bibliotheca Naniana asservatis," (Bononiæ, 1785, 4to) ; and by Dr. Woide, in his memoir, published, after his decease, as an appendix to the fac-simile of the Codex Alexandrinus, (Oxford fol., 1799). By the last-named author it has been shown that this version was most probably executed in the second century, quotations from both Testaments being found in the writings of Valentinus, a Coptic author of the second century, as well as in the works of the Gnostics who flourished during the same period, which quotations have been found to coincide with the fragments of the Sahidic Version now extant.[2] Hence this version is of the utmost importance to the criticism of the Greek text.

Our public libraries, especially the Bodleian, are particularly rich in Coptic and Sahidic MSS., but the only known entire copy of the Coptic Bible, is stated by M. Quatremère to be in the possession of M. Marcel.[3] The Rev. Mr. Tattum, of Bedford, also possesses a fine collection of Coptic MSS. hitherto undescribed.

The great resemblance between the Coptic characters (which supplanted those of ancient Egypt), and those of the Greek alphabet, will not fail to attract attention. Hence, Mingarelli exclaimed, on his first examination of the fragments of which he subsequently published the analysis, "Aperta arcula obstupui; Græcas putabam Ægyptias referi;" adding, that he could not satisfactorily assign the age to any of his MSS., as he had not discovered any indication of a date. The analogy between the Coptic and Greek MSS. in the use of the large round uncial characters, and the large uncials of a more cursive form, will evidently supply a comparative clue to the date of these MSS. In this respect our specimen No. 5, from its close resemblance to the most ancient Greek MSS., may be assumed to be the oldest of the three Coptic fac-similes in our plate. This is copied from a portion of one of the fragments of the Gospel of St. John, written on papyrus, (preserved in the British Museum, having been presented by Sir J. G. Wilkinson in 1834,) the passage being that portion of the 20th chapter which contains the incident of the incredulity of St. Thomas, as may be perceived by the word $\theta\omega\mu\alpha c$ at the end of the first line.

The specimen No. 4, is the commencement of St. John's Gospel, copied from a very fine bombycine codex preserved in the Bodleian Library, of a large quarto size, written in the year of the Martyrs, 890 (A.D. 1173). containing 433 leaves, and comprising the four Coptic Gospels with an Arabic version. Each gospel is preceded by a portrait of its Evangelist, of a large size, executed in colours in the ruder Byzantine style, except that of St. Matthew, which is preceded by a beautifully illuminated page, representing a highly ornamented cross, with the Saviour seated in one of the lower open spaces and St. Matthew in the other, the former figure being copied in our plate. The borders of these drawings are ornamented with rude interlaced ribbon patterns, of which the one before us will serve as a specimen.

Messrs. Silvestre and Champollion have given a very fine series of fac-similes of Coptic MSS., the earliest of which (bearing considerable resemblance to our No. 5 in general appearance, and in the form of the M) is considered to be of the fifth century, and earlier than the Copto-Thebaic and Greek MS. of St. John in the Borgian Collection at Rome, published by Georgii (Fragm. Evang. S. Johann. Rom. 1789, 4to) which Woide refers to the seventh century. With the exception of seven letters derived from the ancient demotic alphabet of Egypt, the Coptic letters are essentially of Greek origin ; and Coptic MSS., with Arabic glosses, are of course more modern than the Arabic invasion and conquest of Egypt.

The specimen No. 6, is copied from one of the MSS. in the Bodleian library, employed by Dr. Woide in his Treatise on the Sahidic Version of the Bible above referred to ; it is of a folio size, with slightly ornamented capital letters and rubricated headings to the various lessons.

---

[1] Gibbon's Rom. Emp. vol. vi. chap. 47, sect. 5. The history of the Copts, their religion, manners, &c., may be found in Renaudot's Hist. Patriarch. Alex., the Chronicon Orientale of Peter a Jacobite, Abraham Echellensis, Paris, 1651, and Assemann, Venet. 1729.

[2] Marsh's Michaelis, vol. ii., part 2, p. 595. Horne, Introduction, vol. ii., p. 227, in the appendix to which, p. 48-49, the author has given a list of the various portions of the Scriptures hitherto published in the Coptic, Sahidic, or Bashmouric versions.

[3] Rech. sur la Langue et la Lit. d'Egypte, p. 118 ; in which work (pp. 114, 115, 134, 135) the author has specified the various portions of the Coptic Bible preserved in the great Continental libraries).

Arabic Ms.

ARABIC GOSPELS.

DESCRIPTION OF THE PLATE.

Title-page of the Gospel of St. Luke, and part of the commencement of his Gospel, from Bishop Butler's MS.

ARABIA, the birth-place of the Mohammedan religion, has, nevertheless, long possessed the means of obtaining a knowledge of the Christian dispensation; the early missionaries having preached the Gospel in Arabia as well as in other countries of the East, although with less success than in Syria and Ethiopia, where Christianity became the established religion of the country. Arabic versions of the Sacred Scriptures are, consequently, of great rarity, and these are not earlier than the 10th century, when the Rabbi Saadias Gaon paraphrased the Old Testament in Arabic at Babylon, of which the Pentateuch and the Prophecies of Isaiah have been published; and a MS. containing Job exists in the Bodleian library; another Arabic version of the Pentateuch (published by Erpenius at Leyden in 1622) appears to have been executed in the 13th century, by an African Jew. The Pentateuch, Psalms, and prophecy of Daniel, were translated by Saadi Ben Levi Asnekot, in the early part of the 17th century. The Arab Christians have also a translation of the Book of Job, and two versions of the Psalms, made from the Peschito, or old Syriac version. All the Arabic books of the Old Testament (except the Pentateuch and Job), printed in the Paris and London Polyglots, were executed from Hesychius's recension of the Septuagint.

Of the New Testament there are many Arabic translations; for, since the Arabic language supplanted the Syriac and Egyptian, the inhabitants of the countries where these had been spoken, have been obliged to annex Arabic translations to the ancient versions, which are no longer understood. These Arabic translations are supposed to have been made at different times between the 7th and 11th centuries. In general, they were not all executed from the original text, but from the versions which they were intended to accompany.[1]

The beautiful MS. which has supplied the materials for the accompanying plate, formerly belonged to the celebrated Bishop Butler, of Shrewsbury, at whose death it became (together with his other MSS.) the property of the nation, having been purchased by the trustees of the British Museum, and now bearing the No. Add. 11856. It is a Codex Bombycinus, consisting of 205 leaves, measuring 10½ inches by 8, with 14 lines in a page, and comprises the four gospels, beautifully written, and in the most excellent state of preservation.

Like the Hebrew, Syriac, and other divisions of the great Semitic class of languages, the Arabic is read from right to left; and, of course, the last page of a MS. is the commencement of the work. At the end, therefore, of the present volume, is an inscription of its former ownership by the College de Propaganda. "Bibliothecæ Collegii Urbani de Propaganda Fide ex dono Illmi. et Reumi. D. Petri Bogdani Archiepiscopi Scuporum ejusdem Collegii olim alumni;"—and the following observation in the handwriting of its late possessor—" Ancient Manuscripts of the Gospels in Arabic are of great rarity."

Each of the four gospels is preceded by a highly illuminated page, containing a few of the first words in the upper and lower compartments; the centre part of each presenting a very beautiful specimen of Moorish ornamental art, precisely similar in the principle of its design to the ornaments of the Alhambra Palace, so splendidly illustrated by Mr. Owen Jones. The specimen copied in the plate, intricate as its centre part appears, will be perceived, when carefully examined, to be produced by four series of straight but interrupted lines crossing each other at an angle of 45°, whereby octagonal spaces of two sizes are produced, which are filled up with *arabesque*[2] foliated patterns, the whole forming, from the admirable blending of the gold and colours, a

---

[1] See Michaelis, Hug, and Horne's Introduction, from which last work the preceding details have been abridged, and whose work contains a Biographical Notice of the printed Arabic versions.

[2] The following observations by M. Langlois on the application of the term *Arabesque* to these and similar ornamental designs, are deserving of consideration :—

" M. Peignot, dans sa curieuse et savante notice sur vingt-et-une

grandes miniatures d'un manuscrit du 15e siècle, lue à l'Académie de Dijon, le 11 juillet, 1832, dit que les ornaments nommés *Arabesques*, que l'on trouve sur des manuscrits, sont bien postérieures aux *Vignettes*, et qu'ils sont ordinairement composés de plantes, d'arbustes, de branches légères et de fleurs, qui s'entrelacent et entourent les pages. Après cette description, qui peut s'appliquer en partie à la flexibilité comme aux directions capricieuses des rameaux de la *vigne*, il ajoute

very rich effect.[1] Each Gospel is also preceded by a portrait of its respective Evangelist, drawn with great rudeness, and as coarsely painted,[2] the figures in all being much too short and broad. St. Matthew is represented holding a book on his breast with his right hand, the head surrounded with a golden nimbus, the face bearded, the feet wearing red sandals, and the upper robe green with a broad edging of gold. St. Mark is represented in the robes of a priest, the golden collar or edge of his robe marked with crosses in front, and seated on a Moorish throne, as is also St. Luke, who holds a book in the right hand, and has another open book placed before him on a stand. St. John is drawn standing, and holding a book in the left hand.

The two lines at the foot of the plate will serve to show the character of the writing of the ordinary text of the volume.

que l'origine des *Arabesques* provient de ce qu'à une certaine époque, on mettait partout des inscriptions arabes comme ornements, et que ces inscriptions, grossièrement copiées, ont dégénéré en simples dessins de toutes sortes d'entrelacements, qui ont conservé le nom d'*Arabesques.* Cependant, en accordant aux *Vignettes* les véritables caractères qui semblent leur assigner les formes du végétal auquel leur nom fait allusion, ces deux mots ne paraissent-ils pas désigner à peu près les mêmes motifs d'ornements ? Quant à celui d'*Arabesques,* quoique probablement assez moderne, il n'en est pas moins vrai qu'il est maintenant universellement consacré à rappeler une foule d'ornements fantastiques, peints ou sculptés, fort en usage dans la haute antiquité, et dont les artistes de la Renaissance, après les avoir exhumés, ont fait si luxuriant emploi. Au reste, comme dans leur application au style de nos monuments gothiques, ces deux mots, *Arabesques* et *Mauresques,* ne se rattachent, dans les doctrines archéologiques, qu'à des idées contradictoires ou fort embrouillées, je ne doute pas que M. Peignot, dont j'honore et la personne et le savoir, ne soit fondé à dire que les *Arabesques* sont des caractères arabes dégénérés en entrelacs bizarres ; il est certain, cependant, que ces ornements, plus ou moins riches de fleurons, plus ou moins artistement combinés, appartiennent à toutes les époques barbares de l'art en l'Europe, et se retrouvent chez des peuples même qui, probablement, n'eurent jamais d'inscriptions arabes à défigurer, en cherchant à les imiter."—*Essai*

sur la Caligraphie, par E. H. Langlois. Rouen, 1841. *p.* 4. Strictly speaking, the term *Arabesque* is applied to the capricious, fantastic, and imaginary ornaments, consisting of fruits, flowers, and other objects, to the exclusion of the figures of animals, which the Moorish religion forbade. It is, however, clearly misapplied, since foliage, griffins and ornaments, not very dissimilar to those of the Arabians, were by no means unfrequent in the friezes of temples, and on many of the ancient Greek vases ; at Herculaneum, and many other places, elegant examples of this species of decoration are to be found. It is, however, to Raphael that we owe the most splendid specimens of the style, which he dignified, and left in it nothing to be desired. Since his time it has been practised with varying and inferior degrees of merit, especially by the French, in the time of Louis XIV.—(*Brande, Dict. of Science.*)

[1] In the original the entire ground of the square is of gold, the blue, red, and black colours, as well as the white letters and lines, being formed with thick layers of opake colours.

[2] This is not surprising, considering that the delineation of living objects was strictly forbidden to the Arabs by the laws of Mohammed, (in order to prevent the possible introduction of the worship of images,) which cannot but have had its effect upon the practice of the art, even by those who had adopted the Christian faith.

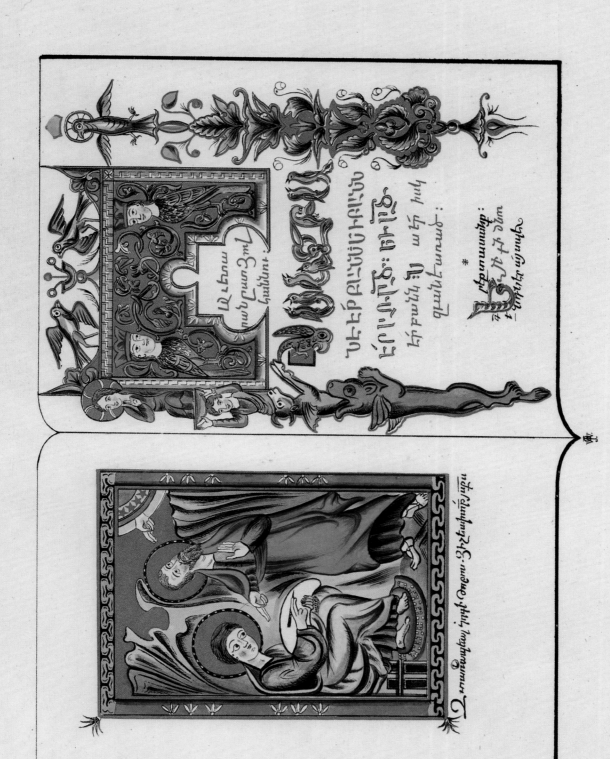

Armenian · Gospels.

THE ARMENIAN GOSPELS.

AFTER the division of Armenia, about the beginning of the fifth century, the western Armenians used the Greek language and characters in their religious offices; but the use of that hostile tongue was prohibited by the Persians in the eastern provinces, which were obliged to use the language of the Syriac Missionaries, by whom the Armenians had previously been converted to Christianity, till the invention of the Armenian letters by Mesrob, Meisrob, Mesrop, or Mesrobes, (which took place shortly afterwards,) and the subsequent version of the Bible into the Armenian language; an event that relaxed the connexion of the church and nation with Constantinople[1], which was soon after entirely broken[2]. The religion of the Armenians, who to this day retain the doctrines of Eutyches, has been briefly described by La Croze[3]; and to their credit it is recorded that, although so constantly suffering under persecution, their zeal has been fervent and intrepid, neither becoming converts to the doctrines of Mahomet, nor reassuming the rites of the Greek or Roman churches; and Etschmiazim, a monastery near Erivan, on Mount Ararat, is still the seat of the Patriarch of Armenia[4].

The Armenian version of the Old Testament is stated by Biblical writers[5], to have been made from the Alexandrian Septuagint, whilst the translation of the New Testament is ascribed to Meisrob and his disciples, by desire of the patriarch Isaac the Great. The latter was not completed till the fifth century. It was thrice translated from the Syriac, and then from the Greek. It appears, however, to have been subsequently altered to correspond with the Romish Latin Vulgate version in the thirteenth century. The first edition of the Armenian Bible, printed at Amsterdam in 1666, in quarto, was also altered to render it conformable to the Vulgate, by the then patriarch of Erivan, which, however, led to its not being cordially received by the Armenian Christians. The most complete version of the Armenian Bible is that of Dr. Zohrab, in quarto, published in 1805, at Venice, (a copy of which is in the library of the British Museum,) and for which its editor collated as many as sixty-nine manuscripts[6].

The present Armenian alphabet contains thirty-eight letters[7], which, although they have been by most writers attributed to Miesrob, have by others[8] been asserted to have been invented by St. Chrysostom, with whom Mesrob corresponded, and in whose time the Bible was translated, and who certainly died in banishment in Armenia. Although the Armenian characters are generally supposed to be derived from the Greeks, their forms are very different, and their number exceeds those of the Greek alphabet by more than one third. Their alphabet contains several letters or marks for sounds, which frequently occur in the Hebrew, Arabic, and Syriac languages, but are not found in the Greek. Like that of the Greeks, whose literature was much cultivated by them, their writing is read from left to right.

Armenian manuscripts are of great rarity in the libraries of the west of Europe. Silvestre illustrates two destitute of miniatures, contained in the Bibliothèque Royale at Paris, the first containing the four Gospels in a large, very regular, black, uncial letter, and which is assigned by him to the eleventh century. It is so precisely similar to the two fragments contained in the Burney Collection, No. 277[9], that it is almost impos-

---

[1] Gibbon, iv. 216.

[2] L'Art de Vérifier les Dates, p. 35. Pagi, Critica, A.D. 535.

[3] Histoire du Christian. de l'Ethiopie et de l'Arménie.

[4] Morier, &c.

[5] Jahn, p. 82; Masch, p. 169-173; Kortholt, p. 304; Horne, ii, p. 233.

[6] Horne, vol. ii., part 2, p. 50.

[7] In the N. Tr. de Dipl. i. pl. 13 x., the alphabet is made to consist of 39 letters, of each of which numerous examples are figured. See also Astle (Orig. of Writing, p. 92) for the letters, with their respective powers.

[8] Angelus Rocha, Discourse on the Books of the Vatican, Sixtus Senensis, and George, Patriarch of Alexandria.

[9] These fragments are portions of the Gospels of St. Matthew and

sible not to believe them part of the same MS. The other MS. is more ornamented, one of the fac-similes from it having a large ornament terminating above in a red Greek cross, and the other specimen with four lines of red letters and a red initial formed of two birds, the remainder being in small black *leaning* uncial letters, somewhat like, but much larger than those in the MS. of the Duke of Sussex. These two specimens are from a menologe written at Ispahan, for the Church of Surat, in India, at the end of the sixteenth century.

Blanchini[1] has given a fac-simile of a most interesting pentaglot Psalter, written in the year 1036 of the Hegira, in Armenian, Arabic, Coptic, Chaldaic, and Ethiopic letters, the Armenian very much resembling that of the smaller characters in the accompanying plate.

The beautiful specimen represented in the accompanying plate is taken from a manuscript of the four Gospels, written in the middle of the thirteenth century, in excellent preservation, and which was one of the chief treasures of the library of his late lamented R. H. the Duke of Sussex. This manuscript comprises 311 leaves of vellum 5½ inches long, by 3½ wide, and is written on both sides in double columns. It is of great value in a biblical point of view, inasmuch as it is of a prior date to those from which the first printed edition was made. It belonged to an Armenian family long resident at Madras, where they settled on their expulsion from Armenia by Tamerlane, and is said to have been highly esteemed by the Armenian Christians.

It commences with eight leaves, on which are inscribed the Eusebian Canons, enclosed within ornamental pillars, and the pages have the margin illuminated with birds, trees, &c. The capitals are written in letters of gold, and the initials of the chapters are composed of fanciful figures of various kinds, and in many of the margins are drawings representing birds, beasts, angels, kings, harpies, &c., in gold and colours. On the page preceding each of the Gospels is an illumination, representing the respective Evangelist; (that of St. Luke has, however, been cut out). I have selected that opposite the commencement of the Gospel of St. John, the two figures representing, as I suppose, the Evangelist when young, writing the Gospel, and as old when he wrote the Apocalypse[2]: the hand coming out of the cloud, is a very ordinary method adopted by the Eastern illuminators to indicate the presence of the Almighty.[3] Mr. Pettigrew has published the figure of St. Mark, seated before a desk writing; but his plate does not correctly represent the details of the picture, especially the instruments for writing, which are placed on the desk before the Evangelist. The art adopted in these drawings is essentially Byzantine. The Evangelist has the *nimbus perlatus*, or golden glory, around the head, with the margin ornamented with pearls. The first page of each Gospel is also beautifully illuminated with an ornamental heading of strange device, and marginal arabesques of gold and various colours. In the former respect, the style adopted in the Greek manuscripts is followed; the latter, however, rarely occurs in such manuscripts. The marginal arabesques are headed by the evangelical symbol, that of St. John's Gospel copied in my plate having the eagle thus introduced, with the head ornamented with the cruciferous nimbus, whilst the opposite side of the page has a marginal design, in which the symbols of the other evangelists are strangely introduced, supporting a figure with a cruciferous nimbus, probably intended for St. John himself. The first line in each Gospel is in capital letters formed of birds, placed in grotesque juxtaposition. The specimen at the bottom of the plate marked with a star is a fac-simile of the ordinary character of the writing and width of the columns, being the commencement of the historical part of the 1st chapter of St. Matthew's Gospel. At the end of the manuscript is an inscription in Armenian, in which the date is introduced, which is said to be A.D. 1251.

The Bodleian Library possesses two small Armenian books of the Gospels (Laud. 34. 35.) the headings and capitals of which are illuminated, but which will not bear comparison with the MS. of the Duke of Sussex. See also the Codex Regius, 83. (Horne, Intr. ii., p. 166.)

Mark, and in the catalogue are referred to the thirteenth century. The following woodcut is a fac-simile of Mark, ch. viii., the beginning of v. 16.

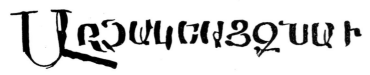

traced from one of the fragments, which are much mutilated, having been

used for the binding of a book: when entire, they must have been of a large folio size, as is the Paris manuscript.

[1] Evangel. Quadrupl., vol. ii., part 2, last plate and specimen but one.

[2] This mode of representing this Evangelist is very rare: it occurs, however, in the Codex Ebnerianus in the Bodleian Library. See Waagen, Art. in Engl. ii. p. 217.

[3] On the signification of the hand stretched from the cloud see N. Tr. de Dipl. iii. 341.

ECCLESIAEQUIDEM ΑΙΜΕΝΟΥΝΕΚΚΛΗCΙΑΙ
UNIUERSAE ΠΑCΑΙ
PEROMNEM ΚΑΘΟΛΗC
IUDAEAM ΤΗCΙΟΥΔΑΙΑC ΦΒ
ETGALILEAM F ΚΑΙΓΑΛΙΛΑΙΑC ΖΥΨ
ETSAMARIAM V ΚΑΙCΑΜΑΡΙΑC ΖΩ
habebant X ΕΙΧΟΝ ΘC
pacem YYZ ΕΙΡΗΝΗΝ ΠΡΙ

MB:

ΟΙCΟΥΚΕΖΟΝΗΝΦΑΓΕΙΝΕΙΜΗΜΟΝΟΙC
ΤΟΙCΙΕΡΕΥCΙΝ : ΤΗΑΥΤΗΗΜΕΡΑΘΕΑCΑΜΕΝΟC
ΤΙΝΑΕΡΓΑΖΟΜΕΝΟΝΤΩCΑΒΒΑΤΩ ΕΙΠΕΝΑΥΤΩ
ΑΝΘΡΩΠΕ ΕΙΜΕΝΟΙΔΑCΤΙΠΟΙΕΙC
ΜΑΚΑΡΙΟCΕΙΕΙΔΕΜΗΟΙΔΑC ΕΠΙΚΑΤΑΡΑΤΟC
ΚΑΙΠΑΡΑΒΑΤΗCΕΙΤΟΥΝΟΜΟΥ

IHC
IHS
ΔΑΥΕΙΔ

2 {

quibusnonlicebatmanducaresinonsolis
sacerdotibus eodem die uidens
quendam operantem sabbato etdixitilli
homo siquidem scisquodfacis
beatuses siautemnescismaledictus
ettrabaricatorlegis

Theodorus Beza

προφητες

ΕΜΕΙC ΔΕΠΟΡΕΙCΟΜΕΘΑ
ΕΝ ΟΝΟΜΑΤΕ ΚΥ ΘΥ ΥΜΟΝ
ΚΑΙ CΥ ΒΕΘΛΕΕΜ
Ο ΟΙΚΟΙC ΤΟΥ ΕΦΦΡΑΤΑ
ΟΛΙΓΟC ΤΟCΕΙΤΟΙ ΕΙΝΑΙ

michias propheta

Norribimur
in nõe dñi dñi nostri...
tu bethlem
domus illius effrata
bezua ẽ ut sit.

3 {

In principio fecit dĩs
caelum et terram
terra tr erat inuisibilis ηπροσιτα
adtende caelum et loquar
audiat terra uerba exore meo

Εν αρχη εποιησεν ὁ θεος
τον υρανον και την γην
Ἡ δε γη ην αορατος και ακατασ και ηας
Προσεχε υρανε και λαλησω
και ακουετω γη ρηματα εκστοματος μου

†
Anni
ab Inca-
rnatione dñi
mu ihu
χρι
M.CCC.II.

4

OQUIRIOSE BASILEUSENAGALLIASTOECE
ONSREGNAUITEXULTETTERRA

Graeco-Latin MSS.

GRÆCO-LATIN ANTE-HIERONYMIAN MANUSCRIPTS.

DESCRIPTION OF THE PLATE.

1. Acts, ch. ix., v. 31, from Archbishop Laud's MS. of the Acts of the Apostles.
2. Luke, ch. vi., v. 3, and the interpolated passage, from the Codex Bezæ, with the Autograph of Beza.
3. Micah, ch. iv., v. 5; ch. v., v. 2. Genesis, ch. i., v. 1, 2; and Deuter., ch. xxxii., v. 1, 2, from the Bodleian Codex, N,E, D. 2. 19.
4. Psalm xcvi., v. i., from the Psalter of Verona.

THE very widely-extended usage of the Greek language[1] at, and for some time preceding, the period of the promulgation of the New Testament, led not only to the execution of the Septuagint Greek version of the Old Testament, about 300 years before Christ, but also to the original composition of the New Testament in the Greek language. Within a very short period after the latter event, the Scriptures were, however, translated into the Latin language; sufficiently proving that the latter was gradually supplanting the Greek as an almost universal tongue.

We have the authority of Sts. Augustine and Jerome in support of the assertion, that numerous translations of the Scriptures into Latin were made in the primitive era of the Church. Thus the former[2] says :— " Qui enim Scripturas ex Hebræa lingua in Græcam verterunt numerari possunt. Latini autem interpretes nullo modo, ut enim cuique primis fidei temporibus in manus venit codex Græcus et aliquantulum facultatis sibi utriusque linguæ habere videbatur ausus est interpretari." And St. Jerome himself states, that " Si Latinis exemplaribus fides est adhibenda, respondeunt quibus; tot enim sunt exemplaria pœne quot codices. Sin autem veritas est quærenda de pluribus; cur non ad Græcam originem revertentes; ea quæ vel a vitiosis interpretibus male edita vel â præsumtoribus imperitis emendata perversius vel â librariis dormantibus aut addita sunt aut mutata corrigimus?"

It will easily be conceived that these versions are of much importance as aids to Biblical criticism, leading to the discovery of the true readings in very ancient Greek MSS. which existed even prior to the date of any now extant.

Amongst these various interpretations, one appears to have acquired a more extensive circulation than the others, and was known in the time of St. Augustine by the name of the "Vetus Itala," or old Italic, on account of its clearness and fidelity.[3] This version, which Jerome mentions sometimes as the *Vulgate*, and sometimes as the *Old*, has been supposed to have been made in the first century; at all events, it was quoted by Tertullian, before the close of the second century.[4]

The MSS. of these Ante-Hieronymian Versions (or those made before the days of Jerome) are, as may easily be supposed, of the greatest rarity, from their great age (the Vulgate Version of Jerome having been almost exclusively adopted since the days of Pope Gregory the Great, in the sixth century)[5]. In the character of their writing, they also betray the highest antiquity; and, whilst we notice the discrepancies which occur in the pages of these versions, we are led at once to the conclusion, that the statement of St. Augustine is precisely confirmed, and also to the more important truth, that the various authors of these Versions must have gone to one common source for the origin of these translations.

In the year 1588, Flaminio Nobili, having collected, with infinite care, all the fragments of the Ante-Hieronymian versions of the Old Testament, quoted in the writings of the Latin Fathers, published the whole in the " Vetus Testamentum secundum LXX., Latine redditum," at Rome.

Subsequently, Sabatier published all the parts of the old Italic Version of both Testaments, which have

---

[1] Cicero says, " Græca leguntur in *omnibus fere gentibus*; Latina suis finibus, exiguis sane, continentur." Orat. pro Archia Poetâ, c. x. ; and Julius Cæsar notices the prevalence of the Greek language even in Gaul. De Bell. Gall. i., 29 ; vi., 14.

[2] De Doctrinâ Christianâ, lib. ii, cap. 2.

[3] Augustine, Op. cit. l. 2 e, 15, quoted by Horne, Introd. 2, 234.

The term *Itala* has, by Casley, Bentley, Bishop Marsh, and some other critics, been considered as misemployed instead of *illa*, but Breyther, Sabatier, and Hug, fully prove the correctness of the former epithet.

[4] Bishop Marsh's Divinity Lectures, Part i., p. 66.

[5] N. Tr. de Dipl. 2, p. 395.

1

survived to our times, in his splendid edition of the " Bibliorum Sacrorum, Latinæ versionis antiquæ seu Vetus Italica," &c., at Rheims, in 1743—49, in three folio volumes, chiefly employing for the text of the Versio Antiqua, the MS. Colbert, 4051.

A more important work, however, as regards the Ante-Hieronymian versions, appeared in 1749, in two folio volumes, published at Rome, by Blanchini, under the title, " Evangeliarium quadruplex Latinæ versionis antiquæ seu Veteris Italicæ editum, ex *Codicibus Manuscriptis aureis, argenteis, purpureis,* aliisque plusquam millenariæ antiquitatis."

The first MS., of which the text is given by Blanchini, is the famous Vercelli Gospels, the writing of which is ascribed to Eusebius himself, with apparent truth, and which bears the inscription—

" Præsul hic Eusebius scripsit solvitque vetustas,

Rex Berengarius, sed reparavit idem,

Argentum postquam fulvo depromsit et auro,

Ecclesiæ Præsul obtulit ipse suæ."

Which fully proves that at the end of the ninth century the volume was an ancient one, and was at that time ascribed to Eusebius. The character of the scription well accords with such a legend, being in slender rounded uncial letters, nearly one-sixth of an inch in height, in narrow columns, with only two or three words in a line[1].

Blanchini's second Codex is a very ancient MS., preserved at Verona, written in uncial letters, very nearly resembling, but somewhat larger than those in Archbishop Laud's MS.

The third MS. in the Codex Corbeiensis, formerly belonging to the Abbey of Corbie (of which specimens are given in the N. Traité Dipl. 3, p. 92, 93).

The fourth MS. is the Codex Brixianus, written upon purple vellum, in silver letters, very similar to those of Archbishop Laud's Codex.

To these were added, in an Appendix, the Codex Foro-Juliensis, preserved at Friuli, and written in moderate-sized uncials, (which is, however, asserted by Michaelis only to contain the corrected version of Jerome), and the Codex Perusini belonging to the Chapter of Perouse, written upon purple vellum, in very massive uncial letters, considerably larger than those of Archbishop Laud's Codex, and which is ascribed by the Italian Palæographers to the beginning of the fifth century.

The following passages, taken indiscriminately from Blanchini's MSS. (to which I have added the corresponding passages from the Versio antiqua of Sabatier, and the Codex Bezæ), will show the nature of the majority of the variations occurring in these Versions.[2]

Codex Vercellensis.	Codex Veronensis.	Codex Corbeiensis.	Codex Brixianus.	Versio Antiqua, ex M.S. Colbert, 4051.	Codex Bezæ.
Matthew, ch. 1., v. 16. Joseph, cui desponsata Virgo Maria, genuit Jesum qui dicitur Christus. Omnes, &c. (So also in C. Sangerm.)	Joseph, cui desponsata erat Virgo Maria, Virgo autem Maria genuit Jesum. Ergo, &c.	Joseph, virum Mariæ, de qua natus est Jesus qui vocatur Christus. Omnes, &c.	Joseph, virum Mariæ, de qua natus est Jesus qui dicitur Christus. (So also in C. Foro-Jul.)	Joseph, cui desponsata Virgo Maria. Maria autem genuit Jesum qui dicitur Christus.	Joseph cui desponsata Virgo Maria peperit Xpm Ihm.
Matthew, ch. 4, v. 10. Vade retro Satanas.	Vade retro me, Satanas.	Vade retro Satanas.	Vade Satana. (So also in C. Forojul.)	Vade retro Satana.	Vade post me Satanas.
Matthew, ch. 6, v. 4. Pater tuus qui videt in abscondo reddet tibi in palam.	Pater tuus qui videt in abscondo reddet tibi in palâ.	Pater tuus qui videt in abscondo reddet tibi. (So also in C. Foro-Jul.)	Pater tuus qui videt in abscondo reddet tibi in manifesto.	Pater tuus qui videt in abscondito reddet tibi in palam.	Pater tuus qui videt in occulto ipse reddet tibi.
Matthew, ch. 8, v. 17. Ipse infirmitates nostras suscepit et languores nostros portavit.	Ipse infirmitates nostras accepit et ægrimonia nostra portavit.	Ipse infirmitates nostras accepit et ægrotationes portavit.	(*Deest.*)—(Et ægritudines portavit; in Cod. Foro-Jul.)	Quia infirmitates nostras accepit et ægrotationes nostras portavit.	(Deest.)

[1] Blanchini and the Benedictines have given a fac-simile of the Text, (N. Tr. de Dipl. 3, 147, pl. 42, iii.) See also Blanchini's " Vindiciæ Canonicæ," and Irici " Sacro-sanctus Evangel. Codex S. Eusebii magni Ep. et Martyr manu exaratus ex Autogr. Basilicæ Vercellensis Mediolani," 1748.

[2] In addition to the works of Nobili, Sabatier, and Blanchini, the following must also be mentioned as containing Ante-Hieronymian Latin versions :—

Scheibel, Codex Quatuor Evangel. Latinus Rehdigerianus, Matthæus et Marcus, cum Textu Gr. et Editione vulgatâ collatus. Breslau, 1763, 4to. From a MS. at Breslau.

Schulz, Disput. de Codice iv. Evangel. Biblioth. Rhedigerianæ in quo vetus Latina versio continetur. Vratislav. 1814, 4to.

Munter, Fragmenta versionis antiquæ Latinæ Ante Hieronymianæ, &c. Copenhagen, 1821, 8vo. (In Miscell. Hafniensia Theolog. et Philol. argum. t. 2.) From a Palimpsest Codex at Wurtzburg.

H. C. Hwiid Libellus Criticus de Indole MS. Græci. N. Test. Vindob. Lambecii, 34. Accessit Textus Latinus Ante-Hieronymianus ê Codice Laudiano. Havniæ. 1785, 8vo.

Of all the Ante-Hieronymian MSS., none have occupied so great a share of the attention of Biblical scholars as the diglot CODEX BEZÆ, so named in honour of Theodore Beza, by whom it was found in the Monastery of St. Irenæus, at Lyons, and presented, in 1581, to the University of Cambridge, in whose public Library it is now preserved, accompanied by the dedicatory autograph letter of Beza, from which the fac-simile in my plate has been copied. It consists of 413 leaves of vellum, measuring 10 inches by 8½ inches, each page containing 33 lines of unequal length, and is written in rather narrow uncial letters, without accents or marks of aspiration, and also without separation of words. It comprises the four Gospels and the Acts of the Apostles, thus arranged—Matthew, John, Luke[1], Mark, Acts; each of which commences with three lines written in red letters, exactly like the remainder of the text, of which the Greek and Latin Versions occupy the opposite pages.

In all these respects (to which it may be added that the alineæ commence with uncial letters in no way different from the remainder of the text), this MS. may fairly vie in antiquity with any known Codex.

Professor Hug, of Fribourg,—who divides the chronological history of the Greek text of the New Testament into three periods, (the first of which extends from the time when the different books were composed to the middle of the third century, when the threefold recension by Origen, Hesychius and Lucian was made,)—taking into consideration the statements of Clemens Alexandrinus, Origen and other Fathers, considers that the ΚΟΙΝΗ ΕΚΔΟΣΙΣ, or common edition, (which had already undergone some alterations,) is, in a great measure, represented by the Codex Bezæ: " If at any time we could find among our literary stock an ancient MS. which was perfectly free from the text of later times, and exhibited those readings which we have just extracted from Clemens, which contained not merely those and several others which elsewhere occur in his writings, but every one of the variations and peculiar readings of the most ancient Fathers, down to the third century, or, at least, a considerable part of them, what else should we say of it, than that it expressed the text of the period or the κοινη εκδοσις which preceded the critical labours? We are in possession of such a MS. : it is the famous Cambridge MS. [2]"

Some difference of opinion has however existed respecting the age of this MS. Dr. Kipling, (who published a splendid fac-simile of the entire Codex,)[3] conjectured that it must have been written in the second century. Michaelis also deemed it the most ancient of the MSS. now extant.[4] Bishop Marsh thought it might have been written two or three centuries earlier than the sixth, and considers it second only, in point of age, to the Codex Vaticanus, whilst Wetstein supposed it to be of the fifth century. The last-named author was further of opinion, that this was the identical manuscript collated at Alexandria, in 616, for the Philoxenian version of the New Testament ; and indeed many of the peculiar readings of the Codex Bezæ, are found in the Syriac,[5] Coptic, Sahidic, and in the margin of the Philoxenian-Syriac versions.

The peculiar scription of the Codex Bezæ will be perceived from the specimen in the Plate numbered 2, in which the C-shaped Σ, the Є-shaped E, the first stroke of the Y elevated above and reaching below the line, the curious-shaped Ξ, the N with the two perpendicular strokes thickest, and the oblique one very slender, the long centre-stroke of the Φ, the tail of the P reaching below the line, and terminating in a hair-stroke, and the ω-shaped Ω are worthy of notice in the Greek text ; as well as the form of the A, the minuscules b, d and l, the uncials E, H, and M, the tailed F, P, R, and Q, the horizontal hair-stroke attached to the end of the tails of these letters, and the curious form of the S in the Latin text.

Both the Greek and Latin texts exhibit many grammatical errors. Thus we have the words ΤΟΝ ΔΕΝΑΡΟΝ—ϹΟΙ ΠΟΙΕΙϹ. ΑΝΥΓШϹΙΝ. ΔΕΗΘΗΤΕ ΟΥΝ ΤΟΝ ΚΥΡΙΟΝ ?—Quando non esset ei filium—super umera—secessit ad marem—spirito sancto—suptus pedes—qualum—coxerunt-macika—karissima-xibunt—fratrorum. But, perhaps, the most singular passage in the volume is the one which, at the kind suggestion of the Rev. John Lodge, the learned Librarian of the University Library, (to whose attentions I have been greatly indebted in the course of this work,) I have given in fac-simile No. 2. It occurs

---

[1] In the heading of the pages of the Gospel of St. Luke we find the name written both Sec. Lucam and Lucan.

[2] Hug. Introd. to N. Testament, by Wait. 1, p. 138.

[3] " Codex Theodori Bezæ Cantabrigiensis," &c. Cantabrig. 1793, 2 vols. fol., which was collated by Porson with the original, and the only fault detected was in a single letter in the margin.

[4] " Cæterum cum sit omnibus indiciis vetustatis insignitus hic codex et fortassis omnium qui nunc supersunt antiquissimus." Proleg. ad Test. Gr., p. 34.

[5] " Textus reperitur Cantabrigiensis Syriacæ utraque versioni maxime admodum convenire." Kipling ; Michaelis Einleitung, p. 583.

at the end of the fourth verse of the sixth chapter of St. Luke; the third and fourth verses being given according to the ordinary version, terminating with the words,

> "OIC OYK EΞONHN ΦAΓIEN EI MH MONOIC
> TOIC IEPEYCIN.

> " Quibus non licebat manducare si non solis sacerdotibus"—

—which it is not lawful for the people to eat, but for the priests alone. Immediately after which is the following singular passage :—

> —— "TH AYTH HMEPA ΘEACAMENOC
> TINA EPΓAZOMENON TΩ CABBATΩ EIΠEN AYTΩ
> ANΘPΩΠE EIMEN OIΔAC TI ΠOIEIC
> MAKAPIOC EI EI ΔE ME OIΔAC EΠIKATAPATOC
> KAI ΠAPABATHC EI TOY NOMOY.

> ——" Eodem die videns
> quendam operantem sabbato et dixit illi
> Homo si quidem scis quod facis
> beatus es, si autem nescis maledictus
> et trabaricator legis."

—The same day seeing a certain man working on the sabbath-day, he said to him, Man, if indeed thou knowest what thou doest, blessed art thou; but if thou knowest not, thou art cursed, and become a transgressor of the law.—Scholtz found this passage only in one other Greek MS. (Nov. Test. p. 231.)

In the margin I have added a fac-simile of the mode in which the name of Jesus is written contractedly in the two versions, and the manner in which the name of David is spelt in the Greek text.[1]

The specimen No. 1 is copied from Archbishop Laud's MS. of the Acts of the Apostles, preserved in the Bodleian Library (F. 82). It consists of 227 leaves of vellum, measuring $10\frac{1}{2}$ inches by 8, and is written in double columns, with only one or two words in each line, the first containing the Latin and the second the Greek text, having twenty-five lines in a page. Like the Codex Bezæ it has the first three lines at the commencement of the book (in both texts) written in red. As a Biblical MS. it is of great value, Michaelis pronouncing it to be "indispensable to every man who would examine the important question, whether the Codices Græco-Latini have been corrupted from the Latin;" and adding, that it was this MS. which convinced him that this charge is without foundation. The Latin text is in one of those versions which differ from that of Jerome. It has been supposed to have been the identical book used by the venerable Bede, because it has all those irregular readings which, in his Commentary on the Acts, he says were in his book, and no other MS. is found to have them. There is an extraordinary coincidence between it and the old Syriac version. It is referred by Astle to the beginning of the fifth century; by Wetstein and Michaelis to the seventh; by Griesbach to the seventh or eighth, and by Hearne[2] to the eighth century.

Both the texts are written in a remarkably fine strong uncial character, the alineæ (as will be seen from the first line of the specimen) commencing with an uncial letter of a larger size than the rest of the line. The B in the Latin text is always written in the minuscule character.[3] The tailed P and R, and the form of the A and L and T, in the Latin text, are also worthy of notice; as is also the want of distinction between the words where two occur in a line. I have added in the blank space fac-similes of those letters which do not occur in the text, as well as the contractions used for the names of *God* and the *Father*.

The specimen is from Acts, ch. ix. v. 31, descriptive of the happy state of the church :—

---

[1] The name Jesus is contracted in most Greek MSS. into J͞C (as in the purple Cottonian MS.). The name of Christ (ordinarily contracted into X͞C) is also written in the Codex Bezæ X͞P͞C.

" 'Le mot Δαβιδ n'a dans les MSS. Grecs que la première et la dernière lettre Δδ de sorte, que il est très difficile pour ne pas dire impossible de savoir aujourd'hui comment les Grecs écriverent ce mot.' Nous l'avons vu ecrire Δαυιδ dans plusieurs MSS. Grecs."—Nouv. Tr. de Dipl. 3. 540 note.

[2] Acta Apost. Gr.-Lat. E. Cod. Laudiano descr. ediditque T. Hearnius, Oxonii, 1715, 8vo.

[3] The same singularity also occurs in the Codex Claromontanus, N. Tr. de Dipl. 3, pl. 42. A minuscule l occurs in the Homilies of Origen (Bibl. du R.) which are written in a hand very similar to that of the Laudian MS. under notice. N. Tr. Dipl. 3, p. 193, and supposed by the Benedictines, to be much older than the 8th century. We have also seen that the Codex Bezæ has the b, l, and d, written in minuscule.

Ecclesiæ quidem universæ per omnem Judæam et Galileam et Samariam habebant pacem.	Αἱ μὲν οὖν ἐκκλησίαι πᾶσαι καθ'ὅλης τῆς Ιουδαιας καὶ Γαλιλαίας καὶ Σαμαρείας εἶχον ειρὴνην.

The two last leaves of the MS. bear various short inscriptions in Greek, including an edict of a Sardinian Prince, Flavius Pancratius (whence it has been supposed that the MS. was written in Sardinia), and the Apostles' Creed, written in Latin uncials, but with various omissions.[1]

The specimens in the lower part of the plate are remarkable for having the Greek version written in Latin characters, a peculiarity respecting which various notices will be found in another article of this work.

The specimen No. 4, is from the Psalter of Verona,[2] written in fine uncial letters, regarded by the Benedictines as of the sixth century, having the words not very distinct, and being destitute of points. It is in quarto, with the two texts written continuously on the opposite pages. The specimen copied is the commencement of Psalm xcvi. (xcvii. according to the Septuagint).

O quirios ebasileusen agalliasto e ge eufrantetosan nesy pollœ nefele ce gnofos cyclo autu diceosune ce crima.	(Ο῎ Κύριος εβασιλεῦσεν αγαλλιαστω η γῆ; εὐφρανθήτοσαν, νῆσοι πολλαι νεφελη καὶ γνοφος κυκλω αυτοῦ, δικαιοσσυν καὶ κρῖμα.)	Dns regnavit, exultet terra jucundentur insulæ, multæ nubes et calligo in circuitu ejus justitia et judicium.

The text follows the Septuagint version, and the MS., like those mentioned below, is very valuable, as preserving to us an authentic evidence of the mode of pronunciation of the Greek language at the time the MS. was written.

The specimens numbered 3, are taken from different pages from the Bodleian MS. N. E. D. 2. 19 (Auct. F. 4, 32), which apparently consists of various fragments collected together, including several pages of Lessons from the Old Testament. This MS. is especially interesting, the characters in which it is written being either Irish or Anglo-Saxon, and which may, I think, be regarded as not later than the eighth century, and because it bears unquestionable evidence of the manner in which the Greek tongue was pronounced in this country. The forms of many of the Greek letters in the upper specimens, are very unusual (except in MSS. written in these kingdoms). The specimens are as follow, the proper Greek text being added above the Greek versions:—

MICHA, ch. iv., v. 5.

ημεις δε πορευσομεθα εν ονοματι κυριου Θεου ημον.
EMEIC ΔE ΠΟΡΕΙCΟΜΕΤΑ ΕΝ ΟΝΟΜΑΤΕ KI ΘI ΥΜΟΝ.

Nos autem ibimus in nomine domini dei nostri.

MICHA, ch. v., v. 2.

Και συ Βηθλεεμ οικος Εφραθα ολιγοστος ει
ΚΑΙ CΥ ΒΕΘΛΕΜ Ō ΟΙΚΟΙC ΤΟΥ[3] ΕΦΦΡΑΤΑ ΟΛΙΓΟCΤΟC ΕΙ
του ειναι.
ΤΟΙ ΕΙΝΑΙ.

Et tu Bethlem domus illius effrata exigua es ut sis.

GENESIS, ch. i., v. 1.

In principio fecit deus cœlum et terram; terra autem erat invisibilis ꝯ incompossita.

Εν αρχη εποιησεν ο θεος τον ουρανον και την γην, Η δε γη ην αορατος
En archi epoeisen o theos ton uranon ce tin gin, I de gi in aoratos
και ακατασκευασος.
ce acatasceuastos.

DEUTERONOMY, ch. xxxii., v. 1.

Attende cœlum et loquar, audiat terra verba ex ore meo.

Προσεχε ουρανε και λαλησω και ακουετω γε[4] ρεματα εχ στοματος μου.
Proseche uranae cae laleso ce acueto gi remata ec stomatos mu.

In the margin is copied, from one of the pages of the MS. containing lunar tables, &c.:—"Anni ab incarnatione dni nri jhu xpi dcccxii."—proving this part of the MS. to have been written in the year 812.

The custom of accompanying the Greek text with an interlineary, or parallel version, was very early adopted, since the Latin Version is in general Ante-Hieronymian. These MSS. are termed Codices Bilingues, or Diglot MSS.; and as there are extant Syriac-Arabic, Gothic-Latin,[5] and Greek-Russian, (Harl. MS. 5723) MSS., it is probable, as Michaelis thinks, that there formerly existed Greek-Syriac, Greek-Gothic, and other MSS. of

---

[1] Credo in Dm patrem omnipotem, et in Xpo Jhu filium ejs unicum Dominum nostrum, qui natus est de Spu sco et Mariâ Virgine, qui sub Pontio Pilato crucifixus est, et sepultus; tertiâ die resurrexit à mortuis, ascendit in cœlis, sedet ad dextera patris, unde venturus est judicare vivos et mortuos: et in Spu sco, sca ecclesia, remissionem peccatorum, carnis resurrectionis.

[2] N. Tr. de Dipl. 3 pl. 42, No. 1, and p. 143.

[3] This word occurs in the Alexandrian, but not in the Vatican Codex.

[4] Thus in the Codex Alex.: ακουετω η γη in the Cod. Vaticanus.

[5] The Harleian MS. 5786, contains a triglot (viz., Greek—Latin —Arabic) Psalter of the twelfth century.

that kind, in which the original and some version were written together. The following, in addition to those above described, are the most interesting Greek-Latin MSS.:—

The Codex Sangallensis, belonging to the library of the famous monastery of Saint Gall, in Switzerland, described by Rettig, in his work, entitled "Antiquissimus quatuor Evangeliorum Canonic. Cod. Sangallensis Gr.-Lat. interlinearis nunquam adhuc collatus ad similitudinem ipsius libri manu-scripti accuratiss. delineadum et lapidibus exprimendum curavit. 4to. Turici, 1836."

The Codex Claramontanus (Bibl. du Roi, No. 107), formerly used by Beza; containing the Pauline Epistles, written in uncials; ascribed by the Benedictines to the fifth or sixth century (N. Tr. de Dipl. 1. pl. 12, f. 8, and 3 pl. 42), but to the seventh by Montfaucon, Champollion, and Silvestre, who have also given a fac-simile of it.

The Codex San Germanensis also contains the Pauline Epistles, written in uncial letters; considered by the Benedictines (N. Tr. de Dipl. 1 pl. 12, f. 12, 13, and 3 pl. 43, p. 165) to be older than the Codex Alexandrinus, but referred by other writers to the seventh century.

The Codex Augiensis also contains the Pauline Epistles. This is a very interesting MS., having been formerly in the Monastery of Rheinau (originally founded by an Irish missionary), and having the Latin version written in Anglo-Saxon, or more probably, in Irish characters, and having, in all probability, been transported by the original founder of that monastery from this country. It is now in the Library of Trinity College, Cambridge. It is important to remark, that the Greek follows the Alexandrian Recension. It also coincides in many respects with the next Codex, and has the names Christ and Jesus contracted, as in the Codex Bezæ. The Epistle to the Hebrews, formerly rejected by the Church of Rome, is only written in the Latin version.

The Codex Boernerianus, in the Dresden Library, also contains the Pauline Epistles (except that to the Hebrews), and having the Latin Ante-Hieronymian text interlined between the Greek; and written, according to Kuster, in Anglo-Saxon, or, according to Doderlein, in Irish characters.[1] A transcript of it is preserved in the Library of Trinity College, Cambridge.[2]

The Codex Ottobianus of the Vatican, written in the fifteenth century (the Latin text in modern Gothic letters), contains the Acts and Epistles, and possesses the disputed passage concerning the three heavenly witnesses (1 John v. 7, 8).

---

[1] It is not only written in the Irish hand, but at the foot of fol. 23 is an inscription in the old Irish language, which is copied in one of Matthæi's Plates.

[2] Epist. Pauli Cod. Gr. cum Vers. Lat. vet. vulgo Ante-Hieron. olim Boernerianus. Edit. a C. F. Matthæi. Misenæ. 1791 (reprinted in 1818). 8vo.

INITIUMEUANGELII
ihuxpi·FILIDI

SICUTSCRIBTUMEST
INESAIAPROPHETA
ECCEMITTOANGELU
ANTEFACIEM TUA·
MEUMQUIPRAE
PARABITUIAMTUA

Ipſe · liber

INPRINCIPIO ERAT UERBUM
ET UERBUM ERAT APUD DM
ET DS ERAT UERBUM

INITIUMEUANGELIIhu
XPIFILIIDIX·;

SICUTSCRIPTUMESTIN
ESAIAPROFETA.
ECCEMITTOANGELUMME
UMANTEFACIEMTUAM·
QUIPRAEPARABITUIATUA

*The Gospels
of
Sts Augustine & Cuthbert*

THE GOSPELS OF SAINTS AUGUSTINE AND CUTHBERT.

AS already noticed in the article upon the Græco-Latin Ante-Hieronymian MSS. of the Bible, there were, "within a few hundred years after Christ, translations many, into the Latin tongue, for this tongue also was very fit to convey the Law and the Gospel by, because in those times very many countries of the West, yea of the South, East, and North, spake or understood Latin, being made provinces to the Romans. But now the Latin translations were too many to be all good, for they were infinite (Latini interpretes nullo modo numerari possunt, saith St. Augustine, de doctr. Christ. lib. 2, cap. ii.). Again, they were not out of the Hebrew fountain (we speak of the Latin translations of the Old Testament), but out of the Greek stream (i. e. the Septuagint) ; therefore, the Greek being not altogether clear, the Latin derived from it must needs be muddy. This moved St. Hierome, a most learned Father, and the best linguist without controversy of his age or of any other that went before him, to undertake the translating of the Old Testament out of the very fountains themselves, which he performed with that evidence of great learning, judgment, industry, and faithfulness, that he hath for ever bound the Church unto him in a debt of special remembrance and thankfulness."[1]

It was towards the close of the fourth century that Jerome, under the patronage of Damasus, Pope of Rome, undertook the task of revising these translations, as well as of making a fresh translation, revising the Old Testament from the Hexapla of Origen, and the New Testament from the original Greek. The Preface which he addressed to Pope Damasus, commencing " Beato Papæ Damaso," is to be found in most of the early copies of his translation. This version, as we learn from Augustine, was introduced into the churches by degrees, for fear of offending weak persons ; but at length it acquired so great an authority from the approbation it received from Pope Gregory I., that ever since the seventh century it has (with the exception of the Psalter) been exclusively adopted by the Roman Catholic Church under the name of the *Vulgate* version,[2] being considered as authentic, of divine authority, and more to be regarded than even the original Hebrew and Greek texts.[3] This opinion, supported as it was by a decree of the 4th Session of the Council of Trent in the sixteenth century, was opposed by the early Reformers, who depreciated this version as much below its intrinsic merit, as by the Romanists it was too highly esteemed. In the present day it is, however, admitted by most critics to be in general a faithful version, and sometimes exhibits the sense of Scripture with greater accuracy than the more modern versions, although in various places it is mistranslated, in order to support the peculiar dogmas of the Church of Rome.[4]

We have seen above that it was chiefly by Gregory the Great that the Vulgate was brought into general use ; and, when his zeal for the conversion of the English to Christianity (which resulted in the mission of St. Augustine) is remembered, it will not appear surprising that he should have forwarded to the missionaries of the British nation copies of that version of the Holy Scriptures which he himself so highly esteemed. We learn, in fact, from the life of St. Gregory the Great, written by Joannes Diaconus, lib. 2. cap. 37, that he sent to St. Augustine, not only assistants, but also " universa quæ ad cultum erant ecclesiæ necessaria ; vasa videlicet sacra, et vestimenta altarium, apostolorum et multorum sanctorum reliquias et *codices multos;*"[5] and

---

[1] Preface to the Bible by King James's translators.
[2] Horne's Introduction, 2, p. 286.
[3] Bishop Lowth's Translation of Isaiah, vol. i. p. 73.

[4] Horne, ut supra, p. 240.
[5] S. Gregorii magni P.P. Opera ed. 2da. Rom. MDCXIII. tom. i. p. 50 ; and see also Bede's Histor. Eccl. 1. cap. 29.

1

in the Annals of St. Augustine's Abbey and the Church of Christ at Canterbury, compiled by a monk of the former establishment in the time of King Henry V. (and preserved among the MSS. at Trinity College, Cambridge), we find described several Codices written in the version of Jerome, and which were always regarded as having belonged to St. Augustine—(the "primitie librorum totius ecclesie Anglicane"). Amongst these MSS. were two "textus Evangeliorum;" one of which was thus described—"In cujus principio X canones annotantur, et vocatur Textus Sancti Mildredi, eoquod quidam rusticus in Thaneto super eundem textum falsum jurans oculos amittere perhibetur;" whilst the other had the 10 Canons, and the Prologus Canonum, at the beginning.[1]

Wanley, who searched for and examined the MSS. of this kingdom with so much care, was led to believe that a copy of the Gospels preserved in the library of Corpus Christi College, Cambridge (No. 286), and another in a similar style of writing in the Bodleian Library (No. D. 2. 14, Bod. 857), are the two identical Gregorian volumes described above: not only because they are two of the oldest Latin MSS. written in pure Roman uncials which exist in this country, but also because they contain Anglo-Saxon entries, now a thousand years old, which connect them with the Monastery of St. Augustine itself.

The specimens in the accompanying Plate, numbered 1 to 5, are copied from these two invaluable MSS.; the first four being from the Cambridge Gospels, which, at the time of the dissolution of religious houses, was preserved by Archbishop Matthew Parker; and the fifth from the Bodleian MS., which bears the signature, on the recto of the second leaf, of "Robertus Cotton Cuningtonensis," and which was subsequently the property of Lord Hatton, amongst whose MSS. it is preserved in the Bodleian Library.

The first of these MSS. is of a quarto form, measuring 9½ inches by 7½, and being about 2¼ inches thick; the parchment is thin; the ink of a faded brown; the text written in fine Roman uncials, in double columns, with 25 lines in a page. The commencement of the MS., containing the Prologue and part of the Capitula, or Synopsis of St. Matthew's Gospel, is wanting, the first leaf being occupied with the latter Capitula; at the end of which is inscribed, in red minuscule characters, "Explicuerunt, Inc. ipse liber," with the Anglo-Saxon addition, "Siᵹeᵹð ⁊ ꝼuꞇe." This minuscule is very clearly and beautifully written, and comes nearest to several specimens given by the Benedictines in their 51st Plate from Gallican (?) MSS. of the 5th and 6th centuries. The occurrence of a minuscule hand at the early period when this MS. was written, is so rare that I have copied part of it in No. 4, in which the f elevated above the line, the l and b with the first stroke gradually clavate, and the peculiar form of the r will be noticed, as well as the dot between the two words placed midway between the top and bottom of the line.

The verso of the second leaf bears the words MATTHEUS HOMINEM, written in Roman capitals, evidently in allusion to the portrait of that Evangelist and his Symbolical Emblem, not now in the book. The beginning of St. Matthew's Gospel occurs at the top of the next leaf, with the heading "*SECUND MATTHEUM*," written in rustic capitals. The first line of this Gospel, "Liber generationis," is written in red letters not larger than the rest of the text; neither is the commencement of the historical part, "Xpi autem generatio," otherwise distinguished than by being written in a line of red letters, as is the case indeed with the first line of each of the principal divisions.

At the end of St. Matthew's Gospels, are the words :—

EXPL. EUANGELIUM
SECUND MATTHEŪ
INCIP. EUANGELIUM
SECUNDUM MARCŪ
DŌ. GRATIAS.

written in alternate lines of red and black capitals.

The verso of this leaf was originally blank, but is now occupied by an Anglo-Saxon document, written about the middle of the 9th century, containing a donation or grant by Ealhburga, a noble lady, to the

---

[1] Smith's Bede's Eccl. Hist. l. i. c. 29, app. p. 690.

Monastery of St. Augustine, at Canterbury, of certain rents and annual proceeds arising out of her estate at Bradanburn.[1]

To this succeed the Prologue and Capitula of St. Mark (the other Gospels being also preceded by similar articles), at the end of which is an entry of an agreement made between Abbot Wulfric (A.D. 949), and Ealdred, the son of Lifing, commencing " In nomine Dni Jesu Christi Heꝑ sputelað on ꝑꝑum," &c.[2]

The specimen numbered 3, represents the beginning of the Gospel of St. Mark (the marginal references to the Ammonian sections, which occur throughout the volume, being omitted in the plate). It is to be read ' Jnitium euangelii jh̄u xp̄i fili d̄i sicut scribtum est in Esaia Propheta ecce mitto angelu̅ meum ante faciem tua̅ qui præparabit viam tua̅.' The false orthography of the words filii and scriptum, the contractions used in the words angelum and tuam, and the manner in which the omission in the sixth line has been corrected, will be observed, as well as the two top lines written in red letters of the ordinary size of the text, which is characteristic of very great antiquity.[3]

Each of the chief divisions, or chapters, commences with two or occasionally only a single line of red letters (independent of its situation on the page), and sometimes only one or two of the first words are thus treated. Often also a single word occupies an entire line of the column. From the character of the writing, and the indistinctness of the words, this MS. may be assigned to the fifth or sixth century at the latest.

The following are specimens of the text of the volume :—

MATTHEW, v. 1—7.—" Videns autem turbas ascendit in montem et cum sedisset accesserunt ad eum discipuli ejus et aperiens os suum docebat eos dicens Beati pauperes spiritu quoniam ipsorum est regnum cælorum. Beati mites quoniam ipsi possidebunt terram. Beati qui lugent quoniam ipsi consolabuntur. Beati qui esuriunt et sitiunt justitiam quoniam ipsi saturabuntur. Beati misericordes quoniam ipsi misericordiam consequentur."

MATTHEW, vi. 9—13.—" Pater noster qui es in cælis, sanctificetur nomen tuum, veniat[4] regnum tuum, fiat voluntas tua sicut in cælo et in terra. Panem nostrum supersubstantialem da nobis hodie et demitte nobis debita nostra sicut et nos demittimus[5] debitoribus nostris et ne inducas nos in tentatione sed libera nos a malo."[6]

JOHN, xxi. 21—23.—" Hunc ergo cum vidisset Petrus dicit jh̄u dn̄e hic autem quid dicit ei jh̄s sic eum volo manere donec veniam[7] quid ad te, tu me sequere, exivit ergo sermo iste in[8] fratres quia discipulus ille non moritur (then, in smaller letters, are interlined, k. et non dicit ei ih̄s non moritur) sed sic eum volo manere donec veniam[9] quid ad te."

The drawings with which this MS. is ornamented are of the highest interest, as being the most ancient monuments of Roman pictorial art existing in this country, scarcely yielding in this respect to those of the Vatican Virgil and Terence, or the Roman Calendar at Vienna, illustrated by Lambecius. In fact, with the exception of a leaf containing miniatures of the Four Evangelists, accompanying a page of the Gospel of St. Luke, *in*

---

[1] The commencement only of this grant being given by Hickes (Thesaurus, vol. iii. Dissert. Epist. p. 10), I have copied it entire :—

In nomine Dn̄i. Ealhburꞅ haꝼæþ ꝅeꞇeꞇ my hyꞃe ꝼꞃeonꝺæ þea hꞇunꝣa þ manælce ꝅeꞃe aꝅyꝼe þam hypū ꞇoꞃꞆæ aꝅuꝼꞇine oꝼ þa lanꝺe æꞇ bꞃaꝺanbuꞃnan. xl ambuꞃa meeꞇꞇeꞅ ꞁ ealbhꞃy ꝺeꞅ ꞁ ꞁꞁꞁ ꝺeꝼeꞃaꞅ. ꞁ xlꞁcc hlaꝼeꞅ ꞁ ane þæꝅe ꞅꞃꞁceꞅ ꞁ cyꞅeꞅ. ꞁ ꞁꞁꞁ ꝼoþꞃo ꝙu ꝺeꞃ ꞁ xx henꝼuꝣla; ꞅꝙꞃꞁceman ꞅe þ lanꝺ hebbe þ aꞅ ꝺꞁnꝅe aꝅyꝼ eꝼoꞃealꝺꞃeꝺeꞅ ꞃaule ꞁ ꝼoꞃ ealh buꞃꝅe ; ꞁ þam þan aꞃ ꞁnꝣan ælle ꝺæꝅe æꝼꞇeꞃ hyꞃa ꝼeꞃꞃe þæne ꞃealmꞃoꞃhꞁa *exaudiat te dn̄s* ꞅꝙæhꝙꞁc man ꞅꝙaꝙꞁꞅ abꞃece. ꞃꞁhe aꞃenꝺen ꝼꞃꞁa ꝅoꝺe ꞁ ꝼꞃꞁa eallum hallꝣū ꞁ ꝼꞃꞁa þan halꝣan þeꞃe. on þyꞃū lꞁꝼe ꞁ on ecneꞃꞃe þon ꞃynꞇheꞃ æꝼꞇ paꞃa manna naman ꞇoꝅepꞁꞇneꞃꞃe þꞁꞃe ꝅeꞃeꞇeꝺneꞃꞃe þ ꞁꞃ þon ꝺꞃꞁhꞇnoþ abꞃꞃꞇ. pꞃ. ꞁ oꞃmunꝺ ꞃꞃb æþelꞃeꝺ pꞃꞁ pynheꞃe ꝺꞁacon. beahmunꝺ. cenheaꝺꞃ. hyꞃe. abꝺa caꝺa beaꞃꞃꝼeꞃꞃ. beaꞃꞃhelm. ealꝺꞃeꝺ. ealhbuꞃꞃh. ealhꞃaꞃu. hoꞃheꞃe. leoꝼe pealꝺhelm. ꝺubꝺe. oꞃa. oꝼe. pꞁꝣhelm. pullaꞃ. eaꝺꞃealꝺ ꝣꞁꝼ hꞁꞇ þon ꞃꞃa ꝅe ꝣæþ ꞃꞃaꞃe nane pyꞃcaꝺ þ hꝙylc bꞃoc on becume þuꞃh hæꝼen ꝼolc oꝙþe

hꝙylce oꝺꞃe eaꞃꝼoꞃneꞃꞃe þ hꞁꞇman nemæꝅe þæꞃ ꝅeꞃeꞃ ꝅelæꝼꞇun aꝣꞁꝼe onoꝙꞃu ꝅeaꞃe beꞇꝙeo ꝼealꝺum. ꝣꞁꝼ þon ꝣꞁꞇ nemæꝅe ꞃylle on ꝺꞃꞁꝺꝺū ꝅeaꞃebeꝺꞃy ꝼealꝺū ꝣꝙꝼ he þon ꝣꞁꞇ nemæꝅe nenelle ; aꝣꞁꝼe lanꝺ ꞁ bec þa hꞁpū ꞇoꞃꞆæ aꝅuꝼꞇine ;

The names of Drithnoth (misspelt Diernodus), Bewmundus, and Winherus, occur in the annals of the Abbey of St. Augustine, preserved in the library of Trinity College, Cambridge, in the middle of the 9th century (Wanley in Hickes' Thes. ii. p. 151). And as it was the custom to write these grants in volumes of the Scriptures belonging to the religious establishments to which the donations were made, we have here abundant evidence that this volume was, in 844, the property of the Monastery at Canterbury founded by St. Augustine himself.

[2] Hickes, vol. iii. Dissert. Epist. p. 10.

[3] The initial letter I of the Gospel of St. John is surmounted with a small cross.

[4] Altered to adveniat.   [5] Altered to dimittimus.

[6] The word Amen is wanting.

[7] The letters am have been scratched out and o substituted.

[8] The letters ter are here introduced above the line.

[9] Altered to venio.

Greek, preserved with the illuminated Greek Pentateuch of the fourth century at Vienna, these are the oldest instances of Roman Christian iconography of which I can find any notice—those of the famous Syriac MS., at Florence, being probably not quite so old as this. No account or fac-similes of these invaluable drawings having hitherto been published, it is with the greatest pleasure that I submit the accompanying tracings from them. Their claim to be regarded as coeval with the MS. rests not only on the style of art which they exhibit, but on the character of the letters used in the explanations of them, and in the identical nature of the leaves of vellum on which they are drawn with those of the text. Unfortunately, only two leaves of these drawings now remain, but it is evident that the whole of the events of the life of Christ, as well as the whole of the Four Evangelists, were originally represented.

The first of these leaves occurs opposite the commencement of the Prologue to St. Luke's Gospel. It is divided into 12 compartments, each 1½ inch square, separated from each other by narrow red margins, and the whole inclosed within a narrow border, painted to imitate bluish marble with red veins. The following are the subjects comprised in these 12 drawings, four of which are introduced into the accompanying Plate :—

1. Christ riding into Jerusalem on the ass, inscribed Osanna filio d̄d̄ benedictus qui venit. 2. The Last Supper. 3. Christ praying in the Garden. 4. Jesus raising Lazarus, inscribed Ih̄s Lazarum suscitavit. 5. Jesus washing the feet of the Disciples. 6. Judas kissing Jesus, the Soldiers fallen to the ground. 7. Christ seized by the Jews, and Peter cutting off the ear of Malchus—the brook Kedron in the foreground. 8. Christ before Caiaphas. 9. Christ led away. 10. Pilate washing his hands. 11. Christ led to Judgment. 12. Christ bearing his Cross.

Although the perspective in these little miniatures is rude, and some of the figures ill-proportioned, their designs are very expressive of the subjects, and some of them are treated with much animation—the figure, of Our Saviour, for instance, in the two miniatures on the left side of my Plate, are not without dignity, whilst that of St. Peter and of the man holding the branch, at the right side of the drawing of the Entry of Christ into Jerusalem, are even spiritedly delineated. The cruciferous nimbus of Christ, the beardless features of all the figures, the position of the two fore-fingers of Christ, in the drawing of the raising of Lazarus, the swathed appearance of the corpse of Lazarus, the rounded dome of the Sepulchre, the hooded dress of the sisters of Lazarus, and the dress and armour of the guards of Christ, are all worthy of attention.

These drawings appear to have been sketched in with a pen and ink, and then filled up with thick opaque colours, destitute of gloss.

The other drawing is that of St. Luke, seated on a throne, within an elaborately ornamented architectural design consisting of marble columns, supporting a rounded arch, and ornamented with the Evangelist's symbol, the Bull, inscribed with the ancient legend, ' Jure sacerdotis Lucas tenet ora juvenci ;' but which is written, ' Jura sacerdotii Lucas tenet ora jubenci.' The substitution of b for v, as in the last word in the line, is of very common occurrence ; but the false orthography of the first two words is, perhaps, to be attributed to the ignorance of the illuminator. This line is written in fine Roman rustic capital letters, the words separated by single dots, placed midway between the top and bottom of the line. The entire design is of great elegance, and the figure of the Evangelist easy and well proportioned. The open book in his hand is inscribed with the 6th verse of the 1st chapter of St. John's Gospel, in minute red uncial letters. In the open space between the two columns, on each side of the Evangelist, in the original, is introduced another series of miniatures, smaller than the preceding, comprising the following subjects :—On the left side : 1. Zacharias troubled at the visit of the angel. 2. Christ upbraided by his parents. 3. Christ teaching from the boat. 4. Peter worshipping Christ on the sea-shore. 5. The dead carried out of the city. 6. Christ ordering Matthew to follow him. On the right side : 1. The doctor of laws questioning Christ. 2. The woman kneeling before Christ. 3. Christ and the fig-tree. 4. Christ and the man troubled with the dropsy. 5. Zacheus in the tree.

I cannot conclude my notice of this MS. without tendering my best thanks to the Rev. J. Goodwin, for his kind assistance in my examination of the C.C.C.C. MSS.

The specimen No. 5 is copied from the commencement of St. Mark's Gospel, in the Bodleian Gospels, referred to above. It is destitute of miniatures, and consists of 172 leaves,¹ measuring 10 inches by 7¼, and is

---

¹ A few leaves, both at the beginning and end of the MS. are wanting.

written in double columns, with 29 lines in a page. The uncial letters in which it is written are comparatively shorter and wider than those of the Cambridge Gospels,[1] and the orthography even more barbarous. The vellum is thin and polished, and the ink is faded brown. The first line of each Gospel, and of the chief divisions, is written in red letters. Sometimes a single word occupies an entire line of one of the columns.

The following are specimens of the text of the MS. which bears corrections in Anglo-Saxon characters :— Matth. v. 22. " Quia omnis qui irascitur fratri suo sine causa."—vi. 9. " Pater noster qui in cœlis es— veniat regnum tuum—Panem nostrum supersubstantialem.—Sicut et nos dimitti (mus inserted by a later hand on an erasure) dev[2]itoribus nostris et ne inducas nos in temptationem sed liv[3]era nos a malo." (Amen wanting.) —xix. 1, 2. " Et factum est cum consummasset iħs sermones istos migravit a Galilea et venit in fini[4]s judeæ trans Jordanen et secute sunt eum turbae multae et curavit eos ibi."

John i. 9. " Hominem venientem in[5] mundum."

The initial letters of each Gospel are plain and red, except that of St. Mark, which is slightly ornamented and surmounted by a cross.[6]

The specimen numbered 6 is copied from a fac-simile of a small MS. of the Gospel of St. John, tradi- tionally affirmed to have belonged to St. Cuthbert, the celebrated Patron Saint of Durham, and Bishop of Lindisfarne (ob. 687), and to have been found in his tomb. The Rev. John Milner has published a notice of this MS. in the 16th volume of the Archæologia, and informs us that it bears the following inscription on the leaf opposite to the beginning of the Gospel, " Euangelium Johannis quod inventum fuerat ad capud Beati Patris nostri Cuthberti in sepulchro jacens anno translationis ipsius," in very ancient handwriting, although vastly inferior to that of the Gospel itself. It was for time immemorial preserved in the family of the Lees (one of whom became Earl of Lichfield, temp. Car. II.), as the undoubted manual of St. Cuthbert. It was given by the last Earl of Lichfield to the Rev. Thomas Philips, who bestowed it on the College of the Jesuits, at Liège, in 1769, whence it was again brought to England after the suppression of their order. The characters of the writing bear intrinsic evidence of an antiquity as high as the age of St. Cuthbert ; the text being without chapters, verses, diphthongs, or points of any kind. The letters are all uncials or capitals, for the most part Roman, but with the N often of the Anglo-Saxon form, with the oblique stroke arising very low upon the first perpendicular stroke. The text is stated by Mr. Milner to be the Latin Vulgate, and to agree perfectly with the text of St. John in the Cottonian Gospels of Lindisfarne, (Nero, D. IV.) but as, in the few passages which he had compared with the present Vulgate, there are certain various readings differing from it, he is inclined to think it is of the old Italic version, which existed previous to the corrections of St. Jerome. It contains the history of the woman taken in adultery. A fac-simile of the first page of the Gospel of St. John accompanies the article, whence it appears that the MS. is of a small size, measuring about 5½ inches by 3¼, and that a page contains nineteen lines of the text. The first word only ' In' is written in red letters—and the passage ' Fuit homo missus a Dō' commences with a capital F, rather smaller than the initial I ; the name Johannes is spelled correctly. I believe it is to this MS. that Dr. Dibdin alludes as being now preserved at Stonyhurst.[7]

The Rev. J. Milner gives extracts from some ancient accounts published relating to the opening of the tomb of St. Cuthbert, in which there is no mention made of any copy of the Gospels being found with the body,[8] but Dr. Lingard (quoting the very ancient and anonymous author of the life of St. Cuthbert, published by the Bollandists, and the Transl. St. Cuth. in Act. SS. Benedict. Sæc. IV., tom. 2, p. 294), states that the Prior Turgot and nine associates, in 1104, upon opening the smaller chest, wrapped in coarse linen cloth and coated with melted wax (in which the body of the Saint was contained), found a *copy of the Gospels* lying on a second lid, which had not been nailed, and which upon being removed disclosed the body apparently entire.[9] That

---

[1] Astle (pl. x.) has given fac-similes of these two MSS., but his plate is coarsely executed, and does not exhibit the characteristic difference in the scription.

[2] Corrected to b.

[3] Corrected to b.

[4] The letters bu added above the line.

[5] The letters hc added above the line in a later hand.

[6] Ornamented initial letters of this date are of extremely rare

occurrence in MSS. The corrections of the word Dī in the second line and of the words scribtum and præparavit are made in a hand considerably more recent than that of the text itself.

[7] Bibliogr. Tour in North of England, i. p. 287.

[8] And see Butler's " Lives of the Saints," March 20, p. 228, and O'Conor, Script. Hibern. i. p. 207.

[9] Lingard, Antiq. Anglo-Saxon Church, p. 267.

the practice of depositing copies of the Gospels in the graves of persons of eminence was not of unusual occurrence we have abundant evidence. In the burial service of the Anglo-Saxons the book of the Gospels and the Cross were placed upon the corpse and covered with the pall ("Feretrum sacrosanctis evangeliis et crucibus armatum").[1] On opening the tomb of Charlemagne, by Otho III., the body of the Emperor was found attired in his robes of state and seated on a marble throne, and in his left hand " a *book of the Evangelists, of gold.*"[2] This and the other insignia were removed by Otho, in order that they might be used at the Coronations of future Emperors. This is the famous MS., written in golden letters, upon purple vellum, long kept at Aix-la-Chapelle, of which a specimen is given by Casley.[3] From the inquiries of a friend I learn that this MS. no longer exists at Aix-la-Chapelle, and therefore presume that it is one of the articles which were removed into the interior of Germany on the approach of the French during the late war, and which have not been restored ; it will probably, therefore, be found with the sword of Charlemagne, at Vienna. The celebrated book of the Gospels of Wurtzburgh (written in a version different from the Vulgate), was also discovered in 743, in the tomb of St. Kilien, who died in 687 It is still preserved with the greatest veneration, and is annually exhibited on the altar of the Cathedral Church on the feast day of the Saint.[4]

---

[1] Wolstan, Vit. St. Ethel. in Act. Benedict. Sæc. V. p. 623.

[2] Lambinet. Edit. 1798, p. 23.

[3] Cat. Royal MSS., pl. xii. No. 1.

[4] Chronic. Godwic. p. 34. Eckhart, 1, 451. N. Tr. d. Dipl. 3, 101, 231, 232.

C

ater noster qui
es inccelis sapce
tur nomen tuum &
ueniat regnum tuum

g l g s i r s

The Gospels of St. Chad.

THE GOSPELS OF SAINT CHAD.

THE Manuscript of the Latin Gospels, from which the accompanying fac-similes have been made, is preserved in the Cathedral of Lichfield, and is highly interesting, not only on account of its very great antiquity, but especially from the numerous entries which it contains written in Latin and Anglo-Saxon, as well as several in the ancient British language untinctured by the latter tongue, which have been considered by Lluyd[1] and other Welsh scholars to be more ancient, by several centuries, than any other relic of the British (or Welsh) language now in existence.

It is on this account that I have preferred giving fac-similes of these curious entries rather than copies of the ornamental details, which entirely correspond with those of the Gospels of Mac Regol, Lindisfarne, and others, in the same style.

The volume measures 12 inches by 9½, and at the present time consists of only 110 leaves, the greater portion of St. Luke's Gospel, and the whole of St. John's, being wanting. It is written on thick strong vellum, and the leaves are, unfortunately, considerably discoloured ; the ink, however, is, as usual, of perfect blackness.

The recto of the first leaf contains the illuminated commencement of the Gospel of St. Matthew—" Liber generationis jhu xpi filii David." The initial letters Lib are of very large size, the L and b being of the rounded form, and the i formed into a j seven inches long, similar in character to the same letters given by M. Silvestre from the Gospels in the Bibliothèque Royale, at Paris. The other letters are 1 inch high, and of the angular form represented in the plate No. 3.

The commencement of the historical part of St. Matthew's Gospel is also elaborately illuminated, precisely in the same style as in the Gospels of Lindisfarne, of which Mr. Shaw has given a fac-simile. The left-hand bottom stroke of the initial X is, however, more elongated, extending to the foot of the page, the letter measuring 9 inches in height. The other letters in this title-page are of the angulated form and 1 inch in height, except the bottom line, of which the letters are rather more than ½ an inch high.

The verso of the 71st leaf is ornamented with a portrait of St. Mark, drawn in the rude style of the early Irish school, as exhibited in the Gospels of Mac Regol, the Book of Kells, &c. The Evangelist is represented as clasping a book with both hands upon the breast, and as clad in robes of many folds ; his head is surrounded by a plain nimbus, over which is extended his symbol, the lion, rudely delineated, but still bearing some resemblance to that animal. The chair, or seat, in front of which the Saint is drawn, (and to the side of which his inkstand is fixed, being supported by a long slender stem,) is of singular form, one side of it representing a quadruped not much unlike a greatly attenuated giraffe, with a long tail, terminated by a curiously folded knot, and the upper part bearing considerable resemblance to the same part of the seat represented in the first plate from the Book of Kells.

The commencement of St. Mark's Gospel occupies the opposite page, and is highly ornamented, the first letters IN being long and narrow, and not less than 11 inches in height.

At the end of St. Mark's Gospel, the Pater Noster is written on a blank leaf in characters rather wider than those of the text of the volume. It is from this page that the specimen No. 2 is taken.[2]

On the following page (fol. 109 v.) appears the portrait of St. Luke, copied in my No. 1. This curious figure affords an excellent specimen of the style of the early Irish school of art, and may be compared with the

---

[1] Archæologia Britannica, 1707.

[2] This writing is remarkable for its size and beauty, as well as for the patches of red and yellow colours, with which many of the letters are ornamented. The text is also curious, the word adveniat being written et veniat. Astle (Origin of Writing, pl. XV., sp. V.) has given a specimen of the writing of the ordinary text of the volume, and other fac-similes from it will be found in the Liber Llandavensis, recently published by the Welsh MSS. Society. The account given of this MS. by the Benedictines (N. Tr. de Dipl. 3, p. 86) is entirely erroneous.

1

Evangelists copied from the Gospels of Mac Durnan, and the Book of Kells. In the original the figure is surmounted by a rudely-drawn winged bull, which has been here omitted for want of space; the cruciferous nimbus, fine-curled hair, short-trimmed beard, and naked feet, of this figure, are worthy of notice, as are also especially the two sceptres[1] which he holds, and the curious seat ornamented with dogs' heads.

The recto of folio 110 is ornamented with the four Evangelical symbols inclosed in square compartments, each measuring 4 inches by 3. These figures are almost the rudest specimens of ancient art now existing in any of the copies of the Gospels. It is, indeed, a most extraordinary circumstance, that whilst these early manuscripts exhibit a most marvellous perfection in the mechanical treatment of the ornamental details, the higher branches of the art were in the lowest possible state; hence the contrast between this page and the one following it, which is entirely occupied by an illuminated cross, ornamented in the same style as those in the Gospels of Lindisfarne, is most striking.[2] The commencement of St. Luke's Gospel occupies the recto of folio 111, the initial letter Q being of large size, the body of the letter forming a highly ornamented oblong square, and the tail of the letter extending to the bottom of the page; the remainder of the page consisting of large angulated letters 1½ inch in height.

The first four and the last pages of St. Matthew's Gospel, as well as all the title-pages of each Gospel, are enclosed within a narrow tessellated border. At the end of St. Matthew's Gospel the scribe has written the words, " Finit, Finit," and at the end of St. Mark the same word singly.

The following passages will show some of the peculiarities of the text of this MS. :—

MATTH. i. 1.—" Liber generationis jhū xpi filii david filii abracham, abracham autem genuit isac, isac autem genuit iacob, iacob autem genuit iudam et fratres ejus, judas autem genuit fhares et zaram de thamar.— i. 16. Joseph virum mariæ de qua natus est ihs qui vocatur xps.—iv. 10. Vade retro satanas.—v. 2. Et aperuit os suum et docebat eos dicens. Beati pauperes, &c. Beati mites, &c. Beati qui lucent, &c. Beati qui esuriunt.—vi. 4. Et pater tuus qui videt in absconso reddet tibi.—viii. 17. Ipse infirmitates nostras accipit et ægrotationes portabit."

The word Johannes was originally written Johannis, but has been subsequently altered. The interpolated passage, Matth. xxvii. 48, occurs in this MS.

The letter f is always employed in lieu of ph, as in farisei, profeta, &c. I is also occasionally used for y, as in sinagoga, ægiptus, &c. Bt are often used instead of pt, as babtizo, babtisma, scribturo. Instances of false orthography are very abundant—e. g., Cessar for Cæsar; temptatio for tentatio; thensaurus for thesaurus; torcetur for torquetur; locitur for loquitur; grauatum for grabatum; Œgeptum for Ægyptum; cocurrit for cucurrit; consulari for consolari; regessi for regressi; delussus for delusus; " stella quem viderant," " he rusolimita," " prohero depatre" for " pro herode patre ; " the prepositions and other particles being almost always joined to the words which they govern.

The text is not divided into sections, but capital letters are occasionally introduced, although not always at the commencement of periods. Three dots thus placed : . indicate a full stop; a dot placed half-way between the top and bottom of the line a short pause; and two dots and a comma (..,) a longer pause.

From the foregoing peculiarities of the text, not less than from the style of the writing and illuminations, I infer that this MS. is one of the productions of the ancient schools of Ireland. Hickes, Lhuyd, Astle, and others have indeed considered it to have been written in England, but these authors were unacquainted with the existence of a school of art in Ireland. Moreover, from a comparison between it and the Gospels of Lindisfarne, Mac Regol, &c., there seems no reason to doubt the opinion of Lhuyd, that it was in his days, 1100 (now more than 1200) years old.[3] The various entries in the margins and open spaces of the MS. are, of course, more recent; but the oldest of these cannot be less than 1000 years old.

Four of the most interesting of these entries are copied in the accompanying plate. The first of these (No. 4), records the purchase of the volume by Gelhi, the son of Arihtuid, from Cingal, for his best horse;

---

[1] From one of the drawings in the Book of Kells, I infer that the instrument in the right hand of the figure before us is intended to represent a branch of a tree. The figure upon the jewel of King Alfred, at Oxford, bears two somewhat similar ornaments.

[2] These singular, but highly beautiful tessellated cruciferous frontispieces, also occur in the Book of Kells, the Autograph Gospels of St. Columba at Dublin, and the Gospels of St. Gatien at Tours, affirmed to have been written by St. Hilarius (N. Tr. Dipl. 3, p. 86)

but which is evidently a very early Irish copy of the Gospels ; now, I believe, no longer existing in France, having been probably destroyed during the revolution, or carried to Russia, as is also believed to be the case with the Anglo-Saxon Gospels of St. Germain des Pres, No. 108.

[3] There is an ancient tradition that it was written by St. Gildas. See Harwood's Hist. of Lichfield, p. 107, and O'Conor Script. Vet. Hibern. 1, p. cxcvii.

and the subsequent dedication of the volume to God and St. Teilo, the patron saint of Landaff.[1] This entry is written in Latin, and is to be read :—

" Ostenditur hic quod emit + gelhi + filius Arihtuid hoc euangelium de cingal et dedit illi pro illo equum optimum et dedit pro anima sua istum euangelium deo et ss Teliaui super altare + gelhi + filius Arihtuid," &c.

The second of these entries is partly in the ancient British language, written in the Anglo-Saxon or Irish minuscule characters—

" Osdendit ista scriptio quod dederunt ris et luith grethi treb guidauc i maliti duch cimarguien eit hic est[2] census ejus,[2] douceint torth hamaharuin ī irham ha douceint torth ī irgaem ha huch ha douceint mannuclenn Deo et scō eliudo D̄s testis saturnnguid testis." Then follow the names of other witnesses. Thus rendered by Lhuyd into Latin and modern Welsh : " Ostendit ista scriptio quod dederunt Rhesus et familia Grethi Trev wydhog . . . (nomen loci) qua itur ad confluentiam Cinchi (amnis). Hic est census ejus. Doy kant torth a maharen yn yr hav, a doy kant torth yn y gâev, a hwch, a doy kant, maniodhen (sev Dyskled ymmenym) Deo et Sco Eluido (viz., Teilaw). Deus testis, Sadyrnwydh[3] testis," &c. Which is thus Englished. " This writing sheweth that Rys and the family of Grethi gave to God and St. Teilo, Trevwyddog, which is on the road to the confluence of Cinchi, and its rent payment is 40 loaves and a wether sheep in the summer, and in the winter 40 loaves, a hog, and 40 dishes of butter, God is witness, Sadyrnwydh witness," &c.

The third of these entries is in Anglo-Saxon, and is to be read :—" + Heꞃ ꞃuꞇelaꝺ an ꝥæꞇ ᵹoꝺƿine eaꞃƿiᵹeꞅ ꞅunu hæꝼꝥ ᵹelæꝺ ꝼulle laꝺe æꞇ þanunꞃihꞇ ƿiꞃe þe leoꝼᵹaꞃ ᵬ hyne ꞇihꞇe ⁊ ꝥ pæꞃ læꝺ æꞇ liciꞇꝼelꝺa." i. e. " Hic declaratur quod Godwinus Earwigii filius se publice et plene purgavit de fornicationis suspicione in quam vocatus erat a Leofgaro Episcopo et quod ejus purgatio facta erat Licitfeldæ." (Hickes.)

We have here evidence of an act performed at Lichfield at the beginning of the eleventh[4] century, at which period it is evident that the volume had been transferred to the cathedral of that city, dedicated to St. Chad, who was the first bishop of that See, in the seventh century. It has accordingly been assumed that it, on this account, received the name of the " TEXTUS SANCTI CEADDÆ." As, however, St. Chad, although by birth a Northumbrian, was educated in Ireland[5], and as the volume evidently emanated from St. Finan's Irish school, of which St. Chad was a celebrated disciple, it appears not improbable that tradition referred the writing of the volume to St. Chad himself. Unfortunately the leaves at the end of the Codex, which possibly contained a notice of the original scribe, are lost.[6]

The specimen, No. 7, is part of a curious Anglo-Saxon and Latin entry, written in Latin characters mixed with Greek, as follows :—O q мн ᐁocyᴇʀɴᴛ ⁊ o qui meis iᐁıꞃniꞅ p̄cibus ⁊ м comenᐁaverunt, which is to be read :— " Omnes qui me docuerunt et omnes qui meis indignis precibus et me commendaverunt."

---

[1] The early connection between Wales and Ireland will account for the volume thus finding its way to Landaff. The curious reader may further consult the recently published " Liber Landavensis," as well as Hickes's " Thesaurus Dissert. Epist." p. xi., and Wanley's description of the volume, in the second volume of the " Thesaurus." St. Teilo succeeded to the See of Landaff in 512, and died 563 or 566.

[2] The curious Anglo-Saxon form of the contractions used for these two words is to be noticed.

[3] This name, Saturnnguid or Sadyrnwydh, appears again in another entry with the additional title of " the preist." I presume this to be the St. Sadwrn to whom the church of Llan Sadwrn in Anglesey is dedicated, and whose sepulchral stone in *Roman capitals* (in which the name is written BEATUS SATURNINUS) still exists in that very ancient church. Archæol. Journ. 1, p. 124.

[4] Bishop Leofgar mentioned in this entry died in 1021.

[5] Beda 1, 403. Ceadda and his brother Ceddi are often confounded together.

[6] See further, O'Conor, Bibl. Stowensis, 2 vols. 4to, 1818 : and Rer. Hibern. Script. vet. i. 194, 196, 203, 211, 275.

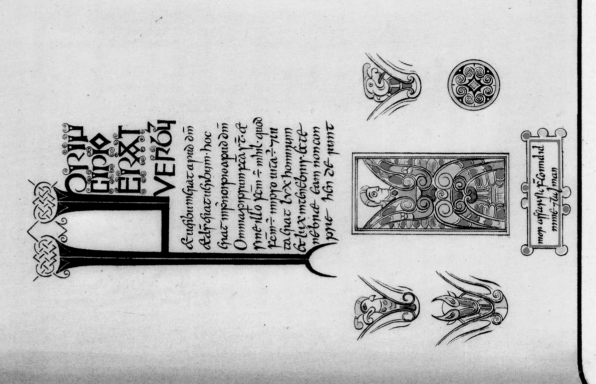

Gospels of Mac Durnan . Pl.1

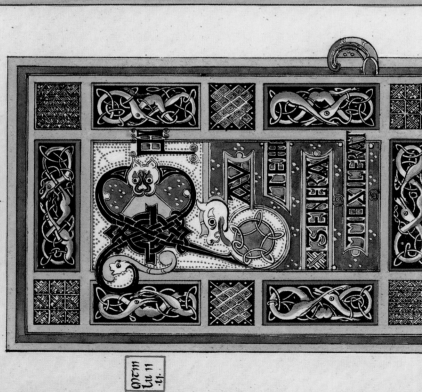

Gospels of Mac Durnan. Pl. II.

✝ MÆIELBRIÐVS MAC

DVRNANI · ISTV · TEXTV

PER · TRIQVADRV · DO

DIGNE · DOGMATIZAT ·

✝ AST · AETHELSTANVS ·

ANGLOSÆXNA · REX · ET

RECTOR · DORVERNENSI ·

METROPOLI · DAT · ÞÆV ·

THE GOSPELS OF MÆIEL BRITH MAC DURNAN.

THE volume from which the accompanying plates are taken appears to me to be so important in respect to the Archæological History of Ireland, that I have been induced to depart from the general plan of devoting a single plate only to each MS., and to publish a more ample series of illustrations from it than will be given from other manuscripts.

In regarding this volume as executed not later than the beginning of the eighth century [1], I am aware that I have to contend against several of our highest authorities in the science of palæography. Thus Mr. Astle, after a careful inquiry into the origin of letters in Ireland, states, more than once, in his work, which is our chief English authority upon the subject, that he " had not been able to discover an Irish MS. older than the tenth century [2] ;" whilst Moore, the favourite bard and historian of Ireland, speaking of the two or three centuries subsequent to the time of St. Patrick, says, " Not a single manuscript now remains, not a single written relic, such as ought to convince that class of sceptics who look to direct proofs alone, that the art of writing even existed in those days [3]." And even of the Gospels of St. Columbkill, to which " Dr. O'Conor [4] triumphantly refers, as affording an irrefragable answer to those who deny the existence of any Irish MS. of an older date than the tenth century," Mr. Moore merely remarks, that his countryman's zeal in the cause of his country's antiquities renders even him, with all his zeal, candour, and learning, not always a trustworthy witness [5]. He accordingly adopts the statement of Mr. Astle as the truth.

If, in addition to these statements, we add the silence of our great authorities, Wanley and Casley, as to the existence of any early Irish MS. ; the difficulty which the worthy Benedictines [6] had to conceive how the Anglo-Saxon characters could have found their way into Ireland (the English having abandoned them in the eleventh century, a century before the English invasion of Ireland) ; the great similarity which exists between the handwriting of the text of the Gospels of Mac Durnan and those of Mael Brigid in the Harleian Library [7], written in the twelfth century ; together with the actual insertion of notices in the volume itself of circumstances which occurred in the tenth century, I fear that I shall be charged with temerity in estimating it to be of the eighth. The proofs, however, on which I rely, will, I think, be deemed conclusive, although the space to which I am, of course, restricted, will render it necessary to condense them, and even to omit many authorities, for the review of which an extended memoir would alone afford sufficient space.

---

[1] Dr. Todd even considers it as a MS. of the seventh century.

[2] Origin of Writing, p. 116-118.

[3] History of Ireland, vol. i. 1835.

[4] Script. Veter. Rerum Hibern. i.

[5] In respect to this manuscript, indeed, Dr. O'Conor (whose name, by the by, is constantly mis-spelt by Moore) has fallen into an error, as the fac-similes which he has given of the Gospels of Columbkill, in the 1st volume of the Script. Veter. Rer. Hibern., are not derived therefrom, but from a different MS., as I am informed by the Rev. Dr. Todd, of Trinity College, Dublin, who states that the former MS. is still in existence, in the University Library, and is a most singular volume.

[6] Nouv. Traité de Dipl. ii. p. 201.

[7] No. 1802. See the elaborate account given of them by Wanley, in the Harleian Catalogue ; and O'Conor's additional remarks in the first volume of his Script. Veter. Rer. Hibern.

1

I shall, indeed, in these introductory remarks, restrict myself to the chief authorities in support of the early introduction of Christianity into Ireland, its flourishing state from the fifth to the eighth and ninth centuries, and the actual statements of the existence of manuscripts executed in Ireland during that period. The former of these is so peculiarly appropriate a subject of inquiry in a work like the present, whilst the early history, both of the Irish Church and Irish learning, is so intimately blended with that of England, that I need scarcely offer any apology in treating the subject in this manner. The introduction of letters into Ireland, which the Irish claim to themselves, and as existing there previous to the introduction of Christianity, and the peculiar characteristics of Irish letters, will be noticed in another article on other sacred Irish manuscripts.

1st. ON THE EARLY INTRODUCTION OF CHRISTIANITY INTO IRELAND.

It is necessary, in the first place, to premise, that by the early historians the Irish were exclusively known by the name of Scots[1], the modern Scots being called Picts.

The statement of Eusebius, that the religion of Christ had been preached in Ireland, has been questioned by Usher as probably originating in the confusion between the name of Hiberia, or Spain, where St. James preached, and Hibernia; but there are other less questionable authorities, even without dwelling on the statements of Theodoret[2], Venatius Fortunatus[3], Nicephorus, Sophronius, or the Greek records quoted by Sir Wm. Betham[4].

St. Irenæus, who was Bishop of Lyons in the second century, affirms that Christianity had been propagated to the boundaries of the world—signifying the Iberian and *Celtic* nations; and Tertullian, in his work against the Jews, written A.D. 209, affirms that the regions of Britain, *inaccessible to the Roman arms*, were subject to the gospel of Christ[5].

"The existence of a church in Ireland before the mission of Palladius, is proved by the evidence of Prosper, Bede, Ado Viennensis, Freculphus Lexoniensis, Ingulphus of Croyland, Hermannus Contractus, Marianus Scotus, Florence of Worcester, Henry of Huntingdon, and others; and mention is made of Albeus, Declan, Ibarus, and Kearan, as four eminent bishops before the mission of Palladius." This passage is quoted from the interesting work of Sir W. Betham[6], who has, moreover, endeavoured at great length to prove, from internal evidence drawn from the Confession of St. Patrick, that the individual by whom it was written was not the St. Patrick of the fifth century, but a missionary previous to the time of St. Jerome; the quotations from the Bible contained in it agreeing with the Ante-Hieronymian version.

The very ancient Book of Armagh likewise mentions the existence of Irish bishops at the time of the coming of St. Patrick.

The Irish Chronicles, entitled the Annals of the Four Masters, and the very ancient Brehon Laws, the authenticity of which is generally admitted, incidentally mention two circumstances which prove that, in the third century, some of the kings of Ireland had become converts to the new religion:—1st. Cormac, after "having turned from the Druids to the adoration of God, was killed by the instigation of the Druids." And 2nd. Donald gained a victory over Congal the Crooked, "because falsehood must always be conquered by truth;" which Dr. O'Conor[8] considers to allude to a religious war between the Christian King Donald and the Pagan Congal.

St. Chrysostom (circa A.D. 388) several times mentions that the knowledge of the Scriptures had passed to Albion and Irene (the ancient name of Ireland), and bears testimony that the British Church maintained the doctrines of Christianity handed down from the apostolical ages[9].

At the beginning of the fifth century, a mission was despatched by Pope Celestine (A.D. 423) to the Scots

---

[1] "Scotia quæ et Hibernia dicitur insula est maris oceani." Canisius Lection. Antiq. t. iv. p. 619. See Usher Primord. and Serinus' ed. of the works of Columbanus.

[2] Tom. iv. p. 610; 2nd Timoth. v. 16 17, and p. 1 16.

[3] De Vita Martini, lib. 3.

[4] Irish Antiquarian Res. vol. i.

[5] "Britannorum inaccessa Romanis loca, Christo vero subdita."

Lib. adv. Judæos, cap. vii.

[6] Irish Antiquarian Researches, vol. ii.

[7] See Mr. Petrie's excellent article on the History and Antiquities of the famed Hill and Halls of Tara. Trans. Royal Irish Academy, vol. xviii. part ii. p. 38.

[8] Cat. of MSS. at Stow.

[9] Opera, tom. vi. Græc. Savil. p. 635.

believing in Christ. The words of Bede, " Palladius ad Scottos in Christum credentes [1] ;" and of Prosper, " Ad Scottos in Christum credentes, ordinatur a Papa Celestino, Palladius, et primus episcopus mittitur [2]," evidently imply the existence of a belief in Christ entertained at that time by the Scots (Irish).

Notwithstanding this mission, but at the same time corroborating the existence of a church in these islands, we find the Irishman, Pelagius " professione monachus, natione non Gallo-Brito, ut Danæus putavit, nec Anglo-Britannus ut scripsit Balæus, sed *Scotus* [3]," with the assistance of his disciples Agricola and Celestius, zealously disseminating his doctrines throughout the British Islands, which led to the synod of Verulam in A.D. 429 ; at which they were triumphantly opposed by Germanus and Lupus, Bishops of Auxerre and Troyes, who had been invited by the orthodox English clergy to dispute with them.

Without entering into the controversy which has existed amongst Irish historians, as to the supposed identity of Palladius and St. Patrick, or the claims of one or other of the missionaries of the latter name who have been assigned as *the* Apostle of Ireland, (and which the elaborate researches of Usher and Lanigan have failed to clear up,) we have clearly sufficient evidence, notwithstanding the extraordinary silence of Bede [4], that in the middle of the fifth century, during the reign of Laogaire, Ireland was visited by a missionary of great acquirements, and who has ever since been regarded as the patron saint of Ireland. He is stated to have died A.D. 465, and to have been succeeded by Benignus, his disciple.

St. Columba, or Columbkill, who was born A.D. 521, and studied in the school of Finnian [5], is another illustrious name, justly revered by the Irish. To him was granted, as a recompense for his labours, the island of Hy, Hii, Iona, Icolmkill, or Icolumbkille, as it has been variously named ; the last of which, derived from that of the saint himself, is retained to this day. Here he established a monastery, which soon became illustrious in the labours and triumphs of the Christian church. He subsequently visited Scotland (A.D. 563), where his success was so great that he was venerated as the national saint of Scotland, until that honour was conferred upon St. Andrew.

From this monastery, Bede informs us [6], that many religious houses were founded by his followers. The history of this saint, by his follower Adamnan, abbot of Hy in 700, is one of the most excellent biographies which have come down to our times. The honourable character given by Bede of the last-named writer, has rendered his name familiar to the readers of British history ; whilst his Cross, which exists to this day upon the royal Hill of Tara, and of which a drawing has been published by Mr. Petrie, proves the reverence entertained for his memory amongst his countrymen.

Columbanus, another almost equally celebrated name, and who is often confounded with the preceding, was born A.D. 559. It was by this missionary and his companions that the monasteries of Luxen and Fontaine in Burgundy, of Dissentis in the Rhetian Alps, and of Bobbio in north Italy, were founded ; and at the last and most famous of which his mausoleum, body, and personal relics are still preserved. He died A.D. 615.

In 605, as we are informed by Bede [7], Lawrence, the successor of St. Augustine in the bishopric of Canterbury, wrote letters to the " Scots who inhabited the adjoining island of Ireland, urging them to conform to the Roman mode of keeping Easter, having learned from Bishop Dagamus, and also Columbanus the Abbot (last mentioned above), that the Scots differ not with the (northern) Britons in their conversation."

Letters also were sent, A.D. 634, to the Scots, both by Popes Honorius and John (the 4th, A.D. 640), upon the same subject, directed to the most dear and holy " Tomiano, Columbano, Cromano, Dinnao, et Baithano," Bishops [8].

The missions of Corman, and especially of Aidan, both monks of Iona or Hii (" the chief of all the religious houses of the northern Scots and Picts," as Bede terms it), to the Court of Oswald, the king of Northanhybria (who in his youth had sought both refuge and instruction in that island), A.D. 635, and the

---

[1] Stevenson's Bede, Engl. Hist. Soc. p. 31.

[2] Prosper, in Chron. an. 431 ; Bass. et Antioch. Coss. Conf. Lanigan, Ecclesiast. History of Ireland, vol. i. p. 9, sec. iv.

[3] Vossius Hist. Pelag., lib. i. cap. 3. Moore is very angry with St. Jerome for throwing into the teeth of Pelagius the *Irish flummery :* " Nec recordatus stolidissimus, et Scotorum pultibus prægravatus."

[4] When we consider that Bede was born and lived so close to Lindisfarne or Holy Island, where, for nearly half a century after the establishment of its monastery, in A.D. 635, Irish missionaries presided,

it is surprising, to say the least, that no notice of the labours of St. Patrick are recorded by him. Bede died A.D. 735.

[5] In this school there are said to have been 3,000 scholars. Martyr. Dungal, ad. 12 Decemb. Morn. 242. Quoted by Moore, Hist. of Ireland, vol. i. The monastery of Bangor, near the bay of Carlingford, in Ireland, which also became a celebrated abode of science, is said to have been founded by Columba.

[6] Hist. Eccl., b. iii. ch. iv.   [7] Id., b. ii. ch. iv.

[8] Stevenson's " Bede," i. 149, gives notices of these bishops.

establishment by Aidan of the bishopric of Lindisfarne, or Holy Island, are so well known and so interwoven with our national history, that I need not detail the circumstances connected therewith.

Finanus, also from Hy, succeeded Aidan in the bishopric, and " he built a church on Lindisfarne, of oak wood and thatch, as the Scotch [Irish] custom was[1]." He was succeeded by Colman, also from Ireland. It was this bishop who conducted the controversy respecting the time of keeping Easter, tonsure, and other equally *important* matters, on behalf of the northern church, held at Strenaeshalch, near Whitby, in 664; when, being worsted in argument, he returned to Iona. And it was not until the beginning of the eighth century, that the northern and Scottish church adopted the Roman custom, under Adamnan, Abbot of Hy, after his visit to the Court of King Alfred.

Alcuin, who flourished at the close of the eighth century, thus mentions the Irish fathers :—

" Patricius, Kieranus, Scotorum gloria gentis,
Atque Columbanus, Comgallus, Adamnanus, præclari patres."

Equally strong evidences of the existence of a church in Ireland, are to be obtained from the records of continental churches; but as the particulars of these will form the subjects of other articles in this work, it will be sufficient to mention, in addition to the founding of the monastery of Bobbio, one of the most renowned throughout Europe, and others, by Columbanus, above alluded to[2], that the famous monastery of St. Gall, in Switzerland, which exists to this time, was also established, and which, as well as the entire canton itself, bears the name of Gallus, an Irish missionary of the middle of the seventh century.

St. Kilian, the apostle and martyr of Franconia, was also an Irishman of the middle of the seventh century. His book of the Gospels, which was discovered in his tomb, and which is stained with his blood, was still preserved at Wurtzburgh, at the time of the publication of the " Chronicon Godwitcense," in which it is stated, that it was annually exhibited on the altar of the cathedral, on the day of his martyrdom[3]. In addition to which, the founding of the monasteries of Seckingen by St. Fridolin, and of Rheinau by St. Fendan, may be mentioned ; and the reader is referred to Moore's History of Ireland, vol. i., for an account of the further labours of Irish missionaries, in the seventh and eighth centuries, in France, Brabant, and the countries bordering on the Rhine.

Ecgbert and Willibrord, two of the early Anglo-Saxon missionaries of Northern Germany (predecessors of St. Boniface) also received their education in the schools of the north of Ireland; and it was from the instructions of Irish missionaries also, that both Aldhelm and Dunstan, two of the most renowned Anglo-Saxon scholars, received the rudiments of their education. The monastery of Malmesbury was founded by Maidulf, an Irishman[4], under whom Aldhelm was instructed, who afterwards became Abbot of the same monastery. It was also by the Irish clergy who served in the church of Glastonbury, that Dunstan was educated, about A.D. 940[5].

The names of Sedulius, Virgilius, Donatus, Maidulph, and John Scotus Erigena, will be sufficient to prove that the fame of the Irish Church was not extinguished in after centuries.

The three centuries, however, which preceded the invasion of Ireland under Henry II. tell a fearful tale in the annals of that country, and fully prove that Ireland had then, as she has now, greater enemies to her welfare amongst her own offspring than the hated Saxons.

2nd. ON THE ANCIENT SACRED MSS. OF THE IRISH.

I now proceed, in the second place, shortly to set forth the historical evidences which remain, in proof of the existence of books in Ireland during these early ages; including, in this branch of our inquiry, a short notice of such actually existing early manuscripts as have been very recently noticed by the Irish antiquaries.

---

[1] Bede, l. iii. ch. 25. This custom appears to have kept its ground in Ireland during several centuries (Vit. St. Malachiæ, auct. D. Bernardi, c. v. xiii.) A curious specimen of a church thus built, still remains at Greenstead in Essex. See Saturday Magaz., vol. i. p. 37.

[2] The following passages sufficiently prove the character of the Irish clergy at this early period :—

" Fatendum est tamen ejusmodi *Episcopos vagantes Hibernos* plurimum Ecclesiæ tum Gallicanæ tum Germanicæ profuisse."—Mabillon, Act. Benedict. sæc. 2, præf. p. xx.

And Osbernus makes the following observation respecting the frequent peregrinations of the Irish : —

" Hicque mos cum plerosque tum vehementer adhuc manet Hibernos ; quia quod aliis bona voluntas in consuetudinem ; hæc illis consuetudo convertit in naturam."—Osb. Vit. Dunstan. p. 91 ; MS. Cleop. B. 13.

" Scotia—[vel Hibernia]—ex quibus *Columbanus* gaudet Italia ; *Gallo* ditatur Alemannia ; *Kiliano* Teutonica nobilitatur Francia."—Canisius, Lection. Antiq. t. iv. p. 619.

[3] See also Mabillon, sæc. 2 ; Benedict, p. 993, No. 2.

[4] Moore finds fault with Dr. Lingard for stating that it was from a *Scottish* monk that Aldhelm received his first lessons.

[5] Lingard, Hist. Anglo-Sax. Church, p. 395.

THE GOSPELS OF MÆIEL BRITH MAC DURNAN.

The existence of schools in Ireland, celebrated both in England and abroad, and the express mention of their ancient manuscripts by historical writers, render the existence of some of them to the present time highly probable. That the Irish must have been provided with manuscripts in great numbers, and that many of these are still in existence, not only in the unexamined stores of our own country, but especially in the libraries in those places abroad where they established themselves, seems to be unquestionable; indeed, the researches of Irish antiquaries during the last twenty-five years have brought to light manuscripts of whose early date no reasonable doubt can be entertained. It would be almost as absurd to contend that a national Church, such as Ireland has been shown to have possessed, existed without manuscripts, as it is to assert that all these precious documents, scattered as they must have been by the Irish missionaries, have perished.

Celestius, the disciple of Pelagius, is expressly stated to have been acquainted with the use of writing: "Cœlestius antequam dogma Pelagianum incurreret, imo adhuc adolescens, *scripsit* ad parentes suos de monasterio *epistolas in modum libellorum tres.*"[1]

The following short extract from the tripartite Life of St. Patrick, (a compilation of the eighth or ninth century, but supposed to have been originally written by St. Evin in the sixth or seventh century, by Colgan, who published a Latin translation of it,) contains two notices immediately connected with our present inquiry.

In describing the visit of St. Patrick and his associates to the Court of Laoghaire, at the halls of Tara, through the midst of the hostile Pagans, attendants of the king, it is recorded, " Sic ergo mirificus vir sociique cum beato puero Benigno *sacrum Bibliorum codicem* in humeris gestanti,[2] per medios hostes salvi et incolumes Temoriam [Tara] usque pervenerunt—Tunc vir sanctus composuit illum *Hymnum patrio idiomate conscriptum* qui vulgo *Feth-fiadha,* et ab aliis *lorica Patricii* appellatur; et in summo abinde inter Hibernos habetur pretio," &c.[3] The manuscript in which this hymn is written, is, notwithstanding the regrets of Dr. O'Conor at its supposed loss, fortunately still preserved in the Library of Trinity College, Dublin: it is a manuscript which, in the opinion of Archbishop Usher, as expressed in a letter to Vossius, was in his time a thousand years old[4]. It is regarded by Mr. Petrie, who has very recently[5], for the first time published a copy and translation of it, as of " singular interest, whether considered as the oldest undoubted monument of the Irish language remaining, or as an illustrative record of the religious doctrine inculcated by St. Patrick." Hoping to be able to give a fac simile of this important document, I shall only observe, that the dialect in which it is written, the language employed, the characters used, and the historical evidences in support of its genuineness, all concur in establishing the opinion of it expressed by Mr. Petrie.

The DOMNACH AIRGID, a renowned and superstitiously venerated reliquary or *Cumdach* described by Colgan[6], and in the tripartite Life of St. Patrick, (ascribed to St. Evin, an author of the sixth or seventh century,) as having been given by St. Patrick to Mac Carthen, the first Bishop of Clogher, has recently been opened by Mr. Petrie[7], and was found to contain a copy of the four Gospels in Latin, written in Irish uncial letters, used in the very ancient manuscripts still preserved in the Library of Trinity College, and which, although agreeing in various respects with the Vulgate, possesses several readings which appear peculiar to itself. Dr. Todd considered, after a careful examination of it with the other ancient MSS. at Dublin, that the contractions which it exhibits might have been in use in the fourth or fifth century; and in a subsequent article he states it to be " probably as old as the fifth century."

The Gospels of Columba, " picturis passim intersertis miri operis et antiquitatis[8]," better known by the name of the Book of St. Columbkille[9], or the Book of Kells, having been mentioned by Tigernach and the IV Masters as existing in the Church of Kells in A.D. 1006, was more recently described by the historians Colgan, (Trias, p. 508,) O'Brien, (sub voce *Cumdach,*) Flaherty, Nicholson, Archbishop Usher, and especially by O'Donel, Prince of Tyrconnel in 1520, who took great pains to collect together all the MSS. he could obtain,

---

[1] Gennadius, De Script. Eccl. Catal., quoted by Archbishop Usher. This, together with the amusingly credulous statement of Bede, that water in which the scrapings of books which had been in Ireland ("rasa folia codicum qui de Hibernia fuerant," Bede, Hist. Eccl. l. 1, c. i. §. 8,) were soaked, was a remedy against the bites of serpents, are incidental proofs that the Irish were at that time familiar with learning and books.

[2] The Bible must have been of tolerable size to require carrying on his shoulders.

[3] Sept. Vit. Tripart. S. Patricii, part 1, ch. lx. Tr. Th., p. 126.

[4] Epist. ad Vossium, in Dissert. de Symb. Antiq.

[5] Trans. Royal Irish Acad. vol. xviii., part 2, 1839.

[6] Vita S. Mac Caerthenni (24 Mart. AA. SS. p. 73).

[7] See Trans. Royal Irish Academy, vol. xviii., part 1, 1838.

[8] Lhuyd, quoted by O'Conor, who regrets the supposed loss of this codex. Dr. Todd, however, assures me that it is still extant in the Library of Trin. Coll., Dublin.

[9] Moore (Hist. of Ireland, vol. i., p. 252) mentions this MS. as having belonged to St. Columbanus; in a subsequent page, however, he correctly notices it as the Gospels of Columbkille.—Archbishop Usher

illustrating the Acts of St. Columba his patron, from which he composed his Life, and amongst which were MSS. by many of Columba's disciples, Baithen, Adamnan, &c. ; and in his days fragments of codices written by Columba himself were still in existence, enclosed in golden and silver cases, and highly venerated.

Amongst the relics of St. Columba, preserved by the O'Donells, was another *Cumdach*, called the CAAH, long highly venerated, and supposed to be endowed with some preternatural merits. On opening this relic, Sir William Betham[1] found it to contain a copy of the greater part of the Psalter, written in a small minuscule Irish character, and agreeing nearly verbatim with the Vulgate version. Lanigan[2] has collected various notices of St. Columba having been employed in copying part of the Psalter, which he directed his disciple Baithen to complete after his decease ; and as the Caah has been handed down for ages in the O'Donell family, of which Columba was a member, Sir W. Betham does not hesitate to regard it as a relic of that saint.

The Missal of St. Columbanus was discovered at the monastery founded by him at Bobbio[3] ; a specimen of it is given by Mabillon and the Benedictines, and ascribed by them to the sixth or seventh century, and of the writing of which it is said by them, that " elle tient peut-être de l'écriture romaine usitée dans les îles Britanniques avant la conversion des Anglois[4]" [by St. Augustine]. This book is now preserved in the Ambrosian Library of Milan ; whilst the Royal Library of Turin contains a copy of Lactantius, written in the Irish characters of the seventh century, and having the following words in the hand-writing, as is supposed, of Saint Columbanus :—" Ex libris Columbani abbatis de Bobbio[5]."

The LEABHAR DHIMMA, or Book of Dimma, first described by Mr. Mason[6], and subsequently by Sir W. Betham[7], and now in the Library of Trinity College, Dublin, is a small codex containing the four Gospels, and the Office of the Visitation of the Sick, in Latin, in small minuscule Irish characters, ornamented with large rude-coloured initials and figures of the Evangelists, and which was found enclosed in another *Cumdach :* at the end of the MS. the scribe has signed his name thus :

FINIT AMEN + DIMMA MACC NATHI + :

i.e. Dimma the son of Nathi. This is a most curious corroboration ; because in the Life of St. Cronan, whose grandfather was also named Nathi, and who died in the seventh century (being, as I presume, one of the Bishops to whom Pope Honorius wrote in 634, as mentioned above), it is recorded, that he employed a scribe of the name of Dimma to write a copy of the Gospels[8]. Sir W. Betham does not hesitate, therefore, in regarding this as the MS. written during the lifetime of Cronan ; adding, that the MS. was preserved, until the dissolution of monasteries, in the Abbey of Roscrea, of which Cronan was the founder, and whose grave-stone, inscribed with his simple name, was dug up in 1826, in making the foundation for a new church at Roscrea.

The Gospels of St. Kilian, still preserved at Wurtzburgh, have been mentioned above, whilst, in the library of Saint Gall, which " surpassed all the other Benedictine establishments in science and literature," are preserved to this day, the manuscripts of its first founders " *Scottice scripti* "—that is, written in Irish characters[9].

The Book of Armagh, written by Aidus, Bishop of Slepten, who died A.D. 698, is still preserved in the Library of the University of Dublin, and has been very fully illustrated with fac similes by Sir W. Betham, in the 2d volume of his Irish Antiquarian Researches. This is, I presume, the identical volume described as the Gospels of St. Patrick, which was preserved in the church of Armagh in the eleventh century, as appears by St. Bernard's Life of St. Malachy.

Mr. O'Conor has described[10] a very interesting Irish MS. preserved within its singular *Cumdach*, or case, in the library of the Duke of Buckingham, at Stow, comprising a copy of the Gospel of St. John, and a missal according to the service of the early Irish Church, which bears evident marks, from the style of the ornamental illuminations, of having been written about the same period as the Book of Armagh. It was obtained from

also describes another copy of the Gospels ascribed to St. Columbkille, which was preserved at Durrow when he published his ' Primordia.'

[1] Irish Antiq. Res., vol. i., pl. l.

[2] Eccl. Hist. of Ireland, ch. xii., p. 14, and ch. xxxii., p. 1, note 40.

[3] The grants made during the first half of the seventh century to this monastery by Popes Honorius I. and Theodore, (Italia Sacra, tom. iv. & v., p. 329), prove that at this early period it had become renowned in the Christian world.

[4] Nouv. Tr. de Dipl. vol. iii., p. 210, pl. 45, sp. II. iii., copied, but not very faithfully, by O'Conor, in the first vol. of his Script. Rer. Vet. Hib.

[5] O'Conor, Picturesq. and Hist. Recoll. of Switz. p. 205.

[6] Trans. Royal Irish Academy, vol. xiii., 1819.

[7] Irish Antiq. Res., vol. i., p. 44.

[8] " Beatus pater Cronanus quendam scriptorem rogavit ut sibi quatuor scriberet Evangelia ; ipse jam scriptor *Dimma* vocabatur." Colgani Act. Sanct., Louv. 1645, vol. i. pp. 16, 17.

[9] Mabillon, Iter Germanicum, p. 6.

[10] Bibliotheca Stowensis, Append., vol. i. The plates illustrating this memoir are published at the end of the 2d volume of his Script. Rer. Hib. Veteres.

Germany, where Mr. O'Conor conjectures that it was carried to the Irish monastery at Ratisbonne, by Tordelbach O'Brian, King of Munster, in A.D. 1130.

Another " wonderful book" was described by Giraldus in the twelfth century, which he saw at Kildare, said to have been written by St. Brigid, who died A.D. 525, containing a Concordance of the Gospels according to St. Jerome's version, ornamented with as many drawings as there are pages in the book. He terminates his flaming account of it by stating, that " vix Apelles ipse similia efficere posset, et manu potius non mortali efformatæ et depictæ viderentur [1]."

The schools of St. Finan and of Bangor, have been already alluded to ; whilst at that of the monastery, built by Colman, at Mayo, for his English followers [2], there were at the time of Adamnan, towards the close of the seventh century, about 100 Saxon or English holy men ; whence it was named Maigh-eona Sassen, or Mayo of the Saxons [3]. Many of these are described as young noblemen, and among them was Edilhun, who " lived in Ireland for learning sake ;" and after his return to England was made Bishop of Lindnesse (Lincoln) [4].

The fame of St. Columbanus and his monastery, at Bobbio, in an after age led Dungal, an Irish missionary, to bequeath a number of books to that monastery, which are now in the Ambrosian Library at Milan, and the Royal Library of Turin.

Aldhelm, the Anglo-Saxon scholar, in a letter which is still extant, addressed to Eahfrida, on her return from Ireland, alludes to the schools of that country in a manner which shows at once his admiration and jealousy of them ; whilst Eric of Auxerre, in his letter to the Emperor Charles the Bald, writes thus :— " Quod Hiberniam memorem contempto pelagi discrimine *pene toto cum grege philosophorum* ad littora nostra migrantem."

The notices of the artistical abilities exhibited by some of the ancient Irish MSS. above described, may appear overdrawn ; but Bede himself gives us incidental evidence of the splendid red colour which was afforded amongst the natural productions of these islands [5]; whilst we also find notices of artists famed amongst the early Irish scholars.

Dagæus, Abbot of Innisceltra, who died A.D. 587 (ten years before the death of Columba), is described as being " scriptorem librorum *peritissimum* [6]." Ultan, who died A.D. 655, was also famous for the like talents, as appears from a metrical epistle of Ethelwolf to Egbert, at that time resident in Ireland, with the view of collecting MSS :—

" Ex quibus est Ultan præclaro nomine dictus,
Comptis qui potuit notis ornare libellos [7]."

Whilst Leland [8] more expressly says of him, " Ultanus *scriptor* et *pictor* librorum erat optimus." Assicus also, the first Bishop of Elfin, is described as having been a skilful adorner of books : " Assicus sanctus Episcopus et Bite filius Assici fecerunt sacros Codices quadrangulares," Triade, p. 134, c. 39. There is evidence likewise in Adamnan's Life of St. Columba, written about the end of the seventh century, that Anglo-Saxon artists were employed in the monastery of Iona : " Religiosus frater, Genereus nomine, *Saxo pictor*, opus pictorium exercebat *in Iona* conversatus insula [9]." Whilst even so early as the fifth century, the decoration of churches is recorded : " Ecclesia Kildariensis, sæc. vto. pictis tabulis et imaginibus depictis ornata [10]."

There still remains another circumstance fully establishing the fact of the existence of a school of caligraphy in Ireland long previous to the end of the seventh century. The style of the drawings and ornaments in the various manuscripts which have been shown above to be of Irish origin, is extremely peculiar, and of which nothing similar is to be met with in Continental MSS. (if, indeed, we except such as bear evident proof of having been either obtained from, or executed by, the Irish missionaries themselves). There is, however, a

---

[1] Topogr. Hib. Francof. fol. 1603, De St. 2, c. 38, p. 730, quoted by O'Conor, who regrets the loss of this fine MS.

[2] Bede, Hist. Eccl. l. iv. c. 4.

[3] Usher, Eccles. Primord.

[4] Bede, Hist. Eccl. l. iii. ch. 27.

[5] " Exceptis variorum generibus conchyliorum in quibus sunt et musculæ quibus inclusam sæpe margaritam omnis quidem coloris optimam inveniunt, id est, et *rubicundi*, et *purpurei*, et *jacintini*, et *prasini* sed maxime *candidi* sunt et cochleæ satis superque abundantes quibus tinctura *coccinei* coloris conficitur cujus *rubor* pul-

cherrimus nullo unquam solis ardore, nulla valet pluviarum injuria pallescere sed quo vetustior est solet esse venustior."—Bede, Hist. Eccl. b. i. ch. 1. Dr. O'Conor's ignorance of natural history has led him to infer that the reflected colours from the pearls found in oysters and muscles, mentioned by Bede, were used as actual pigments.

[6] Vit. Antiq. Dagæi in Actis SS.

[7] Ethelwolph, Epist. Metr. ad Egbert, in Bibl. Stowen. i. App. i. p. 14.

[8] Collectan. ii. p. 364; Harpsfield, Hist. c. 14.

[9] Adamnan, De Vita Columb. l. 3, c. 10 ; Triade, p. 366.

[10] In Triade, p. 523.

great similarity not only in the writing, but especially in the ornamental decorations, of these Irish MSS. and those known to have been executed in England[1]. Of these, the volume of the Gospels of Lindisfarne[2] is, perhaps, the most important MS. which has been preserved to our times, since both the date and place of its execution are well authenticated, it having been written at the close of the seventh century, at the monastery of Lindisfarne, which we have seen was from its establishment, nearly to this period, presided over by missionaries from Iona. Such a volume most clearly proves that the arts of writing and illumination must have been very long practised, whilst the recent establishment of their religion in Northumbria would necessarily allow these Irish missionaries but little leisure for the cultivation of such arts ; so that we cannot but refer them to the parent Irish establishment at Iona, and to a period considerably previous to the date of the Gospels of Lindisfarne. Of the various MSS. mentioned above, which have been recently described, the Book of Armagh comes nearest in point of date to that of the Gospels of Lindisfarne ; and it is impossible to contrast the illuminations of the former, figured by Sir W. Betham, with those of the latter, published by Strutt, Astle, and Shaw, and these again with the illuminated page represented in my second plate, without being convinced of their striking resemblance, and at the same time of their want of resemblance to the ornaments of the Irish manuscripts executed after the tenth century.

The objection that this Book of Armagh, and the Gospels of Mac Durnan, are written in minuscule characters instead of the fine rounded letters used in the Hymn of St. Patrick and the Book of the Domnach Airgid, &c., will be examined in another article.

3rd. DESCRIPTION OF THE GOSPELS OF MÆIEL BRITH MAC DURNAN.

I now proceed to describe the volume of the Gospels of Mæiel Brith Mac Durnan, at the present time one of the chief ornaments of the Manuscript Library of the Archbishop of Canterbury, at Lambeth. It is a small volume, written on vellum, $6\frac{1}{4}$ by $4\frac{1}{4}$ inches in size, and comprises the four Gospels, in Latin, written in minuscule Irish characters. The first leaf of the volume, as now bound, is blank on both sides. On the second leaf, in an Italic hand, of the sixteenth or seventeenth century, are inscribed the following verses in honour of the four Evangelists, and their symbolical representatives :—

DE EVANGELISTIS.

Hoc *Mattheus* agens hominem generaliter implet
Marcus ut alta fremit vox per deserta Leonis
Jura sacerdotis *Lucas* tenet ore juventi
More volans aquile verbo petit astra *Joh(anne)s*
Mattheus instituit virtutum tramite mores
Et bene vivendi justo dedit ordine legem
Marcus amat terras inter cœlumq. volare
Atq. volans Aquila stricto secat om(n)ia lapsu
Lucas uberius describit prelia Christi
Jure sacer vitulus qui menia fatur auita

These lines are very ancient, and were ordinarily placed over the representations of the Evangelists[3]. They are here evidently copied (at the time the MS. was last bound), from the leaf over which, that, on which they are now written, has been pasted. The latter had probably become almost illegible, as we may judge from the omission of two lines at the end applicable to St. John, which had evidently quite disappeared. On the verso of the second leaf are represented, in an ornamental frame-work, the symbolical figures of the four Evangelists, each in a small oblong compartment, having a pretty central star. The four-winged symbol of St. Matthew is copied in my first plate entire, the heads of the three others only being given[4], their bodies and wings being

---

[1] The Psalters, of St. Augustine, of St. Salaberg, and of St. Ouen at Rouen ; the Gospels, of St. Kilian at Wurtzburgh, of St. Boniface at Fulda ; those of St. Germain des Prés (No. 108), of St. Chad at Lichfield, of St. Gall, of Mac Regol at Oxford ; of the Bibl. d. Roi, copied by Silvestre, the Royal MS. 1 E. vi., and the Antiphonarium Benchoriense ; may be mentioned as specimens of this style.

[2] The name of the Gospels of St. Cuthbert, by which this incomparable manuscript has been called, implies, and has actually led to an incorrect date having been applied to it (see Sir F. Madden, in Shaw's Ill. Ornam.). Having been written at Lindisfarne, and not at

Durham, I shall speak of it in this work under the name of the Gospels of Lindisfarne ; the name of the "Durham Book" being, hence also, clearly inappropriate.

[3] The second line on St. Mark will be seen inscribed in gold in my plate of the Coronation-book of the Anglo-Saxon kings. They also appear in a Lombardic MS. of the eighth century, at C. C. Coll. Cambridge, copied by Astle.

[4] The portrait of the lion is not the least extraordinary, proving that the artist had been obliged to have recourse to his own invention in its delineation.

similar to that of St. Matthew's symbol. The extreme rudeness of these drawings render them interesting remains of Irish art. It will be seen that the heads of the man, eagle, and lion, are surmounted by a glory or nimbus of most singular form, for I can offer no other explanation of the appendage[1].

On the recto of the third page is inscribed the commencement of the first chapter of St. Matthew : " Liber generationis jhū xpi," &c., the first two letters only enlarged and richly ornamented, closely resembling the same two letters in the Book of Armagh, copied by Sir W. Betham[2].

The genealogical part of this Gospel, written in the minuscule hand employed throughout the volume, extends to the recto of leaf 4, the verso of which was originally left blank, and upon this we now find written in Anglo-Saxon characters, the inscription copied in my third plate,—

> + MÆIELBRIÐUS · MAC⸗
> DURNANI · ISTŪ · TEXTŪ
> PER · TRIQUADRŪ · DŌ ·
> DIGNE · DOGMITIZAT ·
> ·925 AST · AETHELSTANUS ·
> + ANGLOSÆXANA · REX · ET
> RECTOR · DORVVERNENSI ·
> METROPOLI · DAT · Þ ÆVV :·

Respecting the signification of this passage, Dr. Todd[3], in his notice of this volume, observes— " *Dogmatizare*, in the latinity of the middle ages signifies, to teach, and is generally used in a bad sense to teach false or erroneous doctrine[4]; but it can hardly have that meaning in the instance before us. *Dō* is a contraction for *Deo* or *Domino*. *Triquadrus* when used as an adjective, means *trisected*, divided into three parts; it is not a common word, especially when used as a substantive, as it appears to be here. The meaning of the word *textus* is evident; copies of the Gospels, such as that to which these remarks relate, are always so designated[5]. A learned friend has suggested that *dogmatizat* may, perhaps, mean *sanctions*, *testifies* to the accuracy of this copy of the Gospels; but I cannot reconcile this with *Deo, digne*, and *per triquadrum*. The rest of the inscription is easily translated, ' but Athelstan, King and Governor of the Anglo-Saxons, gives it for ever to the Metropolis of Canterbury.' The adversative *ast* seems difficult to explain on any interpretation of the former part of the inscription : it would seem to imply some opposition between the fact of Athelstan giving the volume to the city of Canterbury, and the dogmatizing of the text by Mac Dornan." It appears to me probable that in this inscription the sense has been slightly sacrificed, in order to preserve the alliterative style, of which the Anglo-Saxons were so much enamoured, and of which it will be seen that this inscription offers a striking example.

Mr. Lewis Morris, an excellent Welsh antiquary, in an article upon this MS.[6], endeavours to translate the inscription in the following manner :—" Mæielbrith, the son of Durnan, does worthily expound this text by references[7], but Athelstan, king and ruler of the Anglo-Saxons, makes a present of the book to the Metropolitan Church of Canterbury for ever." He however admits his inability to determine the meaning of the words, which he reads " per triquadrum Dominum," but which Mr. Samuel Pegge, in a subsequent article[8], conjectures may mean " by the assistance of the Trinity ;" suggesting, however, that *Do* may be a contraction of *Deo* instead of *Dominum*.

Mr. Morris, in the article above alluded to, has claimed this MS. as a production of his own country, stating it to be " written in the ancient British letter now commonly called the Saxon letter. The MS. seems to me to be as old as St. Hierome's time, with whose version, as in print, I find it to agree in most places. There is a note in it in capital letters, in Latin, which looks but modern in comparison to the book, signifying that it was expounded by Mæielbrith Mac Durnan ; and in the margin, in, I think, a still more modern hand, in figures +925, which was probably inserted about the 15th century, when figures came in use, [Dr. Todd ascribes them to the 16th or 17th century]. I take the book to have belonged originally to the Britons, not

---

[1] The heads of the lion and eagle, in the Book of Armagh, have a similar ornament.

[2] Irish Antiq. Res. vol. ii. In the Gospels of Lindisfarne, and of the Bib. Roy. Paris (described by Silvestre as of the tenth century !) the third letter b is added to the ornament.

[3] Brit. Mag. vol. xiv. p. 142.

[4] Du Cange Glossar. in voce.

[5] " *Textus* liber seu codex evangeliorum, qui inter cimelia ecclesiastica reponi solet auro gemmisque ut plurimum ornatus aureis etiam interdum characteribus exaratus."—Du Cange, in voce.

[6] Cambrian Register, 1795, vol. i. p. 358, et seq.

[7] Mistaking the usual Eusebian references for explanations or dogmas of Mæielbrith.

[8] Cambrian Register, i. p. 365.

9

only on account of the character (the same letter being to be seen on our ancient tomb-stones in Wales, erected before the Saxons had the use of letters), but also because Mæielbrith Mac Durnan was also a Briton, as plainly appears by his name; and you may see by some copies of Gildas Nennius, that the Cambro-British kings used on the first coming of the Saxons the appellative of Mac instead of Ab, and Mab."

This slight ground for conferring the scription of the MS. on a Welshman, will scarcely be considered, when it is stated that Dr. Todd has satisfactorily shown from various extracts from the ancient historians of Ireland, that Mæielbrigid (or Mæolbride) [1] Mac Durnan, i. e. the son of Durnan—or, as the Irish write it, Tornan—was Abbot of Derry in the 9th century, and afterwards Archbishop of Armagh, to which see he was promoted in 885, and died A.D. 927. He is spoken of in the highest terms for his piety, charity, and learning. In the Annals of Ulster, the chronology of which differs almost uniformly by a year from that of the Annals of the Four Masters, the death of Mæielbrigid is thus recorded :—

" 'A.D. 926, Maolbrighde, the son of Tornan, comarb [successor] of Patrick and Columbkille, 'felice senectute quievit,' so that he died in the year of the common æra 927.' It was in the year 925 that Athelstan succeeded to the throne of the Anglo-Saxons, so that this volume may have been sent as a present to him by Mæielbrigid on his accession. And if it was then deemed a suitable present for a prince, it must have been even then regarded as a volume of some antiquity and value. Athelstan died in the year 941."

On the recto of the fifth page we also now find a miniature painting of the Crucifixion pasted upon the front of the next leaf, which appears also to have been left blank; the word " ewanglia," *gospels*, copied in Pl. 11, in italic roman capitals, being only visible when held to the light through the superposed leaf. This painting having the background of highly burnished gold, represents the Saviour suspended upon the cross, with the Virgin on one side looking up to his face, and holding a small book, and the favourite Disciple weeping on the other side, also holding a book. In its drawing it very much resembles the same subject in the Arundel Psalter, No. 60, executed at the beginning of the twelfth century; and I presume, that this drawing must be attributed to that or the following century: it was therefore inserted long subsequent to the execution of the volume.

The verso of the fifth leaf contains a front portrait of St. Matthew, vested in a full cope or chasuble, holding in his right hand a long simple crozier, hooked at the top and pointed at the bottom, and in his left a book;—on his feet are black shoes with a pale edging, which also runs down the middle of the front. The general style of this figure and its extraordinary head-dress, is very similar to that of St. John copied in my first plate.

The recto of leaf six, comprises the first five words of the historical portion of St. Matthew, xpi autem generatio sic erat, " now the birth of Christ was in this wise,"—enclosed in a most elaborate border, represented in my 2nd plate. It is a perfect gem of caligraphic art, and exhibits, in miniature, the style adopted in the most costly manuscripts, of which the Gospels of Lindisfarne, the Rushworth Codex at Oxford, and the Golden Gospels of the Harleian Library, are perhaps the most elaborate specimens. The writing is especially interesting, since it shows the adoption in Ireland of the Roman capitals in their fantastical form, such as we see them in the oldest Anglo-Saxon manuscripts; the forms of the A, M, N, O, S, C, and G, (the last being a minuscule transformed into a capital,) are worthy of notice. The initial X, formed of several ribands interlaced together, is especially characteristic of the Irish style; as are also the little curls at the ends of the letters p i ; the latter character is also to be seen in the headings of the gospels of St. Luke and John. The heads of animals so singularly introduced into this design, are common in the early Anglo-Saxon manuscripts, as they are also in the Duke of Buckingham's Irish Codex. It will be seen, that one of them has a strange kind of nimbus placed over it. The pretty circular interlaced ornament at the commencement of the two lines of the word *au-tem*, occurs in the Book of Armagh. The curious long-necked quadrupeds, for such they are, which are so fantastically interlaced at the sides, and the marginal ornaments formed of diagonal intersecting lines, are especially characteristic of the Irish origin of this MS.

On the verso of this leaf the Gospel is continued in the ordinary hand-writing of the volume. The following passages, together with the introductory verses of St. John's Gospels, copied in my first plate, will show that

---

[1] " Maol, pronounced and in modern times written, Mul and Mæl, is a common word in Irish proper names, as Mulpatrick, Mulvany, Mulconry, &c. It denotes a servant or tonsured person, devoted by ton- sure to some saint or religious vow. Mul-bride or Mul-brigid, in Irish, ꝎꞬꞷꝆᛒꞃꝀꝼᛑᛖ, signifies ' the devoted tonsured servant of St. Bridgit.' "—*Todd.*

this MS. is written in a version different from that of the Vulgate in several respects; leading us to infer, in conjunction with the specimens given by Mr. Mason, Dr. Todd, Sir W. Betham, and others, that the Latin versions of the Irish Church differ, in several respects, both from the Vulgate and the Ante-hieronymian versions of Blanchini.

The Lord's Prayer is written as follows :—

" Pater noster q(ui) es in cœlis, s(an)c(t)ific(e)tu(r) nomen tuum. Adveniat regnum tuum. Fiat voluntas tua, sicut in cœlo, et in terra. Panem n(ost)rum cotidianum [1] da nobis hodie. Et dimitte nob(is) debita n(ost)ra sicut et nos dimisimus debitoribus n(ost)r(i)s. Et ne nos inducas in temptatione(m), sed lib(er)a nos a malo.— Amen."

The Beatitudes are as follows:—

" Videns autem jhs tbas, ascendit in montem, et cum sedissit accesserunt ad eum dip ejus et apiens os suum docebat eos dcs. Beati pauperes spu, qm ipsoru ÷ regnum cœlorum. Beati mites, quoniam ipsi possidebunt terram. Beati qui lugent nunc, qm ipsi consolabuntur. Beati qu esuriunt et sitiunt, qm ipsi saturabuntur. Beati misericordes, qm ipsi misericordiam əseqnt. Beati mundo corde, qm ipsi Dm videbunt. Beati pacifici, quoniam filii Di vocabuntur. Beati qui psecutionem patiuntur, ppt justitiam, quoniam ipsorum est regnum cœlorum. Beati estis cum maledixerunt vob homines et psecuti vos fuerunt et dixerunt omne malum advsum vos mentientes ppt me : gaudete et exultate," &c.

These two specimens will show the style of the contractions adopted in the MS., the wanting letters being supplied in the upper extract.

Of the version used in this MS., Dr. Todd observes, that "it would be a matter of some interest to determine, whether it be the modern Vulgate or the ancient Italic, (as it is called,) or Ante-hieronymian text. If it be the latter, the perfect state of preservation in which the MS. is found, will give it considerable value ; but if I may judge from other specimens of the same class of MSS. which I have examined, I should expect the text to be *mixed;* that is to say, a text which exhibits some of the readings of the ancient Vulgate, although in the main agreeing with Jerome's version."

In the lower margin of the page, containing Matthew xxvii. 24—32, there is a gloss or note in the Irish language, copied at the foot of my first plate, and evidently written in the ordinary text of the volume. It appears to be a note or reflection on the indignity with which our Lord was treated by the soldiers before Pilate, and is as follows :—

móṗ aṙṙáṗṙa ꝑ coṫmóṫa
ṅṫṁe ꞁ ṫalṁaṅ.

This inscription Dr. Todd translates, with a doubt as to the second word,—Ꝺoṗ eaṙoṅoṫṗ ṙa ꝑoṗ coṫmóṫa ṅṫṁe aʒuṙ ṫalṁaṅ: "Great dishonour this upon the Incarnate God of Heaven and Earth ;" the word coṫmóṫa being used by the Irish as a name for our Saviour, where, out of reverence, they do not wish to utter the sacred name of JESUS.

At the end of the Gospel of St. Matthew are the words in the hand-writing of the volume, also copied at the foot of my first plate, beneath the portrait of St. John :—" Amen: Do gtias ago." [2] The verso of the leaf on which this was written was left blank originally, but is now occupied by an Anglo-Saxon inscription, commencing thus :—

+ puljṫan aṅceꞇ ʒṗeꞇ cnuꞇ cynṫnʒ

(Wulfstan the Archbishop greets Canute the King.)

[1] St. Jerome altered this version, as given by Cyprian, Ambrose, Augustine, and others, into *superstantialem.* In the Service of the Church, however, the word *quotidianum* was retained.

[2] There is preserved at the Abbey of Fulda a manuscript which has long been regarded as the autograph of Boniface, the apostle of Northern Germany. It is a small octavo volume of the Gospels, written in a hand not very unlike that of the present volume, (which the Benedictines describe as written in " Saxone aiguë *allemande,*" N. Tr. de Dipl. iii. 446, to which, however, it bears no resemblance,) at the end of which the real scribe has signed his name, in these words : " Finit : *Amen. Deo gratias ago.* Vidrug, scripsit." The first few words of St. Matthew's Gospel, of which a specimen is given by Schannat (Vind. Litt. p. 225, and N. Tr. de Dipl. 3, pl. 46, vi. vi.), accord with the version found in the Domnach Airgid, mentioned above, agreeing therewith in the spelling of the names Abracham and Issac, and in the insertion of *autem* (contracted as in Irish MSS., of which the Fulda MS. is, almost unquestionably, one) after Isaac. The volume is the more interesting, as connected with the question of the early date of these MSS., as it bears an inscription, written in the ninth century, stating that it had been restored to Fulda by Arnulfus, king of Germany : thus proving its *prior celebrity* as connected with the Abbey.

11

The recto of the following leaf was also left blank, and is now inscribed with the following statement respecting a grant made by King Canute (the first line of which is copied in Pl. 11): "Cnud rex Anglorum dedit ecclesiæ Christi brachium sancti bartholomei apli cum magno pallio et sui capitis auream coronam et portum de Sandevic [Sandwich] et omnes exitus ejusdem aquæ ab utraque parte fluminis ita ut natante nave in flumine cum plenum fuerit quam longius de navi potest securis parvula super terram projici debet a ministris ecclesiæ xpi rectitudo navis accipi. Nullusque omnino hominum aliquam consuetudinem in eodem portu habet exceptis monachis ecclæ Xpi. Eorum quoque est transfretatio portus et navicula et cheloneum naviculæ et omnium navium quæ ad Sandevic venerint à Pepernessa usque Nordmutha. Si quid autem in magno mari repertum fuerit delatam Sandevic medietatem ecclesia Xpi habebit reliqua vero pars inventoribus remanebit." The grant of an arm of St. Bartholomew, a great ecclesiastical mantle (pallium, not a pall), a golden crown, and the dues of the port of Sandwich with its liberties, form a strange admixture in the grant, noticed in this paragraph[1].

On the verso of this leaf is the portrait of St. Mark; very similar in its style, but smaller than that of St. Matthew and John, holding a book in his left hand. His dress, and the singular ornaments on his head, resemble those of St. John, but his feet are naked. On either side, forming at the first sight merely a slender pillar, stands a monstrously attenuated animal, erect on its hind legs, whilst over the head of the Evangelist, and partly hidden by the ornamental frame of the picture, is the winged lion, with a head not unlike that of a sheep, surmounted with the singular nimbus (?) already noticed in other figures.

The following leaf has been interpolated, being a drawing of the Scourging of Christ by the Jews. The Saviour is represented tied by the wrists to a narrow column in the centre of the miniature, with a figure on each side preparing to strike him. They are dressed in short tunics; and one has on a white skull-cap, and his hair is painted blue; as was common about, or rather before, the period assigned to this miniature, which is contemporaneous with that of the Crucifixion, above described.

The next leaf comprises the commencement of the Gospel of St. Mark (Initium Evangelii, &c.), the first two letters, *In*, being enlarged, and formed like the *In* in my first plate, but more ornamented, the other letters, *itium*[2], of the first word, being much less enlarged, and of an uncial form, the remainder of the page being occupied with the minuscule writing. This is enclosed within a very elegant frame, having a large star at the top and a large dog's head. At the end of this Gospel the scribe has written, "Finit, amen, finit."

The next three pages were left blank, but are now occupied with four Anglo-Saxon charters of King Canute, one of which is copied in my second plate:—

Cnuꞇ cyninᵹ ᵹꞃeꞇ ealle mine ƀ ⁊ mine eoꞃlaꞅ ⁊ mine ᵹeꞃeꝼan on ælceꞃe ꞅciꞃe þe æþelnoð aꞃceƀ ⁊ ꞅeluꞃeꝺ æt cꞃiꞅꞇeꞅ cyꞃcean lanꝺ inne habbað ꝼꞃeonꝺlice ⁊ ic cýðe eoꞃꝥic hæbbe ᵹeunnen hi̅ ꝥhe beo hiꞅ ꞅaca ⁊ ꞅocne ƿyꞃðe ⁊ ᵹꞃið bꞃyceꞅ ⁊ ha̅ ꞅocne ⁊ ꝼoꞃꞅꞇealleꞅ ⁊ inꝼan ᵹeneꞅ þeoꝼeꞅ ⁊ ꝼlymena ꝼyꞃinðe oꝼeꞃ hiꞅ aᵹene menn binnan byꞃiᵹ ⁊ buꞇan ⁊ oꝼeꞃ cꞃiꞅꞇeꞅ cyꞃcean ⁊ oꝼeꞃ ꞅƿa ꝼeala þeᵹna ꞅƿa ic hi̅ ꞇo læꞇan hæbbe ⁊ ic uelle ꝥ ænig mann ahꞇ þæꞃ on ꞇeo buꞇon he ⁊ hiꞅ ƿicneꞃaꞅ ꝼoꞃþā ic hæbbe cꞃiꞅꞇe þaꞅᵹe ꞃihꞇa ꝼoꞃᵹyꝼen minꞃe ꞅaꞃle ꞇo eceꞃe alyꞅendneꞅꞅe ⁊ ic uelle ꝥæꝼꞃe æniᵹ mann þiꞅ abꞃece be minun ꝼꞃeonꝺꞅcipe.

Of which the following is a translation, the law terms employed for the different kinds of tenure not being translated:—

"I Cnut greet all my Bishops and my Earls and my Reves in every shire that Æthelnoth Archbishop and the Convent at Christ Church have land in, friendly. And I say that I have granted him that he enjoy (beo ƿyꞃðe) his saca and socne, and gryth bryces, and hacsocne and forestealas, and infanges theoffes and flymena fyrmthe (so we are to read, instead of fyrinthe) over his own men, within borough and without, and over Christ's church, and over as many Thanes as I have permitted him to have; and I decree that not any man should any thing therein claim but he and his servants, because I have besought Christ's holy authority to forgive my soul in recompense for the land; and I will not that any man break this, by my friendship" (that is, as he values my friendship)[3].

[1] In the Library at Stowe is contained the original grant, dated "anno ab Incarnatio 1023," by King Canute, of his crown, and the duties of the port of Sandwich, to the church of Canterbury (Bibl. Stowensis, ii. 135). The latter, "ab utraque parte fluminis cujuscumque terra sit quam longius de navi potest securis parvula quam Angli vocant Taparcax, super terram projici, Ministri Christi rectitudines accipiant."

[2] The style of this word *Initium* exactly corresponds with that of the Book of Armagh, copied by Sir W. Betham.

[3] The introductory form of this charter was retained so late as the reigns of Henry I. and II. (see specimens of their charters, given by Astle, pl. xx. 9, 10.) From the elongated tops of the f, and the recurved tops of the e, this was evidently written during the reign of King Canute. (See similar specimens in Astle, pl. 21.)

The verso of the third of these leaves contains the portrait of St. Luke, scarcely above half the size of that of Sts. Matthew and John. His head-dress and robes are similar to those of the other Evangelists. In his right hand he holds a short plain crosier, hooked at the top, and blunt at the foot. In his right hand he holds a book, with an ornamented cover—if, indeed, it be not intended for a *cumdach;* and he has shoes on his feet. This is altogether the rudest figure of the four Evangelists.

The next leaf has been interpolated, and is now occupied by a miniature representing the Betrayal of Christ on the recto, copied on my third plate, the verso being still left blank. The drawing is much more spirited than either of the others which have been similarly introduced; and, from the armour and highly-polished back-ground, I apprehend that it must be assigned to the thirteenth century. The outlines are entirely formed by *black* lines, some of which, as in the features, are very delicate, whilst others are very coarse.

Then follows the Gospel of St. Luke, the first two words, *qm.* (quoniam) *quidem,* nearly similar to those at the beginning of St. John's Gospel, the q being enlarged, with its tail extended along the left hand margin of the page. The remainder of the writing in this page is in Irish minuscule, and is enclosed within an ornamental frame-work of twisted snakes. At the end of St. Luke's Gospel is written—" D̄o ḡtias ago."

On the verso of this leaf is the likeness of St. John, represented in my first plate. This rude design will give a good idea of the figures of the other Evangelists, and which in general design, and in the singular distribution of the drapery, correspond with those in the Leabhar Dimma, the Gospel of St. John of the Duke of Buckingham, and in the Gospels of St. Chad, as figured by Hickes in his Thesaurus (vol. i.). They are entirely unlike the drawings of the Evangelists in other early MSS., such, for instance, as those in the Gospels of Lindisfarne, which clearly exhibit traces of Byzantine art; or those in the Purple MS. (Reg. 1., E. 6), which are evidently of Anglo-Saxon origin. They, in fact, more nearly resemble in general style the strange figures of Northern chessmen, represented in Sir F. Madden's learned article in the Archæologia, vol. xxiv. The ornaments of the head in this figure have been carefully copied, and I am quite unable to explain the two curious appendages on each shoulder—for surely they cannot be intended for the vittæ or infulæ of the mitre. I thought they might, from something similar appearing on the heads of the symbolical emblems, be intended for appendages of the nimbus or glory, but the head is here surrounded by a distinct one of a yellow colour[1]. The head of St. Luke in the Leabhar Dimma, and that of St. John in the Duke of Buckingham's codex, have a somewhat similar appendage on each shoulder. The colours are laid on very thick, and have a semi-opake appearance, the face having a thick coat of white, in which the features are represented by black lines. My chief object, however, in selecting this portrait, was to show the articles in his hands which were anciently used in writing; that in his right hand appearing to me to be unquestionably intended for a pen formed of the quill of a bird, some of the web being left at the upper end[2]. The point of the pen is dipped into a small conical utensil, filled with red colour, supported on a long slender stem, reaching to the ground. In his other hand he holds another sharp-pointed instrument. This is a circumstance of much archæological interest, clearly showing (if my idea of the age of the MS. be correct) the employment of the pen nearly two centuries earlier than is represented in any existing drawing.

From a line of Juvenal—

" Anxia præcipiti venisset epistola *pennâ.*"—Satyr iv.

it has been supposed that quills from the wings of birds were in use in his time, but it is more than probable that the poet was but here employing a poetical image. Theodoric, king of the Ostrogoths in the 5th century, is stated to have used a pen to write the first four letters of his name[3]. St. Isidore of Seville, who wrote in the middle of the 7th century, precisely describes the pen as one of the two instruments used in writing, " penna avis cujus acumen dividitur in duo[4]." Mabillon[5] cites a miniature of the time of Louis le Debonaire, (9 sæc.) and another of the 10th, in which the Evangelists are represented with pens in their hands; and the same is to be seen in the Harleian MS., No. 2820, of the 10th century, in which the ink-stand is represented as in this Irish MS.

The thumb of the right hand appears to be ornamented with a ring. The instrument in the left hand may be either a style or a knife; it is unlike any of the instruments used by scribes figured by Montfaucon

---

[1] I find nothing at all analogous to this in M. Didron's article upon the Nimbus in the Révue Générale de l'Architecture et des Travaux Publics.

[2] That it is not intended for a knife, as described by Dr. Todd, is evident both from this circumstance, and from being dipped into the pot of red colour.

[3] Ad calcem Ammiani Marcell. p. 667.

[4] Isidor. Hisp. Orig. lib. vi. cap. 14. [5] De Re Dipl. Suppl. cap. ii. n. 8.

and the Benedictines. The ornaments in the different pannels of the border are especially Irish, and by far more elaborate than, although in the same style as, those represented from the Book of Dhimma, of the Duke of Buckingham's MS.

The next leaf has been introduced, and contains a miniature of the Embalment of Christ on the recto (the verso remaining plain): the dead body of the Saviour being laid upon a table, Joseph of Arimathea pouring ointment into the wound in the side from a globular vessel, and with a handkerchief tied round his head; five figures stand round the table weeping, four with nimbi round the heads, and one with a red skull-cap having a conical erect point in the middle. The execution of this miniature corresponds with that of the three others which were introduced at the same period.

The next page has the commencement of St. John's Gospel, copied in my first plate, inclosed within an ornamental frame. It is to be read: "In principio erat verbum, et verbum erat apud Deum et Deus erat verbum · hoc erat in principio apud Deum Omnia per ipsum facta sunt · et sine illo factum est nihil · quod factum est · in ipso vita est et vita erat lux hominum et lux in tenebris · et tenebræ eam non comprehenderunt." This passage possesses several readings quite unlike any of the ancient versions I have yet examined. The conjunction of the first three letters, as in the Leabhar Dhimma and Duke of Buckingham's MS., is considered by Mr. O'Conor to represent the Trinity in Unity. The letter N thus formed bespeaks the venerable antiquity of this volume. The irregular manner in which the first three words are written is interesting and peculiar, resembling the Gospels of St. Germain des Prés in this respect.— N. Tr. Dipl. v. ii. pl. 18.

The few last lines of this Gospel are written more contractedly than the rest, so as to come into the end of the page without beginning a new leaf.

St. Jerome's prologues to the different Gospels are not copied, and Dr. Todd suggests that the blank leaves left before each were intended to have them introduced. Neither do the tables of the Eusebian Canons appear; the Eusebian Numbers, however, and references to the Ammonian Sections, are given throughout in the margin, enclosed within red lines, as shown in my second plate.

In conclusion, it is to be observed that the MS. has been carefully collated, and the modern chapters indicated by coarse red chalk figures, which appear to me to be in the handwriting of the celebrated Archbishop Matthew Parker, whence I infer that the MS. remained at Canterbury until the dissolution of monasteries by Henry VIII. The MS. is not inserted in Mr. Todd's Catalogue of the Archiepiscopal MSS., published in 1812; but I have not been able to learn from the Rev. Mr. Maitland, the present learned Librarian of Lambeth Palace, from whom, or under what circumstances, it has again fallen into the possession of the Archbishopric of Canterbury.

The Book of Kells. Pl. II.

THE BOOK OF KELLS.

MANY circumstances tend to prove, that, for several centuries, the ancient Christian Church of Ireland formed no integral portion of the Church of Rome; whilst, in various respects its discipline and other peculiarities seem to have been more analogous to those of the Eastern Churches.[1] That the Irish received Christianity at a very early period is perfectly authenticated, independent of the question, whether it came from the disciples of Irenæus at Lyons direct to Ireland,[2] or from Roman or English missionaries during the earlier part of the period that the Romans were in possession of Great Britain.[3] Placed far apart from the rest of the civilised world, religion in Ireland retained unaltered its early forms and discipline.[4] Whereas Rome, at the end of six centuries from the first establishment of the Christian religion, had assumed a dominant character, and had, by degrees, introduced a series of discipline, practice, and doctrines, unknown in the first ages of the Church,[5] and of which consequently the Irish were ignorant.[6] Hence the great disputes which took place between the Irish missionaries in the north of England, and the Romish missionaries and followers of St. Augustine; and hence, whilst the Romish Church, in the sixth century, strenuously endeavoured to substitute the Vulgate translation of the Bible in lieu of the old Italic and Septuagint versions,[7] almost every copy of the Gospels, which, from the style of the writing, orthography, and caligraphy, may be known as having been written in Ireland, now in existence, appears (from the collation which I have made of a considerable number of them) either to be written in a version distinct from the Vulgate, or to have the Vulgate mixed with a preceding version, forming what is termed a mixed text. This circumstance did not escape Archbishop Usher, who states, " certe antiquam Italicam [versionem] in usu fuisse in Hibernia usque ad annum 815." Ware, also, and Sir W. Betham, assert that the extracts from the Bible in the Confession of St. Patrick, contained in the Book of Armagh, written in the year 698, are not in the Vulgate version.[8]

There is still another circumstance which singularly, although in an indirect manner, appears to prove the correctness of the preceding remarks—viz., that at a period when the fine arts may be said to have been almost extinct in Italy and other parts of the Continent—namely, from the 5th to the end of the 8th century —a style of art had been established and cultivated in Ireland, absolutely distinct from that of all other parts of the civilised world. There is abundant evidence to prove that in the 6th and 7th centuries the art of

---

[1] Thus Sir Robert Cotton, Sir Henry Spelman, Camden, and Selden, having been appealed to upon the subject of the early monachism in this country, drew up a report, wherein they declared, that previous to the coming of St. Augustine the Egyptian Rule was only in use.— (" Qui Ægyptiorum mores secuti." Reyner, Apost. Benedict. p. 202. Ledwich, p. 89.)

[2] Ledwich, Antiq. of Ireland, p. 55.

[3] Todd, Church of St. Patrick, p. 13.

[4] " The Scottish [Irish] monks had been taught to respect as sacred every institution which had been sanctioned by the approbation of their ancestors."—Lingard, Antiq. of Anglo-Saxon Church, p. 34.— " The doctrines which they had received from their forefathers they considered as their most valuable inheritance."—Ibid. p. 37.

[5] Thus Irenæus, even in the second century, complained of the innovations of the Roman Church; and Eusebius says, " Εξέναντιας δε των επι Ρωμης τον υγιη της εκκλησιας θεσμον παραχαραττοντων, Ειρηναιος διαφορους επιστολας συντασσει."—L. 5, c. 20.

[6] " Utpote quibus longe extra orbem positis nemo synodalia Paschalis observantiæ decreta porrexerat."—Bede, Hist. Eccl. L. iii. c. 4.

[7] St. Isidore (Ann. 630) states, that " Hieronymi editione gene-

raliter omnes Ecclesiæ utuntur pro eo quod veracior sit."—I. 1. Offic. c. 12.

[8] It is very greatly to be desired that a careful collation should be made and published of the various ancient MSS. of the Gospels written in Ireland, as I have no doubt that some important results would be thereby obtained. That such would be the case may be easily conjectured, when it is mentioned that the slight examination which I have made of the texts of the Dublin MSS. has brought to light, in one of them, a passage in St. John's Gospels, hitherto supposed to be unique in the Vercelli Gospels. I have but little doubt that it will be found that, from the peculiarities of the text, as well as of the caligraphy, the Gospels of MacRegol and MacDurnan, the Book of St. Chad, the Gospels of SS. Luke and John in C.C.C.C., portion of the Royal MS. 2 A. 20 in the British Museum, the Duke of Buckingham's Gospel of St. John, the Gospels of St. Germain des Près, No. 108, also the Gospels in the Bibliothèque du Roi, Lat. 693, the Gospels at St. Gatien at Tours, the Gospels of St. Boniface at Fulda, besides all the ancient Gospels at Dublin (except the autograph Gospel of St. Columba), and several at St. Gall, are all Irish MSS., and not written in the Vulgate version.

1

ornamenting manuscripts of the Sacred Scriptures, and especially of the Gospels, had attained a perfection in Ireland almost marvellous, and which in after ages was adopted and imitated by the Continental Schools visited by the Irish missionaries. The chief peculiarities of this school consist in the illumination of the first page of each of the Sacred Books, the letters of the first few words, and more especially the initial, being represented of a very large size, and highly ornamented in patterns of the most intricate design, with marginal rows of red dots ; the classical Acanthus being never represented. The principles of these most elaborate ornaments are, however, but few in number, and may be reduced to the four following :—1st. One or more narrow ribbons, diagonally but symmetrically interlaced, forming an endless variety of patterns. 2nd. One, two, or three slender spiral lines, coiling one within another till they meet in the centre of the circle, their opposite ends going off to other circles. 3rd. A vast variety of lacertine animals and birds, hideously attenuated, and coiled one within another, with their tails, tongues, and top-knots forming long narrow ribbons irregularly interlaced. 4th. A series of diagonal lines, forming various kinds of Chinese-like patterns. These ornaments are generally introduced into small compartments, a number of which are arranged so as to form the large initial letters and borders, or tesselated pages, with which the finest manuscripts were decorated. The Irish missionaries brought their national style of art with them from Iona to Lindisfarne in the 7th century, as well as their fine, large, very characteristic style of writing: and as these were adopted by their Anglo-Saxon converts, and as most of the manuscripts which have been hitherto described are of Anglo-Saxon origin, it has been the practice to give the name of Anglo-Saxon to this style of art. Thus several of the finest fac-similes given by Astle as Anglo-Saxon are from Irish MSS. ; and thus Silvestre, who has copied them (without acknowledgment [1]), has fallen into the same error; whilst Wanley, Casley, and others appear never to have had a suspicion of the existence of an ancient school of art in Ireland.

In respect to the higher department of art, it was highly important to determine whether a distinct style had also been established, or whether the Byzantine school had pervaded the Sister Island ; such being unquestionably the case with the portraits of the Evangelists delineated in the copy of the Gospels written at Lindisfarne, at the close of the 7th century (Cott. Nero, D. IV.). That the former was the case, there was reason to surmise from an inspection of the grotesque portrait of St. Luke, given by Hickes from the Book of St. Chad, and from those published by Sir W. Betham from the Leabhar Dimma, and by O'Conor from the Duke of Buckingham's Gospels, as well as from analogous specimens given in this work.

With the view, therefore, of determining this question—as well to trace the distinctions between the early Irish and Anglo-Saxon styles, so as to learn how far the latter was indebted to the former for its existence—I have, by the kindness of the Rev. J. H. Todd, the learned Librarian of Trinity College, Dublin, examined the various ancient MSS. in the Library of that establishment.

Ireland may justly be proud of the Book of Kells. This copy of the Gospels, traditionally asserted to have belonged to St. Columba, is unquestionably the most elaborately executed MS. of early art now in existence, far excelling, in the gigantic size of the letters in the frontispieces of the Gospel, the excessive minuteness of the ornamental details, the number of its decorations, the fineness of the writing, and the endless variety of initial capital letters, with which every page is ornamented, the famous Gospels of Lindisfarne in the Cottonian Library. But this MS. is still more valuable, on account of the various pictorial representations of different scenes in the life of our Saviour, delineated in a style totally unlike that of every other school, and of which, I believe, the only other specimens are to be found in the Psalter of St. John's College, Cambridge, and at St. Gall ; the latter, however, being far inferior in execution to those in the Book of Kells. When it is further stated, that this magnificent volume is now for the first time described and illustrated, the reader will not be indisposed to underrate the interest of the present article as an addition to the history of the Fine Arts hitherto neglected by all previous writers. [2] In my two Plates such portions of the ornamental details as are peculiar to the volume have been selected, rather than such as are similar to those in the Gospels of MacRegol and Lindisfarne.

---

[1] The mode in which Silvestre has attempted to give a greater air of faithfulness to his copies of Astle's fac-similes, without having seen the originals, is quite fictitious. Thus he has printed the writing in faded brown ink, whereas the ink used in these MSS. has retained its blackness in a wonderful degree.

[2] I believe an intention has been entertained by the Society of Antiquaries of publishing fac-similes of the ornamental pages of the Gospels of Lindisfarne. I would, however, beg leave to suggest that the volume now under description is far more worthy of such an undertaking, more especially as the annual grant to the Royal Irish Society quite precludes such a step being taken by that body.

The volume consists of 339 leaves of very thick and finely glazed vellum, measuring (although sadly cropped) 13 inches by 9½, a page of the text containing 16, 17, or 18 *lines*, the writing occupying 10 inches by 7.

The recto of the first leaf contains in the first column (surrounded by an ornamented border), various Hebrew words with their significations in Latin (the early part of this Glossary being wanting); whilst the second column is occupied by the four evangelical symbols, singularly drawn, but almost obliterated, holding books in their hands. Then follow the Eusebian Canons, which occupy several pages. They are written in narrow columns, inclosed between highly ornamented pillars, in which all the peculiar styles of ornament above described are to be found; these support rounded arches and circles, which are inclosed by larger rounded arches, the open spaces bearing the evangelical symbols in a variety of strange attitudes, according in number with the number of the Evangelists in the several Canons.

To these succeed several Charters in the Irish language, written in the strong ordinary Irish minuscule characters, containing grants of lands to the Abbey of Kells, the Bishop of Meath, and the Church of Kells, by Melaghlin, King of Meath, dated A.D. 1152.

The verso of fol. 7 contains the drawing of the Virgin and Child, copied in Plate 1, which is inclosed within a highly elaborate border composed of intertwined lacertine animals with dogs' heads. This singular composition is interesting from the proof it affords of the veneration of the Virgin Mary in the early Irish Church; the large size in which she is represented, as well as the glory round her head (which singularly bears three small crosses), evidently indicating the high respect with which the Mother of Christ was regarded. The infant Saviour, it will be observed, is destitute of the nimbus; the seat on which the Virgin is seated is not devoid of elegance, terminating above in the dog's head with an immensely elongated interlaced tongue. The drawing of the whole is entirely puerile, whilst the ingenuity displayed in the intricate patterns at the sides and upper part of the drawing is quite remarkable. This singular interlacing of the limbs of human figures is peculiarly characteristic of the Irish MSS., and it is accordingly found in the Gospels of MacRegol and the Book of St. Chad. The instrument held by the Angel, at the right hand of the foot of the drawing, is worthy of remark, being analogous to one of the sceptres held by St. Luke in the Book of St. Chad.[1] These are followed by the " breves causæ" and " argumenta" of each of the four Gospels (which extend to fol. 25), part of which is beautifully written in a narrower and more recent hand and in various coloured inks, the first page being highly ornamented and containing the words " Nativitas Xp̄i in Bethlem iudae. Magi munera offerunt et infantes interficiuntur, regressio—;" these words being written in rows of angular letters of different sizes separated by highly ornamented bars, the first word (except the large initial N) being formed of lacertine letters, copied in my second plate. The headings of the breves causæ and argumenta of each of the other Gospels are also ornamented with one or two rows of large similarly formed letters.

The 20th leaf is misplaced, being the commencement of the Glossary of Hebrew words, the other part of which occurs in the first leaf of the volume. The recto of the following leaf contains two inscriptions in the Irish language, containing grants of certain glebe lands in perpetuity for three ounces of gold to the Monastery of Arbraccan, made by King Moriertach O'Laghlyn, and others, witnessed by Gilmacbag, Archbishop of Armagh; Erthro, Bishop of Meath, and many others.[2]

The verso of this leaf is occupied by drawings of the four evangelical symbols, singularly delineated and ornamented, and inclosed within broad elaborate square borders. The verso of the next leaf is entirely occupied by a full length portrait of St. Matthew (seven inches high), inclosed within a highly ornamented border, his head surrounded by a rich nimbus, his right hand placed, beneath his robe, on his breast, and his left hand (naked) holding a book, and with naked feet.

The recto of folio 29 contains the first two words of St. Matthew's Gospel " Liber Generationis," in the same style as, but larger and infinitely more elaborate than in the Gospels of Lindisfarne. The Saint himself is again represented standing in the lower part of the page, holding a book in his left hand, wearing shoes similar to those in the Gospels of MacDurnan. The genealogical history extends to fol. 31, v. The following leaf has on its verso another portrait inscribed, on an erasure, with the name of Jesus Christ in a modern hand, but it is evidently misplaced, and is intended for one of the two Evangelists, whose portraits are

---

[1] Mr. Petrie showed me an ancient Irish relic, which I consider to have been the handle of one of these instruments. Can this be intended for the " flabellum muscarium," used in the early church " ad muscas a sacrificio abigendas?"

[2] Dr. Todd is occupied at the present time in editing these inscriptions.

wanting. This figure holds a book in his left hand, which is covered with his robe, and supports the top of it with his naked right hand. It is inclosed within an ornamented border of lacertine animals. The verso of the following leaf is covered with a tesselated ornament in the same style as those of the Gospels of Lindisfarne. The excessive intricacy and delicate execution of this and other similar pages is quite marvellous.

The opposite page contains the commencement of the historical part of St. Matthew's Gospel " Xp̄i autem generatio," magnificently ornamented; the initial letter X being nearly thirteen inches high and nine and a half broad; the Xp̄i, in fact, occupy almost the entire page; every part of the open spaces of the letters, as well as the bodies of the letters themselves, being most minutely ornamented and coloured, the whole forming the most elaborate specimen of caligraphy which was perhaps ever executed. To this succeeds the text of the Gospel of St. Matthew, written in a fine large hand in a *mélange* of uncial and minuscule characters; a specimen of which, being St. Matthew, v. 4, 5, is given in Plate 2, together with a series of separate letters, in order to complete the alphabet. Each verse or short paragraph is commenced by a finely ornamented, but singularly drawn, initial letter, chiefly formed of strange-looking animals, intertwined in the most ingenious and often elegant manner, no two throughout the volume being alike, and several, often many, occurring on each page. Several portions of the latter part of this Gospel are also elaborately ornamented, thus the recto of fo. 114 contains a drawing of Christ seized by two Jews (St. Matthew, xxvi. 30). The Saviour is represented with a beard and curling hair, 7½ inches high, the Jews being only 5½ inches, the latter wearing mustachios turned up towards the eyes, and pointed beards. The design itself is however puerile. The whole is inclosed between two highly ornamented columns, supporting a rounded arch, the crown of which terminates in two large dogs' heads. The verso of the same leaf is occupied by the following verse, ' Tunc dicit illis ih̄s omnes,' &c., written in large square ornamented letters, inclosed in ornamental borders, the initial T similar to that represented in Plate 1; the fourth line in Plate 1 being copied from this page, and containing the letters ' (di)cit illis ih̄s om(nes)' in which the B-like form of the H, the D-like O, and the M, are especially to be noticed. The commencement of the 38th verse of the 27th chapter (Tunc cruciferant, &c.), is illuminated in the same manner upon f. 124 recto. The first two words are copied in Plate 1.[1] The initial T is formed of a most singular quadruped, vomiting forth horned serpents. The first two words of the 28th chapter are also similarly written.

At the beginning of St. Mark's Gospel (fo. 129, v.) is another representation of the evangelical symbols, copied in Plate 2, but inclosed in a large highly ornamented square, and each accompanied by various singular sceptres, &c. The first few words of this Gospel, Initium evangelii Ih̄u Xp̄i, occupy the entire page (fo. 130, r.), the letters INI being more than a foot high, with all the open spaces minutely ornamented. The 25th verse of the xvth chapter of this Gospel also occupies an entire page, being written in large square and red letters, inclosed within tesselated ornaments, the head of an angel represented at the top of one side, and his feet at the bottom of the illumination : one of the lines of which, hora ter(tia), is represented in Plate 1. The last page of this Gospel is decorated with two most singular dragon-like monsters, forming lateral diagonal ornaments to the page, an angel and a lion occupying the open side spaces.

The first page of St. Luke's Gospel, or rather the single word Qn̄iam, occupies an entire page (fo. 188, r.), the first letter, Q, filling nearly two-thirds of the page; it is of an oblong form, with semicircular projections from the middle of each of the four sides, and with a short narrower space terminating in a large circle, extending from the middle of the under side of the square. The words ' Fuit in diebus Herodis,' as usual, are written of a large size in the following page in square letters but little decorated. The genealogy of Christ (Luke iii.) occupies 5 pages, every line commencing with the word Qui, (fuit, &c.), ornamented in an endless variety of forms, with a pretty arabesque at the end of the chapter across the bottom of fo. 202.

The controversy of Christ (who is here figured with a cruciferous nimbus similar to that of the Virgin in Plate 1.) and the Devil (Luke iv.) is represented in a most extraordinary drawing, which occupies, with its decorated border, the entire fo. 202, v. The Devil is represented of small size, extremely attenuated, with two wings, and is painted black, he however is destitute of the usual caudal appendage : Christ is attended by a number of his disciples on his right side, and two angels hover over his head.

The first verse of the 4th and the first verse of the 24th chapters of this Gospel are also highly ornamented, and occupy separate pages. It is to be observed that the word ' Finit' is not written at the end of

---

[1] The false orthography of the word crucifixerant is to be noticed. The Vulgate reading is Tunc crucifixi sunt.

4

the several Gospels according to the common Irish custom, but at the end of St. Luke's Gospel is inscribed " Explicit evangelium secundum lucam Explicit evangelium secundum johannem," the latter word, showing the mode in which a space at the end of a line was ordinarily filled up by widening the letters, is copied in Plate 1.

The four evangelical symbols are again represented at the beginning of St. John's Gospel, (fo. 290, v.) inclosed in a highly ornamented square framework, and the following leaf bears the portrait of St. John, part of which is copied in the annexed engraving. The nimbus in this drawing is most splendidly orna- mented, part only being here copied. The flowing curls of the hair are here particularly to be noticed illustrating (as Mr. Petrie informs me) the ancient habit of the Irish, but the chief object in giving this figur e(which will serve as a specimen of the other Evangelists), is to exhibit the pen which is held in the right hand, and which confirms the opinion which I expressed concerning the instru- ment in the hand of St. John in the Gospels of MacDurnan. The Saint is represented seated on a large ornamented cushion, and wears sandals on his feet.

The commencement of this Gospel " In prin- cipio erat verbum et verbum," occupies the recto of fo. 292, the INP being of gigantic size and conjoined together, in the same style as the begin- ning of the other Gospels. The latter part of this Gospel is wanting.

The various readings of this MS. are as im- portant as its ornamental details. In the first place I may mention that I detected in it the celebrated passage asserting the divinity of the Holy Ghost, which has hitherto been considered as unique in the silver Gospels at Vercelli. It occurs in St. John iii. 5, 6, (fo. 297, v.) and is as follows: " Quod natum est ex carne caro est quia de carne natum est et quod natum est ex spū sps̄ est quia ds̄ sps̄ est et ex dō natus est." These words were struck out by the Arians, and Father Simon[1] asserted that there was no Latin MS. in existence in which they were to be found.

MATTHEW i. 1-3. Liber generationis ihū X̄pi filii david filii abracham. abracham autem genuit isac isac autem genuit iacob iacob autem genuit iudam et fratres ejus iudas autem genuit fhares et zarad de thamar, fhares autem &c.—Ch. i. 16. Joseph virum Mariæ[2] de qui natus est ihs̄ qui vocatur X̄ps.—Ch. i. 23. Ecce virgo in utero habebit et pariet filium.—Ch. iv. 10. Vade retro Satanas.—Ch. v. 1. Videns autem ihs̄ turbas ascendit in montem et cum sedisset accesserunt ad eum discipuli eius et aperiens os suum docebat eos dicens. Beati pauperes spū quoniam ipsorum est regnum cælorum. Beati mites quoniam ipsi possidebunt terram. Beati qui lugent nunc quoniam ipsi consulabuntur. Beati qui essuriunt et sitiunt iustitiam quoniam ipsi saturabuntur.—Ch. v. 22. Omnis qui irascitur fratri suo reus erit iudicio.—Ch. vi. 4. Pater tuus qui videt n absconso reddit tibi.—11. Panem nostrum supersubstantialem[3] da nobis hodie.—13. *Amen* wanting.— Ch. viii. 17. Ipse infirmitates nostras accipit et egritudines portavit.—Ch. xix. 1. Et factum est cumsummasset ihs̄ sermones hos transtulit se a galilea et venit in fines iudeæ trans iordanem et saecute sunt eum turbæ multæ et curabit eos ibi.—Ch. xxvii. 48. Alius autem accepta lancea[4] pupungit latus ejus et exiit aqua et sangis.

JOHN i. 1. In principio erat verbum et verbum erat apud dm̄ et ds̄ erat verbum hoc erat in principio

[1] St. Ambrose in libro de Spiritu Sancto ; Simon, Hist. Crit. du Texte, p. 355 ; Blanchini Vindicia, Roma, 1740, p. 373.
[2] The diphthong is written with e and a cedilla.

[3] Cotidianum in St. Luke's Gospel.
[4] The letter τ with three dots occurs after the word " lancea."

apud d̄m̄ omnia per ipsum facta sunt et sine ipso factum est nihil quod factum est in ipso vita erat, &c.—Ch. i. 4. Fuit homo misus a d̄o cui nomen erat johannis hic venit in testimonium ut testimonium perhiberet de lumine ut omnes crederent per illum non erat ille lux sed ut testimonium perhiberet de lumine Erat lux vera venientem in mundum, in mundo erat et mundus per ipsum factus est et mundus eum non cognovit.

The following is all the historical evidence I have been able to collect relating to this Volume. Giraldus Cambrensis must evidently have had it before him when he thus described a book of the four Gospels, at Kildare, in the twelfth century, his description so exactly according with it.

" Liber mirandus inquit tempore Virginis Brigidæ ut aiunt Angelo dictante conscriptus, continet IV. Evangelistarum juxta Hieronymum Concordantiam ubi quot paginæ fere sunt tot figuræ diversæ variisque coloribus distinctissimæ. Hic Majestatis Vultum videas divinitus impressum. Hinc mysticas Evangelistarum formas nunc senas nunc quaternas nunc binas alas habentes. Hinc aquilam, inde vitulum, hinc hominis faciem, inde leonis aliasque figuras pæne infinitas quas si superficialiter et usuali more minus acute conspexeris, litura potius videbitur quam ligatura nec ullam attendens prorsus subtilitatem ubi nihil tamen præter subtilitatem. Sin autem ad perspicacius intuendum oculorum aciem invitaveris et longe penitus ad Artis arcana transpenetraveris tam delicatas et subtiles, tam actas et arctas, tam nodosas et vinculatim colligatas, tamque recentibus adhuc coloribus illustratas notare poteris intricaturas ut vere hæc omnia Angelica potius quam humana diligentia jam asseveraveris esse composita. Hæc equidem quanto frequentius et diligentius intueor semper quasi novis obstupeo, semperque magis ac magis admiranda conspicio, nec Apelles ipse similia efficere posset et manu potius non mortali efformatæ ac depictæ viderentur." [1]

The Codex appears to be the identical volume alluded to in the Annals of the IV Masters in the Records of the Church of Kells in the year 1006 :—" Soisccel mor Cholaimcille do dubhgoid issin oidhche as in Erdomh iartharach an Doimhliacc moir Cenannsa Prim mind iartair Domhain ar aoi an chumtaigh daenda ⁊ a foghbhail dia fichetadh for dibh miosaibhiar ngaitt dhe a oir⁊ foid thairis "—i.e. " Evangelium Magnum Columbæ Ecclesiarum furto ablatum nocte ex sacra domo inferiori Cathedralis magni Kellensis Præcipua reliquia occidentalis mundi ad juramenta præstanda fuit ista contra perjuria hominum et inventum est sub cespitibus post duos menses postquam furto ablatum esset ejus aurum et cespite involutum."

Dr. O'Conor, who by some strange oversight was unaware of the existence of this magnificent volume, has misapplied this passage to a smaller copy of the Gospels also preserved in Trinity College, Dublin, reported to have been written by St. Columba himself. Archbishop Usher had evidently both these MSS. before him when he says of the monastery of Durrow " inter cujus κειμήλια Evangeliorum Codex vetustissimus asservabatur quem ipsius Columbæ fuisse monachi dictitabant ex quo et non minoris antiquitatis altero eidem Columbæ assignato quem in urbe Kelles sive Kenlis dicta Midenses sacrum habent." Lhuyd also describes this volume as being " miri operis et antiquitatis qui liber Colum Kill vulgo dicebatur." [2]

It only remains to mention that from a comparison of this volume with the Gospels of Lindisfarne (known to have been written at the close of the seventh century), and bearing in mind that Lindisfarne was colonised by the Monks of Iona, or Icolumkille, in 634, only forty years after the death of Columbkill himself, there seems to be no good reason for doubting that this volume might have belonged to that celebrated Saint.

---

[1] Girald. Topogr. Hibern. Francof. fol. 1608, Dist. 2, p. 730.   [2] Archæolog. Oxford, fol. 1707, p. 436 and 432.

IRISH

IRISH MANUSCRIPTS.

THE famous BETH-LUIS-NION, upon which the Irish pride themselves so highly, as affording a proof that they possessed the use of letters before their conversion to Christianity, derives its name from the three first letters of their alphabet, b, l and n ; the names of these, and indeed of all their letters, being also those of different trees, which are of common occurrence in Ireland ; and upon the bark of which, it is asserted, that they were accustomed to write. This alphabet differs from those of all other modern nations, in the names, order, number, and power of its letters ; and consists of only eighteen letters, thus agreeing with the most ancient Phœnician, Pelasgic [1], Greek, and Roman alphabets.

The Irish alphabet consists of the following letters, arranged Roman-wise :

ᴀ b c ᴅ e ꜰ ᴣ ʜ ɪ l ᴍ ɴ o ᴘ ʀ ʀ ᴛ ᴜ

And although in writing Latin Theological MSS. they used the other Latin letters, they rejected, and still reject them to this day, from their own alphabet.

The famous scene in the Pænulus of Plautus, (act v. sc. 1), wherein Hanno utters a triplicate soliloquy in the Punic, Lybian, and Latin languages, and which has ever excited, since the revival of literature, the attention of the learned, received, during the last century, an additional interest, in consequence of an attempt made by Colonel Vallancey, the Irish antiquary, to explain the passage, on the principle of a supposed affinity between the Punic and Irish languages. The following are two of the verses contrasted with each other in these two languages :

PUNIC.	IRISH.
Bythlym mothym noctothii nelechanti dasmachon	Beth liom ! mo thime noctaithe nielach an ti daisic mac coinne
Yssidele brym tyfel yth chylys chon tem liphul.	Is i de leabhraim tafach leith chilis con teampluibh ulla.

This is a most striking coincidence ; but the elaborate memoir on this passage by the Rev. J. Hamilton has fully proved the " affinity, or rather indentity, of the Punic with the Hebrew and the Cognate dialects [2] ;" and that the eleven Latin verses which Plautus gives at the end of the Lybian lines, comprise a translation of the Punic ones.

It has indeed been asserted by Vallancey (Irish Grammar, 2nd Edit., p. 4), that the Druids employed the Ogham characters, which the Irish retained for writing in cipher or secret, and which consist of lines placed in various positions, but chiefly diagonally or obliquely, in connexion with a principal or horizontal line ; and indeed the several Ogham alphabets, collected by Astle (Plate XXXI.), commence with the letters b (bacht), l (lacht), f (fecht), s (secht), and n (necht), and which might thence be assumed to be the characters of the Beth-luis-nion ; but no such Druidical writings have ever been seen either by Vallancey or others, nor do the more sober Irish antiquarians consider the Oghams [3] as an ancient invention.

---

[1] On the summit of Tory Hill, or Hill of the Sun, is a circular druidical erection, on one of the stones of which is inscribed BELI DIUOSE, in ancient Pelasgic letters (which in Britain were only known to the Druids), proving that the Sun, worshipped under the name of Beal, was also there known under the appellation Diunosos. Camden, p. 306 ; Wood in Trans. Royal Irish Acad., vol. xiii. p. 58.

[2] Trans. Royal Irish Acad., vol. xviii. Part 1.

[3] Vallancey says that authors are at a loss for the derivation of the word Ogham, which occurs in no Irish dictionary. It has since been suggested that the word was derived from the name of the Gallic or Celtic God of Eloquence, Ogmius, as we learn from Lucian, (Pict. Hist. Engl. i. p. 120.) I find, however, that Ogmius was the Celtic

The fate, and indeed even the existence, of the Beth-luis-nion[1] as a distinct and written alphabet, is enveloped in darkness, for no inscriptions nor coins have hitherto been found in Ireland executed previous to the coming of the Romans into Britain ; and, however it may please the national pride of the Irish, to affirm that the Romans had no intercourse with Ireland, it seems unquestionable that their acquaintance with the only letters which they can be proved to have ever used, and their knowledge of the Christian religion, were contemporary ; and were derived, either immediately or indirectly, from the Roman missionaries, who in the earliest ages of Christianity (probably long before the mission of St. Patrick), diffused a knowledge of the latter through these islands. Thus, Mr. Petrie argues, that it is difficult, if not impossible, to conceive how the minute and apparently accurate accounts found in various MSS. of the names and localities of the Atticotic tribes of Ireland, in the first century, could have been preserved, without coming to the conclusion, that they had been committed to writing in some work, whatever may have been its original name, within a century or two of the times to which they relate[2]. And Innes, who on many other points connected with the asserted antiquities of Ireland was so sceptical, says, that "It may have very well happened, that some of the Irish before that time [even before the introduction of Christianity into Ireland], passing over to Britain, or other parts of the Roman Empire, where the use of letters was common, might have learned to read and write[3]."

The agreement which exists between the early state of the Roman alphabet and that of the Irish, moreover, appears sufficient to prove that it was from the Romans that the Irish received their letters: thus, Mr. Wood informs us, that—

By the ancient Romans,—	By the ancient Irish,—
C was used for G.	CC was used for G.
D " " T.	D " " T.
F, B, and V, commutable.	In all Irish words derived from Latin words, beginning with V, F is used for V ; but
CV pronounced like C for Q.	in pure Irish words, BH " " V. By the Irish, C.
No J.	No J.
P and B, commutable.	P and B, commutable.
H, often omitted.	H, used only as an aspirate.
CS, used for X,	And sometimes by the Irish.

As to the form of the letters of the Irish, as they appear in the most ancient MSS., there is no reason for doubting that they were not derived from the Romans[4]. It is true that both the large round-hand species of writing, which O'Conor regarded as the ancient "unadulterated" Irish hand (as it appears in the Gospels of Lindisfarne and St. Chad, St. Columba's, at Dublin, and the Missal of Columbanus, at Milan, &c.), and the smaller narrow hand, which Sir W. Betham calls the "pure Irish character" (as it appears in the Leabhar Dimma, Book of Armagh, and Gospels of Mac Durnan, &c.) are all minuscule characters ; the former bordering upon the round uncial characters, and the latter on the cursive. If, therefore, we were to adopt the opinion so long prevalent, that the Romans were unacquainted with minuscule writing[5], we must regard the Irish characters as the genuine productions of the Irish school, or adopt the opinion of others, that they received them from the Anglo-Saxons, with whose writings they bear so complete an identity. The fact, however, of the existence

name of Hercules. (Mercure de France, 1756, vol. ii. p. 112.) Would it not be more in accordance with the views of many Irish antiquaries to consider the name as derived from Ogga, the Phœnicean surname of Minerva?—Chompre, Dict. abr. Fabl. Paris, 1833, p. 329.

[1] Innes, indeed, delivers it as his opinion, that the Beth-luis-nion was nothing but an invention of the Irish Seanachies, who since they received the use of letters, put the Latin alphabet into a new arbitrary order, and assigned to each the name of some tree, (Essay on the Antiquities of Scotland and Ireland, p. 446) ; but to this it may be replied, in the words of Moore, that "if they had letters first from St. Patrick, would they have diverted from the forms of the letters? would they have altered the order? would they have sunk seven letters? for in every country they have increased rather than diminished the number of letters." Moore's History of Ireland, vol. i. (in Lardner's Cab. Cycl.) p. 55. If the Phœnician theory of Sir W. Betham (see his Etruria Celtica, 2 v. 8vo, 1842) and others be admitted, it might be assumed that the Irish, on the introduction of the Christian religion and Roman letters, adopted only so many of the

latter as were equivalent to those which they had received from the Phœnicians. It must, however, be borne in mind, that several of the letters not found in the Irish alphabet (as k, q, v) occur in the Phœnician, Pelasgic, Punic, Etruscan, and most ancient Greek and Roman alphabets.

[2] Trans. Royal Acad. of Ireland, xviii., Part ii., p. 46.

[3] Essay on the Antiquities of Scotland and Ireland ; and see Sir J. Ware's Antiquities of Ireland, Edit. Harris, vol. ii. passim, and Astle on the Origin of Writing, pp. 115—123. (2nd Edit.)

[4] Moore implies the reverse when he says, that the letters adapted by them after the coming of St. Patrick, though differing from the Roman in number, order, and power, bear a considerable degree of resemblance to them in shape. Hist. of Ireland, p. 65.

[5] Even Casley was of this opinion, observing (Cat. reg. MS., p. vii.) that "a small alphabet seems to have been first contrived in the seventh century," and that "in Jerome's time there were no other characters made use of for writing but capitals."

amongst the Romans both of minuscule and cursive characters, almost identical in form with those of the Irish, has been so fully proved by the Benedictines[1], that it is as unreasonable to deny that these characters are derived from the Romans, as to assert, with O'Conor, that those Irish MSS. only which are written in the large round-hand of the Gospels of Lindisfarne, are to be regarded as the most ancient. It is indeed no more to be supposed that the Irish scribes would not, for dispatch, employ a smaller and more cursive character, than that the Romans, in their ordinary affairs, would waste the time which writing in capitals or uncials would require.

At the time when, in writing the article upon the Gospels of Mac Durnan, I suggested the certainty that numbers of Irish MSS. of great antiquity were still in existence, "not only in the unexamined stores of our own country, but especially in the libraries of those places abroad where they (the Irish Missionaries) established themselves," I little supposed that within so short a period I should be able, in the pages of this work, to afford ample evidence of the truth of the remark. It may therefore be easily imagined with what pleasure I learned, not only that in the Monastery of St. Gall, in Switzerland (founded by, and named after, one of the Irish Missionaries of the seventh century), are still preserved a number of invaluable MSS. of the Irish school, but that, by the exertions of the Record Commission, fac-similes of many of them, both illuminated and plain, have been obtained, and are now in the custody of the Master of the Rolls. It was with still greater pleasure that I discovered amongst the MSS. in the Library of St. John's College, Cambridge, a Latin Psalter, executed, as it appears to me, unquestionably to have been, in Ireland; and which, from the style of the writing and illuminations, may, I think without doubt, be referred to the eighth or ninth century. In the catalogue which has recently been published of portion of the MSS. of this College, it is described under the No. C. 9, and merely as a Psalter written about the year 800, very much glossed about the year 1200. It is a handsome volume, of the quarto size, containing the Psalter, Canticles, &c., the text written in a semi-uncial or rounded minuscule kind of hand, of which the specimen, No. 2, in the accompanying plate will serve as a specimen. It is the commencement of one of the Canticles which the Church of England has retained in her Service, and is to be read, "Benedicite *omnia* op*era* d*omi*ni d*omin*um *hymnum* dicite et s*upe*r exaltate eu*m* in sec*ula*,"—the letters printed italics being omitted. The ornamental initial is intended for a minuscule b formed into a capital, and is an example of the initials throughout the volume. It will be observed that the mark of contraction of the word opera is placed beneath the line attached to the tail of the p; that the y in the word *hymnum* is of a very singular form, although not uncommon in Irish and Anglo-Saxon MSS.[2] The reading of this specimen will also be seen to differ from the ordinary version, which runs as follows: "Benedicite omnia opera Domini *Domino, laudate* et super exaltate eum in sæcula." The word *et* will be seen to be written in the form in which it appears in our oldest Anglo-Saxon Codices.[3]

The hand in which this MS. is written accords well with its presumed antiquity; since, although it more nearly resembles that of the Gospels of St. Chad, at Lichfield, of the Cottonian Gospels, Nero D. IV., and those at Corpus Christi College, Cambridge, (all figured by Astle,) than any other MS. hitherto described, in the roundness of its letters, the e not elevated above the line, the δ-form of the d—the Roman capital form of the r and s; yet the n shape of the n, the straight top of the second stroke of the a, and the numerous contractions, bespeak a somewhat more recent date. The mode in which the slender stroke of the x is divided is also worthy of observation.

It is, however, in its illuminations that this MS. offers the greatest interest to the archæologist, as it possesses several miniatures drawn in a style which, for singularity and rudeness, is not to be exceeded by that

---

[1] See especially the 29th Plate in the 2d volume of the N. Tr. de Diplom., of itself sufficient to have rendered unnecessary all Mr. Ottley's laborious arguments on this subject.

[2] The Benedictines, in their four most surprising plates of general Alphabets, N. Tr. de Dipl., vol. ii., pl. 20—23, have not represented above half a dozen specimens of y thus formed, and these chiefly Gallican or Merovingian. Some idea may be formed of the laborious nature of these four plates, when it is stated that there are no fewer than 464 different figures of the letter y, whilst of other and more commonly used letters the number of specimens given is more than trebled.

[3] The contraction &, used for the word "and" at the present day, will at once be perceived from this specimen to be no other than the two letters e and t joined together, as in the Minuscule Roman and Anglo-Saxon manuscripts, the loop at the top of the & being, in fact, the elevated closed top of the e.

of the drawings of the most uncultivated nations. It was not without some hesitation that I could bring myself to believe that the drawing represented in the accompanying Plate, numbered 1, was intended for a delineation of the Crucifixion of our Saviour. The extended arms, the sponge, and spear, held by the grotesque objects at the sides of the chief figure, and the angel above the head of the latter, leave no room to doubt that this is really the case. This drawing is worthy indeed of particular notice, as it is unquestionably the most ancient specimen of Irish pictorial composition which has hitherto been given to the public, or indeed, as far as I can learn, which exists in this country. The large size of the principal figure was intended to indicate that a kind of respect was shown to it.[1] The extraordinary propensity of the Irish school for marginal rows of red dots, and for twisting every possible thing into interlaced and ornamental patterns, will be evident from this drawing of our Saviour's habiliments, eyes, ears, hair, &c.; whilst the singular acuteness of the thumbs in all the figures—the grotesque profiles of the soldiers,[2] and the chequered dresses of all the figures, will not fail to create a smile at that poverty of pictorial art, which was able only to delineate the most solemn event which the world has hitherto witnessed, in a manner so liable to be regarded almost as a burlesque. In the original, this and the other miniatures are surrounded by borders, in which we see the singularly *intricate diagonal* Chinese-like patterns, such as occur in the Leabhar Dimma, the Duke of Buckingham's Gospel of St. John, and especially in the Lambeth Gospels of Mac Durnan, in which last, however, these patterns are far more intricate than in any other I have hitherto seen. I doubted, at first, whether the two figures at the sides of the Saviour's head were not intended for the two thieves, but I am now able to state that they are also intended for angels; on the authority, first, of an elaborately carved ancient cross found at St. Patrick's, County Louth,[3] in which the Crucifixion is treated precisely in the same manner; and, second, of a fac-simile of one of the St. Gall manuscripts, obtained by the Record Commission, in which we have also the same general design, but far superior in point of drawing.

The specimen numbered 3 in the accompanying plate is taken from a small Cottonian manuscript, which was almost consumed in the deplorable fire by which so many of the choice manuscripts of that collection were destroyed. It is marked Galba A. 5; and, in Smith's and Planta's catalogues, is recorded to have formerly belonged to King Orwin.[4] It is written in a very cramped minuscule hand, full of contractions,[5] and (although it is very difficult to determine the date of Irish manuscripts) cannot, in my opinion, be older than the eleventh or twelfth century.[6] The initial letters throughout are ornamented in the style of the one prefixed to my fac-simile, which is also a minuscule b enlarged into a capital. The passage consists of the first four verses of the 33rd Psalm, and is to be read as follows: " Benedica*m* domine [7] in omni tempore sem*per* laus *ejus* [8] in ore meo. In d*omino* laudabit*ur* a*n*ima m*e*a, audia*n*t ma*n*sueti et [9] l*ae*tent*ur*. Magnificate D*omin*um mec*um* et exaltem*us*[10] no*men ejus* in idips*um*. Exquisivi Dominum et exaudivit me et ex *omni*bus tribu̎lationibus meis eripuit me." In addition to the peculiarities mentioned in the foot-notes, it will be sufficient to direct notice to the forms of the r in the words *ore* in the first and *eripuit* in the fifth line, to the elongated terminal i in the word mansueti in the second line, and to its small size in the middle of the word Exqsivi in the fourth line, and to the form of the q in the same word, to the form of the a in the word magnificaͭe, to the divided slender line of the x, and to the occasionally elevated e.

The fac-similes numbered 4, 5, and 6, are taken from a MS. in the Harleian Collection (Brit. Mus. No. 1802), which has given rise to a very extended discussion; but which may now be satisfactorily regarded as having been written in the year 1138, and consequently as of great value in affording the means of determining the character of contemporary Irish MSS.

---

[1] So also in the portrait of Dunstan, drawn by himself, kneeling at the side of our Saviour, (Bodl. MS. N. E. D. 11. 19); the latter is represented of so large a size compared to the former, that Dr. Dibdin was led to think that the former was *in the back-ground*. Other examples of this practice are needless.

[2] A still more grotesque treatment of the human profile will be given in the illustrations from the Irish Gospels of Mac Regol, preserved in the Bodleian Library.

[3] Engraved in Britton's Dictionary of Ancient Architecture, in which great doubts are expressed as to its age, although it is stated to be most probably of the twelfth century. I apprehend this Manuscript will go far to prove it to be several hundred years older.

[4] I find no record of any Irish king of this name in O'Conor's great work.

[5] A fac-simile of another portion of this Manuscript was given by Casley in the Catalogue of the Royal MSS.

[6] Casley, 110 years since, described this Manuscript as written in an Irish hand 900 years old.

[7] For Dominum.

[8] Observe the singular contraction used for this word.

[9] Contracted by ꝗ throughout.

[10] The terminal us in this and other words in the specimen is contracted by a mark, as usual, something like a tailed z.

[11] Mis-spelt tbubulationibus.

It is a small Codex, measuring 6½ inches by 5, written upon parchment, consisting of " the four Evangelists, written in the Irish character, by Brigidianus, or Maol Brighte, for the use of Gilla, Coarb or Vicar of the Church of St. Patrick, and supposed by Father Simon[1], to be 800 years old ; though Mr. Wanley will not allow it an earlier date than the 12th century. But whatever difficulties may have arisen in ascertaining the exact date of this curious MS., it is on all hands acknowledged to be one of the most authentic copies of the Latin Gospels which the Irish have ever sent out of their island. It also contains St. Jerome's Prologue of the Canons of the four Gospels, and explanation of such Hebrew and Syriac names as occur in the Gospels ; a Hebrew, Latin, and Irish vocabulary, and the usual prefaces ; an interlineary Gloss, and a Catena Patrum. The singularity of this MS. has induced Mr. Wanley to favour us in the Catalogue with a very accurate account of it ; and in a laborious and judicious criticism to fix its true age, and explode the opinions of Father Simon, as well in regard thereto as to the characters in which it is written." [2]

The Volume commences with the ordinary Prologue, addressed to Pope Damasus by St. Jerome, beginning " Novum opus facere me cogis,"—followed by the Argument of St. Matthew's Gospel. Then follows the genealogy of Christ (being the commencement of St. Matthew's Gospel) with notes, quite distinct from the historical part of the Gospel, the commencement of the latter part—" Christi autem generatio"—being illuminated like the headings of the other Gospels. This is not an unusual plan in other ancient copies of the Gospels written in Ireland. Then follow the Prologues of the other Gospels, with the Glossary and explanation of the Hebrew names, Notes from the Fathers, the Comparison of the Apostles to the Elements, &c., and some verses on the Twelve Apostles. To these succeeds the text of the four Gospels, with a Catena Patrum, and an irregular interlineary Gloss ; those of St. Mark and St. Luke being preceded by a very rude figure of a lion (" made by one who never saw the creature," as Wanley quaintly remarks), and of a bull.

In one or two places the name of St. Luke is written Lucanus, according to the ancient custom.

The initial letters of each Gospel are illuminated in the manner usual in the later Irish MSS., of which the specimen No. 4 will serve as an example. The letters Xpi at the beginning of the historical portion of St. Matthew's Gospel are larger than the other initials, the X exhibiting a very coarsely drawn and coloured interlaced pattern, terminating in knots and dogs' heads. The lion of St. Mark (fol. C0, v.), (of which I have given a fac-simile, numbered 6) and the bull of St. Luke (fol. 86, v.), are surrounded by an ornamented border, in which the intricate *diagonal* patterns of the Irish school are rather loosely drawn. The fac-simile No. 4 (being the commencement of the Gospel of St. Mark) is to be read as follows :—

INItium euangelii ihu xpi
*fi*lii *d*ei *sicut* scriptum *est* in issaia *proph*e*ta* Ecce mitto angelum m*eu*m an*te* facie*m* tuam qui preparabit via*m* tuam Vox clamantis in deserto parate viam domini rectas facite semitas ejus. Fuit johann*e*s in deserto babtizans.

Here (as well as in the first word of St. John's Gospel, " In ") we have the first two letters conjoined, as in the Gospels of MacDurnan ; the next letter, I, is, however, distinct and fantastically drawn : the remainder of the line are smaller capitals (such as are used for the commencement of the verses), gradually degenerating into minuscules. They are not materially different from the alphabet of capitals given in my second Plate of Mac Durnan's Gospels. The remainder of the specimen is written in a comparatively distinct minuscule character, resembling ordinary Anglo-Saxon. The mode of contraction of the words, " sicut " and " est," in the second line, is worthy of notice ; as is also the orthography of the words, " issaia," for Isaiah, " johannis,[3]" subsequently corrected to johannes, and " babtizans ;" and also the forms of several of the letters—as the x, in the first line ; the a and q, in the fourth line ; and the long i and the z, in the last word.

[1] Bibliotheca Critica, tom. 1, p. 271.

[2] Preface to the Harleian Catalogue, vol. i., p. 12 ; and see also

Bishop Nicholson's Preface to his " Irish Historical Library," pp. 11, 12.

[3] The word, thus written and uncorrected, occurs in fol. 128.

The version in which this MS. is written will be perceived by the following extracts :—

Matt. vi. verse 11, " Panem nostrum supersubstantialem da nobis hodie."

Matt. xix. 1., " Et factum est cum consummasset jhs sermones istos migravit a Galilea et venit in fines Judæ trans Jordanum, et secutæ sunt eum turbæ multæ et curavit eos ibi," as in the Vulgate.

Matt. xxvii. after v. 49, a space of a line and a half erased, in which was written the interpolated passage copied in my specimen, No. 7, some of the words being still partially visible.

John i. 1—" In principio erat verbum, et verbum erat apud deum, et deus erat verbum, hoc erat in principio apud deum : omnia per ipsum facta sunt, et sine *ipso* factum est nihil quod factum est, in *eo* vita est et vita erat, (in ipso added afterwards), lux hominum et lux in tenebris lucet et tenebræ eam non comprehenderunt."

John xxii. 21—" Domine hic autem [1] quid, dicit ei ihs sic e⸱ volo manere donec venia quid ad te tu me sequere ; exiit ergo sermo iste int fres quia discipul ille n mori-r. ru[2]s sic eum volo manere donec venia. Hic est discipulus," &c.

The letters o and u are sometimes confounded together, as in the words *parabula* and *diabulus*. The aspirate H at the beginning or even in the middle of a word is commonly expressed thus ⱶ, elevated above the line, a peculiarity which, although not noticed by Mabillon, Mr. Wanley has shown[3] was the use of almost all the ancient Latin grammarians, as Isidore of Sevil, Aulus Gellius, and Quinctilian ; and hence Mr. Wanley considers that it was from the Romans that the Irish received this character[4].

This Manuscript in the comments and glosses, with which it is crowded between the lines and in every vacant space, exhibits some of the allegorical and symbolical ideas which were so common in the twelfth and thirteenth centuries ; for instance, at the head of the Evangelists, the reason which is given that they are four in number is, that they represent ONE church, which is to be extended over the four quarters of the world. The Evangelists themselves are compared to four fluids—St. Matthew, to honey (" Matthæus, melli ") ; St. Mark, to wine (" Marcus, vino ") ; St. Luke, to milk (" Lucas, lacti ") ; and St. John, to oil (" Johannes, oleo ") ;—and various mystical reasons are then given for these similitudes. So, also, they are referred to the four elements and the four seasons of the year.

Some of the glosses are ascribed to Manchanus, an Irish writer of the middle of the seventh century,[5] one of which, on the subject of Transubstantiation, is as follows (fol. 54) :—" Primo quæritur si hæc assumptio Panis et Calicis, *figura*, an *historia*, an *sensus*? *Figura est :* fractio enim panis figurat Corpus ejus fractum a militibus in cruce et in omnibus sanctis iteratur Passio ejus dum patiuntur a Cristo usque ad finem mundi, sed tamen non ut fiebant figuræ legis quæ cessaverunt ; hæc vero figura codidie iteratur."

But the entries at the foot of the different Gospels, written by the scribe by whom the volume was copied, form the most interesting particulars in an archæological point of view. At the end of St. Matthew, the following is inscribed (fol. 60) :—

Oⱜ ᵭo ⱳælbⱜⱑ5ᴄe ⱦ ⱱcⱜⱑbⱨᴄ hc̃ lⱑbⱜū[6]
JS ⱳoⱜ ⱳ5ⱳⱳ Coⱜⱳc̃ ⱳc̃ CaⱜᴄhaⱭ5
ᗪo ⱳaⱜbaᗪ o Ɫaⱜᗪelbach .ⱨ. bⱜⱭaⱑⱳ

Meaning, " Pray for Moelbrigte, who wrote this book. Great was the crime when Cormac Mac Carthy was slain by Tardelvach O'Brian." At the end of St. Mark, the first of these lines is repeated, as it is also at the end of St. Luke, with an addition, as copied in my specimen No. 5,—

Oⱜ ᵭo ⱳælbⱜⱑ5ᴄe ⱦ ⱱcbⱨᴄ ⱨ .l. in xxviii anno,
ⱷᴄaᴄⱑⱱ ⱱuae IN ᗪaⱜa blⱑaᗪaⱑ ⱑ ⱦⱜⱑ 5oe ᴄhaⱭ5 ⱳoⱜ ⱱeⱑ.

Which means, " Pray for Moelbrigte, who wrote this book in the twenty-eighth year of his age and in the second year after the building of the great house ;" but at the end of St. John's Gospel there is a much longer entry

---

[1] Contracted in the ordinary Irish and Anglo-Saxon manner.

[2] " Dīx ei ihc̃ ñ morīt," is added by a later hand in the margin.

[3] Hickes Thes. (Catal. Libr. Sept.), p. 156.

[4] The Greeks also used this ⱶ for the aspirate, and this ⱶ for the soft form of H, and it has been suggested that it was from the union of these two forms that the H was produced.

[5] See Ware de Scriptor. Hibern. Dubl. 1689, lib. 1, p. 27 ; O'Sullevan's Histor. Cathol. Ibern. Compend. Usher Brit. Eccles. Antiq. Dubl. 1639, p. 864 ; and the References to MSS. given by Wanley, loc. cit.

[6] The words " q. scribsit hc̃ librū," being in Latin.

(copied in fac-simile by O'Connor in the first volume of his great work), containing a great variety of historical particulars, some of which induced Mr. Toland to infer that the volume was written in the year 908; but which led Mr. Conry (whose opinion was confirmed by many circumstances collected by Wanley) to state that it was copied about the year 1140, being the same year wherein Cormac Mac Carthay was slain by Turlough O'Briain, the second year after the building of the great house, when Donchad O'Kervall was King of Argiall; Murchad the son of Neil, son of O'Loghlin, was King of Olichia; Cunlad O'Connor, King of Ulidia; Murchad the son of Malachias, King of Meth; Dermot Mac Morough, the King of Leinster; Connor O'Brian, the King of Munster; Tirlough O'Connor, King of Connaught; and Gilla, the son of Liach, a dignitary of the Cathedral Church of Armagh. The determination of this date is a question of great interest, as it will not only afford the means of comparison, as to the age of contemporary Irish MSS., but will also serve indirectly to confirm the histories preserved in some of their Annals. Its solution accordingly exercised the researches of Mr. Wanley and his friends to a very considerable extent, as will be seen in the second Volume of the Catalogue of the Harleian MSS.; and a similar date has again been assigned to the MS. by Dr. O'Connor[1] from the concurrence of the historical particulars above inserted, which will apply to no other year than A.D. 1138.

The specimens numbered 7 and 8 are copied from the Harleian MS., 1023, in the British Museum, which is a small quarto Volume, containing the Four Gospels in Latin, but written in strong-set Irish minuscule characters, and in the Vulgate version, with, however, various readings. The greater portion of St. Matthew's Gospel is wanting; at the end of which are some verses upon our Saviour, commencing—

" Sola divina salvandus sum Medicina."

Then follow the Gospels of St. Mark, Luke, and John, preceded by the ordinary Prologues, and by rude delineations of the Lion of St. Mark and the Eagle of St. John. The MS. also contains some short questions respecting Eve, &c., probably from Alcuin; a Table of Succession of the forty-two Egyptian Kings, called Pharoahs; some Verses on the books of both the Old and New Testaments; and the Names of the Seven Sleepers. The initial letters of each Gospel are in the same style as, but much less elaborately ornamented than in the preceding MS. The specimen No. 7, from St. Matthew, chapter v., is to be read as follows:—

" Ceteri vero dicebant sine videamus an veniat helias liberare eum. Alius autem[2] accepta lancea pupugit latus ejus et exiit aqua et sanguis. ihs autem iterum clamans voce magna emisit spiritum." The interpolated passage in this extract (" Alius—sanguis ") occurs in most of the copies of the Gospels written in Ireland.

The ordinary Irish contractions of us at the end of the words videamus, alius, and latus, and of the words et, autem, and ejus, occur in this extract. The name Johannes is correctly spelt; and the passage, John xxi. v. 21—23, is as follows:—" Dñe hic autem qīd. dt ei jhs sic ego e volo manere donec venia qd ad te tu me seqre. Exivit °⁄g sermo iste it fratres q discipulus ille n morit et n dix ei ihs n morit s sic e volo manere donec venia. Hic est discipulus," &c. Each of the Gospels is terminated by the usual—" Finit, Amen; finit, Amen," as copied in the specimen No. 8.

---

[1] Script. rer. Hibern. vet., vol. i., prol. p. cxlv.   [2] Written in the ordinary Irish contraction.

Irish Mss. Pl.2.

IRISH BIBLICAL MSS.—PLATE II.

THE series of manuscripts from which the fac-similes in the accompanying plate have been copied (in conjunction with the Book of Kells), constitute a series of actual proofs, *still preserved in Ireland,* of the existence of religion and a national school of art in that country, at a period when the rest of Europe was almost involved in mental darkness; and I believe I may fairly affirm that a more varied series of illustrations, or one constituting a more valuable selection of materials towards the history of writing in any individual country, has rarely been exhibited in a single plate. The majority of these MSS. are preserved in Trinity College, Dublin; and it is by the kind permission of the Rev. Dr. Todd that I am enabled to add this series to the preceding plate of Irish MSS., although in point of age the MSS. now under notice have greatly the precedence over those contained in the former plate.

The earliest of these MSS. is represented in No. 4, which closely agrees in its characters with various Gallican and Merovingian MSS. of the sixth and seventh centuries, given by the Benedictines. This MS. is in the library of Trinity College, Dublin, and contains an Antehieronymian version of the Gospels, written upon leaves of vellum, of a small quarto size, and which require careful mounting and editing. They are destitute of illumination, except that on one page there is a plain representation of a cross, accompanied by the Greek letters **A** and **ω**. The specimen No. 4 consists of part of the 39th and 40th verses of the eleventh chapter of St. Luke, " Quod autem intus est vestrum plenum est rapina et iniquitate; stulti nonne qui fecit quod foris est," &c. The indistinctness of the words, the want of contractions, and the form of many of the letters (as e, n, r, s, &c.) are especially to be noticed in this MS.; and it is on this account that the really Irish origin of the MS. may perhaps be questioned.

The specimen No. 3, in the short thick character of the writing, somewhat approaches the former; but the peculiar form of several of the letters, as the g, r, d, &c., and the numerous contractions, bespeak the Hibernian school. This specimen is copied from a very ancient MS., preserved in the library of Trinity College, Dublin, and which belonged to Archbishop Usher; it measures 9½ inches by 7, with 26 lines in a page; the writing is rude, and destitute of patches of red colour, so common in Irish MSS. The words and often the syllables are broken at the end of the lines. The MS. is very imperfect, containing only 86 leaves, the vellum being thick and coarse, almost resembling horn. The first three words of St. Matthew's Gospel (" Xpi autem gene—ratio "), and the " Initium eua(ngelii) " of St. Mark, are represented of a large size (each occupying an entire page, in the style of the Gospels of MacRegol and St. Chad), but far more rudely designed, figures of the Saints being introduced into the body of the ornamental page, each being about three inches in height, and drawn nearly in the style of those in the Gospels of MacDurnan. The headings of the other Gospels are wanting. The specimen of the text in No. 3, is copied from St. Luke vi. 23, 24. " Gaudete et exultate in illa die Ecce *enim*[1] merces vestra multà in cœlo *sæcund*um *hæc enim* facebant *profetis* patres eorum *verun*tamen væ vobis divitibus (qui habetis consulationem vestram)."

This MS. abounds in false orthography, as " profetis — discendiens — vidians — diciens — essuriunt — langoribus habundaverit — hirascitur — nissi — johannis — pussillis — farisseorum — relincimus — puplicani," &c. Of the text, the following passages are specimens :—Ecce virgo in ut*ero* habebit—omnis qui hirascitur fratri suo reus &c. The interpolated passage, St. Matthew xxvii. v. 48, is contained in this MS.

---

[1] The words printed in italics are singularly contracted in this MS.

1

The specimen, No. 1, is copied from a MS. of the four Gospels, also preserved at Trinity College, Dublin, written, as is asserted, in an entry in the MS. by St. Columbkille himself, in the space of twelve days. It consists of 248 leaves of vellum, 9½ by 6 inches in size, with 25 lines in a page. At the commencement of the volume, and preceding each of the four Gospels, are pages entirely covered with tessellated interlaced ornaments, as in the Book of Kells, &c., the pattern being, however, much larger than in any other MS. which I have examined. Each Gospel is also preceded by a drawing of the symbolical animal of the several Evangelists, inclosed within an ornamental border, occupying the entire page, the four symbols being also represented together in a separate page at the beginning of the book. These drawings are probably the rudest and most grotesque delineations of the sacred symbols ever executed; the latter are copied in the wood-cut at the end of this article.

The Epistle of Jerome to Damasus (Novum opus, &c.), a series of explanations of Hebrew names, the Eusebian canons (not inclosed within ornamented columns), the "breves causæ" of the Evangelists, and a page of Irish concerning St. Columbkille, occupy the first thirteen leaves; the remainder of the volume being occupied with the Gospels. The commencement of the Epistle of St. Jerome, and of the Gospels, "Liber genera*tionis* ihu xpi filii dauid filii abracha," "Xpi autem generatio," "Initium evangelii ihu xpi," "Quoniam quidam multi—," "Fuit in diebus herodis," and "In principio erat verbum et verbum erat apud dm," are written in large ornamented letters, of which my specimen No. 1, and the two fac-similes given by O'Conor (Script. vet. Rer. Hibern.) from the beginning of St. Luke, will afford an idea, the remainder of the page being in the ordinary writing of the volume, which, it will be observed, is in large rounded characters, similar to those of the Book of Kells, Gospels of MacRegol, &c. The fourth line of my fac-simile contains various words and differently formed letters, and the fifth line is part of the head of St. John's Gospels, "verbum erat apud ΔM," the last contracted word deum being in Greek capitals. It will be perceived that the style of the ornaments of this MS. is that of the finest early Irish codices, and especially resembles that of the Gospels in the Bibliothèque du Roi figured by Silvestre * (as of the 10th century!). A few passages will serve to show the text of this volume, which, from its agreement with the Vulgate, constitutes a remarkable exception to the other ancient Irish gospels. "Joseph virum mariæ de qua natus est ihs qui vocatur xps—Ecce virgo in utero habebit et pariet filium—vade Satanas—aperiens os suum—qui irascitur fratri suo reus erit iudicio."—Pater tuus qui videt in absconso reddet tibi—panem nostrum supersubstantialem—ipse infirmitates nostras accepit et egritudines portavit—fuit homo misus a dō cui nomen erat johannis—venientem in mundum – the *lancea* passage in St. Matthew xxvii. v. 48 is correctly wanting.

Originally this volume was inclosed within a silver case, made by the orders of Flannius, son of Malachy, King of Ireland, circ. A.D. 916, as appears from the Irish inscription on the ancient cover, which was to this effect:—"The prayer and benediction of St. Columb Kille be upon Flannius, the son of Malachy, King of Ireland, who caused this cover to be made."

The specimen, No. 2, is copied from the ancient "Liber Hymnorum," cited by Archbishop Usher and others, and now contained in the library of Trinity College, Dublin, and noticed in the article upon the Gospels of MacDurnan. It consists of 34 leaves of very thick smooth vellum, measuring 10½ inches by 7, with 28 lines in most of the pages; written in large Irish characters, partly in Latin, and partly in the most ancient known dialect of the Irish language, called the Bearla Feine, in which the Brehon Laws are written; the latter portion being in a more cursive character than the Latin. The large ornamental initials are very complicated and interlaced, but they have none of the elegance of those of the Book of Kells, &c.; they are indeed in a style which does not appear so ancient as in those MSS., according rather with the capitals in the Harleian Gospels of the 11th century, the Brehon Laws in the British Museum, and Bodleian Library at Oxford. Archbishop Usher, however, considered it, in his time, to be at least 1000 years old.

The volume consists of 29 short hymns, prayers, and other religious compositions, amongst which are the Magnificat and Benedictus, portion of which is copied in the two lower lines of No. 2. "Quia fecit mihi magna qui potens ēst et s*anct*um n*o*men ējus Et m*i*ser*i*cor*d*ia *ejus* in progenies et p*r*ogenies timentib*us* *eum*."

The two upper lines in this fac-simile are copied from the commencement of the Hymn of St. Patrick,

---

* Like the volume before us, the MS. in the Paris library has the large letters at the commencement of each Gospel, occupying only a portion of the page; and each Gospel is preceded by its symbolical animal, the calf being very similar to that in the Gospels of St. Columbkille. I find also, on examining the Paris M.S., that it agrees with the Dublin one, in being written in the Vulgate version.

described by Mr. Petrie as the very oldest undoubted monument of the Irish language remaining, whilst it is equally valuable as an evidence of the religious doctrine which St. Patrick inculcated. The specimen is to be read :

' A Tomriug in diu murt trentogairm trinoit cretim treodataid foisin oendatad ī dulemain dail.'

i. e. ' At Temur (Tarah) to-day I invoke the mighty power of the Trinity. I believe in the Trinity under the Unity of the God of the Elements.' [1]

The various fac-similes in the right hand division of the accompanying plate are copied from MSS. preserved in the Cumdachs, or ancient silver cases, and which have for centuries been regarded with superstitious reverence, until, in fact, the knowledge of their contents had become entirely lost. To open one of these cases was indeed considered an act of the greatest sacrilege, which would be certainly attended with evils of the direst nature. The prying curiosity of modern antiquaries has, however, overweighed the fear of unknown evils, and discovered in these cases copies of the Psalter or Gospels, accompanied in some cases by prayers for the visitation of the sick.[2]

Sir W. Betham gives in his ' Irish Antiquarian Researches,' a very graphic account of the alarm which was occasioned by his desire to open the CAAH, one of these venerable relics, which was found to contain the PSALTER OF ST. COLUMBA. This inestimable MS., with its Cumdach, is now, by the kind permission of Sir W. O'Donell, placed in the rich Museum of the Royal Irish Academy. A short notice of it will be found in the 6th page of the article upon the Gospels of MacDurnan. The volume is of a moderate 8vo size, written in small minuscule characters, with the words indistinct, with the first letter of each Psalm of a large size, but destitute of colours, and but slightly ornamented, and the two or three following letters, also larger than the text, of which the specimen, No. 8, is a fac-simile, being the commencement of the 91st Psalm : " Qui habitat in adjutorio altissimi in protectione Dei cœli commorabitur,"—in which it will be seen that the d and s are written in their roman form ; occasionally, however, the d is of the uncial form, and the s of the f form, with the topand bottom extending very slightly above and below the line ; the r is of the n shape, with the second stroke more oblique, the i final is generally straight, but prolonged below the line.

The specimens under No. 7 are copied from the LEABHAR DIMMA, noticed in the article on the Gospels of MacDurnan (p. 6), and recently purchased from Sir W. Betham by Trinity College, Dublin, for 200*l.* The MS. measures 7 inches by 5½, and is irregularly written, having 30, 40, or nearly 50 lines in a page, written in double columns. Each Gospel is preceded by a rude representation of the Evangelist, except the last ; in which the eagle, with four wings, is represented instead of St. John, each being inclosed within an ornamental border, rudely executed in interlaced ribbon patterns. Sir W. Betham has given copies of these drawings, as well as of the commencement of St. John's Gospel, and of part of the prayers for the sick, at the end of the volume, the whole of which latter he has also published, although not quite correctly.

The first page of St. Matthew's Gospel is written in a smaller hand, and more carefully than the remainder, the scribe not having used any lines. The genealogical introduction occupies the first column (being itself written in double columns), the historical part commencing at the top of the second column of the first page. The

---

[1] The following are extracts from this singular production, as translated by Mr. Petrie in the Transactions of the Royal Irish Academy :—

" At Temur to-day may the strength of God pilot me, may the power of God preserve me, may the wisdom of God instruct me, may the eye of God view me, may the ear of God hear me, may the word of God render me eloquent, may the hand of God protect me, may the way of God direct me, may the shield of God defend me, may the host of God guard me against the snares of demons, the temptations to vices, the inclinations of the mind against every man who meditates evil to me, far or near, alone or in company.

" I place all these powers between me and every evil unmerciful power directed against my soul and body, as a protection against the incantations of false prophets, against the black laws of Gentilism, against the false laws of heresy, against the preaching of idolatry, against the spells of *women, smiths, and druids*, against every knowledge which blinds the soul of man. May Christ to-day protect me against poison, against burning, against drowning, against wounding, until I deserve much reward.

" Christ be with me, Christ before me, Christ after me, Christ in me, Christ under me, Christ over me, Christ at my right, Christ at my left, Christ at this side, Christ at that side, Christ at my back.

" Salvation is the Lord's, salvation is the Lord's, salvation is Christ's. May thy salvation, O Lord, be always with us."

The magical spells attributed to women, smiths and druids, continue, according to Mr. Petrie, in the belief of the people in various parts of Ireland up to the present time.

[2] Most of these Cumdachs and their contents are noticed in the article on the Gospels of MacDurnan ; besides these, another Cumdach (from which the contents had been unfortunately abstracted) is described in Sir W. Betham's Irish Antiq. Res., and was in the possession of the late Duke of Sussex ; at the sale of whose effects it was purchased for the lately established College of St. Columba, near Drogheda. Another Cumdach, containing the Gospels of St. Mulling, is described in a subsequent page of this article.

specimens copied from this page are to be read, " Liber generationis—iac*ob* autem *genuit* ioseph vir*um* mariae de qua nat*us* est ih̄c xp̄s cui disponsata virga m*a*ria maria autem *genuit* ihm̄ qui d*icitu*r xps," (the scribe jumbling together two different readings), " Xp̄i autem generatio sic erat cum esset disponsata mat͞er maria ioseph antequam."

Below this, from a subsequent page, are copied the following lines :—" Fuit iohannis in̄ deserto babtizans et p*r*edicans." At the end of the Gospels the scribe has written his nam̄e, also copied in the plate, " Finit Amen . . ,✠Dimma macc nathi✠ . . ,"—with two lines of Irish, of which the following is the translation made by Mr. Eugene Curry :—

> " I desire for myself, in reward of my labour,
> The tending of herds with all attention.
> Nuts, not poisonous, I will crack,
> And a righteous habitation.

At the end of St. Matthew's Gospel he has also inscribed his name :—" Finit. Pray for Dimma, who wrote by the Lord God's benediction."

The following are a few of the readings of this MS. :—" Virgo in utero habet et pariet filium "—" vade retro Satanas "—" qui irascitur fratri suo reus erit judicio "—" panem nostrum cotidianum͞ "—" ipse infirmitates nostras accipit et egretudines nostras portavit." The " *lancea* " passage in the xxvii. Chapter of St. Matthew, v. 48, also exists in this MS., which does not contain any of the Hieronymian Epistles, or Eusebian Canons.

The specimens No. 6 are copied from a MS., also preserved with its Cumdach in the Library of Trinity College, Dublin, containing the four Gospels written by St. Mulling, who flourished in the 7th century.[1] The Cumdach was described in Vallancey's Collectanea, under the name of the Leath Meisicith, and Leath Fial, or Stone of Destiny. It was presented to Trin. Coll. Dublin by Mr. Kavanagh, in whose family it had been preserved with religious veneration for ages, and who was descended from the O'Kavanaghs, the chiefs of the district in which St. Mulling flourished.[2] Of the volume itself no account has hitherto been published. It measures $6\frac{1}{4}$ inches by $4\frac{3}{4}$, and is written in double columns in very neat minuscule characters, full of contractions, with 28 to 36 lines in a page. Many parts of the MS. are discoloured by the action of the metal pins which have been driven into the case from time to time. The scribe has so arranged his text that each Gospel forms a distinct packet of folded leaves (the volume not having any binding). The last and part of the preceding pages of the packet containing St. Mathew's Gospel having been left blank, the *original scribe* had filled them up with the Office for the Visitation of the Sick. Each of the Gospels commences with the first word, or first few letters, of a large size (2 or 3 inches long), in the style of the Gospels of St. Chad, *not coloured*, but with double marginal rows of red dots.

The specimens before us are to be read—" (X͞pi) autem generatio," being part of the heading of the historical part of St. Matthew's Gospel, each word occupying a separate line of the first column of the verso of leaf 1 ; also the Lord's Prayer as follows :—"Pater noster qui es in cœlis s͞cificet nomen tuu͞ adueniat regnu͞ tuu͞ fiat voluntas tua s̄i in cœlo et in terra Pan͞e nostru͞ supsubstantia-lem da nobis hodie et remitte nobis debita nostra s̄i & nos remittem͞s debitorib͞s nostris et *ne patiaris nos induci in temptationem* sed libera nos a malo."

The following are a few of the readings of this MS. :—" Jacob autem genuit joseph cui disponsata erat . . . . . q. genuit ihm̄."—Ecce virgo in utero concepiat et pariat filium."—" Vade retro Satanas."— " Qui irascet fr̄i suo reus erit," &c.—" Pater tuus q͞ui vidit in absconso reddet tibi."—" Ipse infirmitates nostras accipiet et egritudines nr̄as portabit."—" Et factu̅ est cum consumasset ih̄s sermones ih̄s sermones istos transtulit se a galilea & venit i̅ fines iudeæ trans jordanem secut. st eu̅ tb̄æ multæ & Ɛ curavit eos ibi."—The *lancea* passage (St. Matth. xxvii.) is also here interpolated ; but each word is marked above with three small dots, placed in a triangle.—" Fuit homo missus a do cui nomen erat iohannis."—" Erat autem lux vera q̄ inluminat quæ inluminat omnem venientem in h̄c mondum in hoc monds erat et mondu̅ per ipsum factus est et mondus eum non cognovit."

At the end of St. Matthew and St. Luke, the scribe has written, " Finit Amen finit ; " at the

¹ See Ware's Bishops, Ferns.
² It is not determined whether the Corp Nua or Corp Naomh of the Abbey of Tristernach was a reliquary or a Cumdach. It was described by Vallancey. The Meeshac, also described by Vallancey and Sir W. Betham, who figured it, is now in the possession of the New College of St. Columba, as above mentioned.

end of St. Mark, "finit;" and at the end of St. John, "ΦINIT Amen ΦINIT" (copied in my plate). "O Tu quicunq. scripseris v̄el scrutatus fueris v̄el et ī͞a videris h̄ volumen," &c.; and four other lines almost illegible, "Nomen aūtem scriptoris Mulling dicitur. Finiunt quatuor euangelia" (also copied in the plate).

There is also an inscription on the verso of the last page in the same hand as the text, containing the Magnificat, part of the Sermon on the Mount, Apostles' Creed, "Patricius ēp͞is," and a circular table with inscriptions.

In the same box was also found the Epistle of St. Jerome to Pope Damasus; the articles on the four Evangelists ("Hic est Johannes Evangelista," &c.); the numerical tables of the sections of the Gospels, and three full-length drawings of the Evangelists, in the style of those in the Gospels of MacDurnan; each holding a book, and one a pen with an ink-stand by his side; each also with a circular nimbus, and one with the long curls of hair(?) hanging over his shoulders; all of which evidently formed portions of the Gospels of St. Mulling. In addition to these, was also found a fragment of St. Mark's Gospel from another MS., of which the specimen No. 5 is a fac-simile of the commencement; and which is remarkable, not only for the curious forms of the capital letters in the first line, but also for the variation in the reading of the second line. It is to be read, "INItium euangelii i͞h͞u x͞p͞i filii d͞i sicut scriptum est in p̄rofetis ecce mitto angelum meum ante facīe."

It remains to notice the two singular specimens represented under the Nos. 9 and 10, which are copied from the Book of Armagh, written at the close of the seventh century, and which, in several of its ornaments, is very similar to the Gospels of Lindisfarne (Cott. Nero, C. IV.) of the same date. The text however is written in minuscule characters, very similar to those of the Gospels of Mac Durnan, the volume being of the 8vo size. It moreover contains the whole of the New Testament, and also "the Confession of St. Patrick," and has been fully described by Sir W. Betham, in the second volume of his Antiquarian Researches, with fac-similes of some of the drawings and ornamental initial letters.*

The specimen, No. 9, is part of the word "Apocalipsis," at the commencement of the Book of the Revelations, the Ap being omitted, or rather, minutely delineated at the commencement of the fac-simile, the A measuring nearly five inches in length, and highly ornamented. I do not recollect any other instance in which the large square form has been applied to a word not written in capitals—these letters being in fact large square minuscules.

The specimen, headed No. 10, "KaTa MATTHYM," is the Lord's Prayer in Latin, written in singular-formed Irish-Greek letters, in which capitals and minuscules are strangely mingled together.

"ΠaTHR NOCTER KYI EC IN KaeλιC CKIΦIKHTYR NWMEN TYYM aΔVENIaT REΓNYM TYYM ΦIaT VoλYNTaC TYa CIKYT IN Kaeλω ET IN TERRA ΠaN͞E NOC-TRYM KOTIΔIaNYM ΔA NWβιC hoΔIE ET ΔIMITTE NWβιC ΔEβITA NOCTRA CIKYT ET NWC ΔIMICCIMYC ΔEβιTWRIβYC NOCTRIC ET NH ΠaTIaRIC NWC INΔYKI IN TEMΠTaTιWNEM CEΔ λιβeRa NOC a Maλω."

It will be seen that this MS. has the same singular reading of the penultimate paragraph as occurs in the Gospel of St. Mulling.

It has been affirmed that the ignorance of the ancient scribes led them to write Greek in Roman characters; but we have here abundant proof not only of their learning, but also of their piety, since we cannot but suppose that the circumstance of the Lord's Prayer being thus distinguished resulted from a desire entertained by the scribe to treat that particular portion of the Gospels with a greater mark of reverence.

Other instances however of this usage may be quoted. The Benedictines (after Gori and Maffei) have given copies of two deeds of sale on papyrus written at the close of the sixth century, which, although in Latin, are written in cursive Greek letters, almost unintelligible. (N. Tr. de Dipl. 3, pl. 63, No. II., 2, 3.) The Abbey of Fulda possesses an ancient parchment written in the same style, with the M formed as in our specimen

---

* I learn from Mr. Petrie that this volume is in the possession of a private gentleman in Dublin, and is not in the library of Trinity Coll.

(Henselius Sinops. Univ. Philolog. p. 95.)   I have no doubt that it would be found that this is the production of an Anglo-Saxon or Hibernian scribe, Fulda having been founded by our missionary, St. Boniface.

The Benedictines have also given other specimens in Pl. 40, II. xi., (p. 128), Plate 45, VI. vii. (p. 192), Pl. 59, V. iii. (p. 442), written towards the beginning of the Ninth Century, in a Latin Bible of the Library of St. Germain-des-Prés.   There is another example given by the Benedictines (Ibid. Pl. 37, II. viii., p. 85) from that singular MS. the Sacramentarium of Gelloni of the eighth century, being the Hosanna.   But the practice was not confined to MSS., for it occurs in charters and in lapidary and marble inscriptions, whereof the same authors have collected a number of examples in the second volume, pp. 635—642, observing (Ibid. p. 66)—" On trouve plusieurs signatures grecques dans les actes publics d'Italie.   Des ecclésiastiques de divers autres pays, soit par vanité, soit par quelque autre motif, souscrivent quelquefois en grec."   " Les caractères grecs, dit M. l'Abbé Lebeuf, et même des mots entiers, étaient employés dans les lettres formées par les évêques." Ibid. vol. iii., p. 128, where are collected a number of additional references.*

This employment of Greek characters by the learned ecclesiastics at this early period was almost a necessary consequence of the flourishing state of the Byzantine Empire during the sixth and seventh century, when so decided a movement was made to disseminate the Christian religion ; and that numbers of such instances (as are alluded to in our pages) should be found in the early MSS. of the United Kingdom, is only a further proof of the intimacy and connexion which must have existed between the Church here and in the East, of which our early ecclesiastical annals offer so many instances, and of which one, given by Archbishop Usher, must in the present place suffice.   Speaking of Virgilius (an Irish bishop of the eighth century), who visited the Holy Land, he states " *Pontificem* secum habuit proprium Dobdam nomine *græcum* qui ipsum secutus ex patria— mirarer vero ex Hibernia nostra hominem græcum prodiisse nisi scirem in agro Midensi apud Trimmenses (Trim. Com. Meath) *ædem sacram* extitisse quæ GRÆCÆ ECCLESIÆ *nomen ad hunc usque diem retinet.*" (Epist. Hibern. Syllog. Note xxi.)

The wood-cut at the foot of this article is a copy of the drawing of the Evangelical Symbols, from the Autograph Gospels of St. Columba described above.

* The Latin inscription on the Gaulish tomb of Gordianus given by Fabretti, in the third century, is also written in strange Greek characters.   N. Tr. de Dipl. i. 705.

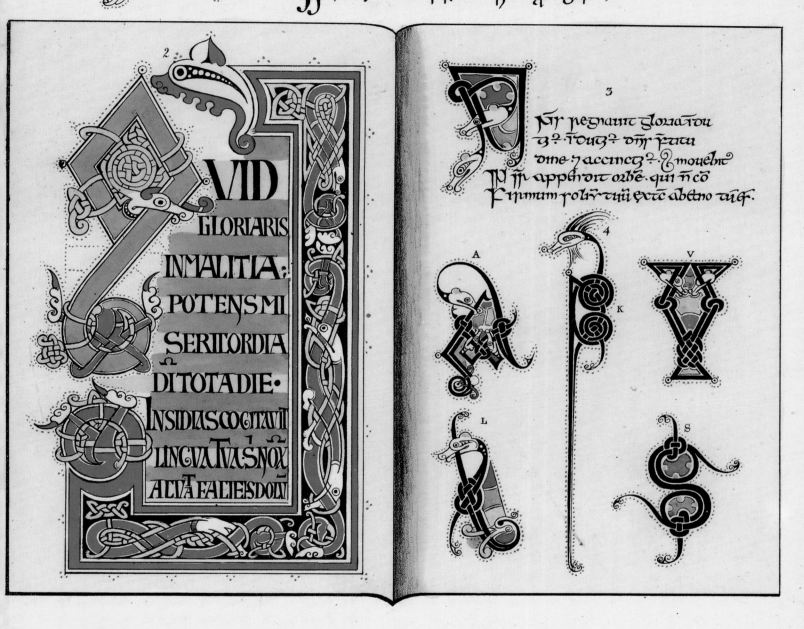

Psalter of Ricemarchus &c.

THE PSALTERS OF ST. OUEN AND RICEMARCHUS.

THE intimate connection which existed for many ages between Ireland, Wales, Cornwall and Armorica, will enable us to account for very many peculiarities, which may be traced from one to another of those countries. Thus of Pagan relics, we find many in these countries perfectly analogous ; such, for instance, are the hare (or boundary) stones of Cornwall [1], the maen hir of Wales, and the men hars in Armorica [2]. Hence, too, we have such analogous places of defence as Castle an Dinas and Caer Bran, in Cornwall, and Castel Dinas Bran, near Llangollen, in North Wales; and also similar Druidical circles of stones, both in Wales and Ireland, bearing in the language of the people the names of astronomers' circles ; and hence, to descend to less important matters, the similarity between the coracle (cwrwgyl) of the Welch and the currach, as the common boat is to this day termed by the Irish, and which, like the coracle, is shaped like a walnut-shell, and rowed by one paddle ; whilst the extraordinary proficiency both of the Welch and Irish on the harp, is well known to all. Indeed, some of the most learned Welch antiquaries admit that their national music is of Irish origin ; and the proficiency of the Irish in church music in the seventh century was so great, that the daughter of King Pepin of France sent to Ireland for persons qualified to instruct the nuns of the Abbey of Nivelle in psalmody.

The political independence so long maintained by the Irish, Welch, and Cornish, against the Anglo-Saxons, necessarily preserved to them their national characteristics; whilst the long struggles which they made to maintain the religion of their forefathers distinct from that of the Anglo-Saxons converted to Romanism, gave to them a common tie of interest. Of the religious independence of the Britons, we have abundant proof in the accounts recorded of the failure of the negotiations between St. Augustine and the Welch clergy, and the protest of the latter against the Papal supremacy, recorded in Spelman's Concilia [3] ; whilst their connection with the Irish Church [4] is equally proved by the identity of their tenets, as affirmed by Bede [5].

In like manner, as Camden informs us, " The people of Cornwall have always borne such veneration to Irish Saints who retired there, that almost all their towns have been consecrated to their memory," and as St. Patrick is asserted by some historians to have been born [6], and also to have laboured for the propagation of the Gospel, in Cornwall,[7] two parishes in that county to this day retain the names, of Petroc-Stow, (contracted into Padstow) and Little Petheric,[8] and hence, the Irish Saint Kieran, or St. Piran, who also laboured in Cornwall, is commemorated in the little church overwhelmed by the sand, thence named ' Sci Pyerani in Zabulo' or ' Sabulo,' and popularly Perran Zabuloe.

From what has been observed above, it will be at once apparent why so intimate a resemblance should be

---

[1] King's Munimenta Antiqua.

[2] See Hamper, in Archæolog., v. 25 ; and especially Higgins' work on the " Celtic Druids."

[3] Fuller, Book II., Cent. VII., Sec. iii.; and see Stillingfleet's Orig. Brit., p. 359.

[4] See the Rev. J. Williams' recently published work on the Ecclesiastical Antiquities of Cymry, its history, doctrine, and rites, p. 263, and *passim*.

[5] " Scoti nihil discrepabant in conversatione a Britannis—similem

vitam et professionem egisse ; " and see Hanmer's Chron., p. 9, for the connexion between the Irish and Welsh.

[6] Other authorities give Wales or Armorica as the place of his birth.

[7] Even the Saxon name of the county itself, Corn-Wealas, proves the early connexion between the Cornish Britons and those of Wales or Wealas.

[8] See the Rev. W. Haslam's very interesting little work on Perran Zabuloe, recently published, p. 13.

1

traced between the ecclesiastical relics of ancient art still existing in these several divisions of the empire. This is to be found in the remains of the most ancient stone buildings now existing—in the ancient stone crosses scattered so abundantly through all these parts, and in the ornamental details with which they, as well as other relics, are often most elaborately enriched.

I believe the opinion that there were no native stone erections in Ireland, England, or Wales, previously to the ninth or tenth century, to be wholly untenable. Where wood abounded, doubtless it would be preferred for building, but in stony districts the natives would, surely, make use of stone for their structures. A careful examination, during the past summer, of the mode of building adopted in several of the most ancient of these remains in Ireland, as at Monaster-boice and Glendaloch,[1] as compared with the Rev. Mr. Haslam's detailed account of the church at Perran Zabuloe, recently dug out of the sands; and the Rev. H. L. Jones's character of the most ancient of the churches in Anglesea[2], clearly proves an identity both of design and workmanship, quite distinct from Anglo-Saxon or Norman remains[3].

The Crosses, for the most part formed of single blocks of granite, equally indicate the connection between Ireland, Wales, and Cornwall; and at the same time afford a further proof of the early relations existing between the Irish and British Churches, in the *Greek* form of the Cross carved upon these granite slabs[4]. Some of the later of these Crosses are, indeed, more elaborately ornamented; and as the ornaments correspond with those of the illuminated Irish MSS., we have an *hitherto unnoticed corroboration* of the date of the former. Some of these contain in the centre part of the Cross a representation of the Crucifixion, more or less rude in design, and sometimes (as in some of the Crosses in the western parts of Cornwall[5]) reduced to the rude sculpture of a single human figure, with the arms extended[6].

Specimens of the more elaborate of these Crosses occur at Monaster-boice, Tuam, and Clonmacnois, in Ireland; at Margam and Lantwit, in Wales; at Lanherne, in Cornwall; and at Inverary, in Scotland (brought, I believe, from Iona[7]).

Some of these Crosses have the shaft divided into compartments, wherein are sculptured various scriptural events or ornamental work; and I presume that the sculptured stone at Kilcullen, engraved by Ledwich, and the elaborately carved shaft at Bewcastle, in Northumberland, described by Sir F. Palgrave, in his "History of England," which has so much puzzled antiquaries to account for its origin, are parts of two of these Crosses[8].

Two similar crosses, 26 and 18 feet high, ornamented with stories or ranges of sculptured bishops, &c. formerly existed at Glastonbury, which it will be remembered was frequented by the Irish.

In addition to the ancient carved crosses we may also refer to the ornamental carvings figured by Ledwich as existing in his time at Glendaloch[9], and which were unique of the kind in Ireland, although exhibiting the interlaced patterns and other analogous Irish designs; to the tomb of Cormack, long used for waking the clergy in

[1] This subject will be treated at great length in Mr. Petrie's forthcoming prize essay on the Round Towers.

[2] Archæolog. Journal, i. p. 120. The original church of St. Gervais, at Rouen, which is, I believe, the oldest Christian (Ante-Norman) erection remaining in France, and which now forms the crypt of that church, also perfectly agrees with Mr. Jones's description of the Anglesea churches.

[3] Mr. Bloxam, in his Principles of Ecclesiastical Architecture, considers Perran Zabuloe to be "probably not of earlier date than the twelfth century." Mr. Haslam, by treating the subject in connexion with its history and analogies, has most satisfactorily refuted this opinion.

[4] Haslam, *ut supra*, p. 18.

[5] The number of these Crosses in this part of the country must be very great, as Mr. Haslam states that every parish in Cornwall contains several, and almost every churchyard has one at least; and Pennant informs us that in Iona there were as many as 360.

[6] I am aware that it is the opinion of writers on Christian Iconography (Milman, Hist. of Christianity, vol. i.; Didron, Iconogr. Chrét. p. 260, *et seq.*) that representations of the Saviour, in his degraded and crucified state, were not executed previous to the tenth century. The several articles in this work upon the Syriac and Irish MSS., and that upon the Gospels of St. Augustine, are sufficient to disprove such an opinion.

[7] The Eyam and Bakewell Crosses, in Derbyshire, are probably not of British origin, the ornaments on the former not corresponding with those of the Irish school.

[8] Some sagacious writers, finding on the Bewcastle shaft chequered or tesselated patterns (in addition to the human figures and interlaced ribbons), have come to the conclusion that they were intended for the arms of the family of Vaux, and that the stone was erected by some of them!

[9] It is to the disgrace of the Irish that these stones no longer exist at Glendaloch. On a recent visit I was not able to find more than one or two of the least interesting. One of these stones afforded Ledwich an opportunity of reviling the Irish clergy; but a very little knowledge of Christian Irish iconography would have afforded a truer explanation. The centre figure holding a book is not a Bishop or Priest, but Christ, or one of the four Evangelists. The "Pilgrim leaning on his staff," is a Bishop, with his short pastoral staff, or cambatta; and "the young man holding a purse to commute it for penance," is an Ecclesiastic, with the sacred bell used in Ireland. One of these bells is preserved in the collection of the Royal Irish Academy, inscribed in fine large round letters—

ᴏᴘᴏɪᴄ ᴀᴘᴄħᴜᴍᴀᴘᴄᴀᴄħ ᴙ ᴀɪʟᴇʟʟᴏ

Pray for Archummascach, the son of Ailello.

Cumasach, Œconomist of Armagh, died A.D. 904.—Archæol. Monast. Hibern. Co. Armagh, p. 19. The Welch Saint Illtyd's Bell, inscribed 'Sancte Iltite, ora pro nobis,' was lately discovered at Lantwit. Williams' Church of Cymry, p. 188.

Cashel cathedral, which exhibits in its carvings the serpentine animals with long interlaced top-knots and tails [1]; and to the ornamental details upon the cross of Cong, the pastoral staff of the abbot of Clonmacnois, and other beautifully carved metal relics preserved in the collection of the Royal Irish Academy, as well as to the more ancient parts of the silver covers of the Irish cumdachs.

Ledwich, indeed, and others,[2] consider the ornamental interlaced patterns, spiral lines, Chinese-like diagonal patterns, and intertwined animals, as " Runic knots and Scandinavian superstitions," and as the work of Danish or Saxon workmen. It appears to me, however, to be far more correct to refer them, as Mr. Britton is inclined to do, to the civilised Britons (and Irish). The Cross of Adamnan, on the Hill of Tara, described by Mr. Petrie, is evidence of their existence centuries before the Danes invaded Ireland; whilst the identity in the ornamental details with the undoubted Irish MSS. of the seventh, eighth, and ninth centuries, and the total absence of Runic characters in Ireland, as well as the inscriptions which occasionally appear on the crosses, both in Ireland and Wales,[3] in the ancient large rounded Irish or British character; all prove a common origin, distinct from the Anglo-Saxon or Danish, and which may be traced to the early Christian schools of Ireland or Wales.

The preceding observations have appeared necessary, in order to enable us to obtain a more precise idea of the origin and date of the MSS. copied in the accompanying plate, than would have been gained without an inquiry into the relations existing between Ireland and the other countries above referred to.

The specimen No. 1 is copied (after Astle [4]) from a MS. of St. Augustine's Treatise " de Trinitate," in the library of Corpus Christi College, Cambridge, " written by John de Gente Ceretica (or Cardiganshire), in the time of Sulgen, who was Bishop of St. David's in the reign of King Edward the Confessor."—(Astle ut infra, p. 104.)

It is to be read—" Incipit nunc prefatio sive prologus [5]. Domino beatissimo et sincerissima auctoritate venerando sancto patri et consacerdoti Pape Aurilio Augustinus in domino salutem."

The Minuscule character used in this MS. is called by Astle, set Saxon; whereas the historical and palæographical circumstances set forth in this and other articles of this work, clearly show it to be of Irish origin; and that this character " was used in Wales longer than in England," as affirmed by Astle, is only the necessary result of the situation in which the two countries were respectively placed, and the connection which doubtless still subsisted between the Irish and Welch Ecclesiastics. The form of the initial letter in this fac-simile is especially interesting, when compared with the capitals of the same period, given in our plates of Anglo-Saxon psalters, and those in our plates from Irish MSS.

Nos. 2, 3, and 4, are copied from a small Psalter in the Library of Trinity College, Dublin, which belonged to Ricemarchus, Bishop of St. David's (Menevia,) in the year 1088, as appears by some Latin verses at the end of the volume. It measures $6\frac{1}{4}$ inches by $4\frac{1}{4}$, and is $1\frac{3}{4}$ inches thick, each leaf containing 24 lines. It commences with the spurious Epistles of Jerome to Choromatius and Eliodorus, notices of the Apostles, with Explanations of their names; a very long Calendar, and Lunar Tables, partly written in Greek initials, and several other Epistles and Prefaces of Jerome. The Psalter is written in the Minuscule character, with many contractions, of which No. 3 is a specimen, being the commencement of the 92nd (93rd) Psalm, which is to be read " Dominus regnavit gloria indutus est* indutus est* dominus fortitudine et* accinctus est*.[6] Insr appendit orbem qui non commovebitur : firmum solium tuum ex tunc ab eterno tu es." Each Psalm commences with an ornamental initial, of which several are represented (No. 4). Three of the Psalms have, however, the commencement more elaborately illuminated, namely—the 1st, 51st (52nd), copied on the plate No. 2, (which is to be read " Quid gloriaris in malitia : potens misericordia Dei tota die, insidias cogitavit lingua tua sicut

[1] One of the capitals in Shobdon Church, Herefordshire, is ornamented with a lacertine animal with a long top-knot intertwining round the body, precisely as in the Irish MSS. and carvings (Archæol. Journ. i. p. 235). The position of this church seems sufficient to indicate that this carving, instead of being a specimen of " Norman ornamental sculpture," was derived from some tradition of the Irish or Welsh school of art; and Mr. Gage Rokewood's suggestion of the resemblance of the neighbouring Kilpeck sculptures to the costume of the ancient Britons, supports this opinion. Mr. Wright, in the article above referred to, rejects this suggestion, but observes, that a good work on the architectural antiquities of the churches of the borders of Wales is much wanted; it would, however, render the subject far more complete to contrast the whole of the Welch ecclesiastical remains

with the Anglo-Saxon on the one side and with the Irish on the other. In this respect the Rev. Mr. Jones's figures of the Anglesea sculptures are extremely valuable; and it is to be regretted that he omitted to figure the " early and highly curious crossed stone standing in the park at Penmôn."

[2] " It is certainly Danish." " These figures are Runic knots."— Ledwich. Hickes pronounced them to be magical.

[3] I have not been able to trace the inscription on Eliseg's Pillar, near Valle Crucis Abbey, in N. Wales, described by Lhuyd.

[4] Origin of Writing, tab. 20, spec. iv.

[5] Astle misread this ' incipit ne prefatio.'

[6] The words marked with an asterisk are contracted in the usual Irish style.

nov*acula* acuta faciens dolu*m*;") and the 101st (102nd) Psalm (commencing " Dne exa*u*di orationem meam et clamor meus ad te veniat̄ N̄ abscondas faciem tuam a me in die tribulationis meæ inclina ad me aurem tuam.")

It is interesting to observe, that the version in which the text is written is not the Gallican which was chiefly employed in MSS. written in England in the eleventh century.

At the end of the MS. are written some extracts from Bede, on the Psalms and the Latin verses above referred to, written by Ricemarchus in the characters of the text, commencing —

> " Filius Isai David cui patria Bethlem
> Pastor crismatus ter, miles, Rex, citharedus,
> Ymnidicus. Psalmista potens cantorque propheta
> Gesta canit po*pu*los erudit moribus altor (*vel* nutritor)
> Sponsu*m* dat thalamo cui sponsus pacifer uno
> Terrea contempnit vultus ad sidera tollit.
> *   *   *   *   *   *
> Ergo in nostra qui dicor gente RICEMARCHI
> SULGENI genitus necnon Johannis adelphus [1]
> Ithael asscripsit studium cui n̄ inaurat
> Psalmorum proceres depinxit rite Johannes
> Ille sit inscriptus gemma sub pectore natis (*vel* sacerdotis)
> Hunc capiat hirubin templi pictura sub alis .., "

These verses (for a copy of which I am indebted to the Rev. J. H. Todd), in addition to the conformity of the style of the ornamental initials of this and the preceding MS. fully confirm its Welch origin, as well as its date, viz., about the middle of the eleventh century. These initials are singular, but not destitute of elegance, and consist of interlaced ribbons, terminating in the heads of animals.

The border in the larger illumination consists of the head and body of a strange animal (made up of smaller lacertine creatures), terminating beneath the *q* in two legs and claws; the large *q* is also formed of a similar animal, the hind top-knot forming the interlacing in the open part of the letter, the body terminating in a pair of red legs and claws.

The specimen No. 5 is taken from the Psalter of St. Ouen, a MS. preserved in the Library of the Hôtel de Ville, attached to the ancient Abbey of St. Ouen, at Rouen, and which has much perplexed the French palæographers as to its real origin and date. By Silvestre and Champollion it is considered as of the seventh or eighth century, and as written in the " écriture minuscule saxonne de France ; " whereas a comparison with the preceding specimens in my plate will, I think, satisfactorily prove it to be of Irish or Welch origin, probably not earlier than the tenth century.

It consists of 309 pages, measuring 9 by 6½ inches, with 30 lines of different lengths across the page ; and contains a double version of the Psalter ; namely, the Gallican and that made by St. Jerome from the Hebrew : the former written in Roman demi-uncials, and the latter, on the opposite page, in a fine minuscule of Irish or Anglo-Saxon characters. This distinction, pointed out to me by M. Pottier [2] (the learned librarian of the Bibliothéque de Rouen), is carried through the volume ; but the text is interlined with a multitude of notes, written in extremely minuscule letters, precisely in the style of the Harleian Gospels, No. 1802, copies of several of which are given by the Benedictines, tom. iii., pl. 59, p. 444, 445.

Our fac-simile is the commencement of the 5th Psalm, and is to be read as follows :—

Gallican Version.	*Hebrew Version.*
Verba mea auribus percipe dn̄e	Verba mea audi dn̄e
intellige clamorem meum	intellige murmur meum
Intende voci orationis meæ	Rex meus et ds̄ meus
Rex meus et deus meus	

The heading of many of the psalms is written thus, " In finem Ψalmus David," &c., the Greek capital being used instead of the letters Ps.

The capital letters (whereof an extensive alphabetical series is given by the Benedictines [3]), are not ornamented with colours, but simply drawn with ink with the greatest precision ; neither are any of the Psalms (not even the 1st) distinguished by more elaborate initials. Some of these capitals are precisely similar to those of the Psalter of Ricemarchus.

---

[1] Sulien and his sons Rhyddmarch and Joan are honourably recorded in the Annals of the Welch church, at the end of the eleventh century. Williams' Ch. of Cymry, p. 162.

[2] M. Pottier has illustrated this MS. very fully with fac-similes in his forthcoming catalogue of the MSS. in the library under his care.

[3] N. Traité de Dipl., 2 pl. 18.

Exinde coepit ihs praedicare
et dicere poenitentiam agite
adpropin quauit enim
regnum Caelorum bffrz6

Purple Latin Gospels of the Anglo-Saxon School

PURPLE LATIN GOSPELS OF THE ANGLO-SAXON SCHOOL.

REFERENCE TO THE PLATE.

Portrait of Saint Mark.—First two Words (Quoniam quidem) of Saint Luke's Gospel, and Chap. iii., v. 1 and 2 of the Gospel of Saint Matthew.

THE Royal Manuscript preserved in the British Museum (marked 1 E 6,) must be esteemed one of the most precious monuments of early Anglo-Saxon caligraphy and illumination which have come down to our times. Its noble size (18 inches by 14), the clearness of the writing, united with the circumstance that several of its leaves are stained of a very dark purple colour, might lead almost to the presumption that this was the identical copy of the Gospels which St. Wilfred presented to the Church of York, and which his biographer Eddius described as a thing almost miraculous. From an inscription on the fly-leaf in a hand about 500 years old, the volume appears to have belonged to the Monastery of Saint Augustin, at Canterbury.

In its present state it comprises the greater portion of the four gospels in Latin, a few leaves having been sacrilegiously abstracted; but from the numeration of the quaternions (the first of which marks now remaining appears at the foot of the page containing the 10th Chapter of St. Matthew's Gospel, and is numbered lxxx; the last page of St. John's Gospel bearing the number lxxxviii), I presume that in the original state it must have contained the entire Bible. At present only 77 leaves remain, written on both sides in double columns, each containing forty-two lines. Both Casley [1] and Astle [2] concur in considering it to have been written in the 7th century. The first leaf is stained dark purple, on the reverse of which is inscribed, in letters an inch high, " Hæc est speciosa quadriga luciflua aiae [for animæ] sps gratia per os agni Di inlustratā in quo quattuor proceres consona voce magnalia dica [for dicant]." These form eight lines, which are alternately of gold and silver; and I have not the least doubt that, in the original splendid state of the volume, they were intended to apply to an illumination on an opposite purple leaf containing the symbolical representations of the four Evangelists. The majority of the letters in the inscriptions on this and the other purple leaves are tall Roman capitals well proportioned, with both ends of the thick strokes slightly dilated, and with the F, G, and P short-tailed, but they are intermixed with numerous uncial, and occasionally with square, letters, especially the C and G, the diamond-shaped O, and the S often appearing in its reversed Z-like form. The M is occasionally formed of three perpendicular strokes, the first and second united by one or two transverse bars, and the second and third by a single one. Casley (Cat. Roy. MSS., pl. xii.) has given a short specimen of these letters, copied by the Benedictines (N. Tr. de Dipl., vol. iii. pl. 37, IV. iii.), and Astle (pl. 18, v.) has also given a number of these capitals, but many of the most curiously formed ones are still unpublished.

The second leaf commences with the Epistle of Jerome to Pope Damasus, the inscription " Beato Papæ Damaso Hieronimus," being in large red uncial letters, forming three lines, and the initial N [3] of the first word. (Novum) is ornamented with a row of red dots on the sides of each stroke, the remainder being in the same hand as is employed throughout the Gospels. The last three lines of the Epistle, as well as the first five lines of the following page, containing the Capitula of the Gospel of St. Matthew, are also in red letters.

The tables of the Eusebian Canons commence on the recto of leaf 4, preceding which, however, are small portions of two leaves which have been cut out, one of a dark purple colour. The Canons are inscribed within narrow columns, most elaborately ornamented, a foot in height, supporting rounded arches, all being elegantly adorned with knots and scrolls, forming intricate patterns in numerous compartments, and with singular dragon-

[1] Cat. MSS. King's Lib. p. 12.
[2] Origin of Writing, p. 99, pl. 18, No. 5.
[3] The commencement of this epistle has been copied in fac-simile by Astle (pl. 18, v.); but he has omitted the red dots round the initial N which are so peculiarly characteristic of the Anglo-Saxon style.

1

like monsters, in the style of the Anglo-Saxon school, and margined with rows of red dots.[1] Five pages are occupied by these ten canons, after which it is evident that several pages have been abstracted, some of which were most probably purple and illuminated, containing the portrait of St. Matthew, and the commencement of his Gospel, as the 7th leaf commences with the passage "Joseph autem vir ejus," &c. being the 19th verse of Chap. i. of this Gospel.

The Gospel of St. Matthew terminates on the verso of leaf 28, and is followed by the ordinary "Evangelium sec Mattheu explicit. Incip Evangl sec Marcum, feliciter"—which are written in large red capitals; the contractions being, as usual, marked by a bar above the word, and followed by a small triangular red dot (occasionally radiated) placed half way between the top and bottom of the lines.

The next leaf is occupied with the introductory observations on St. Mark's Gospel, and is followed by a leaf of vellum stained of a dark purple colour, on the recto of which is inscribed, "Hic IHS baptizatus est ab Johanne in Jordane cœlis apertis Spu Sco in specie columba discendente sup eum voceq. paterna filius alti throni vocicatus."

These words (which were evidently intended to refer to a drawing of the Baptism of Christ in the River Jordan, which must have been cut out from the volume), are written in alternate lines of gold and silver, in capitals an inch high.

The verso of this purple leaf is occupied by a portrait of St. Mark, seated between two flesh-coloured, rudely daubed columns, supporting a rounded arch, and bearing a shield at the top, within which is a winged lion painted green, having the base of the wings red, and holding a book in the fore-feet; it is from a portion of this illumination that the portrait of St. Mark in my plate is taken. The Evangelist is represented as seated on a red cushion, holding in his hands a long scroll, which is given to him by a hand extended from a cloud in the top of the drawing, the scroll extending below his feet, where it is very rudely represented as wound round a roller. On the other side at the top of the drawing hangs a curtain looped up at the side. The colours are thick, and of course opake, and glossy, as though mixed up with some kind of varnish. The under robe of the Evangelist is of a dirty apple-green, and the upper one white, in which the only attempt to represent the folds of the drapery is effected by a number of dark brown or black lines, without any shading; on the under robe the lights are formed by a paler yellow body-colour, but still with the folds indicated by the single lines. The feet are naked, and like the hands greatly attenuated, according to the fashion of the Anglo-Saxon artists. The naked flesh is represented by an opake very pale salmon colour, relieved by opake white laid on in stripes, giving the flesh almost a tattooed appearance.

The whole picture is contained within a border of various colours about an inch broad, portions of which are foliated; the angles and centres with circular ornaments, which will, however, bear no comparison with the ornaments of the Eusebian Canons.

The Gospel of St. Mark (of which the first three verses are wanting, but which were evidently written originally on another purple ornamented leaf), commences on leaf 31 and extends to leaf 41, when it terminates at the 39th verse of the xvth chapter, the remainder (as well as from chap. iii. v. 32, to chap. v., 14) being cut out. Then follow the Capitula of St. Luke's Gospel (leaf 42), and these by two purple leaves, before which, however, two others have been cut out close to the binding.

The first of these two dark purple leaves is occupied by two most elaborately decorated columns supporting a rounded arch ornamented at the top with a miniature, which Casley considers to be that of St. Luke himself, but which appears to me to be intended for God the Father (as it is most probable that the portrait of St. Luke, painted in the same style as that of St. Mark, occupied one of the stolen purple leaves). This portrait represents an aged man with flowing hair and a short beard, and with the first and second fingers of the right hand extended. Beneath this miniature is painted a winged bull, the emblem of St. Luke; and in the middle of the leaf are written the two first words of St. Luke's Gospel, copied in my plate—

QNIAM
QUIDEM;

[1] The style of the ornaments of these columns is very similar to those given in the N. Traité de Dipl., vol. ii. pl. 18, in the initial letter of St. John's Gospel, from the famous Gospels of St. Germain des Prés, No. 108.

in letters of the most fantastical character, the initial Q exhibiting an excellent specimen of ornamental Saxon letters [1].

In this illumination, we perceive the strong taste of the Anglo-Saxon school for contrasts, not only appearing in the alternation of golden letters in a silver border and silver letters in a golden one, but also in the colouring of the opposite compartments in the rounded part of the Q. The strokes terminating in the heads of animals, with the elongated tongues twisted into interlaced ornaments, and the ornaments at the top of the long stroke of the Q, are particularly characteristic of Anglo-Saxon ornaments which were so much admired and imitated by the early Continental illuminators. The more abundant use of gold in the ornaments of this volume and the Psalter of Saint Augustine, distinguishes them from the Gospels of Lindisfarne and Mac Regol.

The second purple leaf is occupied by the inscription, in gold and silver capitals, " Hic Gabriel angelus Zachariæ sacerdoti in templo Dni apparuit almumq; prae cursore magni regis ei nasciturum prædixit,"—which evidently applies to a drawing now no longer in the book, representing the visit of the angel Gabriel to Zachariah.

Then follows the Gospel of St. Luke, extending from leaf 45 to leaf 67, the first four verses wanting, which evidently were originally written on another purple ornamented leaf.

At the end of St. Luke's Gospel another leaf is cut out, and then follow the Capitula of St. John's Gospel, and the Gospel itself; all the illuminations at its beginning being no longer found in the book. The first five verses, and all after chap. xi., v. 37, are also wanting.

It will be seen from the specimen at the foot of the plate, as well as from those given by Casley (copied in N. Tr. de Dipl., pl. 55, viii. iv. 2), and Astle (pl. 18, v.), that the text is written in a hand which may be considered partly semiuncial and partly minuscule. My specimen, containing the call to repentance by John the Baptist (Matth. iii., 1, 2), is to be read " Exinde coepit Ihs praedicare et dicere paenitentiam agite adpropinquavit enim regnum caelorum ;" in which we observe—1st, that although the diphthong oe is used in the second word, it is inaccurately altered to ae in pœnitentiam and cœlorum ; 2nd, that the name Johannes is contracted, like that of Jesus, into Ihs; and 3rd, that the version does not agree with the Vulgate [2]. Of the writing it is to be observed, that although Astle gives this MS. as a specimen of Roman Saxon (or that kind of Saxon writing which is very similar to the Roman, and may be deemed the oldest, and of which the Gospels, Cott. MS. Otho C. 5, and Reg. 1, B. 7 ; the Codex Rushworthanus, and the Charters of Kings Sebbi, A.D. 670, and Uihtredus (Withred), A.D. 693[3], are specimens) ; yet we nevertheless here see the transition to the more fixed Saxon characters exemplified ; the r, for instance, assuming its ꝑ or n form, and the e sometimes losing its rounded uncial Roman form, and appearing with the top elevated above the line ; the forms of the a, f, g, n, (in enim and regnum) &c., are also worthy of notice[4]. The s, on the contrary, retains its Roman form throughout. The larger letters at the beginning of each paragraph are chiefly uncial, as shown in my specimen, but various other-formed letters are also used, of which Astle has given an extensive collection (pl. 18, v.). In part of St. John's Gospel they are painted in the open parts with yellow and green, with marginal rows of red dots.

The first page of this Gospel offers a few specimens of the errors, &c., not unfrequently to be met with even in the finest early MSS. : thus,—Chap. i., v. 10, is written, " Et mundus per ipsum fuctus (for factus) est et mundus per ip eum non cognovit." The scribe having discovered his error in again writing per ip after the second word mundus, has not erased those letters with the knife, nor struck them through with the pen, but placed a row of dots above them. The word est is often contracted thus ÷ . " Mosen " is written for Moysen. " Dm nemo vidit umqua " for unquam. The word Johannes, rightly spelled as a nominative, has been repeatedly altered to Johannis[5], by a stroke through the e and a small i written above: e. g. " vidit Johannᵉs jhm," John seeth Jesus. The letter b is also often used for v, as in " serbasti " for servasti, in the MS. under notice.

[1] In some of the impressions of the plates the purple ground is represented of too light a tint.

[2] The Beatitudes, Matthew, v. 3–11, are as follows, according with the Vulgate version :—

" Beati pauperes spū quoniam ipsorum est regnum cœlorū.

" Beati mites, quō ipsi possidebunt terrā.

" Beati qui lugunt, quoniam ipsi consolabuntur.

" Beati qui esuriunt et sitiunt justitiā, quō ipsi saturabuntur.

" Beati misericordes, quō ipsi misericordiam consequentur.

" Beati mundo corde, quoniam ipsi Dm videbunt," &c.

And the Lord's Prayer (Matth. vi. 9–13) is as follows :—" Pater noster qui es in cœlis, scificetur nomen tuum. Adveniat regnum tuum. Fiat voluntas tua sicut in cœlo et in terra. Panem nostrum super substantialem da nobis hodie; et demitte nobis debita nostra sicut et nos demittimus debitoribus nostris. Et ne nos inducas in temptationem, sed libera nos a malo."

[3] A.D. 697, teste O'Conor Bibl. Stow. 2. 112.

[4] The single letters at the end of the specimen represent b, e, f, y, z, and &c.

[5] This erroneous spelling is occasionally met with in other very

3

From the portions which still remain of the present MS., it is evident that each Gospel was preceded by at least four purple leaves, on which were painted a large portrait of the Evangelist and an historical subject more especially described in an opposite inscription in gold and silver letters, together with one or two pages occupied by the first few verses of each Gospel. The loss of these drawings is greatly to be regretted, as they would have afforded a better idea of the style of early Anglo-Saxon composition and higher design than is afforded by any other coeval manuscript of the Gospels now existing.

In consequence of researches made since the above has been in part printed off, with a view to determine the identity of the manuscripts sent by Pope Gregory to St. Augustine, I infer that the MS. now under notice is no other than the remains of the Gregorian Bibl e described at the head of these manuscripts, by a monk of the Abbey of St. Augustine, in the time of Henry V., in a MS. History of the Monastery of Augustine, and the Church of Christ at Canterbury[1], and where Wanley[2] considered it most probable that the MS. remained until the time of Henry VIII.

It is true that Casley, Astle, and Sir F. Madden, describe this MS. merely as a copy of the four Gospels, without any intimation of its being but a small portion of a more extended codex; the last-named writer having, in an opposite note[3], alluded to the Gregorian Bible and its stained leaves. The following description will, however, be seen to accord completely with the MS. before us :—" Imprimis habetur in librario, BIBLIA GREGORIANA, in duobus voluminibus: quorum primum habet rubricam in primo folio de capitulis libri Genesis: secundum volumen incipit prologo beati Jeronimi super Ysaiam prophetam. In *principio vero librorum in eisdem voluminibus inseruntur quædam folia, quorum aliqua purpurei aliqua rosei sunt coloris*, quæ contra lucem extensa mirabilem reflexionem ostendunt[4]."

Of all the Augustine MSS.—(the " primitie librorum totius ecclesie anglicane "—as they are called by the annalist above mentioned ;) Wanley justly observes that the " Biblia Gregoriana duobus voluminibus scripta agmen ducunt[5];" adding that these volumes were in existence no long time previous to his researches, since, in the Apologetic Petition of the Catholic Laics, presented to King James I. in July, 1604, they were expressly described in these words :—" 𝕿𝖍𝖊 𝖇𝖊𝖗𝖞 𝖔𝖗𝖎𝖌𝖎𝖓𝖆𝖑 𝕭𝖎𝖇𝖑𝖊, 𝖙𝖍𝖊 𝖘𝖊𝖑𝖋𝖘𝖆𝖒𝖊 𝕹𝖚𝖒𝖊𝖗𝖔 𝖜𝖍𝖎𝖈𝖍 𝕾. 𝕲𝖗𝖊𝖌𝖔𝖗𝖞 𝖘𝖊𝖓𝖙 𝖎𝖓 𝖜𝖎𝖙𝖍 𝖔𝖚𝖗 𝕬𝖕𝖔𝖘𝖙𝖑𝖊 𝕾. 𝕬𝖚𝖌𝖚𝖘𝖙𝖎𝖓𝖊, 𝖇𝖊𝖎𝖓𝖌 𝖆𝖘 𝖞𝖊𝖙 𝖕𝖗𝖊𝖘𝖊𝖗𝖛𝖊𝖉 𝖇𝖞 𝕲𝖔𝖉'𝖘 𝖘𝖕𝖊𝖈𝖎𝖆𝖑 𝖕𝖗𝖔𝖛𝖎𝖉𝖊𝖓𝖈𝖊." Which words were also cited by Sutcliffe, in his answer to the same petition (p. 87). Hence it is evident that Wanley, who travelled through the whole of England, in order to discover MSS. of the Anglo-Saxon age, had failed in discovering any traces of them, and no subsequent author has succeeded in recognising them.

The inscription also at the beginning of the volume, " Liber Sancti Augustini Cantuariensis," evidently alludes to the tradition of the book having belonged to St. Augustine himself. If, however, the MS. be portion of the Bible of St. Augustine, it is clear that it is not of Continental origin, both from the writing and ornaments : but that it was not executed in England in the time of St. Augustine[6], and might not actually have belonged to him, is by no means so clear. We may, indeed, easily conceive that our Apostle would have been most anxious to provide his disciples with a standard copy of the Holy Scriptures, upon which he would employ all the talents of his immediate followers.

---

ancient MSS. It occurs, in a collection of Canons, made and written in the middle of the 6th century (see N. Tr. de Dipl. 3, pl. 51, III. 3, iii.) and a specimen from the Anglo-Saxon Gospels of St. Germain des Prés, No. 108, is given in the last-mentioned work, 3, pl. 47, VI. 3, ii., in which the word was originally written with a capital I, but which has been altered to a square capital E ; as is evident not only from the want of space, but also because all the rest of the letter E's are of the rounded form. It also occurs in the Irish MS. called the Leabhar Dhimma, which Sir W. Betham considers as of the 7th century ; in the Cambridge Gospels of the 6th century, (Astle, pl. 15, ii. ;) in the Irish Harleian Gospels, No. 1802, and even in the Papyrus Act of

Donation to the Church of Ravenna in the 6th century, preserved in the Vatican (N. Tr. de Dipl. 3, pl. 64).

[1] The MS. containing this History is preserved in the library of Trinity Coll., Cambridge, and is described by Wanley in Hickes' Thesaurus, vol. ii. p. 172.

[2] Hickes Thes. ut supra.

[3] Introd. to Shaw's Ill. Ornaments, p. 4, 5, in notes.

[4] Smith's Bede, App. p. 690.

[5] Hickes Thesaurus, vol. ii. p. 173.

[6] Sir F. Madden refers it " unquestionably to the 8th century," Mr. Shaw (Alphabets, pl. 1) to the 10th.

ASCENSIO DÑI

VIRI GALILEI

MA RIA

E
A
TVS
VIR

qui

NON ABIIT IN CON SI
LIO IMPIORUM

&inuiapeccatorum non st&it &incathe
dra pestilentiae non sedit

The Psalter of King Athelstan.

PSALTER OF KING ATHELSTAN.

THE little volume, from which the accompanying fac-similes have been taken, is one of the most interesting of all the Cottonian MSS.; first, in consequence of portion of it having been written (as is supposed) in this country so early as the year 703; and, secondly, because it appears sufficiently evident that the Psalter belonged to King Athelstan, the first page bearing an inscription to that effect in the handwriting of "Thomas Rector de Cobbrok, Wynton, 1542." Moreover, on the reverse of the same leaf we find the same fact stated by Sir R. Cotton himself; the second leaf also bears an interpolated beautiful illumination, apparently of the early part of the 15th century (let into a marginal border of the 16th), representing a King kneeling to the Creator, who appears in the clouds, and bearing the inscription in gold letters, on a blue ground, " Psalterium Athelstani Regis," written in Roman capitals, but almost effaced, and the blue colour partly peeled off, disclosing a *set-off* of the modern gothic writing, which was written upon the back of the vellum, on which the miniature of the King is drawn. This treatment is precisely similar to that which the Coronation Oath Book of King Athelstan (Tiberius, A. 2) has undergone; whence, as well as from the similarity in the calligraphy, we are led to suppose that the part of this MS. containing the Psalter proceeded from the same school, and passed through the same hands as that volume; the entry in this Psalter of the deaths of Charlemagne, Pippin, &c., will further account for its having come into possession of King Athelstan, from his connection with the Emperor Otho.

The volume consists of three parts. 1st, the Calendar, with the various rules for finding Easter, &c., lunar tables and other matters of that kind, written in early Anglo-Saxon characters; 2nd, the Psalter, with its prefaces written in a later beautiful Caroline minuscule hand; and, 3rd, a series of short Prayers, (one for each Psalm,) at the end of the volume, written in early Anglo-Saxon characters.

This manuscript contains 200 leaves of vellum, measuring 5 inches by $3\frac{3}{4}$; the early part of the MS. contains 22 lines, the Psalter, 19, and the Prayers at the end, 19 or 20 lines in a page.

The verso of the 2nd page is occupied by a drawing of Christ, seated on a throne, ornamented with a crucifix, and with a chorus of angels on each side of the upper part of the page; a chorus of Prophets, occupying the lower part of the drawing. Most of the figures wear the hair parted in front, but one has the crown of the head tonsured; the two middle compartments are occupied only by heads of some of the Prophets. The corners of the frame-work are ornamented with lions' heads. The style of this drawing is rude, the outlines formed by thick strokes of a pen; and the colours (except the blue), dull, heavy, and opaque. The drawing copied in my figure, No. 1, although bound up with the later part of the MS. is unquestionably from the same school as the earlier portion, agreeing with the miniature on the verso of leaf 2, as well as with the drawings in the Calendar, in style, execution, and colours. This miniature of the Ascension is a far more pleasing composition than the former, and, as a very early specimen of art in this country, is particularly valuable —being totally unlike the later Anglo-Saxon style, and exhibiting none of the awkward attenuation of limbs, and fluttering of draperies, by which the drawings of the 10th and 11th centuries were so particularly distinguished. Herein, in fact, we recognise more of the style of Eastern art; and it is interesting to trace the traditional mode of pictorially treating the Ascension, as exhibited in this drawing [1].—In my account of the Syriac [2] MSS. will be

---

[1] The Ascension, in the famous Bible of Charlemagne, at Rome, is treated quite differently; see D'Agincourt's Peint., pl. xliii. fig. 4.

[2] I have in the same article also alluded to the similarity between the ornaments in the ancient Syriac MS. of Rabula, and those in the most ancient Anglo-Saxon MSS., and may here further mention that the very peculiar and common pattern found in early Irish and Anglo-Saxon MSS., formed of several slender spiral lines united in the centre of the circle, with the ends dilated, is evidently identical (although on a smaller scale) with the pattern which the artist of the drawing of the Miracle at the Pool of Bethesda (copied in my plate) has employed to represent the waves in the pool. These apparently trifling circumstances seem to me to prove more forcibly than the most laborious arguments, the connection between the early Christians in these islands, and those of the East, so strongly insisted upon by various writers.

found the description of a very ancient drawing of the same subject, which greatly resembles this in style, but contains representations of the flaming chariot and winged symbols of the Evangelists. In the drawing before us, we however notice, that the nimbus of Christ is cruciferous, and the right hand raised in the act of benediction, but with all the fingers extended, (contrary to the practice in the Romish church). Here, too, as well as in the other miniature copied in my plate, we find the Saviour represented according to the most ancient type of Christ, as a young man, and without a beard.

A calendar, with figures of the zodiacal signs at the head of each month, and with ornamental initial letters (KL), and *tail-pieces*—extends to the verso of leaf 15. The style of these drawings will be seen from my figures, 2 and 3, the former of which represents an Ecclesiastic habited in a blue dalmatica, (rather than a chasuble), a pallium without any ornament, and with the alb(?) and the two ends of the stole(?) visible above the feet; the head is not tonsured, although an evidently later hand has endeavoured to supply that distinction by a black stroke over the forehead, which I have omitted. In another of these little drawings, however, we find the crown of the head represented properly as tonsured[1].

The festivals and Saints' days are introduced into this Calendar in Latin verses, which hence possess considerable interest.

To these succeed various rules and directions for finding the epacts, lunar tables, paschal moons, &c. &c., amongst which is the article copied in my fac-simile, No. 5, which is to be read as follows:

" Argumentum ad inveniendum quotus sit annus Domini."

" Si nosse vis quot sint ab incarnatione Dñi scito quot fuerint ordines indictionū ut puta v. anno tyberii cæseris xlvi. hos per xv multiplica fiunt dcxc. adde semper regulares xii quia iiii indictionū [e] secundum dionissiū dñs natus[2] est indictione q̄q̄. cujus volueris ut puta in presenti i fiunt dcciii. isti sunt anni nativitatis dni."

This rule was considered by Sir R. Cotton as proving that the MS. was written in the year DCCIII. It is to be observed, however, that we find this rule and example in MSS. of a much later date than the one before us, as in the Cottonion MS. Jul., A. 6, which was evidently written about the end of the 10th century (and most probably at Hyde Abbey), so that we ought perhaps rather to consider this as a formula to be adopted, with an example, than as a proof of the year in which this part of the MS. was written, which must, however, be referred to the eighth century.

The 21st leaf is occupied by a miniature of Christ, seated within the Vesica piscis (copied in my figure 6) and surrounded by the choruses of martyrs, virgins, &c. This drawing is entirely in a different style to the two other miniatures, being far more carefully drawn with opaque colours, a brick-red being especially prevalent. This drawing I apprehend to be coæval with the Psalter, and to have been executed on the Continent. We possess too few Frankish monuments of art of this early period in this country, to allow of an extended comparison therewith, but this little drawing is far superior as a work of art to the miniatures in the Alcuin Bible, or the Golden Gospels in the British Museum.

To these succeed various prayers on the 22d and 23d leaves, written in Caroline minuscule characters, and on the 24th are entries of the deaths of " Carolus imperator, Pepinus rex, Bernardus R., Woradus dux," and " Himildruda comitessa," written in a kind of Lombardic minuscule. These are followed by prefaces to the " Psalterium de translatione lxx. interpretum emendata a Sco Hieronymo presbytero in novo," which extends to the 162d leaf, on the verso of which is written the apocryphal Psalm of David, when he fought with Goliath.

This is followed by various canticles from the Old and New Testaments, the Lord's Prayer, Athanasian Creed, Te Deum laudamus, Gloria in excelsis, &c., which extend to the 182d leaf, the whole being written in a delicate Caroline minuscule character, the nearest resemblance to which occurs in a specimen given by the Benedictines of the time of King Pipin.[3]

The titles of the different prefaces to the Psalms are written in large golden Roman capital letters, each occupying an entire page; and the commencements of the 1st, 52nd, and 102nd Psalms are also written in golden capital and uncial letters, the initial being highly ornamented, the first of these being copied in my plate (No. 7), at the foot of which two lines from the next page are added to show the ordinary character of the writing of this part of the MS.,—the words of which are often not distinct; the et conjoined, and the f sometimes extending below the line. The style of the splendid initial letter (b) resembles that in the Coronation

---

[1] I am inclined to think that this is by far the earliest drawing of an Ecclesiastic hitherto published.

[2] See Beda, De Temporibus, n. 14.

[3] N. Tr., De Dipl. pl. LIII. iii. 3.

Book of the Anglo-Saxon kings; but the initials of the two other Psalms mentioned above are much more foliated in their terminal ornaments. The specimen is to be read—

BEATUS VIR QUI NON ABIIT IN CONSILIO IMPIORUM
et in via peccatorum non stetit et in cathedra
pestilentiae non sedit.

The remaining leaves are occupied by short Latin collects upon each Psalm, which are written in Anglo-Saxon characters, the last leaf containing the litany according to the Greek Church, the Lord's Prayer (without the Doxology), the Apostles' Creed, and Trisagium; these articles being in the Greek language, but spelled according to the pronunciation of the time, and written in Anglo-Saxon letters—a peculiarity already noticed in the article on Græco-Latin MSS. The fac-simile numbered 4 is the Lord's Prayer, which is to be read as follows, the proper Greek being here introduced above the lines:—

[Πατερ ημων ο εν τοις ουρανοις αγιασθητω το οναμα σου ελθετω η Βασιλεια σου γενηθητω το θελημα σου ως εν ουρανω και επι της
Pater imon o yn ys uranis agiastitu to onoman su elthetu e basilia s genitthito to theliman su oss en uuranu. ke pi as

γης τον αρτον ημων τον επιουσιον δος ημιν σημερον και αφες ημιν τα οφειλημματα ημων ως και ημεις αφιεμεν τοις οφειλεταις ημων και μη
gis ton arton imon ton epiussion doss imin simero ke affis imin ta offilemata imon os ke imis affiomen tas ophiletas imon ke mi

εισενεγκης ημας εις πειρασμον αλλα ρυσαι ημας απο του πονηρου.]
esininkis imas is perasmon ala ryse imas api tu poniru.

Dr. Lingard, who has given a (not quite correct) copy of this translation, considers, notwithstanding the evident errors which it presents, that it may hence be inferred that not only the vowel ι, but also η, and the diphthongs ει and οι were generally sounded alike, and expressed by the Anglo-Saxon i; and that the diphthong αι had the long slender sound of the present English a, and therefore was always expressed by the Anglo-Saxon letter e. In these respects the pronunciation of our ancestors appears to agree perfectly with the pronunciation of the modern Greeks.[1]

The custom of writing one language in the characters of another, is of great antiquity, and the instances of its occurrence in manuscripts and inscriptions are of great rarity. Origen wrote the Hebrew text of the second column of his Hexapla in Greek characters; and even the Jews themselves sometimes employed the same usage.[2] Maffei speaks of some books written in the German and Italian languages, printed in Hebrew text; and has published, at the end of his "Diplomatic History," some compositions written in Latin upon papyrus, but in Greek characters, observing that the early Christians often wrote in this manner. Even at the present time, when the Pope performs Mass, the Epistle and Gospel are read both in Latin and Greek, in honour of the Greek Church; and Maffei quotes the following passage from a MS. of the twelfth or thirteenth century:—"Leguntur in quibusdam ecclesiis xxiv. lectiones, xii. græce et xii. latine: græce propter auctoritatem lxx. interpretum quorum auctoritas floruit in Græcia; latine propter auctoritatem Hieronymi cujus translatio prevaluit in Italia." And as the Greek language was but little studied in the West, it became necessary to write it in Latin for the use of those who were ignorant of the Greek, so as to enable them to recite such passages in the latter language; and hence the Hymns, Creed, &c., and other Greek articles written in Latin characters, found in ancient books of the Service of the Roman Church. Hence, also, Mabillon derives the ancient practice of saying the Mass in Greek and Latin, in the Abbey of St. Denis, in France,[3] on the five chief feasts of the year.

The Bodleian Library possesses a very interesting and ancient MS., "De Officio Missæ," written in early Anglo-Saxon or Irish characters, which also notices this diglot usage in the Church, and which thus commences:—"Primum in ordine misse antifona ad introitum canitur *antifona græce latine vox reciproca interpretatur*."[4]

[1] Lingard, Antiq. of Anglo-Saxon Church, p. 521, who quotes De la Rocca, Précis historique sur l'Isle de Syra, p. 159, Paris, 1790. "Dans ai, ei, oi, η, υ, les Ellénistes de Paris, prétendent qu'il faut prononcer les trois premières comme si elles étoient deux lettres aï, eï, oï; à l'égard des deux autres la première comme e, la seconde comme i. Nous prononçons au contraire la première comme e, et les quatres autres comme i."

[2] Maffei, oposc. eccles. col. 64.
[3] De re Diplom. p. 367.
[4] MS. Bodl. Hatton 56, and see Hickes' Thes. vol. i. 176, for a fac-simile. The ornamental initial letter is very similar to that at the beginning of the Kalendar in the Psalter of King Athelstan; part of the tail of the P is however omitted by Hickes.

That this custom of writing Greek in Latin characters was not so entirely caused by the ignorance of those for whom the MSS. were written, seems evident from the circumstance that the occurrence of Latin written in Greek characters is more frequent than the reverse case. In many cases, indeed, the custom appears to be but the result of the fancy of the moment, and seems to indicate that the scribe and his readers were as well versed in one as the other language. Instances in support of this opinion, as shewn in the employment of Greek words and letters in Latin inscriptions, and indeed the substitution of Greek for Roman letters in entire passages, will be found in another article of this work.

The following, in addition to the instances mentioned in the article on the Græco-Latin MSS. and the Psalter of King Athelstan above described, are the only notices I have found of the use of Roman instead of Greek letters:—

The Cottonian MS., Titus, D. 18, contains the Lord's Prayer, a Hymn, and short Greek Liturgy, all in the Greek language, but written in Roman characters.

Hickes, in the Preface to his Thesaurus (p. 19), has also given the Lord's Prayer in Greek, but written in Roman characters, from a MS. in the public library of Cambridge, and also from a Sacramentary at Rome.

Mabillon [1] has given a specimen from the Codex Dyonisianus, supposed to be of the 9th century, which also shows that this mode of writing Greek was not peculiar to the inhabitants of these islands. It is as follows, the true Greek text being here interlined:—

[Πιστευω εις ενα θεον πατερα   και εις το πνευμα το αγιον το κυριον και ζωοποιον το εκ του πατρος.]
Pisteugo is ena theon patera . . . . ke is to pneuma to agion to kyrion ke   zoopion to et tu patros.

And

[Gla in excelsis do et sup ra pax.]
Doxa en upsistys theo ke epi gis irini.

The Benedictines have given a few specimens in which Greek was written in Latin characters, as in the Bible of St. Germain des Prés, No. 17, written about the year 822, where we find the Greek Doxology thus written:—DOXA PATRI KE IO KE AIO PEUMATI KE NIN KE AI KE IS TOS ENISTOS. AMIN. KE being written for και, IO for υιω, AIO for αγιω, PEUMATI for πνευματι, IS TOS ENISTOS for εις τους ενιαυτους. Thus showing the mode in which Greek was pronounced in France in the reign of Louis le Débonnaire.[2]

Another not less curious instance occurs in the singular MS. called the Sacramentary of Gelloni, written in the 8th century, and of which a fac-simile is given by the Benedictines (plate 47, iv. i.). It is as follows:—

[Ου της βασιλιας ουκ εστι η τελος και εις το πνευμα το αγιον κυριον και ζωοποιον το εκ του πατρος επορευομενον.]
U this basilias uc esti e thelus ke his tho pneuma to agion kyrion ke os opion tho ec tu patros ecporegomenon.

The Benedictines have moreover given numerous examples of inscriptions upon very ancient coins and marbles in which the Latin and Greek letters were intermingled together, both in writing Greek and Latin (N. Tr. Dipl. ii. p. 636, et seq.); and have shown that this practice prevailed in France, Spain, and England, as well as in Italy, from the 5th to the 9th or 10th centuries.

[1] De re Diplom. p. 382 and 383 ; tab. 12, fig. 3.   [2] N. Tr. Dipl. 3, 129.

Scōm Lucam

M
QVI
DEM

multi conati sunt ordinare
narrationem. quae innobis

☩ In nomine dñi nr̄i ihū xp̄i Hen is appiten.
Cnutes. kynges nama þe is ure leofa
hlaford for populde.] ure zastlica broðor
forzode.] harold ðæs kinges broðor.

The Gospels of K. Canute.

THE LATIN GOSPELS OF KING CANUTE.

DESCRIPTION OF THE PLATE.

Commencement of the Gospel of St. Luke, beneath which is the inscription relating to King Canute.

THE handsome manuscript from which the accompanying Plate is taken is preserved amongst the Royal MSS. in the British Museum, where it is marked 1 D. 9. It consists of 150 leaves of vellum, measuring 13½ by 10½ inches, and in a full page comprises 26 lines. It consists of the four Gospels, with the ordinary prologues of Jerome, but without the tables of the Eusebian Canons (the last leaf of the Gospel of St. John wanting), and which are followed by the Index of the Dominican Gospels, as appointed to be read throughout the year. The hand in which it is written is a firm-set Saxon, strongly tinctured with the Caroline minuscule. The two lines in the Plate printed in gold will serve to show the style of writing adopted throughout. The small *a* (occasionally, as in the second syllable of the word narrationem) and the *t* retain their Saxon form, but the *r* and *s* are nearly of the ordinary Roman form. The first two words in the Plate, *Secundum Lucam*, are written in rustic capitals, and the *Quoniam* quidem in Roman majuscule characters. The N at the beginning of the word narationem retains its ancient Anglo-Saxon form.

Before the commencement of St. Mark's Gospel is the following Anglo-Saxon inscription, apparently written in a different hand from the text of the volume, being, as we learn from Wanley[1], a certificate or testimonial of the reception of King Canute and others into the family or society of the Church of Christ at Canterbury.

"In nomine dni nri ihu xpi. Heꞃ iſ aꞃꞃiten Cnutes kẏnᵹeſ nama þe iſ uꞃe leoᵹa hlaꞃoꞃð ꞃoꞃ populðe ꞃ uꞃe ᵹaſtlica bꞃoðoꞃ ꞃoꞃᵹoðe ꞃ haꞃolð ðæſ kinᵹeſ bꞃoðoꞃ.

"Ðoꞃð uꞃe bꞃoðoꞃ Kaꞃtoca uꞃe bꞃoðoꞃ Thuꞃi uꞃe bꞃoðoꞃ." i. e.

In the name of Our Lord Jesus Christ. Here is written Canute the king's name. He is our beloved Lord worldwards, and our spiritual brother Godwards; and Harold this king's brother; Thorth our brother; Kartoca our brother; Thuri our brother.

On the next leaf is the entry of a Charter of the same king, also in the Anglo-Saxon language, confirming the privileges of the same church, as follows :—

"Cnut cinᵹ ᵹꞃet lẏꞃinᵹ aꞃceᵬ. ꞃ ᵹoðꞃine ᵬ. ꞃ ælmeꞃ abb. ꞃ æþelꞃine ꞃciꞃman ꞃ æþelꞃic. ꞃ ealle mine þeᵹneꞃ tꞃelꞃhẏnðe. ꞃ tꞃihẏnðe ꞃꞃeonðlice. ꞃ ic cẏðe eoꞃ ꝥꞃe aꞃceᵬ ᵹꞃæc to me ymbe xpeꞃ cẏꞃcean ꞃꞃeolꞃ. ꝥ heo hæꞃð nu læꞃꞃe munðe þon hiꞃ hꞃilan æꞃ hæꞃðe. þa lyꞃðe ic him ꝥ he moꞃte nꞃꞃne ꞃꞃeolꞃe ꞃettan on minam naman. þa cꞃeð he to me ꝥ he ꞃꞃeolꞃaꞃ ᵹenoᵹe hæꞃðe ᵹẏꞃ hi aht ꞃoꞃꞃtoðan. þa nam ic me ꞃẏlꞃ þa ꞃꞃeolꞃaꞃ ꞃ ᵹeleðe hi uppan xpeꞃ aᵹen peoꞃoð on þæꞃ aꞃceᵬ ᵹe ꞃilnyꞃꞃe. ꞃ on þuꞃkilleꞃ eoꞃleꞃ. ꞃ oꞃ maneᵹꞃa Goððꞃa manna þe me miðꞃætꞃion to ðan ẏlcan ꞃoꞃe þeaꞃðan þe hit æþelbyꞃht cinᵹ ᵹeꞃꞃeoðe ꞃ ealle mine ꞃoꞃe ᵹeneᵹan. ꝥ næeꞃꞃne nan man ne ꞃẏ ꞃꞃa ðyꞃꞃti. ꞃy he ᵹe haðoð. ꞃẏ he læꞃoðe ꝥ æniᵹ þaꞃa þinᵹa ᵹe lythe þe on ðam ꞃꞃeolꞃe ꞃtænt. ᵹẏꞃ hit hꞃa ꝥ ænne ðo. ꞃy hiꞃ liꞃ heꞃ ᵹeꞃceꞃt. ꞃ hiꞃ þununᵹ on helleᵹꞃunðe butan he hit þe ꞃtiðlicoꞃ ᵹe bete æꞃ his ænðe be þæꞃ aꞃcebiꞃceoꞃeꞃ tæcinᵹᵹe."

These entries, together with the circumstance that the volume was certainly written about the beginning of the 11th century, and that its splendour well merited the ownership of royalty, have evidently led to the tradition of its having been the property of King Canute himself, who most probably bestowed it upon the Cathedral at Canterbury, to which, as we have seen in the article on the Gospels of Mac Durnan, he was a great donor. Indeed, from his donations as well as his devotion to the church he was surnamed the Pious[2]. His pilgrimage to Rome, and his munificence to the two great monasteries in St. Omer's, and other churches, have been recorded by the grateful recipients of his bounty[3].

---

[1] Hickes' Thesaurus, vol. ii. p. 181.
[2] Turner, Anglo-Saxons, iii. p. 280 ; and Hickes, in Dedication to Thesaurus.
[3] See Matth. Westm. 404, 405, 409 ; Wise's Asser. 126 ; Encom.

Emmæ, 173, &c. His donations of an arm of St. Bartholomew, and of an arm of St. Augustin, to different churches, have been recorded, as well as the great sums he paid for these relics.

1

The first few words of each Gospel are written in golden letters, the initial being of large size, and inclosed in a magnificent border, each varying from the rest, and also having its different divisions ornamented with different patterns. The very peculiar character of these ornaments, so entirely unlike those of the earlier Anglo-Saxon school, in which the pattern was composed of elaborate interlacings, and at the same time so different from the illuminations of any other country, will best be learned by an inspection of the accompanying Plate. They may perhaps be most appropriately described as an attempt to combine the taste of the richer Roman architecture, in which variations of the antique acanthus make the chief figure, with the earlier inter-laced style of the Anglo-Saxons; for it will be perceived that the foliage is not only made to fold over and under the different bars of blue and gold, but also to interlace with the adjacent leaves. This style of ornament was not confined however to manuscripts, for we find it appearing in the capitals of some of our early English churches, as in St. John's, Chester, and in Steetly church, in Derbyshire; as also on the ornament at the top of the crozier of Archbishop Ataldus, who died 933, and which was found in his tomb, placed in the choir of the cathedral at Sens, figured by Willemin.

The Gospel of St. Matthew commences on the 6th leaf, the initial L in the first word (*liber*) being of large size, and of the rounded form common in early manuscripts. This, as well as the initial I at the beginning of each of the Gospels of St. Mark and St. John, is ornamented somewhat in the style of the initial letter of the Coronation Book of the Anglo-Saxon Kings. Mr. Shaw having copied one of the letters, I, in the fifth subject of his " Dresses and Decorations," I have selected the Q, especially as it affords a good example of the Anglo-Saxon style of drawing, and wherein the attenuated extremities and fluttering drapery are conspicuously treated. The gold in this MS. has apparently been applied in leaves, and which has tarnished in parts. The colours are laid on very thick and glossy, the lights being generally produced by opaque white or yellow colours.

The number of MSS. executed in the style of that now under consideration, with which we are acquainted, is very small. The noblest is, unquestionably, the Benedictional of Ethelwold, belonging to the Duke of Devonshire, written about 980; and which, Dr. Waagen says, surpasses, in the number and splendour of the pictures and the rich ornaments of the borders, all the other Anglo-Saxon MSS. which he had seen in England. This volume has been fully described in the 24th Volume of the Archæologia, wherein outline fac-similes of all the illuminations are published, as well as by Dibdin[4], Waagen[5], and others.

Another MS. of the Gospels, of exquisite richness and dazzling splendour, in the same style, is in the library of Trinity College, Cambridge, and which, in the style of its execution, is far superior to the Gospels of Canute. This is likewise adorned with miniatures of single figures, as of Christ, and the four Evangelists. There are also two celebrated MSS. in the same style in the public library at Rouen, which have been described and illustrated in the Archæologia (vol. 24), and by Dibdin, Turner, Sylvestre, Willemin, and others. Both these MSS. have the advantage of being adorned with miniatures of scriptural subjects, such as the Nativity, Flight into Egypt, &c., and as it is nearly certain that both are of English origin, they are important monuments of art, as it appeared in this country at the beginning of the eleventh century.

The British Museum possesses two other examples of this style (but destitute of gold in the illuminations), namely, the Arundelian Psalter, No. 83, and Cottonian Psalter Tiberius, C. 6; but as both these are furnished with an Anglo-Saxon interlineary version, they will be described in another article of this Work.

The following notice, by William of Malmsbury[6], seems almost especially to refer to the artist, by whom the book before us was executed[7]. " Habebat tunc [Wolstanus] magistrum *Ervenium* nomine inscribendo et quidlibet *coloribus effingendo* peritum. Is libros scriptos, sacramentarium et psalterium quorum principales *litteras auro effigiaverit,* puero Wolstano delegandos curavit. Ille preciosorum apicum captus miraculo, dum pulchritudinem intentis oculis rimatur, scientiam litterarum internis hausit medullis. Verum doctor ad sæculi spectans commodum spe majoris pretii *sacramentarium regi, tunc temporis Cnutoni, psalterium Emmæ reginæ, contribuit.*"

---

4 Bibl. Decam. 1, p. lix.

5 Art and Artists in England, iii. p. 232.

6 In his life of St. Wolstan, who was bishop of Worcester in 1062.

7 An occasion will occur in another article of this work to mention some particulars respecting other contemporary artists.

Insto
Anno
Tuildo
tanus
Rex ka
Rolus
Ausem
Perum
Hbap
tizatus
est fi
lius
eius
pippi
nus Adom
no A
Posto
lico

EVANGELISTARIUM
Charlemagne

Finit Deo Gratias
Hoc opus eximium francho
rum scribere Carlus:;
Rexpius egregie hildgarda
cum coniuge iussit;

DEFUNCTO AUTEM
HERODE ECCE ANGE
LUS DNI APPARUIT
IN SOMNIS JOSEPH
INAECYPTO DICENS

THE EVANGELISTIARIUM OF CHARLEMAGNE.

DESCRIPTION OF THE PLATE.

Miniature of Christ, group of birds and ornamental details, together with the large golden initial letters at the commencement of the volume (In illo tempore), portion of the text (Matth. ii. 19), and of the Latin verse at the end of the volume, together with the entry concerning the baptism of the emperor's son Pippin at Rome, in the year 781.

THE entire social disorganization naturally consequent upon the destruction of one great empire, and the establishment of another in its stead, cannot be otherwise than accompanied by a general neglect of the more refined arts of mankind. Hence it is, that from the period of the final overthrow of the Roman empire, in 476, by Odoacer, until the middle of the eighth century, the arts of writing, drawing, &c., were almost at the lowest possible ebb. The few manuscripts of this period which have survived to our times are full of examples of barbarous Latinity, and the writing itself is almost as bad as it became during the reign of the miserable modern gothic style.

The establishment of the empire of the West by Charlemagne's subjugation of the Lombards, Bohemians, and Huns, was accompanied by a revival of learning under the auspices of that great emperor, whose zeal for the propagation of religion and letters has been rewarded by the applause of all subsequent historians. To his fostering care the universities, of Paris (the mother of all the academies of the west), Pavia and Bologna owe their origin; whilst his patronage of Willehad, the Anglo-Saxon missionary of Friesland, and of Alcuin, the greatest Anglo-Saxon scholar of his day, gives him a claim to our national respect.

The protection afforded to the Church by Charlemagne, the imposition of tithes made by him for the support of the clergy, churches, and poor; the forcible conversion to Christianity of the conquered Witikind and his Saxon followers, and the confirmation of the patrimony of St. Peter to the Popes of Rome (being the foundation of their temporal sovereignty), are all evidences of his zeal for the diffusion of religion; whilst of his care for the welfare of letters, it is said by one of the most competent writers, " Charlemagne fit à la vérité changer la face de la littérature—L'orthographie prit un état de consistence qu'elle n'avoit point éprouvé jusqu'alors."[1] And in one of his letters, which has been preserved, he himself says, " Because it is our care that the state of our churches should ever progress in improvement, we have laboured by vigilant study to renovate the sources of literature, almost obliterated through the negligence of our forefathers, and by our example to incite to the study of the sacred Scriptures."[2] Not content with correcting with his own hand the MSS. of his age[3] (and of which the title bestowed upon him by his contemporaries, " Studiosus in arte librorum," bears ample testimony), he ordered that all priests should make themselves familiar with the Greek and Latin languages, and that every bishop, abbot, and count should retain a secretary to write correctly; and that only persons of mature age and skill should be allowed to copy the Gospels, Psalter, or Missal.[4] Hence the form of the letters themselves was greatly improved or renewed.[5] The fine old Roman capitals were again employed,[6] and the uncial and minuscule were so greatly polished in appearance that they have acquired a distinct name in the science of diplomatics—namely, that of the CAROLINE.

These ample claims on the good services of the ecclesiastics of his time are proved by the many fine volumes offered by them to the emperor on different occasions, and which exhibit the state of the arts of the time, as we may suppose, in its highest state of development; as such, they are therefore important landmarks in the history of the sciences of caligraphy and artistic design.

The manuscript from which the fac-similes in the accompanying plate were copied, is justly regarded as one of the most precious of the Charlemagne relics. It is an Evangelistiarium, or copy of those portions of the Gospels (about two hundred and forty in number) used in the service of the Church, and is throughout written in golden uncial letters upon leaves of stained purple vellum, in double columns, surrounded on all sides and separated by ornamental borders about half an inch wide, the space outside the borders not being stained

[1] N. Traité de Dipl. iv., 497.
[2] Mabillon, Annal. Benedict. ii., p. 328.
[3] A MS. of Origen's Commentary on the Epistle to the Romans, corrected by Charlemagne, is described by the Benedictines as being still preserved in the Bibliothèque de l'Empereur.
[4] Hist. Littér. de France, t. 4, p. 19 ; Baluz. Capit. i., 237.
[5] Mabillon, De Re Dipl., p. 50.
[6] N. Tr. de Dipl. ii., 530.

purple. It measures 12¼ by 8½ inches, and consists of 127 leaves, with 28 lines in a page. At the commencement of the volume are six curious illuminations, each occupying the entire page, very rudely drawn and coloured. The first of these is an architectural ornament or temple, inclosing a mystical fountain, surrounded by birds and animals, from which portions are given at the head of my plate, being one of the groups of birds, part of the ornamental frieze, and one of the capitals of the columns of the temple, together with a lamp suspended from the middle of it : the colours are thick, opaque, and dull, or discoloured. To this succeed representations of the four Evangelists, each seated upon a bolster-like cushion, and attended by his respective symbolical animal, drawn with great rudeness ; the last of the illuminations containing a full-length figure of the Saviour seated upon a scarlet cushion, relieved with gold and white. The footstool is of gold, and the hair is intended to be flaxen ; the figure, as will be seen from the upper portion of it, copied in my plate, represents the Saviour as young and beardless, with the right hand in the act of benediction, in the mode adopted by the Romish Church. The back-ground of this drawing is filled up with arabesques, rudely drawn, and with the letters IHS.XPS of large size, in gold : the whole is surrounded by a border of various patterns of arabesques in red, blue, gold, &c.

The Gospel lessons commence on the following page, with the large and elegant majuscule letters on the right side of the plate, being the usual commencement of the lessons, " IN ILLO TEM(PORE)." The interlaced style of these ornamental letters evidently bespeaks the influence of the Anglo-Saxon or Irish caligraphy ; whilst the purely Greek or Roman scrolls introduced into various parts give a charming variety to the patterns. With the exception of an eagle, drawn with considerable taste in an open space at the foot of one of the leaves, (copied by Willemin in his Monumens Inédits), there are no other ornaments throughout the volume than those mentioned above.

The specimen of the text, copied in the plate in uncial letters, is to be read—" Defuncto autem Herode ecce angelus dni apparuit in somnis Joseph in Œgypto dicens". (Matth. ii. 19.)

At the end of the Gospel-lessons is a calendar from the year 775 to 797, in the margin of which, opposite to the year 781, is written, in small rustic capitals, the evidently contemporary entry copied in the middle of the plate—" In isto anno ivit Dominus Rex Carolus ad scm Petrvm et baptisatus est filius eius Pippinus a Domino apostolico"; from which it has been conjectured that the volume was written to commemorate the baptism by Pope Adrian of the Emperor's son, Pippin.

The two last pages are occupied by Latin verses, written in golden minuscule letters, strongly tinged with the Lombardic style in the clavate tops to the l, d, &c., and evidently written before the improvements introduced by Charlemagne had come into use.

From these verses (which will be found reprinted in the Décades Philosophiques) we learn that the volume was finished in 781, that it took seven years to complete it, and that it was written, by order of Charlemagne and his wife Hildegarde, by Godescalc, or Godschalcus, [1] who is probably identical with Godescalc, Deacon of Liege, mentioned in the middle of the eighth century, [2] in the Hist. Littér. de la France, iv., p. 57 ; and it is evident that these verses indicate that the volume was finished in 781, to commemorate the victories of Charlemagne over Didier, King of Lombardy, in 774, when he went with his wife to Rome, where he was received with the honours of a triumph by his friend, Pope Adrian.

The volume was long preserved in the Abbey of St. Servin, at Toulouse, in a richly-embossed and massive case of silver. During the French revolution the case was, however, stolen ; and in 1811 the volume was presented to Napoleon, in the name of the city of Toulouse, on the occasion of the baptism of his son ; it has since been preserved in the private library of the King of France, in the Louvre ; and it is by the kind permission of M. Barbier, who now occupies the situation so long and worthily held by his father, that I am enabled to offer the accompanying fac-similes of this inestimable MS. It is proper to add, that Dr. Dibdin, in his Bibliogr. Tour, has given a beautiful fac-simile engraving of the entire painting of the Saviour,[3] and that

---

[1] The following are the lines in which these circumstances are narrated :—

" Septies expletus fuerat centessimus annus
Octies in decimo sol cum cucurrerat anno
Ex quo Christus Ihesus secla beaverat ortu
Exuerat totum et tetra caligine mundum.

*　　　*　　　*　　　*　　　*

" Septenis cum aperit felix bis fascibus annum
Hoc opus eximium Francorum scribere Karlus
Rex pius egregia Hildegarda cum conjuge jussit.

*　　　*　　　*　　　*　　　*

" Ultimus hoc famulus studium complere Godescalc."

[2] Sir F. Madden, in Gent. Mag., 1836, p. 587.

[3] The heavy black outlines are too much weakened in Dr. Dibdin's plate.

copies of all the illuminations are contained in M. Du Sommerard's work, Les Arts du Moyen A'ge, and also in the Voyages Pittoresques dans l'Ancienne France (Languedoc, art. Toulouse). It is also to be observed, that as Alcuin's recension of the Scriptures was not completed till the year 799, the volume above described exhibits that text of the Vulgate which Blanchini terms its *second* state; namely, the version of St. Jerome much corrupted, and before its correction by our Anglo-Saxon scholar, Alcuin.

The following MSS. are also interesting from their connexion with the Great Emperor of the West.

A volume of the Gospels given by Charlemagne to Aix-la-Chapelle, written in golden letters upon purple vellum, which was found resting upon his knees when his tomb was first opened, and which was until lately preserved at Aix-la-Chapelle; it was, however, removed into Germany with other relics of Charlemagne during the war—and is now probably at Vienna. A fac-simile of the text is given by Casley (Plate XII., spec. 1), and it appears to be but rudely written.[1] (See Lambinet, edit. 1798, p. 23).

The Codex Witikindi, being a copy of the Gospels given by Charlemagne to Witikind, on the (compulsory) conversion of the latter to Christianity. This MS., as I am informed by a friend, is now preserved at Berlin. It is said by the Benedictines (N. Tr. de Dipl. 2, 104) to be written in letters of gold, and to have been preserved in the College of St. John, at Herford (Erfurt?).

The Golden Gospels of St. Médard de Soissons, presented to that Abbey by Charlemagne (as stated by Count Bastard). This fine MS. very closely resembles the Golden Gospels of the Harleian Library, and is written in golden uncials. It contains portraits of the Evangelists, preceded by an illuminated page, containing a representation of a mystical fountain surrounded by stags, birds, &c., drawn with considerable skill, and infinitely superior to the illuminations in the Evangelistiarium of Charlemagne, or the Golden Harleian Gospels. Silvestre has published a plate from the text; and Count Bastard has given not less than six plates of fac-similes from this MS., which is preserved in the Bibliothèque du Roi.

The Psalter written by order of Charlemagne for his friend, Pope Hadrian, in golden minuscule letters and capitals, very similar to those in the Psalter of King Athelstan. Some of the leaves are stained purple. It contains a number of dedicatory Latin lines, commencing, " Hadriano summo papæ patrique beato Rex Carolus salve," &c. This MS. is preserved in the Imperial Library at Vienna. Silvestre has given several fac-similes from it. It was written by Daguefus, and at first dedicated to Charlemagne himself, and was afterwards bestowed by him (in consequence of Pope Hadrian's decease) on the Anglo-Saxon, St. Willehad, first Bishop of Bremen, where it was preserved for eight centuries. (See Thulemas, Bulle Aurée, p. 12.)

Dr. Dibdin mentions another Evangelistiarium given by Charlemagne to the Abbey of Chremsminster, in the 3rd Vol. of his Bibliogr. Tour on the Continent.

The Gospels of St. Riquier, given by Charlemagne to St. Angilbert, and now preserved (as M. Pottier informs me) in the public library of Abbeville,[2] also merits notice and description: neither must the Bible of St. Paul at Rome be omitted, although antiquaries are at variance whether the portrait contained therein be intended for Charlemagne, or his grandson, Charles le Chauve. In many respects the latter corresponds with the Alcuin Bible in the British Museum, and the Bible No. 1, of the Bibliothèque du Roi, presented to Charles le Chauve by Count Vivien; but the text of the Caroline Bible at Rome is not in the revised version of Alcuin, which is the case with the two other Bibles compared with it.

Having already, in the article upon Purple Greek MSS.,[3] and in the account of the Purple Latin Gospels of the Anglo-Saxon school, given some account of the practice of using vellum stained of a purple colour, and golden ink, in MSS. of high rank, I shall take the present opportunity of noticing a few of the most celebrated Latin MSS. written upon vellum of that kind, and which being almost entirely confined to volumes of the sacred Scriptures, and otherwise remarkable for their Palæographical peculiarities, are especially worthy of being noticed in this work.

Of these MSS. those written in silver letters are by far the rarest, and generally of the highest antiquity, several of these containing Antehieronymian versions of the Gospels. Amongst these, the Purple Gospels of

---

[1] This MS. in John xxi. 22 & 23, reads, " Si sic eum volo manere donec veniam " in both places, whereas most MSS. read only sic, without the si (Casley).

[2] See Martene, Voy. Litt. 2e Part. p. 175.

[3] Since this article was published, Don Pascual de Gayangos has published the Second Volume of his History of the Mohammedan Dynasties in Spain, which contains an account of a splendid work, written in gold and silver upon a sky-blue ground, sent in the 9th century by the Greek Emperor to Abdu-r-rahman.

3

Verona, Brescia and Perouse, all published (with fac-similes) by Blanchini, as well as the Codex Bibl. Cæsar., Vindob. (Blanch. 2, pt. 2, DCXXXIII), formerly belonging to the Monastery of St. John de Carbonari, at Naples, are to be noticed, as well as a fragment of a copy of the Gospels preserved (by the care of the Rev. Dr. Todd) in the library of Trinity College, Dublin, which bears considerable resemblance to the Vienna MS., and may be estimated of the 5th century: it measures 14 inches by 10, and is written in double columns, with 20 lines in a page, the first letter in each column being a plain uncial letter, about 1¼ inches high, and indiscriminately being that at the beginning of a paragraph, word, or even syllable, the remainder of the text being written in uncial letters ¼ of an inch high.[1]

All these manuscripts are written in uncial letters, but probably the finest of all in respect to the beauty of the character of the letters, is the famous Gallican Latin Psalter, affirmed to have belonged to St. Germain, Bishop of Paris (A. D. 576), and which is now preserved in the Bibliothèque du Roi; fac-similes of which are given by Blanchini, the Benedictines, (N. Tr. 3, pl. 43, v.) and Silvestre, which is written in silver, except the names of God, and the Diapsalma, which are in gold.

Silvestre has also given a fac-simile from a MS. of the New Testament, written in the ninth century, in large silver Caroline minuscule mixed with uncial and Anglo-Saxon characters, and ornamented with large initials nearly six inches high, and which appears to be the same MS. as is described by the Benedictines, from the library of the Cardinal de Soubise. (N. Tr. de Dipl. 3, p. 122, 196, 351, &c.)

The latest instance of the employment of silver and gold is seen in a large Missal written upon black paper, contained in the Imperial Library of Vienna, written in tall stout gothic letters of silver with initial letters of gold, described by Dr. Dibdin in his Bibliographical Tour, by whom also an Evangelistiarium of the fourteenth century, written in tall, broad, Gothic, golden letters on white vellum, is also described. Montfaucon (Diarium Ital. p. 308), describes a purple MS. of Homilies on the Gospels of the seventh or eighth century.

Of Latin MSS. written throughout in golden letters upon purple vellum, the finest specimen in England is Mr. Douce's Psalter, now preserved in the Bodleian, and of which an account has been given in the recently published catalogue of that portion of the library: several of the pages are occupied with large illuminated capitals and with miniatures (the figures about two inches high), in the style of the illuminations of the Frankish school of the ninth century. The volume is a small quarto, and the text written in Caroline minuscule letters.

The Gospels of St. Germain, No. 663, is entirely written in golden rustic capitals, and is described by the Benedictines (N. Tr. Dipl. ii. 99, iii. 43, 98), and considered by them to be not more recent than the sixth century. On a recent visit to the Bibliothèque du Roi, I was shown a MS. of the Gospels written in similar characters, which I was informed had not been hitherto described, and which appears to me to be of the ninth century, the characters closely resembling those used in the illuminations of the Caroline Bibles. Unfortunately the spaces left for the figures of the Evangelists have never been filled up.

Here, also, may be mentioned the Horæ of Charles the Bald, of which a beautiful fac-simile has been given by Silvestre.

It appears also to have been the custom to introduce a few leaves of purple vellum at the beginning of MSS. of great value, during the ninth and tenth centuries, as in the instance of the Gospels used at the Coronations of the Anglo-Saxon Kings, described in another article of this work—the Golden Harleian Gospels, 2788; and in other fine MSS. of the Caroline period, especially the Gospels given by Louis le Debonnaire to the Abbey of St. Médard de Soissons.

In many MSS. also, one or more lines are alone stained or painted purple, as in the specimen given, from the Alcuin Bible in the British Museum, in another article of this work.

Many other MSS. written in gold upon purple, or in gold upon unstained vellum, are described by the Benedictines, (N. Tr. de Dipl., ii. p. 100-106, iii. 351.) Both Blanchini and Mabillon have given separate chapters to this subject; and others are also mentioned in Lambecius' catalogue of the Vienna Library.

[1] The following extract from the 13th chapter of St. Matthew will serve to show the version used in this MS., which has not been hitherto described:—" Vos autem audite parabolus seminantis omnis qui audit verBum regni et non intellegit venit malus et rapit quod seminatum est in corde eius Hic est juxta viam seminatus super autem petrosam seminatus hic est qui audit verbum et cum gaudio suscipit illum et non habens radicem in se sed est temporalis Facta autem angustia aut perSecutionem propter verbum continuo scandilazatur qui autem in spinis seminatur hic est qui audit verbum et sollicitudo sæculi et divitiarum voluntas suffocat verbum et fit sine fructum. In terram autem bona qui seminatus est hic est qui audit verbum et intellegit."—In the above passage I have preserved the faulty spelling of several of the words.

AVLVS

uocatus apts
segregatus ineuange
lium di

5 { Pro me quis que legas uersus orare memento
Alchume di coregatus sine fine uale .

2 Xps e ueritas . Qn int tres sunt
qui testimonium dant . sps aqua et sanguis . et tres unus sunt.
Si testimonium hominum accipimus

3 Munera dedonis accipe scatuis
Qua pater albinus deuoto pectore supplex
Nominis ad laudem obtulit et cetu .

Pro mequisq: legas uersus orare memento
Alchu medi cor ego tu sine fine uale

4

ADAM VOCAT REDEMTOR

The Bible of Alchuine.

THE ALCHUINE BIBLE IN THE BRITISH MUSEUM.

DESCRIPTION OF THE PLATE.

1. Commencement of St. Paul's Epistle to the Romans.
2. The disputed Passage, 1 John v., 7.
3. The Conclusion of the Verses by Alchuine.

4. Drawing of Adam and Eve charged with the First Sin.
5. The last two lines of the Alchuine verses from the Vallicella Bible.

DURING the dark period which elapsed between the date of St. Jerome's Vulgate revision of the Scriptures and the close of the eighth century, the text of the Sacred Volume had become so much corrupted by the carelessness and wilfulness of transcribers, that a fresh revision became necessary; and which was undertaken by our great Anglo-Saxon scholar Alchuine, (Albinus or Alcbinus,) at the direction of his patron Charlemagne; as appears from a letter addressed by the former to Gisla, the sister of Charlemagne, in 799; wherein he describes himself as still deeply engaged on the emendation of the Old and New Testament, undertaken by order of Charlemagne[1].

Angelom, a monk of Luxeu, in Burgundy, a contemporary of Alchuine, also declares, that he saw and diligently examined the Bible which Alchuine had corrected for Charlemagne[2], and which had been completed under the eye of Alchuine during the year 800, being destined as a present to the Emperor on the day of his coronation as Emperor of Rome, on Christmas day in that year. The letter which accompanied this gift has been fortunately preserved, and is in the following terms:—" After deliberating a long time what the devotion of my mind might find worthy of a present equal to the splendor of your Imperial Dignity, and the increase of your wealth, that the ingenuity of my mind might not become torpid in idleness whilst others were offering various gifts of riches, and the messenger of my littleness come empty-handed before the face of your sanctity; at length, by the inspiration of the Holy Spirit, I found what it would be competent for me to offer and fitting for your Prudence to accept. For to me inquiring and considering, nothing appeared more worthy of your Peaceful Honour than the gifts of the Sacred Scriptures; which, by the dictation of the Holy Spirit and Mediation of Christ-God, are written with the pen of celestial grace—for the salvation of mankind, and which knit together in the sanctity of one glorious body, and *diligently emended*, I have sent to your Royal authority, by this your son and faithful servant, so that with full hands we may assist in the delightful service of your Dignity."[3]

At the present time we possess no means of identifying the volume described in the preceding extract with any of the several Caroline Bibles now in existence. From internal evidence, however, the Bible purchased ten years ago by the British Museum, at the price of £750, appears to have better claims than any of the others to be considered as the volume presented to Charlemagne.

M. de Speyr Passavant, the late possessor of the volume, obtained it from M. Bennot, of Delémont, near Basle, who bought it when the episcopal territory of Basle was occupied in 1793 by the French troops, it having been transferred to Delémont from the monastery of Moutier-Grand-Val, where it was preserved at the close of the 16th century, as appears by an entry on the last page of the Bible. M. Passavant asserts, further, that it was brought to Grand-Val by the Benedictine Monks of Pruem, near Treves, when their convent was dissolved in 1576 (upon which event they retired to Grand-Val); that this is the identical volume given to Pruem by the Emperor Lothaire, grandson of Charlemagne; and that it is also mentioned by Charlemagne in his will: there appear, however, to be no grounds for the last three assertions. The last is entirely fictitious; the preceding rests on the Charter granted to the Superior of Pruem by Lothaire, in which is included " *opus* quod—faciendum curavimus *Evangelium* scilicet "—after which is added, " *Bibliothecam* cum imaginibus et majoribus characteribus in voluminum principiis deauratis."[4] But there is nothing to identify this Bibliotheca (or Book of the Scriptures) with the volume before us, nor is there evidence to prove that the Benedictines of Pruem brought this volume to Grand-Val.

---

[1] " Totius forsitan Evangelii expositionem direxissem vobis si me non occupasset Domini regis præceptum in emendatione veteris novique Testamenti." Opp., t. 1, vol. i., p. 591. It is singular that this important labour of Alchuine is not noticed in Mr. Wright's recently published volume of the Anglo-Saxon portion of the Biographia Britannica Literaria.

[2] Epist. clxxxv., p. 248.

[3] Epist. ciii. Opp. t. 1, v. i, p. 153.

[4] Sir F. Madden, in his elaborate articles upon this volume (in the Gentleman's Magazine for 1836), suggests that the Gospels *and* Bible were both made at the expense of Lothaire, but the word opus (in the singular,) seems to apply rather to the Evangelium alone.

1

THE ALCHUINE BIBLE IN THE BRITISH MUSEUM.

The volume before us (which is now numbered MS. Add., 10546,) consists of 449 leaves of fine vellum, measuring 20 inches by 14¾, written in double columns of small Caroline minuscule characters, with 50 or 52 lines in a full page. It commences with the Epistle of Jerome to Paulinus, the title of which,—" INCIPIT EPISTOLA SANCTI HIERONYMI AD PAULINUM PRESBYTERUM de omnibus divinis Historiæ libris," occupies an entire page, and is written in golden capitals, about one inch high, on bands of purple, inclosed within an interlaced ornamental border[1], with eight large and eight smaller interlaced ornaments in silver in the corners and intermediate spaces; the initial letter of the Epistle, F (Frater Ambrosius), is twelve inches high and five broad; the frame-work being of silver with golden ornaments, and with what appears to be intended for a lantern and a vessel to contain holy oil, represented suspended from the transverse bars of the letter. The first nineteen lines of the Epistle are written in golden uncials. The verso of fo. 5 is occupied by a large illumination, divided into four compartments by purple bands bearing inscriptions in golden *rustic* capitals, and containing representations of—

1. The creation of Adam and Eve.
2. Eve presented to Adam, and the charge given against eating the forbidden fruit.
3. The temptation of the Serpent; breach of the commandment, and shame on being taxed with it by God, (the latter portion of which is copied in the annexed plate); and,
4. The expulsion from Paradise, and employment in tilling the ground and suckling children.

These drawings appear strongly tinged with the Byzantine style of art: the figures, indeed, of the Creator and angels are very similar to the drawings in the famous purple Codex Geneseos, at Vienna, and other early Greek drawings. Moreover, it is to be observed, that the various subjects in the Museum Bible occur in Count Vivian's Bible, in the Bibliothèque du Roi; treated in almost precisely the same manner; the group, for instance, in my plate, appears in the latter volume, but the positions of the different figures are reversed; the Creator being on the right side of the drawing, and not quite so short in its proportions. The same subjects also occur (but with many others) in the Bible of the Monastery of St. Paul at Rome.

The purple bands separating these drawings are inscribed :—

A + ω

ADAM PRIMVS VTI PINGITVR ISTIC̈.
CVIVS COSTA SACRAE CARPITUR EVAE.
XPŪS EVAM DVCIT ADAE QUAM VOCAT VIRAGINE.
AST EDANT NE POMA VITAE ꝑHIBET IPSE CONDITOR.
SVADET NVPER CREATAE ; ANGVIS DOLO PVELLAE.
POST HAEC AMOENA LVSTRANS.   ADAM VOCAT REDEMTOR
VTERQVE AB VMBRIS PELLITVR INDE SACRIS
ET JAM LABORI RVRA COLVNT HABITI.

The preface of St. Jerome to Desiderius commences on folio 6, the title and first lines of which are in capital and uncial letters, alternately, of gold on a purple ground and red; the large capital D is silver and gold, and within it are drawn two cocks, with a vase of flowers between, and beneath two lions. A table of the chapters of Genesis follows, and the book itself on folio 7, with a large initial in gold and silver in the same style as before (copied in Smith's Fac-Similes of Literary Curiosities); and above it the monogram of the name of Jesus, in gold, copied at the top of my plate.

Each of the books of the Bible has a similar table of chapters prefixed, and commences with an ornamental initial, more or less elaborately executed, and with small figures of birds, beasts, &c., in gold and silver in the open spaces of the letters, of which the specimen in the accompanying plate will give a general idea, being the commencement of the Epistle of St. Paul to the Romans; and from which it will be seen that the style of these ornaments agrees exactly with those of Count Vivian's Bible represented in the following plate of this work.

Opposite the first page of Exodus (fol. 25, verso,) is another large illumination, (filling the entire page,) divided into two compartments. In the upper is represented Moses receiving the volume of the law on Mount Sinai from the hand of the Almighty, in the clouds; the hill itself is in a blaze of red. Above, two angels are pouring out fire from golden horns; and at a distance, at the bottom of the hill, stands a figure holding a sceptre terminating in a fleur-de-lis, evidently intended for Joshua. Beneath is the same figure of Moses expounding the law to Aaron and the Children of Israel, Joshua standing behind him holding a sceptre, as in

---

[1] A reduced copy of this border is given in the Pictorial History of England, vol. i., p. 138.

the upper part; the names Moys, Aaron, Filii Israhel, and Josue, being inscribed over the figures; and the following lines being written on a purple band :—

> SVSCEPIT LEGEM MOYSES CORVSCA
> REGIS E DEXTRA SVPERI SED INFRA
> JAM DOCET XPI POPULUM REPLETVS NECTARE SANCTO.

These figures are about four inches high, and are represented standing within a palace, the architecture of which exhibits the debased Roman style, in its fluted columns with foliated capitals, with a door on each side, the entrance covered with a curtain hanging by rings from poles. Moses is clad in a white mantle, with a violet-coloured tunic with a red border; and Aaron, with beard and moustaches, in a scarlet mantle and white tunic ornamented with gold, having a golden crown with fleur-de-lis on his head, and holding a sceptre terminating in the fleur-de-lis in the left hand, and a golden manutergium, formerly used for wrapping the sacred volume in, in the right hand.[1] The remainder of the Old Testament is destitute of illuminated miniatures.

Previous to the commencement of the New Testament are delineated the ten Eusebian Canons, inscribed within coloured arches, supported by curious architectural columns; after which is a large illumination, occupying the entire page (fo. 352 verso). In the middle, within an oval, is represented the Saviour seated on a globe, with a nimbus round the head, the features young and beardless, the right hand raised in the act of benediction, and the left one holding a book.

This figure is exactly six inches high, and, as compared with the same subject illustrated in the article upon the Evangelistiarium of Charlemagne, the one before us exhibits a wonderful improvement in the art of design, as well as a totally different style of colouring, the prevailing tones of this drawing being slaty-blue or ochre-red, relieved with white and gold. On each side is written in capital letters of gold—

> REX MICAT AETHEREVS CONDIGNE SIVE ꝒPHETAE
> HIC EVANGELICAE QUATTVOR ATQ: TVBAE.

Around the oval, and inclosed within a large diamond-shaped space, are representations of the four Evangelical symbols, and outside of the diamond, in the four corners, are the full-length figures of the four greater prophets holding scrolls, and trees.

At the end of the volume is a fourth large illumination, probably illustrative of the Apocalypse. It is divided into two parts, in the upper of which appears the Bible, laid on a sort of ark or altar, and above this is a scarlet curtain, faced with silver. On the right appears the lamb, typical of the New Testament; and on the left the lion of Judah, emblematical of the Old. At the corners are the four Evangelical symbols. In the lower part is represented a figure seated on a chair, surrounded by full-length figures of the Evangelical symbols, that of St. Matthew being at his feet, holding to his lips a horn of silver. The following lines are inscribed in gold upon purple bands in the centre of the page :—

> " SEPTEM SIGILLIS AGNVS INNOCENS MODIS
> SIGNATA MIRIS JVRA DISSERAT PATRIS
> LEGES E VETERIS SINV NOVELLAE
> ALMIS PECTORIB: LIQUANT ECCE
> QUAE LVCE POPVLIS DEDERE MVLTIS."

The leaf preceding this illumination contains certain religious epigrams and verses written by Alchuine, which have attracted much attention. The latter are 44 in number; the last 12 being as follows :—

> " Codicis istius quod [quot] sint in corpore sco
> Depictæ formis litterulæ variis
> Mercedes habeat xpo dominante per aevum
> Is Carolus qui iam scribe jusset eum
> Haec dator aeternus cunctorum xpe bonorum
> Munera de donis accipe sca tuis
> Quae pater albinus deuoto pectore supplex
> Nominis ad laudem obtulit ecce tui
> Quem tua perpetuis conseruet dextra diebus
> Ut felix tecum uiuat in arce poli
> Pro me quisq: legas versus orare memento
> Alchuine dicor ego; tu sine fine vale."

---

[1] Sir F. Madden considers it certain that these figures respectively represent Alchuine and Charlemagne. As, however, the figure of Moses is larger and far more prominent than that of Aaron, and as the latter is bearded (contrary to the fashion of the Frankish princes, as shown in various illuminations published by Count Bastard and others), I consider this supposition very doubtful.

Several of the latter lines are copied in the plate under the number 3.

Sir F. Madden has pointed out, what appears to be, abundant proofs of these lines being the production of Alchuine—as indicated, indeed, in the last verse quoted above ; and has from thence drawn the conclusion that " this very copy of the Bible was made under the superintendence of Alchuine, for the Emperor Charlemagne."[1] It is to be observed, however, that these verses, with certain alterations and additions, occur in another copy of the Bible, preserved in the library of the Fathers of the Oratory called della Vallicella, at Rome, marked B 6 ; also thence supposed to have been written by Alchuine, and presented to Charlemagne ;[2] and that, from a recent examination of Count Vivian's Bible, presented to Charles the Bald (in the Bibliothèque du Roi, described in the following article of this work,) Sir F. Madden is inclined to consider that the volume before us is rather a production of the time of the last-named Emperor. That there is a surprising similarity in the general appearance, style of writing, ornaments, and miniatures of this Bible and that of Count Vivian, is unquestionable ; and it must be allowed that the Charlemagne Evangelistiarium is so much ruder in its details as to lead us to infer that there must have been at least half a century between the period of the execution of the two volumes. It must, however, be remembered that the Bible of Count Vivian was certainly, and the Alchuine volumes in all probability, executed in the Monastery of St. Martin, at Tours (the most learned establishment then in existence, and of which Alchuine was the Abbot); and that the Benedictines (unquestionably the best judges of the ancient character of writings executed in their own country,) consider that the writing of the Bible of Count Vivian is that of the close of the eighth, rather than the middle of the following century.

The specimen No. 2 will give an idea of the character of the writing, being the celebrated passage 1 John, v. 7, omitting the heavenly witnesses—" *spiritus est qui testificatur quoniam* xps e veritas qnm tres sunt qui testimoniū dant sps aqua et sanguis et tres unu sunt. Si testimoniū hominū accipimus" &c.[3]

[1] Gent. Mag. ut supr., p. 475.

[2] As affirmed by Blanchini ; "Alcuinus vir omnium quos ea tulit ætas eruditissimus volumen sacrorum Bibliorum Hieronymianæ editionis utrumque continens testamentum nuncupavit Regi præcellentissimo et qui unus plurimorum instar esse debet, sc., Carolo magno. *Exstat hoc exemplar autographum millenariæ ætatis in nostra congregatione Oratorii Romani bibliotheca* ; "—the last two lines of the Alchuine verses in this Bible are copied in my plate under the No. 5.

[3] It is to be observed that the words sps aqua, &c., to the end of the fac-simile, are written on an erasure, *but by the first hand and ink:* as more clearly appears from the following red alinea, and the numeration of the verses in red roman minuscules,—showing that there is no space for the introduction of the heavenly witnesses.

4

M

INPRINCIPI
OCREAUITDS
CAELUMETTRA

Noteetfibiunufquifq:uel iacentem
lineæuel figna ædiantiu id ē uel
obelof ÷ uel afterifcof ✻ Etubi

Bible of Charles the Bald.

BIBLE PRESENTED TO CHARLES THE BALD,
BY COUNT VIVIAN.

DESCRIPTION OF THE PLATE.

Initial letter Q, with emblematical figures of the Sun and Moon; Miniature of St. Jerome starting from Rome, on his Travels, to correct the Bible;

Initial letter M; commencement of the Book of Genesis, and part of the preface, with medallion portrait of Charles the Bald.

THE zeal displayed by the great Emperor Charlemagne, in the propagation of religion and the improvement of the literature and arts of his time, appears to have had considerable influence upon his descendants and successors. His son, Louis le Debonnaire, also surnamed the Pious, ordered the Bible to be translated into the Theotisc language, " quatenus non solum litteratis verum etiam illiteratis sacra divinorum præceptorum lectio panderetur," [1] and some of his coins bear the figure of a temple, in which a cross is elevated, inscribed XPISTIANA RELIG. (Christiana religio.)

The magnificent Book of the Gospels given to the Abbey of St. Medard de Soissons by this Emperor, is one of the finest relics of the Caroline period, and is now preserved in the Bibliothèque du Roi, fac-similes of which have been given by the Count Bastard, by whom it is stated that it was written for Charlemagne; and by M. Silvestre. It is written in golden uncial letters, very similar to the Evangelistiarium of Charlemagne, and the Harleian golden Gospels, in double columns, some of the leaves being stained purple. Its illuminations of the Evangelists also nearly resemble those in the Harleian MS. The Count Bastard has given a series of fac-similes from another MS. of the Gospels which belonged to Louis le Debonnaire. The initials of the Four Gospels are formed of an angel, lion, bull, and eagle, having the bodies distorted so as to form the letters, which are about 5 inches high. They nevertheless exhibit surprising skill for the period, the Lion of St. Mark standing upright for the letter I, with wings crossing over the head, is especially drawn with great spirit.

A Sacramentarium written for Drogon, Archbishop of Metz, son of Charlemagne, ornamented with beautiful capitals and arabesques, and with minute full-length figures, is also preserved in the Bibliothèque du Roi, and has been illustrated by Count Bastard as well as by M. Silvestre.

The Gospels of Lotharius, the grandson of Charlemagne, Emperor of Italy and Lorraine, containing a contemporary portrait of himself (excellently engraved in Dibdin's Bibliogr. Tour, vol. ii.), is also preserved in the Bibliothèque du Roi. The Count Bastard has devoted not fewer than 9 plates of his extravagant work to this MS., which in its style is very similar to the first Bible of Charles the Bald, and the Alcuin Bible in the British Museum. It was written in the Abbey of St. Martin at Tours; on the verso of the second leaf is a representation of the Creator.

Charles the Bald, another of the grandsons of Charlemagne, appears, however, to have far exceeded any of his relatives in his luxurious taste for illuminated MSS. of the Scriptures and books of devotion; judging from the number of them which still exist as monuments of his zeal for the welfare of the arts. It is indeed stated in some of the accounts of his life, that he and his sister Ada caused many copies of the Gospels to be written in letters of gold.

The Psalter,[2] or Prayer-book, of this monarch is preserved in the Bibliothèque du Roi (No. 1152), and is a small quarto volume, sumptuously bound with carved ivory ornaments. The text throughout is written in golden uncials, upon purple vellum, between the years 842 and 869: as may be judged from the marriage of the prince with Hermintrude, and her death; her name appearing in the Litany at the end of the volume, in conjunction with that of her husband.[3]

---

[1] Præf. in libr. antiq. linguâ Saxonicâ script. Bouquet, tom. 6, p. 256.

[2] Often miscalled the Bible of Metz.

[3] " Ut Hermintrudem conjugem nostram conservare digneris, te rogamus audi nos.—Ut mihi Karolo a te Rege coronato vitam et prosperitatem atque victoriam dones te rogo audi me."

1

BIBLE PRESENTED TO CHARLES THE BALD BY COUNT VIVIAN.

At the beginning of the volume is a miniature painting of King David with his four attendants, Asaph, &c. ; another representing Charles the Bald himself, seated on a throne ornamented with pearls, and blue and red gems, and bearing a globe and sceptre in his hand, the latter surmounted by a fleur-de-lys, and inscribed—

> " Cum sedeat Karolus magno coronatus honore,
> Est Josiae similis parque Theodosio."

Another miniature represents St. Jerome, seated with the calamus in his hand, and his writing utensils before him. The initial B of the first Psalm is in the style of the same letter given in this work from the Psalter of King Athelstan, but far more elaborate; and the whole page is inclosed in a broad border, painted in thick opaque colours, representing pearls, gems, and foliage. The portrait has been engraved, by Montfaucon and Willemin; and a splendid fac-simile of the first page of the Psalms is given by Silvestre.

An Evangelistiarium is described by Dr. Dibdin as having also belonged to Charles the Bald, and now in the same library; the illuminations of which are rubbed and faded, and the writing is in a minuscule character. And another volume of Hours is stated, by Willemin and the Benedictines (N. Tr. de Dipl. ii. 100), to be preserved in the Imperial Library of Vienna, and formerly in the Abbey of Frauenmunster, Zurich; and which was printed at Ingolstadt, in 1585, by the care of Felicien, Bishop of Scalen, and dedicated to Maximilian, Duke of Bavaria.

A copy of the Gospels written in gold uncial letters in 870,[1] splendidly ornamented, and containing a portrait of Charles the Bald, was formerly preserved at Ratisbon; but is now in the Royal Library at Munich. From the magnificent specimens published by Silvestre, it appears to bear considerable resemblance to the golden Gospels of the Harleian collection,[2] although even more gorgeous in some respects.

The BIBLE OF CHARLES THE BALD, from which the drawings in the accompanying plate have been copied, is a noble folio volume, placed at the head of the Latin Bibles in the Bibliothèque du Roi (No. 1), and was presented to the Emperor by Count Vivian and his brethren, monks of St. Martin of Tours, as represented in an illumination at the end of the volume, which has been repeatedly engraved, and which is described in some annexed verses:—

> " Haec etiam pictura recludit qualiter heros
> Offert Vivianus cum grege nunc hoc opus," &c.

The Benedictines, however, contend that the volume was written for Charlemagne, but subsequently presented to his grandson (N. Tr. Dipl. iii. p. 134, note); the miniature and verses at the end being an after addition. The name of *Charles* is also introduced into some verses at the beginning of the volume, written in golden rustic capitals on purple vellum, commencing—

> " Rex benedicte tibi hæc placeat biblioteca Carle," &c.

And in the second and following pages are delineated, amongst the marginal ornaments, two small medallions with busts, one inscribed " David Rex imperator," and the other (copied in my plate), " Karolus Rex Franco." The volume measures 20 inches by 15, and has the text written in a Caroline minuscule, of which a specimen is given at the foot of the plate; the commencement of each book being written in golden capitals, as in the specimen from the commencement of the Book of Genesis (which in the original is written on a purple ground). The initials are highly ornamental, being drawn in a style quite unlike that of the Anglo-Saxon school, and which the Count Bastard terms Gallo-Frankish. The letters Q and M in the accompanying plate will serve as specimens of this style, as shown in some of the smaller initials, others being of a much larger size; the letter F, at the commencement of the usual preface of St. Jerome to the Old Testament, being 10 inches high. The frame-work of many of the pages is also elaborately ornamented with arabesques of great beauty, and even of Grecian purity: and in one of the letters (D), are represented the twelve signs of the Zodiac; whilst in the open spaces of another (B), are the two figures classically representing the Sun and Moon, copied in the upper part of my plate.

---

[1] This date appears in the lines—

> " Bis quadringenti volitant et septuaginti
> Anni quo Ds est virgine natus homo."

Which accords with the 31st year of Charles's reign, as is further stated—

> " Ter denis annis Karolus regnabat et uno
> Cum Codex actus illius imperio ;"

The portrait of the Emperor being inscribed—

> " Hic residet Karolus divino munere fultus
> Ornat quem pietas et bonitatas amor."

[2] See Dissertatio in aureum ac pervet. SS. evang. Cod. MS. monast. S. Emmerani Ratisbonæ, auct. P. Colomanno Sanftl. Ratisb. 1786, 4to.

The volume also contains a series of illuminations of high interest, with reference to the state of the arts in France in the ninth century ; and it is extraordinary that, although the Count Bastard has devoted no less than sixteen plates of his gigantic work to the illustration of this volume, not one of these illuminations (except the often published miniature above described at the end of the volume), has been published by him or any other author.[1] Some of the illuminations for the most part nearly correspond with those contained in the Alcuin Bible in the British Museum, and also, in general design at least, with some of those in the Bible of St. Paul, at Rome.

The first of these illuminations represents St. Jerome's journey from Rome, and his labours in correcting the scriptures—as in the Bible of St. Paul—divided into three compartments ; of which the drawing of my plate offers a fac-simile of part of the upper division. This drawing is especially interesting, as affording a representation of a fortified city defended by its tutelary Deity; a bishop of the ninth century in his robes, and a ship, very similar to those seen on the coins of the Emperor Hadrian. The painting is executed in a thick and shining composition, with a red brick colour very prevalent throughout. Opposite to the first chapter of Genesis is another illumination in three compartments ; containing the Creation, Fall of Man, and Culture of the Earth. Another illumination precedes the Book of Exodus, divided into two compartments ; in the upper of which is represented Moses receiving the Law upon Mount Sinai, which is in a blaze of red paint ; and in the lower Moses is delivering the law to the people—the figures, about seventeen in number, being about four inches high. The drapery is strongly marked, and the drawing is considered by Dr. Dibdin to be a little in the style of late Greek art. The heads and eyes are disproportionably large, and a coarse red colour very prevalent. The illumination at the beginning of the Psalms is inclosed within an oval frame-work of purple measuring 12 inches by 9½, and representing King David in the middle with attendants, and an angel holding a wreath at each corner of the frame.

The tables inclosing the Eusebian Canons at the beginning of the Gospels are highly ornamented ; and opposite to the first chapter of St. Matthew is a representation of Our Saviour in the centre, surrounded by the four Evangelists and four Prophets : the countenance of Christ is not destitute of expression, but the brick-red colour is unpleasantly preponderant.

Opposite to the beginning of St. Paul's Epistle to the Romans is an illumination, in three compartments, representing the leading events of the life of the Apostle ; and at the beginning of the Apocalypse is another, in two compartments : the lower very remarkable, representing St. John seated, holding a white wand, which is made to encircle him, with an angel blowing a horn before him.

The Bibliothèque du Roi also possesses another Bible formerly belonging to Charles the Bald, of great interest, from the peculiar style of the ornaments, which strongly partake of the Anglo-Saxon character in the intricate, interlaced, narrow, ribbon-like patterns, with which the large initial letters are ornamented, and which are quite unlike the ornaments of the genuine Frankish style.[2] This noble MS., of a large folio size, has the text written in a small, close-set minuscule character, and some verses prefixed, written in golden rustic capitals, on a purple ground, from which its date may be fixed with certainty between 865 and 876.[3]

The verses commence thus :—

" Bibliorum seriem Karolus Rex inclitus istam
Contexit chryso corde colens catharo."

The first three pages of Genesis are also written in golden letters, as well as the commencement of each book. The volume was preserved, during 700 years, in the Abbey of St. Denis, whence it was removed in 1595 to its present location.

As a biblical MS. it is of great interest, as having been the text of Stephens' edition of the Bible, printed in 1528. Forty pages were stolen by Aymon from the latter part of the volume,[4] about a dozen of which are now preserved in the Harleian Library, No. 7551, from which the magnificent title-page of the commencement of St. Paul's Epistles to the Romans, has been published by Smith, amongst his fac-similes of Historical Documents, Part VI. ; the initial letter P(aulus) being 11 inches high. Silvestre and the Count Bastard have

---

[1] Willeman has indeed selected one or two trivial groups.

[2] M. Bastard qualifies the peculiar style of ornament exhibited in this volume, by the name of Franco-Saxon. The sacramentarium of St. Gregory at Rheims, of which a beautiful fac-simile is published by Silvestre, is ornamented in the same style.

[3] See Baluze Capitul., col. 1566.

[4] These stolen portions afforded M. Jorand the materials for his Grammatographie de la Bible de Charles le Chauve.

also published other fac-similes of the volume; others representing the ornamental details are given by Willemin, and a series of the smaller curious capital letters by the Benedictines (Vol. ii. pl. 18, and iii, pl. 37 and 41). This volume is destitute of miniatures.

The Bible of the Benedictine Monastery of St. Paul at Rome[1] must here be mentioned, although antiquaries are in doubt whether the portrait and verses contained in it were intended for Charlemagne or Charles the Bald. This is a MS. of large folio size, " ingentis molis pulchritudine et elegantia nulli cedit vere Augustam præfert magnificentiam," as observed by Montfaucon. The text is written in a small Caroline minuscule,[2] and ornamented with capitals of a gigantic size (of which D'Agincourt has given a fac-simile), executed in a style very similar to that of the initials in the Gospels of the Coronations of the Anglo-Saxon Kings, but having the open spaces filled up with foliated ornaments and flowers. The illuminations are of great interest, comprising a portrait of the Prince " Karolus," for whom this volume was written,[3] which has led to much discussion.

In this drawing the monarch is represented seated on a throne crowned, and wearing short moustaches, but without a beard, and holding in his hand a globe, inscribed with the letters CRSNMXRLEH, the interpretation of which has exercised the ingenuity of different authors. Beneath the portrait are, however, written some verses, commencing—

" Rex caeli dn̄s solita pietate redundans
Hunc Karolum regem terrae dilixit herilem, &c."

which, with other verses in the prologue to the volume addressed, to " Rex Carolus," by " Ingobertus referens et scriba fidelis," leave no doubt that it was either for Charlemagne or his grandson that the volume was written.[4] The monarch is attended by two females and two squires, who have been regarded as Hildegarde and her attendant, and Charlemagne's two sons, Carolan and Louis. The lower part of the page contains in three compartments, the labours of St. Jerome in reforming the text of the Bible: the first division, representing him starting on his travels, being very similarly treated to the same subject in the plate at the head of the present article. Fac-similes of this, and several of the other drawings which ornament this MS., occupying entire folio pages, are given by D'Agincourt, who has devoted six plates to their illustration, and who observes that they constitute " un exemple très remarquable de l'état où l'art se trouvait parmi les Latins," at the period of the execution of the volume, the drawing being very indifferent and rude, and the grouping of the figures extremely confused, although, in general, the chief personage is placed in the centre of the drawing. It must be added that this MS. exhibits the Vulgate text in what Blanchini calls its second state, namely, the version of Jerome much corrupted previous to its correction by Alcuin.

[1] Now deposited in the Monastery of St. Calixtus, dependant on St. Paul's.

[2] Blanchini Evang. quad. vol. ii. pt. 2. tab. p. DCXXVI. has given a long fac-simile.

[3] Engraved by Alemanni (De Lateranens. pariet., &c., Rom. 1625 and 1756); Margarini (Inscript. Antiq. Basilic. S. Pauli, Rom. 1654);

Mabillon (Museum Ital. 1, p. 70); Montfaucon (Monum. de la Mon. Franc. 1, 304); D'Agincourt (Les Arts par les Monumens); and Willemin (Monum. inéd. de France).

[4] See N. Traité de Diplom. iii., p. 123—125, for a discussion on the question.

INI TIVM
EVANGELII
ihu xpi filii di

MARCVS
VT ALTA FREMIT VOX
PER DESERTA LEONIS

Pater noster quun caelis es.
scificetur nom entuum
Yeniat regnum tuum

+ ODDA REX

+ MIHT HILD
MATER REGIS

Coronation Book of the Anglo Saxon Kings.

THE CORONATION OATH BOOK OF THE ANGLO-SAXON KINGS.

REFERENCE TO THE PLATE.—All the fac-similes are taken from the Cottonian MS. Tiberius A 2.

THE historical circumstances connected with the manuscript from which the accompanying plate is copied, render a few preliminary observations requisite.

That the rude nations of antiquity should, upon the election of one of their number to administer justice, or to serve as their leader in war, and often to act with an unlimited control over themselves and their fortunes, have required from him the strongest assurances of his determination to perform such duties in the manner most conducive to the welfare of the tribe, is not more natural than that the ministers of religion who first preached its doctrines amongst them, and who would naturally be regarded with veneration and awe, should be called upon to give the weight of their authority to the election so made, and consecrate the choice by ceremonies bearing the mark of Divine original, and for which they were able to refer to the Levitical law, as affording a precedent. The practice of crowning a newly-elected king could not but have been acceptable to the person so elected, for it strengthened and established his authority.

In the article upon Sclavonian Biblical Manuscripts I have noticed the ceremony of raising the newly-elected monarch upon a shield, which was used amongst the northern tribes of Europe; and our early Anglo-Saxon Kings were elevated from the ground at the time of their coronation, and were required to promise that they would duly discharge the duties of their station.

The Oath of King Edgar, (A.D. 958,) reprinted from the Reliquiæ Antiquæ, (vol. ii. p. 194,) where it is given from a contemporary, is as follows :—

Ðis ge-writ is ge-writen stæf be stæfe be þam ge-write þe Dunstan arcb. sealde wrum hlaforde æt Cingestune þa on dæg þa hine man halgode to cinge, ᚼ for-bead him ælc wedd to syllanne butan þysan wedde þe he up on Cristes weofud léde, swa se bisceop him dihte :·

On þære halgan þrynnesse naman. Ic preo þing be-háte cristenum folce ᚼ me under -ðeoddum ; án ærest þ ic Godes cyrice ᚼ eall cristen folce minra ge-wealda soðe sibbe healde ; oþer is þ ic reaf-lac ᚼ ealle unrihte þing eallum hádum for-beode ; pridde, pat ic beháte ᚼ be-beode on eallum dómum riht ᚼ mild-heortnesse þæt us eallum arfæst ᚼ mild-heort God þurh þ his ecean miltse forgyfe, se lyfað ᚼ regað ". Finit.

This writing is copied letter by letter after the writing which Dunstan, the abbot, delivered to our Lord at Kingston on the day on which they consecrated him king, and he forbad him to give any pledge except this pledge, which he laid on Christ's altar as the bishop appointed for him.

In the name of the Holy Trinity I promise three things to Christian people, and bind myself to them : first, that I will to God's church and to all Christian people of my realm hold true peace ; the second is, that I will forbid rapine and all injustice to all classes of society ; the third, that I vow and promise in all [my] judgments justice and mild-heartedness [mercy] that the gracious mild-hearted God, through his everlasting mercy, may forgive us all who shall live and reign.

The Coronation Oath of Ethelred II., at Kingston, in 978, was nearly identical with the above, Dunstan officiating at the ceremony. It will be seen that there is no precise statement in the preceding extract as to the manner in which this Oath was to be taken; but there is abundant proof in the various ancient Coronation services which have been published, that it was taken by the king, his hand at the time being placed upon the Book of the Gospels laid upon the altar, and that it was ratified by the same book being immediately afterwards kissed. The practice has indeed come down to our own times, and it is also used at our coronations; it exists in all Christian countries, and even in Mahometan nations, when an oath is taken, the right hand is placed over, and the left one beneath, the Koran[1].

Marténé, in his large work on the Ancient Rituals of the Church, has collected numerous Coronation ceremonials, from which the following have been selected, as bearing upon the present question.

In the benediction of the Emperor of Rome, it is stated that before he enters Italy, he should take an Oath with his hand placed upon the Gospels, in the presence of the cardinals.

[1] The Library of the East India Company contains a splendid copy of the Koran, on which Sujah Dawlah swore to the treaty of 1768.

Roger of Hoveden, in his Annals, gives the ceremony of the coronation of King Richard; in which the king is directed to kneel before the altar, on which the Holy Gospels and the relics of many saints were placed; and then, as was the custom, to make the Oath. The French kings also, after taking the Oath, are directed to place their hands on the Book of the Gospels [1], whilst the ceremonial of the coronation of Albert, Duke of Austria, and king of Hungary, states, "Hæc omnia super hæc sacro-sancta Dei Evangelia tacta, me veraciter observare juro [2]." The Liber Regalis of Westminster, and the beautiful Coronation Book of Charles V. of France, preserved amongst the Cottonian MSS., (Tiberius, B viii. b), and the ceremonial of the coronation of King Henry VII. [3] may also be referred to as to the practice of swearing upon the Book of the Gospels. The Oath itself was altered by King Henry VIII., and the copy of it, corrected in his own hand-writing, is still preserved amongst the Cottonian MSS., and has been engraved as the frontispiece to Sir Henry Ellis's Letters on English History.

I have entered into the preceding details, in consequence of the doubts which have been entertained by some writers respecting the employment of the volume from which the accompanying plate is taken, as that upon which the Anglo-Saxon kings took their oaths at the time of their coronation, the like honour having been claimed for King Alfred's Psalter in the library of the Duke of Buckingham at Stowe. I can, however, find no instance of the Psalter having been thus employed, whence, independent of other circumstances, this tradition may be disputed. There is, indeed, at Stowe, a Passionale, or " little booke with a crucifixe " on the cover, comprising those portions of the Gospels which record the events of the passion of our Saviour, which is recorded to be the book upon which the Kings and Queens of England took their coronation oath, previous to the Reformation. But this manuscript is stated by Dr. O'Conor [4] to have been written in the twelfth or thirteenth century.

The volume from which my plate is taken consists of 216 sheets of thick vellum, 9 inches by 7 in size, the edges being singed and curled by the Cottonian fire of 1731. It is now preserved in the British Museum, having the mark, Tiberius A 2.

The first page of the volume contains a large illuminated frontispiece; in the centre of which is a youthful king, crowned and kneeling in a church, with two courtiers behind him, and in front of a figure of Christ, naked and wounded on the side. The former has been supposed to represent King Richard II.; but it appears to me to be unquestionably intended for the youthful Henry VI., being, in fact, precisely similar to the miniatures of that king, contained in his Psalter in the same library (Cotton. Domitian, xvii.). In the upper part of the illumination, is an aged crowned king, kneeling in the open country, with the devil at his back. There are also eight coats of arms in various parts of the page, and on a blue slab are inscribed the following lines :—

" Saxonidum dux atque decus, primumque monarcham
Inclitus, Ælfridum qui numeravit avum
Imperii primas quoties meditantur habenas,
Me voluit sacrum regibus esse librum."

This illumination is evidently of the early part of the fifteenth century, and the verses above quoted record the tradition that Athelstan, (the grandson of Alfred,) by whom the English monarchy was consolidated and raised to so much importance in the eyes of Europe, had devoted this volume to the service of the coronation of the Anglo-Saxon kings.

The second and six following leaves are occupied by the two Epistles of St. Jerome to Pope Damasus, and of Eusebius to Carpianus; and the prologue of the Four Gospels. With the exception of the words 'Beatissimo Papæ Damaso Hieronimus,' (which are in large golden roman capitals, the initial B being ornamented in the Saxon style), and a few of the introductory words of the other articles, (which are in small golden rustic capitals,)

---

[1] Ex MS. Pontificali Eccl. Senonensis, annor. 300.

[2] See tom. vi. Anecdot. Bernardi Pez.

[3] See the Rutland Papers, recently published by the Camden Society, edited by W. Jerdan, Esq. See also the Royal MSS. 12 D iii. 6, and 14 C, vi. 4, the Burney MS. 277, and the Cottonian MS. Tiberius B 8, a. The Cottonian MS. Vitellius, A 7, which contained a copy of the coronation oath of the early English kings, was unfortunately destroyed in the fire of 1731. A copy of it is, however, preserved amongst the MSS. of Junius in the Bodleian Library, numbered

60. See Wanley, in Hickes' Thesaurus, vol. ii. and Hickes' Anglo-Saxon Grammar, the preface of which contains a copy of a precisely similar oath from the Anglo-Saxon MS. Cotton. Cleopatra, B xiii.

[4] Bibl. MS. Stowensis, ii. p. 35. Dr. Dibdin (Bibl. Decam. l. liv.) has strangely confounded the Psalter and Passionale as one volume ; but Dr. O'Conor has fully described both. Astle has given a fac-simile of the former, (Origin of Writing, vol. xix. No. 6,) and Vertue made a fac-simile from the latter, which he presented to the Antiquarian Society, pasted in a folio volume of drawings, p. 25.

the writing of these Epistles, as well as of the text of the Gospels, &c. is the caroline minuscule [1], so much adopted on the Continent in the ninth and tenth centuries.

The 9th to the 12th leaves are occupied by the Argumentum and Breviarius (or synopsis of the breves, or paragraphs) of St. Matthew's Gospel; and on the verso of the 12th leaf is the commencement of the apograph of a charter [2] of King Athelstan, dated 927, whereby he grants to the church of Christ in Canterbury the land of Folcestan super mare, where was formerly a monastery and nunnery, and where Saint Eanswitha was buried.

The charter commences thus:—"Anno dominice incarnationis nongentesimo vicessimo septimo Ego Æthelstanus rex premuneratione eterne salutis & p. salute mea, & anime patris mei Eduardi, p quo reverentia et honore archisacerdotis Wlfhelmi concedo eccle xp̄i in dorobernia," &c.; and terminating with the following signatures:—" + Ego Æthelstanus rex, signo crucis confirmavi; + Ego Wlfhelm̃ dorobernensis archi-ep̄s donatione regis, tropheo crucis consignavi; + Ego Theodredus ep̄ūs lundoniensis subscripsi; + Ego Ælfeagus Wintoniensis ep̄s subscripsi; + Ego Odo Scyrburnensis ep̄s subscripsi; + Ego Wlgaruf dux subscripsi." This charter is also written in a caroline minuscule hand, but different from that of the text of the Epistles and Gospels. The latter portion of it is written on the recto of leaf 13 (of which the verso is left blank); but which was of the same texture and was ruled in the same manner as the remainder of the volume, so that it is clearly not an interpolation [3], as is the following leaf 14. This is evident, not only because the latter is differently ruled, but also because on the blank verso of leaf 13 is the ' set-off' of the ornamental pattern of the design, inclosing the Eusebian Canons, which commence on the recto of leaf 15. Now this interpolated sheet contains on the recto a short Latin poem (partly in rhyme) in honour of Athelstan, written in a hand and ink rather different from the rest of the volume, commencing—

" Rex pius Ædelstan patulo famosus in orbe,
Cujus ubique viget gloria lausque manet,
Quem d̄s angligenis solii fundamine nixum,
Constituit regem Terrigenisq Ducem," &c. ;

whilst on the verso is written an entry in a strong Anglo-Saxon hand, in which is a declaration that Athelstan had given this volume to the church of Canterbury. " Volumen hoc Evangelii ÆÐELSTAN Anglorum basyleos & curagulus totius bryttanie [4] devota mente dorobernensis cathedre primatui tribuit eccte xp̄o dicata," [5] &c. Here, therefore, we have an entry, in strong Anglo-Saxon characters, of a circumstance which could not have occurred long before the entry itself was made, and which refers the writing of the volume itself to a still earlier period, namely, the beginning of the tenth century, when, in fact, the caroline minuscule characters were in full employment.

Leaves 15 to 22 are occupied on both sides by the Eusebian Canons, or references to parallel passages in the different Gospels, which are written within ornamental architectural columns, and rounded arches.

The recto of leaf 23 is occupied by an inscription in large golden roman capitals, " INCIPIT EVANGELĪŪ SECUNDŪ MATTHEŪ," and beneath this are inscribed the two signatures copied at the bottom of our plate, " + Odda rex," and " + Mihthild mater Regis [6]." Hence Mr. Turner [7] conjectures that the volume was a present from Otho of Germany, who married Athelstan's sister, and from Mathilda, the Empress of Henry, and mother of Otho. H. Rosvetha, his contemporary, spells Otho's name Oddo (Reub. 164, and N. Tr. Dipl. iii. 368. Pl. 55. iv. 2). This supposition is partially confirmed, as above suggested, by the style of the writing of the volume.

[1] Or small letters, used during the Caroline or Charlemagne dynasty.

[2] The practice of inserting charters in manuscripts of the Scriptures and Liturgies, was common amongst the Anglo-Saxons. Hickes' Dissert. Epist. p. 9, 10 ; and N. Tr. Dipl. i. 106.

[3] Supposing the volume to have been written in Germany (as has been supposed, and as seems most probable from the style of the writing), and sent to England, it is difficult to conceive wherefore this blank 13th leaf should have been inserted between the end of the Breviarius and the Eusebian Canons ; for I presume that the grant of King Athelstan must have been written in England, and not contemplated by the original German writer.

[4] Athelstan was the first who assumed the title of King of all England. Alfred was merely styled " Occidentalium Saxonum Rex."

[5] A fac-simile of a portion of this inscription is given by Casley in the plates to the catalogue of the Royal Library. The employment of the Saxon letter Ð for TH in the King's name is remarkable.

[6] These signatures are evidently written in the same hand, which is very similar to the capital letters in Cædmon's Paraphrase at Oxford, (Astle, pl. 19, spec. 8); neither this circumstance, nor the identity in the form of the prefixed crosses, however, impeaches their validity (see Bibl. Britann. vol. v. p. 333 ; and N. Tr. Dipl. ii. 430). The same formed G, and the three wedge-like marks after the names, appear in the Pontifical of Egbert, Abp. of York, Sæc. X.; now in the Bibl. du Roi at Paris, copied by Silvestre.

[7] Hist. of Anglo-Saxons, vol. iii. p. 98.

3

The verso of leaf 23 consists of a large illumination, representing St. Matthew, (most coarsely painted, and of a larger size than the figures of the other Evangelists,) seated on a seat with a style in the right hand, and a desk with an open book before him. The upper part of the illumination on the right side is occupied by an angel; the ground of the painting is of a dirty blue green, and the whole is inclosed in a rude arch, from which hangs a green curtain festooned at the sides.

The following page has a large square of purple painted in the centre, on which are the three very large ornamented letters L I B; the remainder of the first verse of St. Matthew's Gospel being written beneath in small gold letters, ' Liber generationis jhū xpī filii dei.'

The two next pages are painted dark blue, and the continuation of St. Matthew's Gospel is written thereon in small golden roman uncials; then follows the remainder of the same Gospel to leaf 69, written in the black minuscule hand represented in my specimen, which is the commencement of the Lord's Prayer; (the sentences beginning with small golden capitals), in which will be perceived the custom of uniting the et in the middle of a word (e. g., sanctific*et*ur) into a &, the long stroke following the & being an evident interpolation, and unlike the ordinary t in the text. The Y-like form of the U or V in Veniat is also remarkable, and characteristic of the period assigned to this MS., which follows Jerome's version of the Vulgate.

Each of the other Gospels is preceded by the same introductory arguments and breviaries. The portrait copied in my plate, is that of St. Mark, who is represented as looking back to inspect a book which a Lion in the clouds is holding in its paws; the ground-colour of this illumination, as well as those of St. Luke and St. John, is of a dirty apple-green, and the whole is inclosed within red columns, supporting a portico, within which is written, in small golden rustic capitals, the laudatory words copied in my plate. On the opposite page are the splendid letters copied in the upper part of the plate, being the beginning of St. Mark's Gospel, " INItium Evangelii jesu christi filii dei," the second and third lines being written in fine-proportioned roman capitals, and the fourth in roman uncial characters. The second and third pages of this and the two other Gospels are written in small roman golden uncials on white vellum.

The portrait of St. Luke represents him seated with a desk before him, and his head turned upwards to a flying bull, which is holding a red book. The first page of St. Luke is occupied by a very large and ornamental Q[1], the initial of Quoniam, the first word of that Gospel. St. John is represented seated, with the body greatly bent, and looking up to a flying eagle, which is not ill drawn; and the first page of this Gospel is occupied by a noble initial J, and the commencement of the Gospel written in small golden uncials, of which a fac-simile has been given in the Pictorial History of England (vol. i. p. 169). The remainder of the volume is occupied by the regulations for reading the Gospels throughout the year. Although extremely rude in their design, the figures of the Evangelists betray but slight traces of Grecian art, so often to be observed in the drawings of this period.

I shall only add that as Athelstan was so great a benefactor to the churches and monasteries of his kingdom[2], and as the volume supplies contemporary evidence of having been given by him to the Metropolitan Church, it is most probable, independent of other circumstances, that after his decease a volume obtained under such circumstances would be employed in future coronations at which the Metropolitan Archbishop must be supposed to have officiated.

---

[1] A nearly similar Q is contained in the Vallicellian Bible of Alcuin (Blanchini, tab. viii.), as is also the same letter in the famous Codex Aureus of the Harleian Library, No. 2788.

[2] Mr. Turner (Hist. Anglo-Saxons, vol. iii. p. 98) mentions three volumes which are recorded to have been presented by Athelstan to various ecclesiastical communities, namely, the Cottonian MSS., Tiberius, A 2 (above described), Claudius, B 5, and Galba, A 18. We are now, however, acquainted with three others, which were similarly bestowed by him, named the Cottonian Otho, B 9, the Royal MS. 1, A 18, and the Gospels of Mac Durnan, now in the library of the Archbishop of Canterbury. (See also the Royal MS. 1 B 7). The Bodleian MS. 2719 (Auct. D 2, 16.) also contains a list of the relics presented by Athelstan to the church of Exeter. That such donations should have insured him a " good report " with his historians, who, in their religious character, were participators of his generosity, is not surprising; but, fortunately for his fame, the list of his library has been preserved; and it is recorded of him, infinitely to his greater honour, that, " like his grandfather Alfred, he was exceedingly fond of the Bible, and *promoted the translation of it into the spoken language of the people*." His liberality is also celebrated in the song of his victory at Brunan Buhr.

> Æthelstan cyning   Athelstan, king;
> Eorla drihten,   Of earls, the lord;
> Beorna *beah* gifa.   Of barons, the rewarder—

or *ring*-given; *beah* being considered by some writers to allude to the ancient ring-money of the Celts. (See Gent. Mag. 1837, p. 500). Others, however, translate the line " of barons the bold chief."—Ellis, Early Engl. Poets, i. 15.

IhPAS

ChA·DOMNI

Initiu Sci euan Secun iohan Cap.i

In principio . erat uerbum Et uerbu erat
apud dm &tr erat uerbu, hoc erat Inprin
cipio apud dm . omnia per ipsum facta sunt ?
&sine ipso factum est nihil Quod factum
est . Inipso uita erat . Et uita erat lux homi
num . &lux intenebrir luc& ?&tenebrae
eam nonconpraehenderunt.

(Incip)

Nam dixit thor elux conbustus quem
doer suocauit Incumpum

OVVEAN TIONES

Lombardic MSS.

LOMBARDIC MANUSCRIPTS.

DESCRIPTION OF THE PLATE.

No. 1. Heading of the Gospel for Easter Day ; and
No. 2. Commencement of the Gospel of St. John, from Mr. Douce's Dominican Gospels.

No. 3. The words "(Incip)iunt questiones" and specimen of Lombardic Minuscule, from MS. of St. Augustine on the Pentateuch, in the Bibliothèque Royale, Paris.

THE successful inroads of Alboin from Pannonia into Italy towards the close of the sixth century terminated in the establishment of the kingdom of the Lombards, who thus became masters of the whole of that country, except Ravenna (which retained its Greek Exarchs until the middle of the eighth century) and Rome (which still remained subject to the Bishop or Pope). The kingdom of the Lombards terminated in 774 ; Didier, the last king, having been conquered by Charlemagne. The name Lombardy has still however been applied to the country south of the Alps to the present time ; and, in like manner, the term Lombardic Writing is given to that peculiar character which was used in the north of Italy, from the seventh to the thirteenth or fourteenth century, when it gave way to the modern Gothic of Italy. Roman in its origin, like that of the Anglo-Saxons, Visigoths, &c., it is nevertheless distinguished by a national style, and by peculiar forms acquired during that long period.

The initial letters of books, chapters, and sections or alineæ, which at first were quite simple and scarcely larger than the rest of the text, began in the seventh century to assume a size and variety of form which has rendered them one of the most simple characters, whereby the age and country of a manuscript may be determined. The capitals of the Lombardic MSS. are generally very massive, blazoned with patches of different colours, or sometimes almost representing very coarse mosaic work, without any of that peculiar intricacy of patterns which distinguishes Anglo-Saxon MSS , except where the influence of some of the Irish or Anglo-Saxon missionaries may justly be presumed. Often these Lombardic capitals are merely Roman in their form, but singularly massive in all their strokes, both ends of which are generally dilated, whilst often whole lines of the headings of MSS. have the letters composed of birds, and especially of fish ; and sometimes of leaves. Often the colours are so arranged as to give the appearance of embroidery work ; and, in other instances, we find the colours contrasted with each other.

The illustrations in the accompanying Plate have been selected, in order to represent these different kinds of initial letters. The specimens numbered 1 and 2, are taken from a fine manuscript of the Dominican Latin Gospels, or those portions which were selected for the service of the Sabbath throughout the year. It formerly belonged to Mr. Douce, and is now preserved in the Bodleian Library, at Oxford (No. 176). It is a small folio, consisting of 127 leaves of parchment, measuring $11\frac{1}{2}$ inches by $7\frac{1}{2}$ inches, with 28 lines in a page. The verso of the first leaf is occupied by the inscription in large Zoomorphic and blazoned capitals, " INCIPIT EVANGELIUM DE CIRCULO ANNI [1]." The initials throughout the MSS. are small and plain, except the following. On the verso of leaf 2, occurs the commencement of the Gospel of St. John ; copied in my specimen, No. 2. On the verso of leaf 61, the initial (V.) of the 28th Chapter of St. Matthew (Vespere autem Sabbati), is formed of a dog and fish, tied together by their tails ; and on the recto of leaf 62 appears the inscription at the head of my Plate, being the heading of the Gospel for Easter Day, the two lines consisting of the words, " IN PASCHA DOMINI," beneath which is the initial letter (I) of the Gospel of the day, measuring not less than six inches in length. The peculiar form of the letter A in the second line occurs in many of the specimens of Lombardic capitals, given by the Benedictines.[2]

The first large initial I, as well as the large foliated mark of contraction over the end of the second line, is nearly like one given by Silvestre from a Gallican MS. of the eighth century of the life of St. Wandrigesile. The latter also often occurs in Merovingian MSS. It is, however, entirely from the capitals that I have

---

[1] Copied in one of the Plates of the Catalogue of the Doucean Library, lately published.

[2] N. Traité de Diplom. 3 pl. 36.

considered this MS. as belonging to the Lombardic school; for the text is written in a splendid Caroline minuscule, of, as I presume, the tenth century, and so plain, that I need not transcribe the specimen of it exhibited in No. 2, and shall, therefore, only notice that the e is generally a little elevated above the line; that the words *deus* and *deum* are contracted as usual by the omission of the two middle letters, and that the conjunctive form of *et* is applied to those letters even when introduced into a word, as in the word *lucet*, in the sixth line.

On the cover of this manuscript is affixed a beautifully carved ivory Diptych, on which is represented, in high relief, the figure of Christ, four inches high, holding a cross in one hand and an open book in the other, whereon are inscribed the letters IHS XPS SUP ASP., in allusion to the figures of the asp and lion beneath his feet. Around the principal figure are represented, in twelve compartments, various events in the life of Our Saviour elaborately carved, and exhibiting traces of Byzantine art, especially in the figure of the Angel in the scene of the Annunciation, which is very similar to one of the Angels in the famous Purple Greek Book of Genesis, at Vienna.

The specimens in the lower part of the Plate are copied from one of Silvestre's most elaborate plates, being portion of the heading of a manuscript of the Commentaries of St. Augustine on the Heptateuch, contained in the Bibliothèque Royale de Paris. The entire title-page is occupied by the words :—

" In Dei nomine.   Incipiunt questiones
Genesis beati Augustini in Eptaticum ;"

forming nine lines, each differing from the rest in design and size.

The initial I is very large, and terminates beneath in a strange lacertine animal of large size, twined into various directions and ornamented with knotted designs. The upper line of my third specimen represents the letters IUNT : the last three of which are conjoined together ; the second stroke of the U forming the first of the N, and the last of the N forming the upright stroke of the T ; it will be seen that these letters are ornamented with interlaced patterns, terminating in eagles' heads (ornamented with a kind of crest, similar to that observed in my first Plate of the Gospels of Mac Durnan). From these circumstances this manuscript is stated by Silvestre to be " Saxonne-Lombardique." The minuscule writing in this specimen is very difficult to decipher, but is to be read :—" Nam dixit hoc uxoribus suis quando eas vocavit in campum." In this specimen the singular form of the a, d, and ri, conjoined together in the word uxoribus, is to be noticed. This type of the Lombardic minuscule is of rare occurrence; but there is a fine manuscript of the Homilies of Origen on St. Luke, in the Library of Corpus Christi College, Cambridge, quite similar, not only in the writing and contractions, but also in the ornamental capitals, especially the letter T, as copied by Astle (Plate XIII. spec. iv.).

Silvestre refers this manuscript to the ninth century.

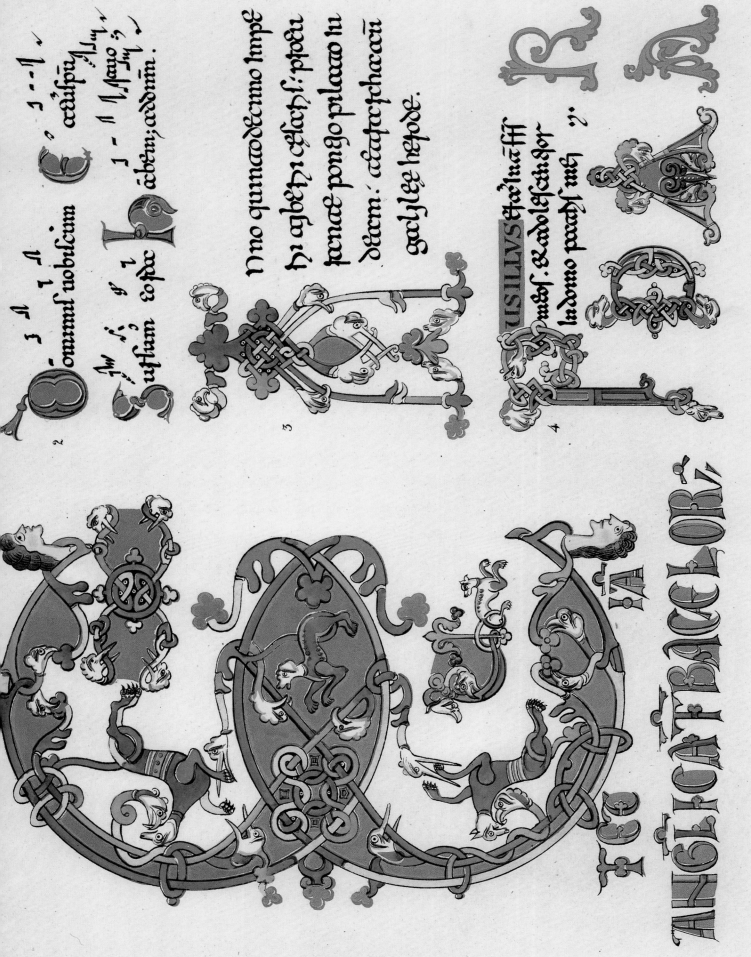

Lombardic   Mss.   Pl. 11.

LOMBARDIC MANUSCRIPTS. PLATE II.

DESCRIPTION OF THE PLATE.

1. The commencement of the "Benedictio Cafrei in Pascha,"— ("Exultet jam angelica turba cælorum");

2. "Dominus vobiscum," &c., accompanied by musical notes; and

3. Commencement of 3rd Chapter of St. Luke's Gospel;—from the Bodleian MS. Canon. Bibl. 61.

4. Commencement of the Apocryphal Psalm of David, with initial letters from Mr. Douce's Lombardic Psalter, in the Bod. Lib.

THE existence of a distinct national system of writing in Italy, notwithstanding all the arguments of the Marquis Maffei [1] and his disciple Ottley,[2] has been fully established by the elaborate researches of Mabillon, the Benedictines, and Messrs. Silvestre and Champollion. It is true that some palæographers, not aware of its characteristics, have confounded it with the Merovingian characters of the French, and even with the Anglo-Saxon styles; [3] some of the peculiarities of which it indeed possesses, especially in its earliest monuments, in common with them, resulting, as may be at once perceived, from their common origin from the Roman minuscule or cursive characters.[4] We are informed by the Benedictines, that the Cardinal Passionei, who, at their suggestion, was occupied for a long period in investigating the history of the Lombardic writings in the most celebrated libraries at Rome, was unable to discover a single MS., written in this character, previous to the eighth century.[5] They accordingly consider that the Abbot of Göttwic, who affirmed that the Lombardic characters were chiefly in use in Italy in the seventh and eighth centuries,[6] mistook the Saxon minuscule for Lombardic. The Liturgies published by Muratori proved its existence in the ninth century; whilst in the eleventh its existence was still admitted, although it was then called Roman.[7] Cardinal Bona, in his work on the Liturgy,[8] informs us that it was the opinion of Italian antiquaries in the middle of the seventeenth century, that the Lombardic characters ceased to be used in the tenth century.[9] The Vatican Virgil, however, No. 1671, is written in Lombardic characters of the twelfth century,[10] which was at first considered by Mabillon to be its limits.[11] In his visit, however, to the celebrated Monastery de la Cava, near Naples, he found two manuscripts which proved that it was still used in 1227. The library of this monastery has remained for the last six or seven centuries in its primitive state, and has afforded to M. Silvestre nearly the whole of his series of specimens of Lombardic writing. Of these the Bible, written in a very minute, distinct, and elegant Lombardic minuscule, of the ninth century, with the headings written in small capitals and uncials; the Treatise of Bede, De Temporibus, of the tenth century; the code of Lombardic laws of the beginning of the eleventh century; a book of Homilies and Hymns in the twelfth century, the Commentaries of Job, of the thirteenth century, the Book de Septem Sigillis, written about 1213, by Benoit de Bari; and the Vitæ Patrum Cavensium, composed at the close of the thirteenth or beginning of the fourteenth century [12] (all except the first being written in the broken Lombardic hand), are all contained in the library of this famous monastery, and prove how long this national character resisted the inroads of the modern Gothic; the ornamented flourished capitals and the

---

[1] Verona illustr. col. 330; Istor. diplom.; and Oposc. eccles.

[2] Archæologia, vol. xxvi.

[3] Thus, Mabillon himself was at first of opinion that the Merovingian of Gennadius, of which he gives a fac-simile, was written in Lombardic (De re Diplom. p. 348, 1349). In like manner Montfaucon considered the writing of a specimen of Papyrus, preserved in the Vatican (written in cursive Roman characters), to be Lombardic, but which Maffei (Oposc. Eccles. p. 60,) determined to have been written in 557, and Keder even in his Commentary on Runic Medals (Acta Erudit. 1705), has confounded the modern Gothic characters with the Lombardic.

[4] "L'écriture minuscule Lombardique n'est qu'une altération de la belle minuscule Romaine, modifiée selon le goût variable de l'Italie,

et sous ce rapport elle peut être considérée comme une écriture nationale Italienne depuis le 7ème siècle jusqu'au XIIIème."—Champollion.

[5] N. Tr. de Dipl. 3, 275. [6] Chronicon Gottw. p. 16.

[7] Mabillon, De re Dipl. p. 52. [8] Lib. 1, Rerum liturg. c. 12, p. 83.

[9] "Ejusdem ævi, decimi nimirum sæculi est Codex Chisius nam caracterem Lombardicum quo scriptus est in fine ejus sæculi desiisse viri periti, a me consulti asseverant."

[10] See "Antiquissimi Virgiliani Codicis fragmenta et picturæ ex bibliotheca Vaticana," dedicated to Pope Benedict XIV.

[11] De re Diplomat. p. 46.

[12] This Manuscript proves, in the style of its ornamental, flourished initials and modern Gothic capitals, that the old Lombardic hand was nearly extinguished by the modern Gothic.

1

headings of the MS. last mentioned, being written in the style which had then, for nearly a couple of centuries, exercised an almost universal sway over the calligraphy of Europe.

The Lombardic minuscule character is distinguished both by the peculiar form of some of its letters, and by the curious mode in which many of them are often conjoined together, so as to present somewhat the appearance of a cursive style. The letter a is generally written with the second stroke curled at the top, more like two letters, cc; the letter c is often formed with a top like our written capital E, the e being similarly formed, but distinguished by a thick horizontal central bar; the g is formed nearly like the Anglo-Saxon 3, but with the top stroke deflexed so as nearly to form a circle. The i is often elevated above the line almost like l; the r is singularly and variously formed, but its variations may be traced (even in its form in the words sursum in my specimen, No. 2 and erā in specimen 4) to the cursive r; it scarcely assumes the Anglo-Saxon form p, neither does the s often take the form of ſ, being generally more like f. The t is perhaps the most characteristic form, having the top stroke of the t produced downwards, and thickened so as to resemble two letters, cc, united by a thick horizontal stroke at the top.

Such are the chief differences in the forms of the minuscule letters, after the Lombardic hand had become most aberrant from its original source. Such is its state in that singular modification which has been termed " Lombardique brisée", from the broken appearance of the strokes of which the letters are composed, and of which the accompanying plate offers several specimens, this character being most evident in the specimen, No. 4.

This hand was commonly employed in the manuscripts preserved in the ancient Benedictine monasteries of Italy, such as Mount Cassen and De la Cava. Such MSS. are unquestionably of great rarity, since the authors of the " Nouveau Traité" favour us, amongst their numerous Lombardic specimens, with but two examples of this style, which had been procured for them by the Cardinal Passionei and the prelate Bottari. D'Agincourt has, however, given nine plates from MSS. at Rome, written in this character, being chiefly liturgical books, from the ninth to the thirteenth century, illustrated with numerous drawings, which are highly valuable as illustrating the state of the art of design in Italy during that period, independent of the Byzantine school. The only drawing contained in the two manuscripts from which the accompanying plate was copied, is a pen-and-ink sketch of the Last Supper in the Canonici MS., of which the following is a copy, and which, as an ancient specimen of Italian art, will be examined with interest.

This drawing as well as the fac-similes, Nos. 1, 2, and 3, in the accompanying plate, are taken from a beautiful MS. preserved in the Bodleian Library, for an acquaintance with which I am indebted to the kindness of the learned librarian of that establishment, the Rev. Dr. Bandinel. It formed part of the Canonici Library, and is marked Can. Bibl. 61. It consists of 198 leaves of vellum, measuring 11¼ inches by 7½, with 19 lines in a full

page ; and (with the exception of a few leaves in an Italian modern Gothic hand, which have evidently been introduced to supply the place of others which had become defaced), is written in a fine Lombardic hand, having the letters only partially broken. It consists for the most part of the lessons from the Gospels used for Sundays and feasts, the initials of which are formed of interlaced ornaments, and rudely-drawn beasts, men, &c., the scrolls terminating in the heads of birds, with long beaks, evidently sketched by the same hand by which the drawing of the Last Supper was executed. A great deal of ingenuity has been shown in diversifying the ornaments of the letter I, which is so often used in the commencement of these lessons, (in consequence of the addition of the words " In illo tempore,"[1]) and which often extend the whole length of the page. The style of these ornamented letters will be perceived in the specimen No. 3, which is the commencement of the 3rd chapter of St. Luke's Gospel, and is to be read " Anno quinto decimo imperii tjberii cesaris; procurante pontio pilato judeam ; tetrarcha au*tem* galjlee herode." The double stroke of the t, the e formed almost as a written capital E, with a bar, and the c sometimes of the same form, but without the bar, the curious form of the conjoined ri, the e with a cedilla for æ, the a formed like cc, the singular form of the r, when written alone, and the i sometimes formed into j, and sometimes like l, deserve notice.

The specimen, No. 1, is the commencement of the Benediction of the Wafer, in the Service of the Mass, which is introduced into the MS., and occupies eight leaves (115 v. to 123), and is accompanied by musical notes. The magnificent initial E is accompanied by a pretty ornament in the open upper space, intended for X, and in the lower space are the letters U and L conjoined, the L formed of the second stroke of the U, united to the dog, which forms the horizontal stroke of the L, the remainder being written in party-coloured Lombardic capitals, "EXULTET JAM̄ ANGĒLICA TŪRBA CÆLORŪM—*exultent divina misteria et pro tanti regis victoria tuba insonet salutaris.*"

The specimen No. 2 is to be read " Dominus vobiscum. Et cum spiritu tuo. Sursum corda. Habem: ad do*minum*," followed by "Gratias agamus dn̄o dō nr̄o. Dignum et justum est. Vere quia dignum et justum est," and which forms part of the Service of the Mass,[2] which the Church of England has retained in the Communion Service " Lift up your hearts. We lift them up unto the Lord. Let us give thanks unto our Lord God. It is meet and right so to do. It is very meet, right," &c. The initial V, of the word Vere, is of large size, in the same style as the E, but having the Lamb of God supporting the cross within a circle in the middle.

The musical notes employed in this MS. are called Neumes, of which the origin dates to the time of Gregory the Great, in the eighth century. They were adopted for the notation of church books, and are of very different forms, of which several examples are given in the course of this work. Here the simple neume consists of a short oblong dash ; but sometimes it is merely a round dot or other well-marked figure. According to its greater or less height above the word, it required a higher or lower intonation of the voice. The relative value of each neume still had to be guessed at, which was avoided by Guido d'Arezzo about the middle of the eleventh century, by placing the neumes on or between red, yellow, or green lines, ruled across the page, the red line indicating that the neume written upon it was the *fa.*

It is difficult to assign a date to MSS. written in these broken Lombardic characters ; but, from a comparison with Silvestre's Plates, this MS. is probably not earlier than the eleventh or twelfth century.

The specimen No. 4 is copied from a charming Latin Psalter, in Mr. Douce's Collection, now in the Bodleian Library, containing 158 leaves, measuring 9 inches by 6, with 20 lines in a full page. The first leaf on both sides contained an inscription, now almost erased, written in alternate lines of red and black Roman capitals upon golden bands. Several leaves have been unfortunately abstracted, amongst which is that containing the first Psalm. The capitals of all the rest of the Psalms, Canticles, &c., are in the style of those copied in my plate, except those of the divisions of the 117th Psalm, which are golden, with red edgings, (two of which are also copied in my plate). All these initial letters are designed with the greatest elegance, the interlaced patterns being arranged with much effect, although far less intricate either than the Anglo-Saxon or Frankish interlaced initials. The verses of each Psalm commence with a small red roman capital, on

---

[1] The Greek Church also commence most of their Dominican Gospel Lessons with the words—" Τω καιρω εκεινω."

[2] This portion of the service of the Eucharistic sacrament was termed the " Sursum corda" from the first two words. It is of the most remote antiquity. St. Cyprian [In orat. Domin.] informs us that the priest prepared the minds of the people by saying " sursum corda" (lift up your hearts), to which they answered, " Habemus ad Dominum", (We lift them up to the Lord).—St. Cyril of Jerusalem, also [Cat. Myst. 5.] St. Chrysostom [Hom. de Encæn.] and St. Augustin [De ver. Relig. cap. 3.] also mention this form.

a small square of gold, and the heading of each Psalm is in red Lombardic minuscule characters. The specimen in my plate is the commencement of the Apocryphal Psalm, which does not occur in Hebrew MSS., nor in the Septuagint version, and is as follows :—" Pusillus er$\overline{am}$ int$\overline{er}$ fr$\overline{atre}$s meos et adolescentior in domo patris mei." In this short fac-simile almost every letter is worthy of the attention of the Palæographer.

At the commencement of the MS. is this note by Mr. Douce :—" This valuable Psalter was written about the year 800 ;" but I should apprehend that it is antedated at least 150 years.

Dominus sicut fortis egredietur et ut uir bellator

HABUCODONOFOR RX

EXPLICIT ECCTA UII LIBRO II
INCIPIT ECCTA UI IN LIBRO II

ngelo filudelfie ecct scribe
hecdicit scs et uerus qui
habet clauem dd qui
aperit et nemo claudit
et claudit et nemo aperit.

The Apocalypse in Visigothic Characters.

THE BOOKS, OF THE PROPHET DANIEL AND OF THE REVELATION, IN VISIGOTHIC CHARACTERS.

DESCRIPTION OF THE PLATE.

The upper line represents a line from a Visigothic Latin choral book marked with musical notes, beneath which is copied Revel. ch. iii. v. 7, having a portrait of Nebuchadnezzar on the left and an armed warrior on the right. At the bottom is a view of the Church of Laodicea, with the angel presenting the book to St. John.

LATIN manuscripts, written in Spain in the Visigothic character, are of very great rarity; for although many such are doubtless contained in the library of the Escurial, of some of which fac-similes have been published by Don Christoval Rodriguez [1], yet elsewhere they are so scarce that the Benedictines were compelled to content themselves with copying Rodriguez' specimens; and even Messrs. Silvestre and Champollion have been able only to give one Visigothic fac-simile, taken from a manuscript, " Louanges de la Vièrge," in Latin, by the Bishop of Toledo, written in the year 989, in Galicia, and which they describe as " un des plus riches et de plus beaux modèles qu'on puisse trouver [2]." This manuscript precisely agrees, in respect to the form of the characters, with that from which the accompanying figures have been drawn, but can bear no comparison with it in point of execution [3].

It is impossible not to be convinced, by an inspection of the accompanying plate, that the Visigoths of Spain adopted the Roman characters, varying them, however, in certain respects. " Les savans conviennent que l'ancien gothique avoit spécialement cours en Espagne. Aldrette, dans son docte ouvrage sur la langue Castellane [4], a publié le modèle d'un MS. de Cordoue. C'est constamment pour le fond l'écriture romaine, quoiqu'elle soit plus nette et plus aisée, comme étant d'une main moins ancienne et plus exacte. L'écriture du missal Mozarabique de Tolède est à peu près la même que la minuscule romaine." [5]

Visigothic capital letters are generally very narrow in form, with the heads of several of the letters elevated considerably above the top of the line. The letters are moreover often conjoined together, as will be seen from the two lines in my specimen, which is to be read—" Explc eccla vᵃ In libro iiº." i. e. Explicit ecclesia 5a. In libro 2do. " Incip. eccla viᵃ In libro iiº " i. e. Incipit ecclesia 6a. In libro 2do.

The elongated tops of the I and L; the tails of the I; the square C, and the conjunction of the letters Inc at the beginning of the second line; the oblique bar of the N, reaching neither the top nor the bottom of the straight strokes, are peculiar. The form of the letters in these two lines closely resembles the first specimen given by the Benedictines, also from a MS. of the Apocalypse, written in the 11th century, in the library of the King of Spain. The MS. before us exhibits many capitals fantastically formed of animals, birds, fishes, leaves, &c. of which the one at the beginning of the paragraph, copied in my plate, is an example, the two fishes uniting to form the letter A.

The Benedictines, notwithstanding their immense researches, were unable to discover a single instance of Spanish Visigothic uncial writing. I have therefore selected two specimens in which it is exhibited; namely, in the name inscribed over the seated monarch Nebuchadnezzar, or, as it is written, " Nabucodonosor rex;" as also in the word Angls (angelus) written over the angel in the lower part of the plate.

The Visigothic minuscule characters are distinguished by several peculiarities. The specimens in the plate are to be read thus :—" Dominus sicut fortis egredietur et ut vir bellator."—The Lord goeth forth like a strong man, and as a man of war.— " Angelo filudelfiæ æcclesiæ scribæ. Hæc dicit sanctus et verus qui habet clavem David, qui aperit et nemo claudit, et claudit et nemo aperit."—(Rev. iii. 7.) And the minuscule inscriptions in the lower drawing are, " Johannes sanctus," St. John, and " ecclesia laudocie," the church of Laodicea. The long heads and tails of some of the letters, the open-topped a, the high-topped e, the e marked with a cedilla for

---

[1] Bibliotheca Universal de la Polygraphia Espagnola, fol. 1738. I have not seen the 13th volume of the Spectacle de la Nature en Espagnol, cited with great praise by the Benedictines, as chiefly executed by the Jesuit B. A. M. Burriell, N. Tr. de Dipl. iii. p. 448, nor the Palæographia Espagnola of Don Terrers.

[2] Palæographie Universelle, livr. 46.

[3] The library of King's College, Cambridge, possesses a fine manuscript Latin Psalter of Orosius, brought from Cadiz, which deserves careful examination.

[4] Del Origen de la Lengua Castellana, fol. 158.

[5] N. Tr. de Dipl. iii. p. 19.

œ, the recurved tail of the *q*, the high short stroke of the *r*, the straight *ſ*, but above all the double-stroked *t*, when written alone, but single when joined in the word *et*, are especially to be noticed. A comparison of these examples with the more ancient ones given by the Benedictines in their 52nd and 60th plates, will show the modifications which took place in the form of these and other letters.

The MS. from which the specimens in the plate have been copied is a most invaluable monument of Spanish art at the close of the 11th century. It comprises a highly illustrated Latin commentary on the Apocalypse, and St. Jerome's treatise on the book of the Prophet Daniel. The authors of the former are stated in the introduction, as follows :—

" In nomine ingeniti prolisque ac pro cedentis co nexa unius semper natura dei tutis. Incipit liber revelationis ipsius domini n̄ſi ih̄u x̄p̄i editus et formatus ab his auctoribus. Id est, iheronimo, agustino, ambrosio, fulgentio, gregorio, liconio, hireneo, abringio, et issidoro."

The volume consists of 279 leaves, in excellent preservation, measuring 15 inches by 9, and on the 277th leaf is given a long account of the history and completion of the MS. itself; from which we learn that it was written in the monastery of Silos, in the diocese of Burgos, in Old Castile; that it occupied twenty years in completion, under the abbacies of Fortunius, Nunnus (Nuñez), and John ; and that it was completed in the year 1109. It was purchased in 1840, for the British Museum, from the Comte de Survilliers (Joseph Buonaparte), and is marked Add. No. 11695.

The first leaf is extraneous, being evidently taken from a coeval choral book; the lines being marked with musical notes as shown in the upper specimen of my plate. The recto of the second leaf is ornamented with a representation of Dives tormented by devils armed with spears and hooks ; and the verso with an arch, elaborately ornamented, within which is a cross supported by a lamb. The verso of the leaf has another beautifully ornamented cross and arch with the monogram **A** and **Ω** (but of the minuscule form **ω**), and the words " Signum Crucis" " Xristi Regis."

The fourth leaf is elaborately ornamented with designs, in which we find the interlacing of the pattern terminating in dogs' heads. The fifth leaf is similarly ornamented with another large cross, inclosed in an arch supported by men, with the monogram **A Ω**, as above, and the words Pax, Lux, Rex, Lex, written in the open spaces formed by the angles of the cross.

The recto of the sixth page is entirely covered with an elaborately tesselated ornament. On the verso of the seventh leaf is a large illumination, representing Christ surrounded by the emblems of the four evangelists in circles ; and the text of the volume commences on the recto of leaf 8.

The text is most profusely ornamented with drawings, which, in many instances, occupy entire pages, amongst which a map of the world, on the 39th and 40th leaves, is a most singular production, in which the Garden of Eden, with Adam, Eve, and the serpent, is conspicuous. On the 222nd and 223rd leaves is represented an attack by armed knights on foot and horseback upon a castle, beneath which is represented King Nebuchadnezzar seated on a chair of state, copied in my plate, and wearing (both here and in many other of the illustrations) a crown of portentous size ; attended by officers who are cutting off the heads and limbs, and putting out the eyes of prisoners. The armed knight copied in my plate is similar to those in this illumination, except that his shield is ornamented and his legs defended by scale armour. My figure is reduced to half the length of the drawing in the original. The rounded form of the shield, destitute of heraldic figures, is worthy of notice, being quite different from the kite shape which prevailed in other parts of Europe about the same period ; especially as we find the other parts of the armour, and particularly the nasal piece attached to the small conical helmet, and the ringed hauberk, precisely similar to those of the Normans and Anglo-Saxons represented in the Bayeux Tapestry.

The drawing at the foot of the plate will afford a tolerable idea of the extremely rude style of art adopted in the execution of the MS. It likewise affords a representation of the Saracenic style of architecture which appears throughout the volume, and which is thus shown to have been as prevalent as it was in the 8th and 9th centuries, in which the celebrated mosque at Cordova was built, wherein the horse-shoe arch is everywhere prominent ; whereas in the Alhambra, which was built between the middle of the 13th and of the 14th centuries, this form of arch seldom appears ; the florid ornaments used throughout the latter erection are in exquisite taste ; and the christian knights represented in the painting of the boar hunt on one of the ceilings appear in plate armour, with visors or ventailles of the 14th century [6].

[6] See Owen Jones' Alhambra, pl. 46, 47, and 48. The Moorish knights represented in these paintings are bearded, turbaned, wearing loose robes with loose sleeves, and swords slung round the neck.

2

Hic est ordo: secundus quem rex debet
coronari pariter inungi. In
primis preparetur pulpitum
aliquantulum eminens inter
magnum altare et chorum ecclesie
beati petri Westmonasterij.

Ce Roy

Regone dei gracia

AMIHHETPR ADPROPINQUABAT eum;
autem dies festus azimorum: qui dicitur pascha, Etquerebant
principes sacerdotum & scribe: quomodoeuminterficerent:
timebant uero plebem Introiuit autem satanas iniudam

The Liber Regalis &c.

THE LIBER REGALIS OF WESTMINSTER AND THE CORONATION BOOK OF RHEIMS.

Illuminated Heading and Miniature of the Coronation of King Richard II., from the Liber Regalis.
Autograph of the same King.

Commencement of one of the Charters of the same King.
Specimen from the Coronation Book of Rheims, at the bottom.

THE Liber Regalis has been justly described as "one of the most curious, authentic, and important manuscripts relating to the coronation of the kings and queens of England which exists." It is, therefore, with much pleasure that I am now enabled, for the first time [1], by the kind permission of the Dean of Westminster, to present a fac-simile of one of its illuminations, representing the coronation of King Richard II., by whom it was presented to the abbots of Westminster, (in the possession of whose successors it has ever since remained,) and at whose coronation, in 1378, it is stated to have been used. When it is recollected that this monarch finished Westminster Hall; that he gave divers sums for rebuilding part of the old portion of Westminster Abbey, together with the revenues of the Priories of Stoke-Clare and Folkstone ; that he likewise granted lands to this church of the yearly value of £200, and gave a ring of great value to St. Bernard's shrine ;[2] that he also bequeathed most of his jewels to the same use [3] (although the injunctions of his will were not allowed to be enforced); that he lies buried in the Abbey, where his monument still remains, and his cognizance, the white hart, is still to be seen, painted of a colossal size, on the wall over the door leading to the east cloister from the south aisle ; and that there is still preserved in the Jerusalem Chamber an original portrait of him, we may easily conceive how much he was attached to Westminster and its noble buildings, which doubtless led to the circumstances which render the volume in question so interesting.

The Liber Regalis is a thin folio of only 37 leaves, or 74 pages, measuring $10\frac{1}{2}$ inches by 7, written in a bold modern Gothic character, with 23 lines in a page. The frontispiece to the volume represents the coronation of the king, copied in my plate. This likeness of the king differs considerably from the portraits which have come down to our times, and which have been published in the Vetusta Monumenta, and by Fenn, Shaw, and others, but more closely resembles his effigy upon his tomb. It is to be observed, that in the other illuminations of the volume the same likeness is preserved. It will be seen that the dresses of the two courtiers are divided exactly in half, one side being blue and the other pinkish red. Now, Chaucer, who wrote during the reign of Richard II., expressly mentions this fashion as being very prevalent ; and in the Cottonian MS. marked D 6, there is an illumination representing John of Gaunt sitting to decide the claims on the coronation of his nephew, Richard II., in which the long robe is divided in half; one side being blue, and the other white, being the colours of the house of Lancaster. The peculiar cut of the sleeves, narrow at the wrist and brought far over the back of the hand, the form of the hat, and short pointed beard, are also characteristic of this foppish period. They may also be seen in the Royal MS., 20 B 6, of the same date.

The back-ground of the illuminations in the Liber Regalis is of highly burnished gold, with scrolls, represented by minute punctures upon the surface of the gold.

The ornamental heading of the accompanying plate represents the commencement of the MSS., written in a fine modern Gothic text ; the directions for the ceremonial being, of course, as was usual, rubricated, (whence the term rubric came to be applied to the directions for the Service of the Church in general,) the prayers being

---

[1] Mr. Strutt, in his "Regal and Ecclesiastical Antiquities," published an engraving asserted to have been made from the Liber Regalis, but which was, in fact, taken from another manuscript belonging to the Dean and Chapter of Westminster, as Mr. Planché has stated in his new edition of that work. [2] Rym. Fœd. viii. 76.

[3] Neale and Brayley's " Westminster Abbey," p. 89.

1

written in black ink. The initial H and the ornamental border are fine specimens of the style of illumination in practice about the end of the fourteenth century, in which we see the golden dots and ivy leaves, daisy buds, punctured gold ground, and the marginal ornaments springing from a slender column formed of two different coloured bars. The ornaments are carried all round the first page, the lower portion forming a very elegant device. The passage copied is to be read :—

" Hic est ordo secundum quem Rex debet coronari pariter et inungi [1]. Imprimis, preparetur pulpitum aliquantulum eminens inter magnum altare et chorum ecclesiæ beati petri Westmonasterii."

After the directions for the mode of fitting up the Abbey for the coronation, it directs that the king, the day before the coronation, shall ride with his head bare from the Tower to the Palace of Westminster, that he may be seen of all his people. The portion relating to the declaration and oaths made and taken by the king is as follows :—

" Finito quidem sermone ad plebem metropolitanus vel episcopus eundem" (sc. regem) "mediocri distinctaque voce interroget, Si leges et consuetudines antiquis justis et Deo devotis regibus plebi anglor. concessas, cum sacramenti confirmatione eidem plebi concedere et servare voluerit, et presertim leges consuetudines et libertates a glorioso rege Edwardo" (sc. Confessori), " Clero populoque concessas." Subsequently the metropolitan inquires of the King, " Servabis ecclesiæ dei cleroque, et populo pacem et integro et concordiam in deo secundum vires tuas? Respondebit, servabo. Facies fieri in omnibus judiciis tuis equam et rectam justiciam, et discretionem in misericordia et veritate secundum vires tuas? Respondebit, Faciam. Concedis justas leges et consuetudines esse tenendas, et promittis eas per te esse protegendas et ad honorem dei roborandas quas vulgus elegerit secundum vires tuas? Respondebit, Concedo et promitto." Then follows the episcopal admonition, after which, " Princeps confirmet se omnia predicta esse servaturū sacramentū sup̄. altare corā cunctis ptiñs prestito."

The ceremonial of the coronation of the king terminates on the 46th page. Then follows the ceremony of the joint coronation of the king and queen, preceded by an illumination, in which each is seated on a chair, and with the like number of attendants as in the drawing of the coronation of the king, who here holds the sceptre and ball in his hands. Next, the various fees to be paid to the Convent of Westminster, and the nomination of certain persons to perform offices on the day of the coronation. The Earl of Leicester is to perform the office of seneschal, though the Duke of Norfolk has claimed the right. This part is very curious, as the coronation of Richard II. affords the first record of the proceedings of a court of claims, holden by John of Gaunt, uncle to the king, as already mentioned above. There is a very curious circumstance in the ritual, concerning the administration of the sacrament to the king and queen. They are to receive wine, but it is explained that it is no part of the sacramental service. The queen is allowed to take it as a sign of *unity.* The coronation of the queen alone commences with the 65th page, and is preceded by an illumination of her coronation, which is almost precisely similar to that of the king, and on page 71 is an illumination representing the king lying in state, beneath a Gothic canopy, crowned, and with the sceptre and ball in his hands, which precedes the ceremony for the funeral of the king.

When Queen Caroline claimed to be crowned with George the Fourth, the Dean of Westminster was summoned to attend the Privy Council, and to produce this book [2].

It may be further mentioned that the late John Dent, Esq. possessed a fac-simile copy of this volume, bearing on its cover the arms of the French dukes of Duplessis. It is thought extremely probable that this manuscript

---

[1] The necessity for the sanctity of the oil employed in the ceremony of anointing the kings, both of this country and France, led to the concoction of some most singular miracles. The Cottonian manuscript Cleopatra, C 4, gives us the version of the words spoken by the Virgin Mary to Thomas à Becket, whilst in banishment at Sens, in France, —" de oleo illo quo reges Angliæ futuri inungendi erunt :" and the circumstances connected with the recovery, in 1825, of some of the precious contents of the " Sainte Ampoule," (brought from Heaven by a white dove at the coronation of King Clovis,) after its supposed destruction after the breaking out of the Revolution, in 1793, almost partake of the ludicrous. The ceremony, although derived from the Jewish laws, does not appear to have prevailed in European nations before the coronation of Charlemagne, (see contra, N. Tr. Dipl. v. 396, note).

[2] In some of the popular accounts of the Abbey, it is recorded, from Malcolm, that, for the regulation of the ceremony of the coronation, a most magnificent book was compiled in very remote times, and kept among the archives of the monastery, but that this was unfortunately burned in 1664, along with many others, but that a copy, or abridgment of it, is contained amongst the Harleian MSS. Is not the Liber Regalis the book here alluded to ?

A small tract entitled, " A Collection out of the Book called Liber Regalis, touching the Coronation of the King and Queen together," was published in 1821. London, 8vo.

was sent to France, to satisfy the scruples of Henrietta-Maria about our coronation ceremonies, previous to her marriage. "In the case of the coronation of Charles I.," said Lord Brougham, in his speech before the Privy Council, "Henrietta-Maria was said to have objected to take any part in it, unless she could be assisted by a popish priest, which the constitution rendered impossible;" and, in fact, at her coronation, she did not take the sacrament with the king.

The signature in the accompanying plate, on the left of the coronation of Richard II., is a fac-simile of his autograph attached to a paper in the Cottonian Library connected with the surrender of the town of Brest. It is stated by Sir Henry Ellis to be the earliest known autograph of any of our kings, and not to have been published. It has, however, since been copied by Nicholls, in his Book of Autographs. The character after the subscription Le Roy R, which Sir H. Ellis regarded as an E, appears to me to be intended for the letter S, (as Mr. Nicholls has also suggested), since it can hardly be supposed that the king, who, as Froissart casually informs us [1], read and spoke French perfectly well, would have written Le Roi Richard of England, instead of Le Roi Richard Second. Indeed, instances of such a formed S are not very uncommon; and one almost precisely similar is given by the Benedictines amongst the letters of the English cursive Alphabet of the 14th century. N. Tr. de Dipl. pl. 33, S. 14 Sæc. No. 5.

The writing on the opposite side of the plate (Ricardus Dei gracia) is from the commencement of one of the charters of Richard II., in the third year of his reign, and is introduced to show the peculiarity of the diplomatic writings of the age. In the original, the initial of the king's name is a very large roman R, the R here copied being the initial of the word Rex in the first line of the charter. It will be seen that the small r in the word gracia still preserved its elongated Saxon character; and the s at the end of the word Ricardus approximates in form to the character after the R in the opposite inscription.

The beautiful manuscript book of the coronation of Charles V., of France, in the Cottonian Library (Tiberius, B 8) forms a fitting companion to the Liber Regalis.

I have, however, thought it more interesting to copy from Silvestre a portion of a fac-simile given by him from a manuscript belonging to the library of Rheims, having for its title "Selectæ Lectiones ad Usum Archi-monasterii S. Remigii Remensis pro festis solemnioribus," and including the Gospels used at the coronations of the kings of France. It is a singular manuscript, and is supposed by Silvestre and Champollion to have been written in the sixteenth, in imitation of the style of writing of the eighth or ninth century. The figures of the evangelists are introduced, but they are not rudely coloured in blue and red patches, but have the drapery elegantly disposed and harmoniously coloured, quite at variance with the style of the drawing of that early period which the writing would indicate. The initial letter I is formed of fleurs-de-lis, an appropriation of that flower as the symbol of France, not in use until long after the eighth or ninth century, whilst the writing affords still stronger grounds for regarding the manuscript as a comparatively modern production: capital, uncial, semi-uncial, and minuscule letters are here blended together in a manner which never occurs in legitimate manuscripts. The form of many of the small letters also betrays a similar origin, the copyist having occasionally used a much more modern form in his letters. The passage is from the beginning of the 22nd Chapter of St. Luke's Gospel, and is to be read, " In ill̄(o) t̄(em)p̄(o)r̄(e) Appropinquabat autem dies festus azimorū(m) qui dicitur pascha : Et quærebant (eum) principes sacerdotum et scribæ, quomodo eum interficerent; timebant vero plebem. Intravit autem Satanas in Judā(m)." In this passage the word *intravit* assumes the greatest appearance of Anglo-Saxon writing; and the diphthong æ is formed of the e with a cedilla.

[1] See Illum. Illustr. of Froissart, pl. 17.

The Psalter of K. Henry VI.

PSALTER OF KING HENRY VI.

EXPLANATION OF THE PLATE.

Miniature containing the portrait of the young king kneeling before the Virgin and Child, at the head of the 38th Psalm.

THE manuscript from which the accompanying Plate is drawn, is justly regarded as one of the choicest treasures of the British Museum, where it is preserved, amongst the Cottonian MSS., with the mark Domitian XVII.

It is a Latin Psalter, written upon 286 leaves of vellum, $7\frac{3}{4}$ inches long by $5\frac{1}{2}$ wide, in a moderate-sized modern Gothic hand, fifteen lines occupying one of the ordinary pages, the illuminated initials at the beginning of each verse being rather small. Each page is inclosed in a border formed of gold leaves, similar to the middle portion of the border on the right hand side of my plate; and as the gold is extremely brilliant, an idea may be obtained of the rich appearance of the volume.

The Calendar occupies the first six leaves, being written in the French language, and composed, for the most part, of French saints, some of which are distinguished by having their names written in gold, amongst which are Sts. Louis and Catherine. Then follow tables for computing the time of the moon's age, dominical letters, &c., the commencement of which is as follows :—" Januarius, Anno Domini MCCCCXX ;" thus fixing the period of the execution of the volume.

The miniatures, of which there are sixteen in number, commence on the verso of leaf 11 ; the first occupying the entire page, and representing the interior of a richly-decorated Gothic church, with a bishop preaching to a congregation of monks.[1] The text of the Psalms commences on the recto of leaf 12, with the well-known " Beatus vir," &c. The illuminated upper part of the leaf, divided into two compartments, represents David and Bathsheba, beneath which is David, playing on his harp, surrounded by his attendants; whilst, at the foot of the page, we have the representation of a child, about ten years old, in a surcoat and mantle of England and France, and crowned, kneeling alone before an altar. The same figure is repeated in four other places— namely, on the recto of leaf 49, in which he is represented kneeling before the Virgin and Child, attended by St. Louis, wearing a crown and the French royal purple mantle, *semé fleur-de-lys*; God the Father, attended by a chorus of angels, enveloped in a scarlet glory, occupying the upper part of the miniature. The drawing copied in my plate occurs on the recto of leaf 74 ; whilst on leaf 176, the same figure occurs, attended by several courtiers ; one of whom is regarded as the Duke of Bedford, Regent of France : and on leaf 205, the crowned child kneels alone in a church, where the service is performed by a number of priests, in various-coloured dresses. Other miniatures, of a devotional character, are interspersed through the volume : such as a representation of the service of the mass, monks at their devotions, nuns in their stalls, (all three of which are engraved in Dibdin's Bibliographical Decameron), the Virgin crowned in the presence of many saints, &c. The pages with miniatures are further ornamented with little grotesques, one of which, in the accompanying plate, represents a child riding on the back of a lion, carrying a toy still used and made precisely in the form here seen. In the miniature before us, the angels attendant on the Virgin are engaged in a concert, one playing on the hand-organ, another on a guitar, and a third on a kind of dulcimer.

A note, at the commencement of the volume, in the handwriting of Sir R. Cotton, states that it was originally in the possession of King Richard II., whose effigy is given in the miniatures of the crowned child ; and the same statement occurs in the description of the volume in Planta's Catalogues, copied verbatim from Smith.

---

[1] The engraving given by Dibdin (Bibliogr. Decamer., 1. p. cii.) is not taken from this illumination, as stated by that author, but from a subsequent leaf.

Mr. Strutt[1] has consequently given a copy of the miniature on the recto of leaf 69, describing it as "Richard II. and his father," but omitting the glory round the head of the Saint; whilst C. H. Smith[2] has copied the child and St. Catherine from the miniature represented in my plate, describing it as King Richard II. with an attendant, supposed to represent Joan Plantagenet, Princess of Wales and Countess of Kent, surnamed the Fair Maid of Kent. The last-named author further observes—

"It is rather remarkable that the illumination from which the plate is copied should have escaped the attention of Mr. Strutt, or that he should have failed to recognise in the portrait the wife of the Black Prince, when he had already acknowledged another similar miniature in the same book for that of her husband. Both represent King Richard before the age of manhood, dressed in a tabard of his arms, and attended by one of his parents, with ducal coronets on their heads, but, from the circumstance of the nimbus that surrounds them, personifying saints. The prince, being habited in a robe semé fleur-de-lys, seems to represent St. Louis. The princess, with a palm branch in her hand, and what appears to be a wheel at her feet, is probably in the character of St. Catherine. Why these two saints should have been selected as tutelary beings to the young king it is not easy to determine."

The difficulty suggested at the end of this quotation, however, vanishes when it is stated, that these miniatures represent King Henry VI., and not King Richard II. The date above mentioned at the head of the lunar tables fully proves this, since Richard II. was murdered in A. D. 1400, whilst Henry VI. was crowned at Paris A. D. 1431, when ten years old. This will account for his being attended by St. Louis[3] in one of the illuminations, whilst St. Catherine attends him in another as his mother's patroness, her own name being Catherine.

Of the style of art in which these miniatures are executed, I shall avail myself of the remarks of an author who has more deeply studied the character of the various states of the art during the Middle Ages than, perhaps, any other living writer.

"The character of the writing," observes Dr. Waagen, "and the pictures, decide for the first half of the fifteenth century. The latter are most delicately painted in water-colours, and breathe the spirit of the school of the brothers Van Eyck, of whom John, the greatest painter of his age, was at that time at the zenith of his art. This Flemish origin is the more easily accounted for, as the Duke of Bedford, who was then Regent of France, and had the greatest influence in all the affairs of the young king, was married to Anne of Burgundy, sister of Philip the Good, Duke of Burgundy, and sovereign of the Netherlands, the great patron of John Van Eyck. The delicacy of the heads is admirable."[4]

---

[1] Dresses and Habits, vol. ii. pl. 84.

[2] Selections of Ancient Costume.

[3] Dr. Waagen, Art and Artists in England, i. p. 143, overlooking the nimbus or glory round the head of St. Louis, describes it as the Duke of Bedford, uncle of King Henry VI. and Regent of France.

[4] I must request the indulgence of the subscribers to this work for the very insufficient manner in which I have endeavoured to furnish an idea of the beautiful original of this plate. It is consolatory, however, to think, that nothing short of a most highly-finished miniature could do justice to the illumination itself.

2

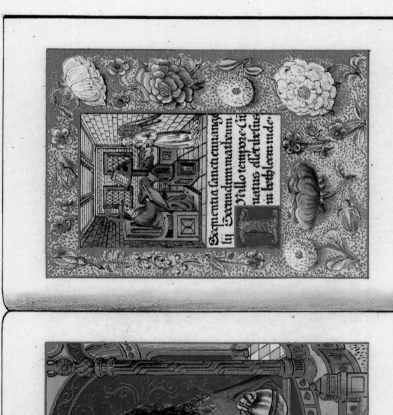

The Prayer-Book of Mary of Burgundy.

THE PRAYER BOOK OF MARY OF BURGUNDY.

DESCRIPTION OF THE PLATE.

Portrait of Christ ; Miniature of St. Matthew writing his Gospel, and Commencement of the Second Chapter of his Gospel.

IN the small but truly select collection of Illuminated Manuscripts, in the Library of the Rev. J. Tobin, of Liscard, near Liverpool, the Prayer Book of Mary of Burgundy holds a very prominent place. Its small size, indeed, will not allow it to compete with the famous Bedford Missal; but the delicacy of its execution and the beauty of its illuminations, together with the historical interest which attaches to it, render it a scarcely less covetable production of middle-age art.

This little volume consists of 422 leaves of fine vellum, measuring 4¼ inches by 3, and commences with the Calendar, which occupies 24 pages surrounded by miniature borders, in which are depicted the occupations and amusements of the several months, which are very simply and animatedly delineated. Interspersed throughout the volume are 55 miniatures of Scriptural subjects, and representations of the Saints (exclusive of those of the Calendar), which are most beautifully executed ; the tone of the flesh is rather inclined to purple, and several may be recognised as the models of certain well-known pictures ; as for instance, in the Christ, copied in my plate, that of the famous Jan Van Eyck, in the Berlin Museum, and in the Virgin with the Child (which is the largest and least elegant drawing in the book), that of Van Eyck's picture, where she is painted by St. Luke, formerly in the Boisserée Collection, now in the Gallery at Munich.[1] Amongst these larger miniatures are several portraits of the Duchess herself, in one of which (fol. 26), she is represented kneeling before a table with an open missal before her, wearing a black velvet head-dress, which falls over the shoulders and back, and attended by St. John the Baptist and an Angel ; reminding us very forcibly of the portrait of Anne of Brittany, in the famous Horæ of that Princess in the Bibliothèque du Roi, engraved by Dibdin.[2] The arms of Mary of Burgundy are represented in front of the Volume.

Some of the representations of female Saints at the end of the Volume are exquisite specimens of art, and equally valuable as illustrating the dresses of the fifteenth century.

The borders of most of these larger miniatures consist of architectural designs, beautifully finished with gold, whilst those of the smaller miniatures generally consist of single buds and flowers, beautifully painted upon a subdued golden ground. Besides these, every page has three little marginal drawings of animals, birds, butterflies, or grotesques, true to nature or full of cheerful humour. The initial letters are of gold, upon a coloured ground, and the writing is in a small but very clear modern Gothic character.

On the whole, this little Volume justly deserves the observation of Waagen, that " it is one of the most delicate and elegant remains of the school of Van Eyck." It was purchased by Sir J. Tobin, for the price of 120*l.*, at the sale of the Hanrott Collection.

The Princess, for whom this little gem of art was executed, was the daughter of Charles the Bold, Duke of Burgundy, being his only child by his second wife, Isabella of Bourbon. She was born at Brussels in 1457, and in 1477 (being the same year in which her father was killed at the battle of Nancy) married Maximilian of Austria (afterwards Maximilian 1st), by which important event the Netherlands and Burgundy were united to Austria. The issue of this marriage was Philip, who married Johanna, heiress of Castile, by whom he had Charles V., and hence the rivalry of France and Spain.

She died in 1482, from a fall from her horse, and the magnificent tombs of herself and her father (which are two of the most elaborate works of monumental art in existence) adorn the church of Notre Dame at Bruges.

---

[1] Waagen (Arts and Artists in England), 3, p. 178.　　　　[2] Bibl. Tour, Vol. ii. frontisp.

My thanks are especially due to the Rev. J. Tobin for his kindness in permitting me to examine, describe, and make drawings from the charming little volume above described ; in addition to which, the gems of his collection are,

The Prayer Book of Francis I. of France (of which a fac-simile of one of the miniatures is given by Dibdin, Bibl. Decam., plate facing clxxix), purchased for 115*l.* from the collection of Sir Mark Sykes ;

The Breviary of Queen Isabella of Spain (of which Dibdin has also given a fac-simile, pl. clxvii, from the drawing of St. John in the island of Patmos), bought at the sale of the Hanrott Collection for 160*l.* ; and, to crown the whole,

The famous Bedford Missal, of which Gough published a long description, with copies of three of the most interesting of the miniatures,[1] and which cost Sir John Tobin 1000*l.*, the late Duke of Marlborough having previously paid 687*l.* 15*s.* for it. Previous to this it was sold, with the rest of the Duchess of Portland's collection, by auction, for 203 guineas.[2] As these three volumes have already been illustrated, I have preferred giving a fac-simile of the little volume above described.

---

[1] Gough's own copy of this descriptive volume, with the coloured copies of the three miniatures, executed with care upon vellum, is now in the British Museum Library.

[2] An interesting anecdote is recorded respecting this sale by Mr. Dawson Turner. Previous to the sale taking place, King George the Third sent for his bookseller, and expressed his intention to become the purchaser. The bookseller ventured to submit to his Majesty that the article in question was likely to fetch a high price— " How high ? "—" Probably two hundred guineas ! "—" Two hundred guineas for a Missal ! " exclaimed the Queen, who was present, and lifted up her hands with extreme astonishment.—" Well, well," said his Majesty, " I'll still have it ; but since the Queen thinks two hundred guineas so enormous a sum for a Missal, I'll go no farther." And at the sale Mr. Evans actually carried off the prize by a bidding of three pounds more than that sum. (Tour in Normandy, vol. i. p. 213.) The good taste of King George III., in endeavouring to secure this historically interesting work of art, led to the preservation and subsequent appropriation to the nation (by gift to the British Museum) of other scarcely less valuable MSS., amongst which is the Missal of King Henry VIII., described in another article of this work.

2

Dmine exaudi ora
aonem meam : et cla
mo2 meus ad te Seniat
on auertas faciem tuam
a me in quacumqz die tribulor In
clina ad me aurem tuam
in quacumqz die Jnuocauie
rote Stloater exaudi me

3

6

Ixi custodiam vias meas vt
non delinquam in lingua
mea olui ori meo custodiã cum

5

Et silon mon affection la supreme sera
en voz prieres ne seray ge z5 oblie
car voz suis   HENRY.   & Jamays

Prayer-Books of K. Henry VII & VIII.

PRAYER BOOKS OF KINGS HENRY VII. & VIII.

DESCRIPTION OF THE PLATE.

1. Illuminated Border ; and
2. Commencement of the 101st Psalm, from Henry VII.'s Missal. Reg. MS. 2 D. 40.
3. Copy of the Autograph of Henry VII., from his Prayer-book in the Duke of Devonshire's Library.

4. Portrait of Mary Magdalen ; and
5. Copy of the Autograph Note of King Henry VIII., from his Missal. Royal (Geo. IV.) MS. No. 9.
6. Fac-simile from the Psalter of K. Henry VIII. Royal MS. 2 A. 16.

KING HENRY VII., amidst all his deep "wisedome and pollicie," so highly praised by Grafton, appears to have been a true son of the Romish Church.[1] "He advanced churchmen," says Bacon, "he was tender on the privilege of sanctuaries, though they did him much mischief, he built and endowed many religious foundations besides his memorable hospital of the Savoy." He appears also to have possessed a strong taste for finely illuminated books of devotion, whereof his Missal, which he presented to his daughter, Queen Margaret of Scotland, inscribing his own gigantic autograph several times therein (and which is now in the possession of the Duke of Devonshire), is described by Dibdin (Bibl. Decameron, i. p. 156). It is of an octavo size, adorned with miniatures, amongst which is a large Head of Christ, highly coloured, but with the chin disproportionately short, and surrounded by a blue radiated back-ground within a border of flowers. Many of the miniatures are half-lengths, of a large size, and among the smaller ones are the Martyrdom of St. Thomas-à-Becket, and St. George on horseback, completely armed. The borders are adorned with flowers and fruits interspersed with Death's heads. The writing is large and Gothic, but the ink is faded. The autograph represented in my No. 3 is copied from Dibdin.

The British Museum possesses another Missal (or rather the remnants of one), which formerly also belonged to the same monarch. It is amongst the Royal MSS., and is marked 2 D. 40. It measures 11 inches by 7, and in its present state consists of only 52 leaves, with very wide margins, only 18 lines being written on a page, the writing occupying 5 inches by 3. It contains portions only of the Psalms, Prayers, and Lessons from the New Testament. The writing is in a late modern Gothic hand, of which the specimen, No. 2, will give an idea. It is the commencement of the 101st Psalm.

The initial letters of each verse are painted in a subdued lilac colour, upon a gold ground, with a crimson margin, the open spaces of the letters occupied by flowers, fruits, animals, &c. ; the initial letters of the Psalms being rather larger than those of each verse, but being similarly ornamented. The borders, however, with which every page is ornamented, constitute the great charm of the Volume. Each consists of a sprig of some flower painted to the life, but accompanied by ornamental foliage, of various colours, most elaborately finished, the introduction of which cannot be deemed in correct taste. Many of these leaves are heightened with touches of gold, the whole being painted upon a deadened gold ground, with shades to each leaf and stem which give great relief, and produce a very natural and most charming appearance. Some of these borders are not so highly finished as the rest, and bespeak a different hand, and the butterflies, and other insects, upon the plants, are entirely the creatures of the artist's fancy.

Our National Library likewise possesses two Volumes of still higher historical interest, having belonged to Henry VIII., and both bearing MS. notes in his own handwriting. One of these subsequently belonged to King George IV., and is now amongst his MSS. at the British Museum, bearing the No. IX.

This beautiful Volume measures $7\frac{1}{2}$ inches by 5, and consists of 288 leaves of very fine vellum, written in a late modern Gothic hand, similar to that in Henry VIIth.'s Missal, with 16 lines in a page, the greater portion of the pages being destitute of borders. It is, however, very richly adorned with numerous miniatures, and the pages where these occur are enriched with elaborate borders, upon a deadened golden ground, with flowers (especially sweet-peablossoms, and red and white roses—the red preponderating), birds, insects and strawberries, and ornamental foliage, of a subdued lilac colour, peculiar to this period.

At the commencement of the Volume is the Calendar, extending over 24 pages, with rather rudely drawn emblems, followed by a representation of the Crucifixion, with the Virgin and St. John standing at the sides, and angels holding chalices, catching the blood falling from the wounds of our Saviour.

[1] The splendid book of Indentures between the King and the Abbot of Westminster (Harl. MS. No. 1498) may be here alluded to.

1

Then follow 15 Prayers to Jesus Christ, and a number of "Commemorations" of Saints, 18 of whose Portraits (half-lengths) are most elaborately painted on the leaves preceding their several Commemorations. Many of these portraits are so highly characteristic, that it seems unquestionable that they were intended as likenesses of some of Henry's contemporaries.

The portrait in my plate appears opposite the Commemoration of St. Mary Magdalen. It has been selected as a good specimen of the series, and on account of the singular style of the head-dress.

Amongst the Saints thus commemorated is Thomas-à-Becket, whose name (unerased) also appears in the Calendar.

One of these portraits (that of St. Katherine, on the 86th page) is especially interesting, representing a fair-featured female, wearing a crown, and with long flowing golden-coloured hair, and habited in a blue dress. This portrait again appears in page 76, as the Virgin bearing the Child, also as the Virgin visiting Elizabeth (page 122), where she is represented without the crown; again in the 102d page, as the Virgin, in the drawing of the Annunciation: in page 156, as the Virgin, in the drawing of the Angels worshipping the new-born Christ: also as the Virgin, in page 176, in the Offering of the Wise Men; in page 184, in the drawing of the Presentation in the Temple; and in page 192, in the Slaughter of the Children. It seems quite evident that this is not intended for an ideal portrait, since at the foot of the 102d page, beneath one of these portraits, we find the following lines, in the handwriting of the King (which have been partially erased, and from which his signature at the foot has been cut):

> " be daly prove you shalle me fynde
> " to be to you bothe louynge and kynde."

Historically considered, these portraits must represent a crowned Queen, a mother and a Roman Catholic, whose Christian name was Catherine, (to whom these lines were addressed,) and who must have lived previous to Henry's abjuration of the Pope. Now, Henry's first wife well answers all these various requisites, and it may be added that her marriage with Henry " was not celebrated with the ceremonies prescribed for widows, but with those appropriated to maids, and that *she wore her hair loose*." I therefore consider that these portraits are intended for Queen Catherine of Arragon, and that the Volume was presented to her by the King.

To these follow the Horæ Beatæ Mariæ Virginis, the Penitential Psalms, the Vigiliæ Mortuorum, the Psalter of St. Jerome (who is represented in the front illumination robed as a cardinal), &c.

The autograph note copied in my specimen No. 5 occurs at the foot of page 434, beneath an illumination representing the Bloody Sweat of our Saviour. It is to be read ' Si silon mon affection la sufvenāce [1] sera en vos prieres ne seray gers [2] oblie car vr̄e suis, Henry R. a jamays," and must, I think, be considered as addressed to the then object of his affections, to whom in all probability he presented the volume.

With the exception of the initial letter of each division of the book (which is prettily formed of broken branches of trees), the capital initials of each verse and prayer are small and of gold, and placed upon a scarlet ground.

The Royal MS., marked 2 A. 16, is a charming Volume, measuring 8 inches by $5\frac{1}{2}$ inches in size, and $1\frac{1}{2}$ inch thick. It consists of the Latin Psalter, beautifully written in small Roman [3] minuscule letters, with small gilt capitals to each verse, placed upon small squares of different colours.

On the first page are emblazoned the royal arms, surrounded by an elegant wreath, with red roses at the corners (the centre leaves of the roses being white), the whole upon a large golden square, followed by a short Latin preface, by " Johannes Mallardus, Regius Orator," addressed to King Henry VIII., whose portrait, seated in his chamber, appears on the verso of the following leaf, at the head of the first Psalm, Beatus Vir., &c. The architectural ornaments and drapery of the curtains in this drawing are delicately painted, and the portrait of the King resembles the ordinary representation of him.

There are six other beautiful miniatures scattered through the volume, in several of which the King is again introduced as David, wearing a flat black velvet cap, edged with white feathers.

Each leaf consists of 17 lines, and almost every leaf bears some mark or short note of the Royal owner of the Volume, in pencil, ink, or red chalk, thus, the verse " Non reliquit hominem nocere eis et corripuit pro eis reges" laconically annotated, " n. bene."

---

[1] Souvenance.   [2] guères.
[3] From this period may be dated the decline of modern Gothic writing, as well as of Gothic architecture.

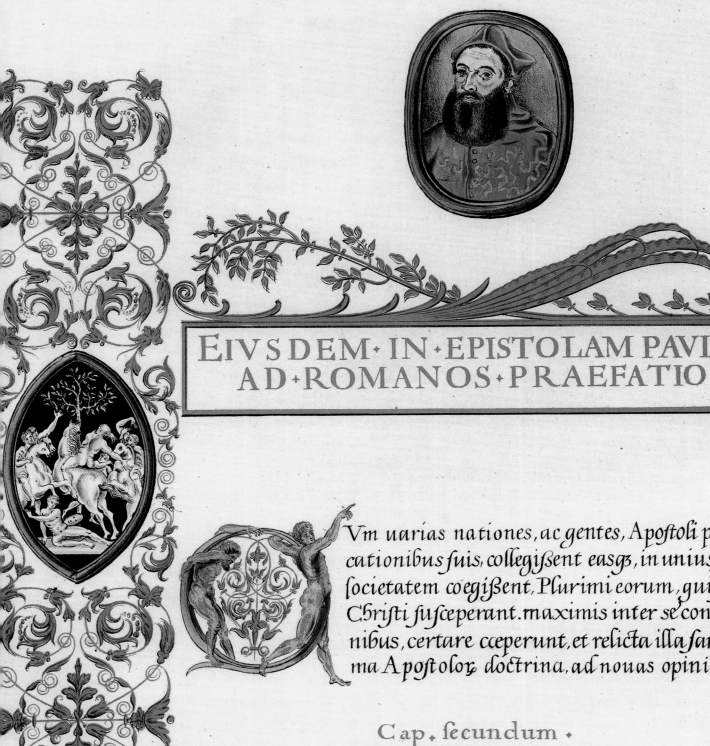

EIVSDEM · IN · EPISTOLAM PAVLI AD · ROMANOS · PRAEFATIO

Vm uarias nationes, ac gentes, Apostoli prædi-
cationibus suis, collegissent easq3, in unius fidei
societatem coegissent, Plurimi eorum, qui fidē
Christi susceperant. maximis inter se contentio-
nibus, certare cœperunt, et relicta illa sanctissi-
ma Apostoloӷ doctrina, ad nouas opiniones.

Cap. secundum ·
PRopter qđ iexcusabilis es o ho ois qiudicas, in quo
·n·iudicas alteӷ teipm cōdénas eadē·n·agis quæ iudicas·

The Soanean Clovio.

THE SOANEAN CLOVIO MS.

DESCRIPTION OF THE PLATE.

Portrait of Cardinal Grimani ; Ornamental border and heading, and commencement of the Cardinal's Preface to his Commentary on the Epistle to the Romans ; with Part of the text of the same Epistle in golden letters.

THE great patronage so nobly bestowed by the Popes and other high dignitaries of the Roman Church, during the 14th, 15th, and 16th centuries upon the fine arts, naturally developed the talents of many Italian painters of miniatures, whose names have come down to us in connection with the productions of their pencils, which were for the most part employed in illuminating Church books or other religious MSS. That Cimabue, Giotto, Simone Memmi, &c., the great restorers of painting in the 13th and 14th centuries, bestowed a portion of their talents upon the illumination of MSS., is more than probable,[1] when the great resemblance between the style of the miniatures in manuscripts, and of the early frescoes, is considered : indeed the progress of the art is as clearly to be traced in Italian miniatures as in the frescoes themselves, and yet the former have been almost entirely neglected. Amongst these earlier Italian miniaturists are to be mentioned Oderico of Sienna, whose name is attached to MSS., dated 1213, in the Library at Florence. Guido of Sienna is also mentioned by Lanzi as having flourished at that same period. Oderigi of Gubbio and his pupil, Franco Bolognese, who died at the beginning of the 14th century, are both immortalised in the 11th Canto of the *Purgatorio* of Dante—the former, for his artistic vanity, being consigned to the infernal regions;

> " ' O,' disse-lui, ' non sè tu *Oderisi*,
> L'onor *d'Agubbio*, e l' onor di quell' arte
> Che alluminar è chiamata in Parisi ?'
> ' Frate,' diss' egli, ' più ridon le carte,
> Che pennelleggia Franco Bolognese :
> L'onor è tutto or suo, e mio in parte.' "

Simone, who died in 1345, Giovanni da Fiesoli (born in 1387), Filippo Lippi, Jacobo Fiorentino, Silvestro, Don Bartolommeo della Gatta, and Gherardo Fiorentino, are also to be noticed as uniting the practices of miniature and fresco painting during the latter part of the 14th and former half of the 15th centuries. During the following century, the splendid talents of Francesco Veronesi, and his son, Girolamo dai Libri, of Vante (the illuminator employed by the famous Matthias Corvinus, King of Hungary), of Francesco Squareione, and of Giovanni Bellini, were for the most part employed in the decoration of books for the Papal library, and which are amongst the most highly prized of illuminated MSS., as, indeed, was also Julio Clovio, the most celebrated of all the Italian miniaturists. This renowned painter was born in 1498, and died in 1578. He was instructed in the art by the famous Girolamo, above mentioned.[2] The following characteristics of his style will be at once perceived in the specimen given in the opposite plate. " His figures, of the most exquisite design and execution, are generally extremely diminutive, though he preserves the expression of the features, &c., with the greatest accuracy. Michael Angelo was his favourite model ; but, with the correctness and grandeur of this master, he combined much of the grace and elegance of Raffaelle, and, although his drawings are not richly coloured, there is a fine effect of chiaro 'scuro in his smallest as well as in his largest productions. He seldom employed gold, and when he did, it was only a slight wash." Nothing can, in fact, exceed the difference between the works of this artist and those of his fellow-countrymen two hundred years before his time. Theirs—for the most part stiff and heavy, with all the characteristics of the worst period of the Byzantine school—and his, amongst the most marvellous copies of nature, perhaps, ever executed.

---

[1] It is, indeed, affirmed respecting Ciambue and Giotto (D'Agincourt, Hist. Art. par les mon. 2 Peint. p. 49) ; and one of the most valuable MSS. in the library of the Arsenal at Paris, contains a number of miniatures reputed to have been executed by Taddeo Gaddi.

[2] Detailed Notices of most of these Artists will be found in the first volume of the Bibliograph. Decameron.

The productions of Julio Clovio are extremely rare in this country. Several are described by Dr. Dibdin[1] with much care ; in addition to which may be mentioned the Strawberry Hill Psalter, being a MS. of small size, with 21 illuminated subjects, and which, at the late sale of Horace Walpole's Collection, was bought in at the price of 441l. ; and the Soanean Volume, hitherto undescribed, and from which the accompanying fac-similes have been made.

This magnificent Manuscript measures 16½ by 13 inches, and contains an unpublished Commentary on the Epistle to the Romans, by Cardinal Grimani, written on 148 leaves of the finest vellum.

The 1st leaf, r, contains the commencement of " Marini Grimani Veneti S. R. E. Cardinalis ac Patriarchæ Aquileiæ Epistola in Commentarios epistolarum Pauli ;" which is inscribed in a transverse slab, coloured to represent grey marble, in golden roman capitals.

The borders of this page are ornamented with elegant Italian arabesques and medallions, with birds, flowers and scrolls, and at the foot of the page is a landscape, with a distant city, mountains, shipping, &c., most delicately finished in colours.

The initial I, at the beginning of the Epistle, is formed of a man standing erect, coloured to imitate bronze, and relieved with touches of gold.

The commencement of the Preface to the Romans, with the very elegant border copied in the plate, occurs on the verso of folio 2, which extends to the 10th leaf, the verso of which is occupied by the frontispiece to the Epistle ; a most noble composition, representing the overthrow and conversion of St. Paul. The Apostle, clothed in Roman costume, fallen to the ground on his back, occupies the left of the picture ; and his astonished companions, on horseback and foot, the right side ; the Saviour, attended by cherubs in the clouds, at the right hand of the upper part of the picture ; and two children, holding the prancing horse of the fallen Apostle, on the left side above. The colouring of the group is delicate rather than rich, but the marginal ornaments are truly gorgeous. These consist in the upper part of naked figures, supporting various pieces of armour and medallions, whilst at the lower part, on the left side, is a female figure, with a green robe, slightly cast round the shoulders and legs, nearly 6 inches high, painted in the most delicate miniature style of art ; at the foot of the picture, naked infants support a small circular miniature of the martyrdom of St. Paul, whilst others carry off various pieces of armour. On a small slab, at the foot of the picture, is inscribed—

" Marino Grimano car. et legato Perusino, Patrono suo, Julius Crovata pingebat."[2]

The commencement of the Commentary occurs on the opposite page. It is entitled,

" Marini Grimani Veneti S. R. E., Cardinalis et Patriarchæ Aquileiæ in epistolam Pauli ad Romanos commentariorum, Cap. Primum ;"

inscribed on a dark marble-coloured slab, supported by infants, with two female figures holding a cross and cup. The borders of this page are illuminated in the same splendid style as the opposite page. The portrait of the Cardinal author himself, copied in my plate, appears in the middle of the right hand border, and beneath him the figure of a Roman warrior, six inches high, most beautifully painted. At the foot of the page, in a small circular slab, are the arms of the cardinal, supported by six naked infants, an angel holding the cardinal's hat. The distant landscape of this little composition is most delicately finished, as are also the two dragons at the sides of the shield ; a scroll at the foot being inscribed with the word Prudentes, whilst another scroll, at the top of the page, (on which are seated a pair of doves,) is inscribed Simplices.

It is quite impossible to convey an idea of the exquisite beauty and finish of these miniatures, which, in the harmonious blending of the tints, resemble the most highly painted china, rather than paintings upon vellum, whilst the design and drawing are equally charming.

The remainder of the volume is entirely occupied by the text of the Epistle, written in verses in golden Roman minuscule letters,[3] and the commentary thereon written in a semicursive Italic hand.

---

[1] Bibl. Decam. 1, 188, particularly a missal belonging to Mr. Towneley, and a series of historical pictures in the library of Mr. Grenville. Vasari describes many of his productions in the continental libraries.

[2] Vasari has given a very different inscription, written by Julio Clovio upon one of his productions.

[3] The fac-simile is the commencement of the 2d Chapter of the Epistle to the Romans—" Propter quod inexcusabilis es, o homo omnis, qui judicas. In quo enim judicas alterum, te ipsum condemnas : eadem enim agis quæ judicas." The curious style of the contractions in this specimen, as well as those of the words easque, fidem, and apostolorum, in the commencement of the preface, are worthy of notice.

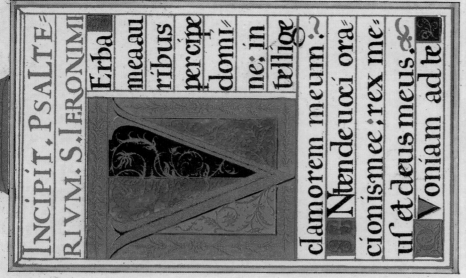

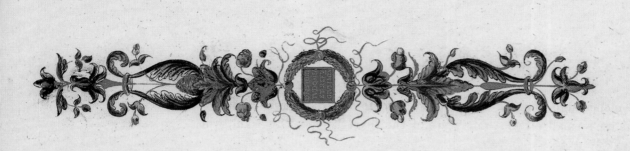

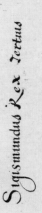

Sigismundus Rex Tertius

Prayer-Book of K. Sigismund.

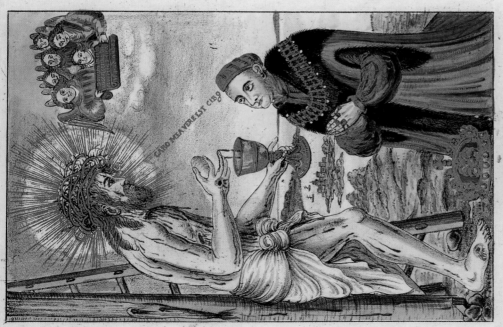

THE PRAYER BOOK OF KING SIGISMUND, OR THE STUART MISSAL.

THE manuscript now to be described is highly interesting, not only for its historical associations, but also for the beauty of the writing, which we perceive to be in the " beaux et anciens caractères romains," the hideous gothic (or modern gothic) letters being exploded about the period assignable to this volume, namely, about the middle of the 16th century.

The volume is of an octavo form, measuring 7 by 4½ inches in size, and forms one of the gems of the library of his late R. H. the Duke of Sussex. It possesses four most exquisitely finished miniatures, one of St. Luke with the bull, writing his Gospel, gorgeously coloured; a second containing the portrait of King Sigismund himself, who is represented kneeling before the Saviour, who stands at the foot of the cross, and presenting the King with the elements of the holy communion, uttering the words " Caro mea vere est cibus." A chorus of angels in the clouds sings, " Domine in cœlo misericordia tua et veritas tua usque ad nubes ;" the distant landscape is very delicately touched with gold. The third miniature consists of the full-length portrait of the Virgin and Child, with the King kneeling at the side of the former. The execution of the folding of the drapery in this miniature is very masterly. The fourth miniature is allegorical. Many of the borders are ornamented with foliated arabesques, very richly painted, and bearing coats of arms, two of which are added on the plate; but in others they are in the Italian style, one of which is copied in my plate, with the words, ' Dn̄s fortitudo mea et refugium meum,' inscribed in small roman golden capitals on a scarlet square.

The specimen of the text copied in the plate is the commencement of the 5th Psalm, " Verba mea auribus percipe domine intellige clamorem meum Intende voce oracionis mee rex meus et Deus meus Quoniam ad te— orabo ; Domine mane exaudies vocem meam," written in the renovated roman minuscule characters, which are here seen to equal in beauty the most elegant modern type (the peculiar shaping of the letter 'a' being worthy of notice), as well as the large and beautifully ornamented initial V. The heading of this page is occupied by the inscription, " Incipit Psalterium S. Jeronimi," in square golden roman capitals ; and above this, on a small oblong scarlet slab, is inscribed in golden minuscule letters, " Salvum fac domine regem nostrum Sigismundum ;" thus indicating that the volume was written for a King Sigismund of Poland, whilst the autograph itself, Sigismundus Rex tertius, sufficiently indicates that the volume was the property of the third King of that name, who commenced his reign in 1587.

At the end of the volume are some additional prayers and invocations of saints, with their effigies, from some other indifferently executed Missal, at the end of which are some leaves filled with entries of dates of births, marriages, &c., of the family of that sovereign: the first being in 1478, of the birth of Isabella Aragone; —the second in 1494, of the birth of Bona fortia, Queen of Poland ;—the third is as follows :—" Die primo Augusti 1520, Cracovie prope diem albescente' pulsata statim septima hora noctis precedentis natus est Illm̄us princeps Dn̄s Sigismundus modernus futurus rex et heres cui sidera faveant nestorea, etatem imperii felicissimi et optabile."

Sigismund the Second commenced his reign in 1540, and Sigismund the Third in 1587. By the marriage of our Pretender James, the son of James II., with Mary Sobieski, this volume came into the possession of the Stuart family, in which it continued till the death of Cardinal York, at Rome, when it passed into the

1

hands of the late Duke of Sussex, with some other Stuart relics. The volume has been unmercifully cropt by the binder, many of the splendid borders being quite cut through, and in many parts, especially the pages containing the penitential Psalms and prayers for seasons of affliction, the writing is almost effaced by frequent usage.

Dr. Dibdin, in his Bibliographical Tour (vol. iii. p. 180, 2d edit.), mentions another very splendid Polish Missal, in 8vo, which also belonged to Sigismund, King of Poland, in the 16th century : the letters, graceful and elegant, but the style of art heavy, although not devoid of effect. It is preserved in the public library at Landshut. If written in the Polish language, as Dr. Dibdin's words imply, it is especially interesting.

1

ⷭⷶⷬⷯ М А Д Е К Е Б РЯ: ьъдⷬ
ⷭ у ⷶ тка
с т р о с т ѣ н м ц н · в а р ъ к р е с у ш мⷬ
въ · въсле дыⷭандашм на
р о д н м н о з н · н о у г н е т
а х о у т д н · н ж е н д е т е р
а с ѫ ц н н ѣ ь т о у е н н е кⷬ

2

3

4

5

Ке сⷩ тнⷣшиа меисти Д' фрарв нот таюⷣарⷯлаиз
Гⷩ · сⷩлоютвоею возвеселитсацрⷭ

6

БЛАЖЕН МУЖ ЕЖЕ НЕ ИДЕ НА СОВѢСТИ НЕЧЕСТВЫИХ

Sclavonic Biblical MSS.

SCLAVONIC BIBLICAL MANUSCRIPTS.

REFERENCES TO THE PLATE.

Specimens 1 & 2 from the "Texte du Sacre."

Specimen 3.—Glagolitique à lunettes, from the Vatican Evangelistiarium.

Ornamental Heading, and Specimen 4, from the Harleian Gospels,
No. 6311.

Specimen 5, from the Harleian Græco-Sclavon. Psalter, No. 5723.

Specimen 6.—Psalm 1. i. from the Royal MS. 16. B 2.

A CONSIDERABLE portion of the savage tribes of Russia, Lithuania, and Poland, who in the sixth and seventh centuries of the Christian era made great inroads upon the Roman and Greek empires, were established about A. D. 550 into the Duchy of Poland under Lech, the chief of the Sclavonians; whilst other portions, after shaking off the yoke of the Avars, became established as the kingdom of the Bulgarians, which lasted until the eleventh century, when they were again reduced to a Greek province. These numerous tribes, however distant or adverse, used one common language [1]. Incapable of fear, and of a roving disposition, they came into frequent contact both with the Greeks and Romans, and from both they obtained a knowledge of the Christian religion, although it may be easily conceived how little their habits would allow them to profit thereby. From the Greeks, too, they derived their letters, which, with some modification, have at length become those of the modern Russian alphabet; Cyril (or Constantine, surnamed the Philosopher, on account of his learning) who converted the Moravo-Sclavonians to Christianity in the latter part of the ninth century, having modified the Greek alphabet, whence the Servian letters are called the Cyrillitan characters.

It has indeed been asserted that Cyril invented these characters; " but it is manifest," says Dr. Henderson [2], " that this invention consisted in nothing more than the adaptation of the ancient characters of the Greek alphabet, so far as they went to express the sounds of the new language, with the addition of certain other new letters borrowed or changed from other alphabets [3] to make up the deficiency. He also substituted Sclavonic for the Phenician names of the letters, on which account the alphabet has been called Cyrillic, after his name." The correctness of this opinion will be evident by comparison of the various letters comprised in my first specimen with those of the ordinary Greek uncials.

1.	The Sclavonian	AS or A . .	is represented in the first letter of the last line of this specimen.			
2.	„	Buki, Booke, or B	„	in the first letter of the sixth specimen.		
3.	„	Viedi, Vadi, or V	„	in the sixth letter of the last line of the first specimen.		
4.	„	Glakol, Glaghol, or G	„	thirteenth	„ fourth	„
5.	„	Dobro, Dobra, or D	„	third	„ fourth	„
6.	„	Jest, Yest, or E	„	eleventh	„ last	„
7.	„	Zelo, Ziclo, or Z .	„	eighth	„ fourth	„
8.	„	Ziviete, Sevetie, or Zothi, form of Z,	} are not represented. Zemla is a small ξ modified.			
9.	„	Zemla, Zemle, a third form of Z,				
10.	„	Ize, Eie, or ï	„	ninth letter of the third line in first specimen.		
11.	„	I, E, or Y	„	fifth	„ last	„
12.	„	Kako, Kawko, or K	„	sixth	„ first	„
13.	„	Ludi, Ludee, or L	„	fifth	„ third	„
14.	„	Muislete, Mislete, or M	„	first	„ first	„
15.	„	Nasz, Nash, or N	„	sixth	„ fourth	„
16.	„	On, Ohn, or O	„	second	„ fourth	„
17.	„	Pokoi, Pokoy, or P is the Greek Π.				
18.	„	Irei, Rlse, or R	„	first	„ fourth	„
19.	„	Slovo or S	„	second	„ last	„
20.	„	Tuerdo or T	„	eighth	„ last	„
21.	„	T or T is not represented, but is formed of three equal upright strokes, united at the top by a horizontal hair-line.				
22.	„	Phert or F is the Greek Φ.				

[1] Gibbon, v. p. 218.

[2] Biblical Researches and Travels in Russia, London, 1826, p. 67.

[3] Half of these however, at least, are considered by the Benedictines to be composed of two or more letters united into one. (N. Tr. de Diplomat. i., p. 707.

SCLAVONIC BIBLICAL MANUSCRIPTS.

23. The Sclavonian Oniku or U is represented in the fourth letter of the fifth line of this specimen.

24.	„	Kher or Czer	„	tenth	„ last	„
25.	„	Ot is the Greek ω.				
26.	„	Ci	„	ninth	„ second	„
27.	„	Sza is formed of three equal upright strokes, united at the bottom by a horizontal line.				
28.	„	Szcza or Stshaw	„	fourth letter in the last line.		
29.	„	Yerr or Jor is a Z with an oblique stroke uniting the middle of the descending line with the extremity of the bottom one.				
30.	„	Ju, } are not represented.				
31.	„	Ftita, }				
32.	„	Ja is represented in the seventeenth letter of the third line.				
33.	„	Jat or Yat	„	fifteenth	„ fourth line.	
34.	„	Jus	„	third	„ of the last line.	

The Benedictines give the characters of four of these alphabets, namely the Servian or Cyrillitan, the Russian printed, the cursive Russian, and the Illyrian or Hieronymian. The first of these consists of forty-two letters: namely, A; B; V; Gh; D; E; K, Y, or Zh; Z; Dz; I; Th or Ph; I; Y; K; L; M; N; X; O; P; Ge; Thc; R; S; T; Y; W; F; Chh; Ps; O; Tz or Cz; Schtsch; Sch; E mute; Ui; I mute; E or Le; E; Ya; You; Yous.

In the preceding alphabets, as well as in that which is named the Illyrian or Hieronymian, being ascribed to a Saint Jerome, it will be at once seen that there are several letters " which seem to be of northern origin, being adapted to sounds peculiar to the languages of the people descended from the Scythians settled in Europe[1]."

In general, the Cyrillitan alphabet was adopted by those Sclavonians who were converted by the missionaries of the Greek church; whilst the Hieronymian alphabet (specially named the Glagolitic, and including that curious species termed the Glagolitique à lunettes) is that of the Sclavonians of the Roman Church[2]; there are, however, some exceptions to this distinction.

The Sclavonian or old Russian version of the New Testament Scriptures, was made from the Greek towards the end of the ninth century, and has been ascribed to the above-mentioned Cyril and Methodius, sons of Leo, a Greek noble of Thessalonica. Of the Old Testament, it has been supposed by Dobrowski that only the book of Psalms was thus early translated: there are, however, frequent quotations from the book of Proverbs, by Nestor, the author of the Russian Chronicle, who died in 1156; whilst the remainder of the Old Testament appears still later to have been translated, a circumstance confirmed by the extreme rarity and recent date of MSS. of the entire Sclavonic Bible[3]; and " Dr. Henderson has shown by actual collation that the Sclavonic text of the Old Testament in the folio Editio Princeps of the Bible, printed at Ostrog in 1581[4], was made with the assistance of the Vulgate, or some ancient Latin MSS., found in the Bulgarian monasteries, or that it was at least revised and altered according to them." Whereas, in the Sclavonian New Testament, the Greek construction is very frequently retained, even when contrary to the genius of the language, and contains at least *three-fourths* of the readings which Griesbach has adopted into the text of his critical edition of the New Testament, and possesses few or no *lectiones singulares*, or readings peculiar to itself. Griesbach has given a list of the Sclavonian MSS. collated for his edition of the New Testament, communicated to him by Dobrowski[5].

Silvestre has given numerous specimens of Sclavonian Biblical MSS., which, on account of their great rarity, merit mention. His first specimen is taken from a History of the " Saints Pères," written in the eleventh century, and contained in the Bibliothèque Royale de Paris. His second is from a Psalter written at the end of the twelfth century, in Cyrillitan characters, during the reign of the Bulgarian king, Assan, and accompanied by a translation of an allegorial commentary, from the Greek, and attributed to Athanasius, from the library of Saint Saviour, at Bologna: the capital letter in this specimen represents a grotesque, griffin-like figure, with a long ornamented snout, and its tail twisted round its neck. His third specimen is from an

---

[1] Astle, p. 58, 91; and Tab. xxvi.

[2] Bishop Walton, in the Prolegomena of his noble Polyglot Bible, states that St. Jerome translated the Bible into the Dalmatian language, that he wrote it in characters approaching those of the ancient Greeks, and that he taught the people of Dalmatia the use of letters. It appears, however, that this was not the great St. Jerome, but a person of the same name, who lived at a much later period.

[3] Henderson, pp. 73, 74; Horne, Introd. ii. p. 245.

[4] " Wiwlia sinetz knigi, wetchago i nowago sawieta pojasiku slowensku;" and see Clement (Bibl. Curieuse, iii. p. 441—444); Dibdin (Bibl. Spencer. v. i. p. 90—); and especially Henderson, Biblical Researches.

[5] Michaelis, v. ii. p. 153—636; Griesbach, Prolegomena, v. i. p. cxxvii.; Beck, Monogrammata Hermeneutices, Nov. Test. 108; Hug. vol. i. pp. 513—517, referred to by Horne, op. cit. p. 246.

2

ancient copy of the Sclavonian New Testament, attributed to the twelfth or thirteenth century, from the Royal Library of Vienna, and written in large square black and red characters. His fourth specimen is from a selection from an Evangelistiarium of the thirteenth century, in the Vatican, written in Cyrillitan characters, containing lessons from the Gospels throughout the year. By Assemani this MS. has been attributed to the eleventh century; but Dobrowski assigns it to the thirteenth century, as it contains lessons not in use in manuscript lectionaries of so ancient a date as is assigned to it by Assemani.

Silvestre's fifth plate of specimens (from which my first and second examples are copied) is taken from a MS. Evangelistiarium of great interest, belonging to the "Bibliothèque Communale de Reims, vulgairement nommé Texte du Sacre," the commencement of which is ascribed to the eleventh, and the latter portion to the fourteenth century, and which Silvestre describes thus:—" Un des plus précieux monuments de notre histoire nationale; car ce serait sur ce même livre que les rois de France auraient prêté serment *par le saint évangile touché*, le jour de leur onction religieuse dans la cathédrale de Reims." This assertion appears to have originated in the statement of the Abbé de la Pluche [1], and to have been partially adopted by the person who made the inventory of the effects of the Cathedral in 1790, attested by the signature of several of the canons of that time; but M. Paris, Librarian of the Cathedral (who has published a long account of this MS.) [2], has questioned this usage; supposing that it may, in its original state, when bound in gold and relics (which disappeared at the Revolution), have been used for the Oath Book of the French kings; but adding that there is also another ancient Latin Evangelistiarium at Rheims, which has also lost its precious covering, and which might also have been thus used, and the two thus confounded [3]. When, however, we consider that the former manuscript was, (as appears from the inventory of relics and other valuable articles belonging to the Cathedral at Rheims) not only enclosed in a silver-gilt cover, but also enriched (as it is stated) with a cross formed of the real crucifix [4], a piece of the sponge and girdle of our Saviour, and other relics, of St. Peter and St. Philip the Apostles, and various saints, and that it traditionally belonged to Saint Jerome himself, and was said to have been brought from the treasures of Constantinople, when ravaged by the Turks;—we can scarcely doubt but that such a volume (presented to the Cathedral by the celebrated Cardinal de Lorraine, in 1574) should have been adopted as the book most fit for the usage which has been attributed to it. Moreover, the principle "omne ignotum pro magnifico" must likewise be supposed to have had some weight in the matter; for the contents of the volume, and even the language in which it was written, were unknown until some of the attendants of Peter the Great, who paid a short visit to Rheims in 1717, asserted that the book which was shown to him as one of the precious relics of the Cathedral, contained in the former part of the volume a Sclavonic Evangelistiarium; although the latter part of the MS. was undecipherable by them. Since that period the volume has occupied the researches of many writers. Aller [5], Silvestre de Sacy [6], Dobrowski [7], M. Kopitar [8], M. Jastrzebski [9], and Eichhoff [10], having published various notices respecting this manuscript.

It is a volume of a small quarto size, written on forty-seven sheets of vellum in double columns, on both sides of the leaves. The first part of the volume (sixteen sheets) is in the Sclavonic language written in Cyrillitan characters, containing various lessons from the New Testament, according to the Greek catholic church. The specimen marked 1 in my plate is from the third page of this part. The second part of the manuscript (thirty-one sheets) is in the same language, but in angular Glagolitic characters, and likewise contains lessons from the Gospels for Sundays, commencing with Palm Sunday. The second specimen given in the accompanying plate is from the first page of this second part, which is terminated by a notice, dated in 1395, stating the nature of the volume, and that the Cyrillitan portion was written by the hand of St. Procopius himself, and that the Ruthenique version was given by Charles V., Emperor of the Romans, to a monastery dedicated to St. Procopius, and to the Sclavonian St. Jerome.

M. Silvestre has given a considerable number of additional Sclavonian specimens in the Cyrillitan character.

---

[1] Spectacle de la Nature.

[2] Chronique de Champagne, 1837, pp. 401 et seq.

[3] The latter was first published by G. Estau, under the title of Consecratio et Coronatio Regis Franciæ, MDX.

[4] The oath of the French king at his coronation, as Grand Master of the Royal and Military Order of Saint Louis, and of the Royal Order of the Legion of Honour, was taken, at least until the revolution of 1830, "on the holy cross and the holy gospels."

[5] Mélanges de Philologue et de Critique, Vienna, 1799.

[6] Magasin Encyclop. de Millin, v. année 1799, t. vi. p. 457—459.

[7] Institutiones Linguæ Slavicæ Dialecti Veteris. Vindob. 1822, 8vo.

[8] Glagolita Clozianus etc. Vindob. Gerold, 1836.

[9] Notice sur le Texte du Sacre, Journ. du Ministère de l'Instruction Publique, 1839.

[10] Histoire de la Langue et de la Littérature des Slaves.

—more recent however than those mentioned above,—one of which is a copy of the Gospels at Vienna, of a folio size; the upper portion of the leaf occupied by a splendid square illuminated ornament, with knots interlaced together. The first line in most of these later MSS. has the letters long, attenuated, and distorted, and chiefly gilt, as in my fourth specimen.

In addition to these M. Silvestre has given several specimens of Glagolitique manuscripts from the Royal Libraries of Paris and Vienna, of the fourteenth century, and one of that peculiar species of Glagolitic which is termed à lunettes, and which is employed in the most ancient manuscripts (of which a specimen from M. Silvestre's plates is represented in my third specimen) being part of an Evangelistiarium and Menologe in the Bulgarian language, belonging to the Vatican Library, which has been attributed to the eleventh and thirteenth centuries, and which, although written in the Glagolitic character, is arranged according to the rites of the Greek church, contrary to the general method adopted in the writings of the two churches, and which has led M. Kopitar to believe that the Glagolitic character, à lunettes, was used by both churches in the earlier days of the Christian Sclavonian church.

The authors of the Nouv. Tr. de Diplomatique, t. i. p. 708, pl. xiii. col. ix., have given an alphabet from a fragment of this character, which they term Bulgarian, contained in the Royal Library at Paris (No. 2340).

Sclavonian MSS. are of great rarity in this country. There are, however, several in the Harleian Collection in the British Museum. From one of these, (No. 6311) a codex bombycinus, or small quarto MS. of the four Gospels on silk-paper, of the fifteenth or sixteenth century, the beautiful ornament represented at the head of my plate is taken, together with the fourth specimen, in large golden capitals, being the first line of the beginning of St. Luke's Gospel; the text being written in Cyrillitan characters. Each of the Gospels is followed by a rudely-drawn hand holding a crucifix, with a superscription in large letters and a rudely-drawn star-like ornament on each side.

The singular interlacing of the patterns adopted in this and the majority of Sclavonian illuminated MSS., calls to mind the Anglo-Saxon school; but the drawings are made with far less precision and regularity, although great taste is often employed in their design. One of them, copied by Silvestre, representing the interlacing of a narrow white ribbon, with golden edges and a blue line along the middle, has a charming effect. These ornaments at the head of the page are derived from the Greek illuminators. For higher art the Sclavonians may well be deemed to have had but little taste, and we accordingly possess scarcely any remains of their skill in design. D'Agincourt[1] has, indeed, given specimens from a fine MS. of the Bulgarian Chronicle of the thirteenth or fourteenth century, preserved in the Vatican, which, as well as an illumination from the Byzantine Chronicle, translated into Bulgarian of the fourteenth century, copied by Silvestre, are absolutely Greek in their style of art.

The Harleian MS. 5723 is a small Psalter, of the fourteenth century, written in red Cyrillitan characters, with a Greek interlineary translation in black letters; it is destitute of illumination, the capitals alone being very slightly ornamented. My fifth specimen is taken from this manuscript.

Numbers 3389 and 7630 in the same library, are also Biblical MSS., as is also, I believe, a single fragment in the Burney collection, No. 277; whilst the Royal Library, No. 16, B 2, has furnished my sixth specimen, being a copy of the first verse of the First Psalm, given in this MS. as a specimen of the writing employed in Russia about 200 years ago. This specimen is to be read thus:—

| Blazen | muz jēze ne ide | na sowisty | neczestiwich. |
| Blessed (is the) | man that not goeth | in the council | (of the) ungodly. |

[1] Les Arts, par les Monum. Peint., pl. 61. One of D'Agincourt's engravings from this manuscript represents the custom adopted amongst the Teutonic and other northern nations of elevating and carrying a newly-elected king on a shield, whereof the chairing of newly-elected members of Parliament; the "lifting" of newly-married couples upon hurdles amongst the shepherds of the South Downs, and carrying them round a flock of sheep; and the Easter custom of lifting, described by Hone, in the Every-Day Book, p. 423, are perhaps to be considered the only surviving relics. D'Agincourt has also given an engraving from a medal, in which a king thus elevated holds in one hand a sceptre, and in the other a sword. Another engraving represents a king thus elevated in the act of being crowned by a priest, who also stands on a shield; whilst a fourth engraving, which is also given in Montfaucon's Anti-quities, represents the king, elevated on a shield, crowned by a figure in the back-ground, wearing a civic crown of oak leaves. In Navarre, it was the custom for both the king and queen, after being anointed, to set their feet on a shield emblazoned with the arms of the kingdom, and supported on six staves, on which they were then lifted up before the high altar of the cathedral. Imperial Rome and Greece also long retained the same custom, which was likewise adopted by the Visigothic kings of Spain, as we learn from an ancient law of Don Pelargo. By some writers, our King's Bench is deemed to have had its origin in the rude elevation of the kings on a marble or stone bench. This, perhaps, ought rather to be considered as a trace of the mode of election and enthronement of the early Danish and Swedish kings.

MÍ ÐEMO
VSSER MÍA.
cuſſe ſiner mín
det. D. ſco ge-
hétter mir ſine ctionſt
r̄.pphetaſ: nu cûme er
ſelbo. unte cuſſe mih
mit déro ſñoze ſines
euangelii.

SCV
LEI

me oſculo
oriſ ſui.

PASSIO·DOMINI

Osfrunk thuc themrm
con thuo rika drohton umbi
theſaro werolder ginuand
mordon talda huo thru foreh
farud than lung thefia furniobarn

Qucurque mite
rum celeſtr nectiurcequum dhazrgheut lnhhechurum.
ordazr héear nu œughi clom

16 – I – A – 15

PREFATIO LIBRI IIII

Nuthie êinagron binôti mâchont thaz grazi
Nob xpec ctoderthuruh nôc therluczſih hab & guênot :·

Theotisc MsS.

THEOTISC MANUSCRIPTS.

THE Theotisc or ancient language of Franks, from its intimate affinity with the Anglo-Saxon tongue,[1] is highly interesting to the English student ; but, unfortunately, its relics are of the greatest rarity, very few being in existence previous to the time of Charlemagne. It has indeed been inferred, both from the assertion of Tacitus, " Literarum secreta viri pariter ac fœminæ ignorant," and the statement of Otfrid, the contemporary of Charlemagne, that the Teutonic, German, or Frankish tribes had not adopted the use of writing to polish their language.

The famous Silver Book of the Gospels, published by Junius, written in the ancient Gothic characters (being chiefly a mixture of Greek and Roman letters slightly modified), and justly regarded by Mabillon[2] and Godefroy Von Bessel[3] as the most ancient monument of Teutonic literature, as well as the Runic characters employed by these nations, prove however that the use of written characters was not unknown among them. The researches of recent philologists in Germany have also brought to light fragments of MSS. written in the vulgar tongue of the period, supposed to be long previous to the reign of Charlemagne, when the renovated Roman minuscule characters were adopted. The Cathedral of Wurtzburgh[4] possesses several manuscripts written in a Saxo-Teutonic minuscule (originating in the Roman), older than the reign of Pepin the Short (A.D. 752—768).

It is worthy of remark that in the different fac-similes of Theotisc MSS. hitherto published we find scarcely any traces of the peculiar forms of the Anglo-Saxon letters.

Most of these ancient MSS. are biblical ; the oldest being considered to be portions of a version of the Gospel of St. Matthew, of which only two leaves were for a long time known, and which were published by Eckhart in 1720; recently, however, Endlicher and Hoffmann have succeeded in discovering fifteen more leaves of this version, which had been cut into strips and employed in the binding of other volumes now preserved in the Imperial Library of Vienna.[5] These particles, which have been arranged with the greatest care, contain on one side the Theotisc, and on the other the Latin version, written in a Roman minuscule character, strongly tinged with Lombardic, a specimen of which, given by M. Silvestre, is regarded by Champollion as of the middle of the eighth century. The a is formed like the two letters cc, the r not produced below the line, the letters ri, et, en, eri, conjoined as in Lombardic MSS., the words distinct, separated from each other by a point, and destitute of abbreviations. The specimen given by Silvestre commences thus " Man auh *sin* tun angila so fama au*h* daz gas am*n*otun enti fyur forbreum itun so selp, &c., translated by Endlicher and Hoffmann :—" Messores autem angeli sunt. Sicut ergo colliguntur zizania et igni comburuntur, &c." Matth. xiii. 39.

Louis le Débonnaire, the son of Charlemagne, ordered that the Gospels should be translated into the Theotisc language, in order that the Francs of his vast empire might the more easily be made acquainted with the Sacred writings, and Otfrid, a Monk of Wiessenburgh, in Alsatia, the disciple of Rhaban Maur, first Abbot of Fulda, and contemporary with Charlemagne, anxious to ameliorate the rugged language of his countrymen,[6] composed a Messiad, or History of Christ, in the Theotisc language, in which were harmonised

---

[1] According to Weekes, the Franco-Teutonic, which was spoken in Germany and Gaul, is derived from the Mæso-Gothic formerly spoken in Bulgaria.

[2] De Re Dipl. p. 46.

[3] Chronic. Godw. p. 66.

[4] Chronic. Godw. 1 pl. i. f. 34.

[5] Fragmenta Theotisca, ed. Endlicher et Hoffmann, Vindob. Gerold, 1834, fo.

[6] " Lingua inculta et indisciplinabilis atque insueta capi regulari freno grammaticæ artis."—Otfrid's Epistle to Luitbert.

1

the Four Gospels. This work, which has been greatly famed, is noticed by Trithemius, in his book " De Scriptoribus Ecclesiasticis." It is preceded by a prologue dedicated to Luitbert, Archbishop of Mayence, and was written by desire of a worshipful matron named Judith :—" ut aliquantulum hujus cantu lectionis ludum secularium vocum deleret." It is also preceded by three Epistles in Theotisc verse, dedicated to King Louis of Germany ; Salomon, Bishop of Constance ; Hartmuat and Werinbert, Monks of St. Gall.

There exist only three MSS. of Otfrid's work, namely, at Vienna, Munich, and Heidelberg. It is from M. Silvestre's fac-simile from the first of these MSS. that the Nos. 1 and 2 in the accompanying plate have been copied. It is considered to be of the middle of the ninth century. The text is written in ordinary Caroline minuscule. In the original the preface is written in verses of lines of different length. The two lines in the accompanying plate being as follows :—

Nu thie éuuarton bi nóti máchont thaz giráti
Ioh x͞pec (d)tódes thuruh nót ther líut sih habet giéinot.

It will be seen that the two hemistichs of each line rhyme together; and, in the original, each alternate line is commenced by a large plain red uncial capital.

The drawing represents the entry of Christ into Jerusalem, and from the architecture, costume, and form of the cross, is supposed by Silvestre and Champollion to have been copied from a Byzantine model. It has been selected in order to allow comparison with the drawings of the same subject given in this work from the Anglo-Saxon Psalter of the Cottonian Library, and the little miniature from St. Augustine's Gospels at Cambridge.

The Munich MS., of which a fac-simile is also given by Silvestre, differs from the preceding in having the text written in double columns, each line being divided into its two rhyming hemistichs, which are thus separated from each other.

The Vatican copy of Otfrid's version, written A.D. 889 (Cod. Palat. Vatic. 52), from which a fac-simile, together with a particular description of this MS., was given by Blanchini,[1] and also by the Benedictines,[2] has subsequently passed to the library of the university of Heidelberg.

This poem of Otfrid has been repeatedly published, the most recent edition being by M. Graff, under the title of Krist, at Kœnigsberg, 1831, in 4to.

The Gospel of St. Matthew in the Theotisc language, is also preserved in the library of St. Gall, and has been collated by Schmeller,[3] from a MS. Gospel Harmony of the ninth century, with the Codex Argenteus, and other portions of the Gothic Gospels discovered by Mai and Count Castiglioni.

The specimen No. 4 is copied from a manuscript in the Cottonian Library (Caligula, A 7), justly regarded as one of the gems of that collection. It is of a moderate octavo size, measuring about 5½ by 8 inches. It has been recently rebound with great care, and contains at the beginning a series of eight drawings, highly coloured and gilt, executed about the time of King Stephen, representing the early scenes of the Gospel history, evidently taken from some other MS., probably of the Psalter (it being much the custom at that period to introduce such a series of drawings at the heads of Psalters). But the greatest part of the volume consists of a Harmony of the Evangelists, written in the tenth century, in the old Frankish or Theotisc language, and said by James to have once belonged to King Canute. The volume is thus described by Hickes :[4]—" Extat quoque in Bibl. Cotton. quasi ex quatuor Evangelistis consarcinatus, codex unus harmonicus, poeticus, et para-phrasticus quem sive Francico-Theotiscus sive Anglo-Theotisc sit, plurimi facio ; tum quod cæteros omnes Franco-Theotiscè scriptos, verborum copia, et dictionis magnificentia antecellit ; tum quod vetustate purissimi sermonis proxime accedit ad ' Codicem Argenteum' cui soli me judice, a veterum linguarum Septentrionalium studiosis post habendus est." See also Hickes' Gramm. Franco-Theot. cap. 22, and Gram. Anglo-Sax. et Mæso-Goth. p. 189.

The text is written in a fine large minuscule character, strongly tinged with German-Caroline,[5] and

[1] Evangel. quadrupl. p. DC.

[2] N. Tr. de Dipl. 3, p. 126, pl. XL.

[3] Evangelii secundum Matthæum versio Francica sæc. ix. necnon Gothica sæc. iv. quoad superest. Ed. J. A. Schmeller, Stuttg. und Tubing. 1827, 8vo.

[4] Gram. Franco-Theotisca, p. 6.

[5] Astle has given a very indifferent fac-simile from this MS., Origin of Writing, pl. 27, 1, and places it at the head of the modern Gothic writing.

2

quite distinct from the Anglo-Saxon. The letter thorn is here replaced by th, and the wen by uu, as in the words uueroldes and uuordon. The letter ð occurs, however, sometimes at the end of a word.

With the exception of a few initial letters, in the style of the one in the accompanying specimen (from fol. 126, r.), the text is destitute of illuminations. The character of this initial S agrees with that of various Anglo-Saxon MSS. written about the time of King Canute.

The attention of the learned was especially directed to this MS. by Hickes, at the beginning of the last century, who made great use of it in his Franco-Theotisc Grammar. Shortly afterwards another copy of it was discovered at Wurtzburgh, which, however, having been long lost, was re-discovered by the Abbé Gley, in the library of the cathedral at Bamberg, whence it has passed into the royal library of Munich. In this MS., as well as in the Cottonian one, the verses are written without any separation in long lines, so that it is difficult to determine the measure. A fac-simile from this MS. is also given by Silvestre.[1]

Another very valuable document for the study of the ancient German or Theotisc language is preserved in the Royal Library, Munich, being a glossary or series of interpretations of the Vulgate Bible, written in Latin, with the translation in Theotisc. This MS. is written in the same character as the preceding, and has been edited by M. E. G. Graff.[2] A fac-simile of this MS. has also been given by Silvestre.

The Royal Library of Munich also possesses another MS., written by Adalram, Archbishop of Salzburg, at the beginning of the ninth century, for Louis, the third son of Louis le Débonnaire, containing portions of one of the Sermons of St. Jerome, accompanied by a Theotisc translation at the foot of each page, which has been edited by M. Schmeller, and of which a fac-simile has been given by Silvestre.

The Bibliothèque du Roi, at Paris, possesses a MS. written partly in the Theotisc language, the text of which has been regarded by the German scholars[3] as anterior by two centuries to the Messiad of Otfrid. It consists of the Epistle of St. Isidore against the Jews and Arians, the Latin text being written in one column, and a Theotisc version in the second, written in Lombardic minuscule, mixed with a mélange of Saxon and Caroline, and which is considered by M. Champollion as of the beginning of the ninth century. The MS. measures $9\frac{1}{2}$ inches by 6, a page containing 22 lines. It is from Silvestre's fac-simile from this MS. that the two lines in No. 5 have been copied.

M. Silvestre has also given a fac-simile from another MS. contained in the Royal Library of Munich, containing a short Prayer or Hymn in the Theotisc language, which has been termed Das Wessobrunnen Gebet, the Prayer of Wessobrunn, and which has been published by the brothers Grimm, and also by M. Wackernagel, and which in its composition resembles the Anglo-Saxon Paraphrase of Cædmon. The leaf of parchment on which it is written is attached to a volume, in the same hand, and is regarded as being of the ninth century.

The Franconian Abbot Willeram, of Ebesperg, who died in 1085, was the author of a work which has long been greatly esteemed amongst the learned in Germany, entitled " De Nuptiis Christi et Ecclesiæ," being a double paraphrase on the Song of Songs, one being in Latin, and the other in Theotisc, of which there exist ancient MSS. in the Libraries of Heidelberg, Breslau, Vienna, and Munich. It is from M. Silvestre's fac-simile from the last of these MSS. that my specimen No. 3 is copied, the Latin commentary, which in the original is placed at the left hand of the quarto page, being omitted. The commencement of M. Silvestre's fac-simile is as follows, the Latin commentary being written in rhyme :—

Quem sitio votis	Oscu-	Cusser mih mit
nunc oscula porrigat oris	letur	(de mo) cusse
quem mihi venturum	me osculo	sines mundes
promiserant organa vatum	oris sui	Dicco ge hiezzer
		mir sine cuonst
		per prophetas, &c.

The translation of the Theotisc paraphrase being given by the Abbé Gley as follows :

" Osculatur me osculo sui oris sæpius promittebat ipse mihi suum adventum per prophetas," &c.

[1] See also Langue et Littérature des Anciens Francs, par G. Gley. Paris, 1814, 8vo.

[2] Trésor théotisque, Berlin, 1834, and Diutiska, t. 1, p. 490, Berlin.

[3] Schilter. Thesaurus antiq. Teutonic. Jo. Frickii præf. gener. p. XIV. Pulthenius Tatiani harmon. Theotisc. G. Gley, Lang. et Littér. des Anc. Francs.

The MS. is written in a fine Capetian Roman minuscule of the eleventh century, this copy being considered by Freher as having been corrected by Willeram himself; the capitals are generally either uncial or Roman, but the initials of the different divisions are elegantly ornamented, although only drawn with red ink.

The Breslau MS. has been edited by Scherzius, in Schilter's Antiq. Teutonic, 1.

An early Version of part of the Psalms (Ps. 89—95) in the German language, contained in a MS. of the eleventh or twelfth century, has been also recently discovered.[1]

Eckhart has given a fac-simile[2] from an historical MS. written in the Theotisc language, in the ordinary minuscule characters, but having the Anglo-Saxon letters thorn (ð) and wen (p); and several other German MSS. of the thirteenth and fourteenth centuries are represented by M. Silvestre.

---

[1] See Iac. Grimm, Gött. Gel. Anz. für Marz. 1833.

[2] Copied in the N. Tr. d. Dipl. 3, pl. 55, p. 384.

4

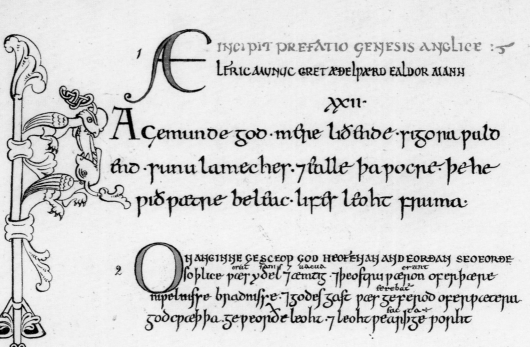

INCIPIT PREFATIO GENESIS ANGLICE :-

ÆLFRIC MUNUC GRET ÆÐELPÆRD EALDOR MANN

1

XCII·

Ðacemunde god· mihte liðthde· rigona puld
tho· runu lamecher· 7 ealle þa pocne· þe he
pið þætne beluuc· lifæt leoht 7 numa·

2

ON ANGINNE GESCEOP GOD HEOFENAN AND EORÐAN   SEOEORÐE
erat sanis 7 uacua   erant
soþlice þær ydel 7 æmtig· 7 þeostru pæron ofer þære
                                         ferebat
nipelnysse bradnysse· 7 godes gast þær gefenod ofer þwæru
                                         sic͞a·
god cpæð þa· gepeorðe leoht· 7 leoht peurðe gepoþht

Metodi cpað· adam slep þe is pife 7 hi gestpinde sunel
7 dolupa·

5

Ðacpæð drihten tocaine· hpær is abel ðinbroðor: ða and
rpapode he 7 cpæð min at· regit ðu rceoldv ic minne
broðor healdon· ðacpæð drihten tocaine· hpæt dydert ðu·
þiner broðor blod clypað uptome oreorðan·

6

HERONGY NÐ SEOBOC ÐEISGENEMNED ONEBREISC· YALE
IMBER ÐÆT IS ONLEDEN NUMERUS· AND ON ENGLISC· GETEL·

Anglo-Saxon Books of Moses.

ANGLO-SAXON BOOKS OF MOSES, &c.

PREVIOUS to entering upon the history of the ancient versions of the Sacred Scriptures made in this country (before the invention of printing), and more especially of those executed during the Anglo-Saxon period of our history, it will be convenient, and indeed necessary in a palæographical point of view, to inquire into the opinions which have been entertained as to the origin of writing itself amongst us; and to notice those letters which are especially peculiar to Anglo-Saxon literature.

1. ON THE INTRODUCTION OF LETTERS INTO GREAT BRITAIN.

Without entering into the question of the usage of Phenician characters (or the identity of these with the Oghams of the Irish) by the Druids, or dwelling on the assertions, both of Cicero and Julius Cæsar, that this singular body of men used Greek letters[1], we have abundant evidence, that the conquest of the southern portion of Britain, and the long sway of the Roman conquerors, led to the diffusion of the Latin language and letters amongst the Britons[2]; and Tacitus tells us, that he took measures for having the sons of the chiefs educated in the liberal arts; and the poet Ausonius, who flourished in the fourth century, mentions a contemporary British author, whom he names Sylvius Bonus, and whose writings must have been in Latin, or they would not have been understood by the Romans. The most ancient British coins, when bearing inscriptions, are inscribed with Roman capitals[3]. Numerous monumental and other inscriptions[4], likewise, sufficiently attest the prevalent usage for such purposes of the old Roman capital letters. Hence, as Mr. Astle observes[5]—"from the coming of Julius Cæsar, till the time the Romans left the Island in the year 427, the Roman letters were as familiar to the eyes of the inhabitants as their language to their ears." He gives it as his opinion, however, that writing was very little practised by the Britons till after the coming of St. Augustine, about the year 596.

The long period between the departure of the Romans at the beginning of the fifth century, and the coming of St. Augustine at the close of the sixth, is so much enveloped in obscurity, that no positive statements can be made as to the condition of letters during that time. The history of religion comes to our aid in a slight degree, and teaches us that during this period there were still some learned men in the country; as Pelagius, Celestius, Gildas the Wise (our earliest historian), the Welsh bard Aneurin, and the historian Nennius, who may be mentioned in proof of the assertion, that letters were never entirely lost during this period; and as most of these authors (some of whose compositions are still extant) wrote in the Latin language, we may infer that they used the old Roman characters.

---

[1] Cæsar expressly says of them "Neque fas esse existimant ea literis mandare quum in reliquis fere rebus publicis privatisque rationibus *Græcis literis* utantur." De Bell. Gall. VI. 13, 14.

[2] "The useful invention appears from the coins of Durmun, Eburo and Eisu to have reached into the kingdom of Darobriges in the West, and of the Brigantes in the North, before the victories of Vespasian in the one, and of Agricola in the other."—Whitaker Hist. Manchester, (2nd edition,) vol. ii. p. 147.

[3] Pegge's Dissertation on the Coins of Cunobelin; Akermann's Coins of the Romans, relating to Britain; Davie's Essay on British Coins.

[4] Borlace, Hist. of Cornwall, pp. 391, 396; Warburton, Vallum Roman. 1753; Pictorial Hist. of England, I. 51, 72, and 106.

[5] Origin of Writing, p. 96.

It was during this interval (A.D. 450) that the Saxons conquered the ancient Britons; but the questions, whether they adopted the letters which they found in use amongst the Britons, being themselves previously ignorant of them; or whether they brought letters with them on their arrival; or, thirdly, whether they obtained their knowledge of letters from the Irish schools of learning,—have been the subject of much discussion amongst our historians.

The Rev. Mr. Whitaker[1] very strenuously adopted the first of these views, quoting a passage from Tacitus[2] in support of his opinion, that the Saxons in the wilds of Germany were ignorant of letters; and insisting that the letters which were used by the Anglo-Saxons were adopted by them *in* this island, and treating, as unreasonable, the opinion of Hickes and Wanley, that the Saxons, instead of borrowing their letters from the Britons, even communicated their own to them[3]. He, accordingly, considers that the Anglo-Saxon characters are in general either Roman, or that the seemingly foreign ones, such as ᵹ ƿ ſ ꞇ ρ, and the contractions for *and, or, th,* and *that,* are probably *Roman*-British, and are all to be referred to the Roman-British modes of writing at the Saxon Conquest.

In support of his opinion, he also mentions the epitaphs of Pabo, Eneon, and Cadvan—Welsh Princes, who were buried in the sixth century—discovered in the Isle of Anglesea,[4] and written in the language of Italy[5]; in the last of which inscriptions we find the Є, ρ (shaped more like n) ſ and ꞇ; whilst the M has nearly the very peculiar form it presents in the oldest Anglo-Saxon manuscripts—namely, three perpendicular strokes united by two nearly horizontal ones. Mr. Whitaker then endeavours to trace (without much success) the Anglo-Saxon forms of the Ð ð þ ƿ ρ and ᚷ, as well as the ordinary contraction for the word or, to the Roman letters which they represent; and concludes by asserting, that all the letters of the Anglo-Saxons were really Roman in their origin, and Italian in their structure, at first, but were barbarised in their aspect by the British Romans and Roman-Britons.

These opinions of Mr. Whitaker have been fully adopted by Mr. Astle[6], but they are opposed to the views of other eminent authors, especially of Hickes and Wanley, whose eminent attainments in the philological learning of the northern tribes of Europe, render their views worthy of the highest respect. These authors contend that the Anglo-Saxons, instead of receiving from the Britons or Irish a knowledge of the letters and learning of Rome, were not so rude as has been affirmed, but brought with them into the country a complete alphabet of Runic letters, which, in ancient times, were in use in those parts of the North of Europe; some of which letters are found mingled with Roman letters in the most ancient Anglo-Saxon MSS., and two of which, namely, the wen (ƿ) and thorn (þ Ð ð) were subsequently actually adopted into the Roman Alphabet, as Wanley observes, "ob singularem utriusque potestatem, quod ad edendos quosdam sonos valebant qui per nullam Romanarum literarum exprimi potuerunt[7];" whilst, as to their knowledge of the Roman letters, these authors contend that they, as well as the Britons and Irish, received them from the Romans themselves, or in other words, that the Anglo-Saxons obtained an acquaintance with the Christian religion and Roman letters simultaneously, upon the coming of St. Augustine[8].

A third opinion which has prevailed on the subject is, that it was from the Irish that the Anglo-Saxons received their knowledge of letters. Thus Camden says, that "Anglo-Saxones ab Hibernis rationem formandi literas accepisse cum initio eodem plane charactere usi fuerint qui hodie Hibernis est in usu[9]:" and in one of the latest and most valuable histories of our country which has been published, the same idea has been retained[10]. The learned Dr. O'Conor has also laboured to prove the same opinion to be correct, in his invaluable work on the ancient writers of Ireland; asserting, that "Nihil itaque a Britones mutuati sunt Saxones, non ita vero

[1] History of Manchester, vol. ii. p. 329.

[2] De Mor. Germ. c. 19, and c. 2.

[3] Lhuyd's Letter At a Kimri, in his Etymologicon, translated in Guthrie's History of Scotland.

[4] Mona, pl. 9 and 10.

[5] Mr. Whitaker exemplifies the usage of the Roman language amongst the higher classes, by the parental appellations *papa* and *mama,* used in genteeler life, whilst *dad* and *mam* of the vulgar are genuine British.

[6] Origin of Writing, p. 96.

[7] Wanley, in Hickes' Thesaurus, Pref. vol. ii.

[8] " Cum fide Christiana Majores nostros Romanarum literarum scientiam et usum accepisse."—" Ab adventu Augustini sensim inolescere apud Anglo Saxones cœpit Romanarum literarum et literaturæ usus." Wanley, ut supra.

[9] Gough's Camden, t. 3, p. 467.

[10] " As the forms of the Saxon alphabetical characters are the same with those of the Irish, it is probable that it was from Ireland the Saxons derived their first knowledge of letters."—Pictorial History of Engl. i. p. 304.

ab Hibernis a quibus prima literarum Nordanhymbriensium epocha procul dubio derivata est[1];" this first epoch being the Anglo-Saxon period previous to the incursions of the Danes.

From the facts which have come down to our own times, aided by the assistance which an extended knowledge of the Palæographia of our country may afford, I think that, on reviewing these conflicting opinions, we are warranted in adopting the following conclusions :—

1. That the knowledge of letters introduced by the Romans, was not entirely lost amongst the Britons after their departure.

2. That the Saxons, on their arrival in this country, were unacquainted with Roman letters[2], which they found in partial usage amongst the conquered Britons, and with which they were afterwards more fully made acquainted by St. Augustine and his followers in the South, and by the Irish Missionaries of Lindisfarne in the North.

3. That the Saxons, on the contrary, brought with them a system of Runic letters which were long retained and partially employed, and that two of these Runic letters were introduced into the Roman alphabet as being more fitted for the delineation of certain Saxon sounds than any single or compound Roman letter.

4. That the similarity existing between the peculiar forms of the Irish and Anglo-Saxon letters results, not from the latter having been first taught them by the former in their schools in the North of England, which were not established until fifty years after the coming of St. Augustine (whose labours in disseminating the Christian religion over the island is well known, and must have been attended with a diffusion of learning), but rather from the circumstance that both people received them from the Roman missionaries; and that most of those forms of letters, which have been supposed to be especially Irish or Anglo-Saxon, occur in the most ancient minuscule manuscripts of other countries, particularly in the Lombardic and Gallican MSS., thus clearly showing one common origin, namely, the Roman minuscule or cursive hands.

5. That, consequently, the distinctions[3] which have been proposed by Dr. O'Conor between the writings of the Northern schools of England and those of the South, are not historically correct; indeed, some of our most ancient documents which exist, to which unquestionable dates (previous to the year 740) can be attached, were written in the middle, eastern, and southern parts of the country, and are in the well-set Anglo-Saxon minuscule, which has been generally considered as peculiarly Irish, and similar to that in which the Book of Armagh, the Gospels of Mac Durnan, and the Leabhar Dimma are written, and which Sir W. Betham calls "the pure Irish character[4]," and to which Camden alludes as being "*hodie* Hibernis in usu;" whilst King Wihthred's charter to *Canterbury Cathedral* (A.D. 697) is written in wide detached upright minuscule characters, quite like those of the Irish Gospels of Mac Regol and St. Chad, and the Gospels of Lindisfarne, written within a few years after the establishment of the Irish School in that island, which latter hand Dr. O'Conor considered as the most ancient "unadulterated" Irish character[5].

---

[1] Epist. Nuncup. p. ccii.

[2] Had the contrary been the case, we should find the peculiar Anglo-Saxon characters in the most ancient MSS. and inscriptions in the North of Germany, which is not the case, except in the schools of the Anglo-Saxon missionaries.

[3] Bibl. Stowensis, vol. ii. p. 117, and in various parts of the first volume of his Script. veter. rer. Hibern. See the Indexes.

[4] Had Dr. O'Conor been acquainted with any of these books, he would have been under the necessity of entirely altering his views of the national distinctions of the Irish and Anglo-Saxon writings.

[5] " Those Saxon MSS. of the seventh century, written in the parts of England where the Irish schools prevailed, are all written in the old Irish characters, without the least affectation of the Saxon style, which latter can be traced chiefly in *Kent*, and amongst the schools of the southern Saxons, whilst the unadulterated Irish prevails in the MSS. of St. Cuthbert [that is, The Gospels of Lindisfarne, Cotton. MS. Nero D. iv.] and St. Chad, both agreeing with St. Columba's Gospels in Dublin, with the Gospels at Durham, and Columbanus' Missal at Milan." O'Conor, Bibl. Stow. ii., p. 117. The charter of King Wihthred, above mentioned, at once disproves this assertion. The learned author is, moreover, in error in uniting the Gospels at Durham with the rest, as they are written in fine Roman uncials. See Astle, pl. xiv. B. If, indeed, O'Conor were correct in asserting the Durham Gospels to have been written in Ireland, or the North of England, I may at once refer to the Charter of King Sebbi (A.D. 570), conveying a piece of land to the Abbess of Barking in *Essex*, and which is in precisely similar characters, (see Casley Cat. Reg. MSS. pl. 1, where the Charter is given entire,) but Dr. O'Conor was evidently misled as to these Gospels having been of northern origin by their being preserved at Durham, so near to Lindisfarne, whereas they were formerly in the Cottonian Library (Otho B. 9,) and are stated by Smith to have been given to the Dean and Chapter of Durham. (Cat. MSS. Cott. 1696, p. 44.) These Gospels, therefore, as well as the Charter of Sebbi, I presume to have been written by some of the Roman missionaries, and not by native scribes.

2. ON THE LETTERS PECULIAR TO THE ANGLO-SAXONS.

The following is the Alphabet as used by the Anglo-Saxons :—

CAPITAL	A Ã	Æ	B	Ƚ	D	E Ꞓ	F	GⱢ	HꞶ	I	K	L	Mꟽ	N	O	P	Q	R	Sꟗ	T	U,Ʋ	U-U,Ƿ	X	Y	Z	Ð Ƿ

MINUSCULE	a	æ	b	c ꝺ	e	ꝼ	ȝ	h	ɩ	k	l	m	n	o	p	q	ꞃ	ꞅꞃ	ꞇ	u	u-u,ƿ	x	ẏ	z	ð þ	þ[1]	ꝩ[2]

| NAME[3] | a | — | be | ce | de | — | ef | ge | ache | — | ca | el | em | en | — | pe | cu | er | es | te | — | wen | ex | wi | — | thorn | thet | and |

| POWER | a | æ | b | c | d | e | f | g | h | i | k | l | m | n | o | p | q | r | s | t | u | w | x | y | z | th | that | and |

On referring to the minuscule, or ordinary alphabet, given above, it will be seen that the letters most unlike the ordinary Roman minuscule characters are the ꝺ ꝼ ȝ ꞃ ꞅ ꞇ (the last four of which Spelman considered as pure Saxon letters), and the supplemental letters, p, þ, Ð, ð, and þ. It requires but little effort to trace the first six letters above mentioned to their true Roman prototypes, when written cursively: the ꝺ, indeed, hardly requires comment; the ꝼ is a small long-tailed f, with the upper part of the long stroke made separately, more obliquely, and not carried above the line, and with the bar placed along the lower part of the line, and the ꞃ is similarly formed, but wants the bar; the ȝ is a cursive capital g, slightly altered, for celerity in writing; the ꞃ is a small r, with the first stroke carried below the line, and the second stroke or dot elongated to the bottom of the line, or, rather, it is a capital R, with the first stroke elongated below, and the second part of the letter written quickly, without the angle in the middle; the ꞇ is a kind of hybrid between a capital T and small t.

It remains to notice the supplemental letters, which, being in fact absolutely national ones, merit our attention as to their origin and use. Whitaker and Astle, we have seen, consider them no other than Roman letters metamorphosed—the p, for instance, being supposed to be only a v, with the first stroke straight, not oblique, and carried below the line, and the top of the letter closed; and the þ only a T and h conjoined, the tail of the second stroke continued below the line, and united to the long straight tail of the first stroke.

The p and the þ are, however, pure Runic letters, and are absolutely named as such in various ancient manuscripts[4]—namely, p, or wen (w), and þ, or thorn (th). The latter of these, with a mark or bar of contraction above it (thus, þ), indicates an addition to the letter, and stands for the word "that." Ð and its minuscule ð are also employed with the same power as þ, namely, th. I have hitherto met with no attempt to explain the origin of this letter, which may have been introduced in the following manner:—When the propensity of the Anglo-Saxons to conjoin their capital letters is considered, it will at once appear that the Ð is no other than a capital T united with the straight stroke of the D. Td, however, are not Th; we must, therefore, recur to the pronunciation of these letters, which we find nearly similar; and hence, in the early Anglo-Saxon MSS., written before the Anglo-Saxon names had settled down, so to speak, into an uniform orthography, we find Th and Td often employed in lieu of each other. The Charter of Æthelbald, King of Mercia, dated A.D. 736 (Bibl. Cott. Augustus 2, 2, olim 3), offers complete evidence of this. Here we find the king's name spelled AETDILBALT, EDILBALT, ETHITBAL(T); and in the indorsement Æþelbalð[5], and another similar name, spelled AETHILRIC; we find also the word norðꞇꞃup twice written on the back of the Charter. The indorsed names I presume to be of a more recent date than the Charter itself, because I cannot find that ð or þ were used so early as 736. This will appear by the following notices selected from the early charters in the British Museum :—

A.D. circ. 670. (Cott. MS., Aug. 2, 29, olim 26[6].) Charter of King Sebbi and his son Œdilred (K. Ethelred?). Written in Roman uncials. Grant of a piece of land named Widmundesfelt to Hildelburga, Abbess of Berking. Here we find *Wid*mundes-felt, Ercnwaldus, and *W*ilfridus, spelled with uu instead of w; but the Saxon names, *W*ritolaburna and Caentincestrio*w* are both written with the Ƿ instead of w.

---

[1] " Hec litera þ Anglica *thet* est nominata et ponitur pro *quod.*" Wanley in Hickes' Thesaurus, v. 2, Præf.

[2] Hec litera ꝩ Anglica *and* est vocata, & ponitur pro istis sex conjunctionibus, *&, quia, at, atque, ac, ast.*"—Wanley in op. cit.

[3] This series of names is from the Cottonian MS., Titus, D. 18, except that of the ꝩ

[4] Cotton. MS. Titus, D. 18. Otho, B. 10, (Hickes' Th.)

[5] Astle gives a fac-simile of another charter of this King, in which the name is spelt Aedelbald.

[6] The numbers of all these Charters have, most inconveniently, been altered since Casley published his fac-similes from so many of them, so that I have been unable to discover some of them under their present numbers, and am therefore compelled to be silent respecting them.

A.D. 679. (Cott. MS., Aug. 2, 2, olim 1.) Charter of Hlotharius, King of Kent; dated from Reculver. Written in Roman uncials. The names of the King and of Theodore are spelled with *th;* and that of the land, called *Westan,* is spelled with uu. The name Reculver is spelled Recuulf.

A.D. 680. (Cott. MS., Aug. 2, 86, olim 81.) Written in narrow moderate-sized Anglo-Saxon minuscule. Grant of Cœdwalla, whose name is spelled with uu, instead of w or ρ.

A.D. 685. (Cott. MS., Aug. 2, 88.) Charter of King Wihthred. Written in open Anglo-Saxon minuscule characters. This is stated not to be an original document in the Cottonian Catalogue: uu are constantly employed in it, instead of w or ρ; the names of the Queen Œthelburga and of Theabul are spelt with th; but, in the body of the Charter, we find the word paeð thus written.

A.D. 693. Grant of K. Wihthred to Canterbury. Written in large round minuscule. In the Library of the Duke of Buckingham, at Stow. The letter ρ is stated by O'Conor to be once used in it. (Astle, pl. 21, 1.)

A.D. 704. (Cott. MS., Aug. 2, 82, olim 77.) Grant by Sueabred to Peohthat of land at Twickenham (Tuicanhom, Tuicoanham, in Middelseax), attested by Coenred, King of Mercia. In this we find the name Waldhario spelled palðhaριο and uualðhaριο; and the names ρceϝτριne and pæoᵹthaᴢh spelled as written, the latter also spelled Peohthat.

A.D. 736. (Cott. MS., Aug. 2, 3, olim 2.) Charter of King Ethelbalt, above mentioned, written in uncials; with the name of Wilfrid spelled UUILFRIDUS.

A.D. 741 and 781. Casley (Plates II. and III.) gives fac-similes from two Latin charters, in which the name, written in Anglo-Saxon characters, of Athelbert is spelled with the th, instead of ρ or ð.

A.D. 749. (Cott. MS., Otho, A. 1: burnt in the Cotton fire.) Astle, Plate XV., iii., written in large round Anglo-Saxon minuscule, without either ρ, ð, or þ.

A.D. 764. (Cott. MS., Aug. 2, 27.) Grant of lands in Middlesex. Written in Anglo-Saxon minuscule, in which we find the word ριchuma.

A.D. 779. (Cott. MS., Aug. 2, 4.) In this charter, th and uu are alone employed.

A.D. 790. Casley (Plate III.) gives a fac-simile of a charter of King Ethelbert, in which his name is spelled Aeðᵫlbeaρhτ.

A.D. 802. (Cott. MS., Aug. 2, 87, olim 82.) Grant by Cuthred (Cuðρeð), King of Kent, to Ϝulϝρeð.

A.D. 808—811. (Cott. MSS., Aug. 2, 98, olim 94, and 47, olim 42.) Grants by Coenwulf, whose name is spelled Coenuulϝ; but Casley (Plate IV.) gives a fac-simile, from another grant by the same king, in which the name is spelled Coenρulϝ.

A.D. 814. (Cott. MS., Aug. 2, 74.) Grant by Coenwulf to Wulfrid, of lands in Kent. Written in a close, small, upright Anglo-Saxon minuscule. In this the names Coenwulf, Coelwulf, and Eadwulf, are written with uu, instead of wu or ρu; but we find the words ρeρτan ριðδe written thus, and the Queen's name, Aelϝþρyþ.

Same year. (Cott. MS., No. 77.) Grant by Coenwulf, King of Mercia, to Archb. Wulfrid. Written in Saxon minuscules. The names of the parties are written Coenuulfus, uulfredo, uulfhard: the þ is repeatedly used in the description of the land granted; and we find the þ and ð, also, several times introduced into the middle of the text, as in the words þanon, lanᵹριðe, oðþone, oρðone, onðone.

These two grants are, therefore, the earliest instances in which we find the Runic letter þ introduced into the Anglo-Saxon alphabet in lieu of th, or tð (ð); and it will be perceived, by the last quoted words, that the þ and ð were used indiscriminately[1].

After the last-mentioned period, we find ρ, þ, and ð more constantly employed, as in the Testament of Elfred, of which a fac-simile is given by Astle (Plate XXI.), written about A.D. 888; and in the 10th and 11th centuries, during the Dano-Saxon period, these letters came into general use—uu (for w), and th, being very rarely found written. I believe William the Conqueror introduced the W. It, however, appears in the Theotisc Gospels, in the Cottonian Library.

The series of Charters, &c., copied by Hickes (Thesaurus, Vol. I., p. 169) corroborate these remarks. In one dated 788, we find þ and ð often used. In the indorsement, we find the same letters, and also the þ in the

---

[1] It has been asserted by Spelman and others, that þ had a hard sound as in *these,* and ð a softer sound as in *that;* but this is denied by Hickes; and the specimens last given above, as also the words ðιn and þιneρ in the fac-simile No. 5, in the accompanying plate, sufficiently disprove the former opinion.

words þæʃ and þa. It is not improbable, however, that, as usual, the indorsement is more recent than the document itself.

I have entered into these details, in the first place, because the subject is a national one, which I have not found satisfactorily treated by previous writers; in the second place, because the circumstances above mentioned will, I think, afford one means of determining the age of early Anglo-Saxon MSS.; and, thirdly, because it may be supposed, also, to afford a proof that the Runic characters were not in frequent use previous to the beginning of the ninth century, and thus enable us to approximate to the true date of these strange inscriptions, which have so much perplexed philologists.

3. THE SACRED POEMS OF CÆDMON.

It is to the Venerable BEDE [1], the pride and ornament of the Anglo-Saxon period, that we are indebted for a notice of the first attempt made in this country to render the Word of God intelligible to the ignorant, by translating it into the vernacular language.

In his account of the monastery at Whitby (Sʒpenaeʃhalh) given in the "Historia Ecclesiastica," he states, that during the period whilst its foundress, Hilda, was the abbess [2], between 660 and 680, there was a certain brother extraordinarily honoured with a divine gift, whereby *whatsoever* he learned through clerks, of the HOLY WRITINGS, he, after a little space, would usually versify, adorning it with the greatest sweetness and feeling, " et in sua, id est *anglorum*, lingua, proferet "—and bring it forth in his own, that is, the *English* [3] tongue.

After stating how that this cow-herd, as he was, had become disgusted with the convivial society [4] of his associates, the narrative records, that in a dream he heard a voice, crying " Cædmon, canta mihi aliquid"—Cædmon, sing me something—whereupon, although he " had never learned any poem," yet (as the statement proceeds),—

BEDE.	BISHOP MORE'S MS.	KING ALFRED'S TRANSLATION.[6]	MR. THORPE'S TRANSLATION.
Historia Eccles. Lib. IV. cap. xxiii. Circ. 730 (Bibl. Cott. Tib. c. 2.5)	Now in the public Library at Cambridge (K K. 5. 16), supposed to have been written A.D. 737.	Circ. A.D. 895.	(Cædmon's Metr. Paraph., 8vo, Lond., 1832.)
statim ipse cœpit cantare in laudem Dei Conditoris versus quos nunquam audierat quorum iste est sensus :—	Pʃimo canʒauiʒ Cæðmon iʃʒuð capmen·	ða ongan he ʃona ʃinʒan in heʃeneʃʃe ʒoðeʃ ʃcýppenðeʃ· þa ʃeʃʒ ˥ þa poʃð þe he næʃʃe ne ʒehýʃðe þaʃa ende býʃðneʃ iʃ þiʃ·	then he began forthwith to sing in praise of God the Creator, the verses and words, which he had never heard, the order of which is this
Nunc laudare debemus Auctorem regni cœlestis, potentiam Creatoris, et consilium illius, facta Patris gloriæ. Quomodo ille cum sit eternus Deus, omnium miraculorum auctor, extitit qui primo filiis hominum cœlum pro culmine tecti :	Nu ʃcýlun heʃʒan· heʃaen ʃicaeʃ uaʃð· meʒuðeʃ mæcʒi· enð hiʃ moðʒiðanc· ueʃc uulðuʃʃaðuʃ· ʃue he uunðʃa ʒihuaeʃ· eci ðʃicʒin· oʃa ʃʒeliðæ· he æʃeʃʒ ʃcopa· elða baʃnum· heben ʒil hʃoʃe· haleʒ ʃcepen·	Nu pe ʃceolan heʃian· heoʃon-ʃiceʃ peaʃð· metoðeʃ mihʒe· ˥ hiʃ moð-ʒeþonc· peʃa pulðoʃ-ʃæðeʃ· ʃpa he punðʃa ʒehpæʃ· ece ðʃýhʒen· ooʃð onʒealðe· he æʃeʃʒ ʒeʃcéop· eoʃðan beaʃnum· heoʃon ʒo hʃoʃe· halig scýppend·	Now we must praise the Guardian of heaven's kingdom, the Creator's might, and his mind's thought, glorious Father of men ! as of every wonder he Lord eternal formed the beginning. He first framed for the children of the earth the heaven as a roof, holy Creator !
dehinc terram, custos humani generis omnipotens, creavit.	ʒha miððun ʒeaʃð· moncýnneʃ uaʃð· eci ðʃýcʒin· æʃʒeʃ ʒiaðæ· ʃiʃum ʃolðu· ʃʃea allʒnecʒiʒ·	þa miððanʒeaʃð· moncýnneʃ peaʃð· ece ðʃýhʒen· æʃʒeʃ ʒeoðe· ʃiʃum ʃolðan· ʃʃea ælmihʒiʒ·	then mid earth, the guardian of mankind, the eternal Lord, afterwards produced the earth for men, Lord Almighty !

[1] Born 672, died 735.

[2] The reader will find some curious particulars respecting the double monasteries, such as Whitby, governed by females, in Lingard's Antiq. Anglo. Sax. Church, p. 120.

[3] King Alfred, in his Translation, translates this by the term enʒliʃc.

[4] " Convivio," translated by King Alfred into ʒebeoʃscipe, literally beer-ship. See " Leges Inæ " apud Wilkins, p. 16, and Tacit. Germ. 22, 23, quoted by Mr. Thorpe.

[5] I consider this MS. as having been written not later than the end of the eighth century. The capital letters in the first page of the History, and the ornaments in the large initial, more closely resemble those in the Purple Gospels (MS. reg. 1. E. 6, of which I have given a fac-simile) than any other MS. I have hitherto seen ; but the hand-writing is a rough minuscule, of the genuine Anglo-Saxon style, with the letter ð constantly used, although uu are employed instead of p.

[6] Chiefly taken by Mr. Thorpe from a Manuscript in the Library of C. C. Col., Oxford. There are other MSS. in C. C. C. C. and the public Library, Camb. The Cotton. MS., Otho B xi., was burnt.

6

Bede admits that although he thus gave the sense of the verses, it was impossible to transfer their sublimity into any other tongue. This thing being told to the Abbess, Cædmon was ordered to repeat his verses before her, and the " most learned men and learners ;" by whom some holy history was then expounded to him, which by next morning he had adorned with the best poetry. Thereupon he was prevailed upon by the Abbess to turn monk ; and " all that he could learn by hearing he meditated within himself, and as a clean animal, ruminating, turned into the sweetest verse," the substance of which (as particularly concerns our present inquiry), is thus stated :—

(BEDE.)	(KING ALFRED.)	(TRANSLATION.)
Canebat autem de creatione mundi, et origine humani generis, et tota Genesis historia de egressu Israel ex Ægypto et ingressu in terram repromissionis, de aliis plurimis sacræ scripturæ historiis, de Incarnatione dominica, passione, resurrectione et ascensione in cœlum, de spiritus sancti adventu et apostolorum doctrina. Item de terrore futuri judicii et horrore pœnæ gehennalis ac dulcedine regni cælestis multa carmina faciebat ; sed et alia perplura de beneficiis et judiciis divinis in quibus cunctis homines ab amore scelerum abstrahere ad delectionem vero et sollertiam bonæ actionis excitare curabat.	Song he æꝼest be middanᵹeapdeᵹ ᵹesceape. ⁊ be ꝼꞃuman moncýnneꞃ ⁊ eall þ ꞃtæꞃ ᵹeneꞃyꞃ þ iꞃ ꞃeo æꝼeꞃte moiꞃeꞃ bóc. ⁊ eꝼt be utgonge iꞃꞃaela ꝼolceꞃ oꝼ æᵹýpta londe. ⁊ be inᵹonᵹe þæꞃ ᵹehat-londeꞃ. ⁊ be oðꞃum moniᵹum ꞃpellum þæꞃ halᵹan ᵹepꞃiceꞃ canoneꞃ bóca. ⁊ be cꞃꞃꞃteꞃ menniꞃcneꞃꞃe ⁊ be hiꞃ þꞃopunᵹe. ⁊ be hiꞃ úp-aꞃciᵹneꞃꞃe on heoꝼonaꞃ. ⁊ biᵹ þæꞃ halᵹan ᵹaꞃceꞃ cýme. ⁊ þaꞃa apoꞃtolaꞃ láꞃe. ⁊ eꝼt bi þam eᵹe þæꞃ copeaꞃban dómeꞃ ⁊ be ꝼyꞃhto þæꞃ ciꞃtꞃeᵹlican piceꞃ. ⁊ be ꞃpecneꞃꞃe þæꞃ heoꝼonlican ꞃiceꞃ he moniᵹ leoð ᵹepoꞃhce. ⁊ ꞃpýlc eac oðeꞃ moniᵹ be þam ᵹoðcundum ꝼꞃemꞃumneꞃꞃum ⁊ dómum he ᵹepoꞃhce. on eallum þam he ᵹeoꞃnlice ᵹýmde þ he men acuᵹe ꝼꞃam ꞃýnna luꝼan ⁊ mán dæða ⁊ to luꝼan ⁊ to ᵹeoꞃnꝼullneꞃꞃe apehce ᵹoðꞃa dæða.	He first sung of earth's creation and of the origin of mankind, and all the history of Genesis, which is the first book of Moses ; and then of the outgoing of the Israelite-folk from Egypt-land, and the ingoing to the land of promise, and of many other histories of the Canonical books of Holy Writ ; and of Christ's incarnation, and of his passion, and of his ascension into heaven, and of the coming of the Holy Ghost, and the doctrine of the Apostles, and also of the terror of the doom to come, and the fear of hell torment, and the sweetness of the heavenly kingdom he made many poems ; and in like manner many others of the divine benefits and judgments he made ; in all which he earnestly took care to draw men from the love of sins and wicked deeds, and to excite to a love and desire of good deeds.

Cædmon is supposed to have died in the year 680, or a little later ; and Mr. Conybeare [1] gives the year 670 as the date of the poem of which the above fragments are all that have been preserved.

The lines copied above from King Alfred's translation of the Ecclesiastical History have been considered by most authors as a retranslation of Cædmon's Hymn from Bede's Latin,[2] and not the original hymn itself. The question is one of some interest, involving the state of the language of the Anglo-Saxons 200 years before the time of Alfred and the inroads of the Danes ; and, consequently, long before it can be supposed that the language of the latter could in any manner have modified the old Anglo-Saxon tongue. Now it happens that, with the exception of the boundaries of property set forth technically in early Anglo-Saxon charters, we possess no other specimen of the genuine old Anglo-Saxon language, except this hymn of Cædmon. " Nulla, proh dolor ! istius ævi [Anglo-Saxonici, i. e. the period previous to the coming of the Danes] literaria monumenta neque membranis inscripta neque lignis saxisve incisa extent quæ scio præter veri Cædmonis fragmentum quod in lib. iv. cap. 24, Eccl. Hist. Bedæ regia versione extat[3]."

Hickes, it will hence be seen, regarded Alfred's version as containing the genuine hymn of Cædmon, and the version quoted above from Bishop More's MS. confirms this opinion. As, however, Mr. Conybeare [4] raised a doubt concerning the age of the verses, as given in this MS., observing, that there appeared to him strong

---

[1] Illustrations of Anglo-Saxon Poetry, p. 36.

[2] Sir H. Ellis in Archæologia, v. 24, p. 331. Thorpe, Preface to his 2nd edition of Cædmon's Paraphrase.

[3] Hickes' Thesaurus, 1. 88. The Theotisc Gospel Harmony, of the Cottonian Library, can scarcely be deemed an example of this era, being evidently a continental production. The few verses spoken by Bede shortly before his decease, and quoted by Cuthbert of Jarrow, his disciple, must not, however, be overlooked. They are given by Stevenson in his recent edition of the Historia Ecclesiastica, from nearly contemporary Anglo-Saxon MSS., now preserved at St. Gallen in Switzerland. It is probable that the attention of Raske was not directed to these lines, nor to those of Cædmon contained in Bishop More's MS., and hence it is not surprising that in the Anglo-Saxon

works hitherto published, he should have found no variation of dialect, because all that he had seen were of the Dano-Saxon period of Hickes. We must, however, remember that King Alfred was not very likely to have adopted any Danisms into his translations ; and if the same dialect was retained until the Norman Conquest, it is evident that the subsequent settlement of the Danes in England made but little impression on the old language. Mr. Thorpe asserts that the only MSS. which exist, in which a provincial dialect can be traced, (Pref. to Cædmon,) are the gloss in the Cottonian Gospels (Nero, D. 4), and in the Psalter (Vesp. A. 1), the Ormulum and a fragment of Bede, to which he refers, but which I am unable to find in his volume.

[4] Illust. of Anglo-Saxon Poetry, p. 6.

grounds for thinking them the work of the eleventh or twelfth century; it is necessary to examine whether this supposition is not entirely groundless.

The MS. itself is described by Wanley[1] as being written in very ancient characters, and " ad calcem hujus codicis legitur (si non eadem saltem *manu æque antiqua*) canticum illud Cædmonis" copied above. At the end of which is the statement " Primo cantavit Cædmon istud carmen." Then follow three Latin words with their corresponding names in Anglo-Saxon; and the latter part of the volume is occupied by historical notices, reaching down to the year 737, and is written " eadem manu qua scribitur Codex."

It is to be observed in the first place, that Wanley who had more practice in the examination of Anglo-Saxon MSS. than perhaps any other person who has yet studied them, could not have mistaken a MS. of the eighth century for one of the eleventh or twelfth; such a supposition is of itself unworthy of a moment's consideration.

2ndly. It is expressly stated, that this was the hymn as first sung by Cædmon himself. It is written just where it might have been expected to have been found, and evidently by a writer who had the hymn in his mind long before the birth of King Alfred.

3rdly. It is scarcely possible that the words of a hymn which Bede had rendered so famous should have been lost between his days and those of King Alfred.

4thly. The language in which it is written, although almost corresponding word for word with King Alfred's version, differs from it both in the orthography and the grammatical form of some of its words, which appear to be in a ruder dialect than in the later version of the royal author. Mr. Conybeare alludes to one or two of these peculiarities, as being similar to others found in a more recent period; but I believe it will be found that the orthography bears a much closer resemblance to the ancient Theotisc language. Thus the word in the 10th line, which in later Anglo-Saxon MSS. is always written bearn (child, vulgo bairn), is here found spelt barn; and in the Theotisc Gospels (Cott. MS. Cal. A. 7) it is also spelt barn; so also the Anglo-Saxon word ælmihtig (almighty, from æl, all) in the last line is here spelt with a simple a, as it is also in the same Gospels. I thus infer that at the time when this MS. was written, the Anglo-Saxon language was more of a Theotisc or continental character than in King Alfred's time. Moreover,

5thly. These lines are here found written throughout without either p, þ, or ð, which is of itself a sufficient proof that they were not written in the 11th century, and, as I have already shown in speaking of the usage of these letters, that they must have been written long before the days of King Alfred.

4. THE METRICAL PARAPHRASE BY THE PSEUDO-CÆDMON.

About the middle of the 17th century the celebrated antiquary, Archbishop Usher, presented to the equally celebrated Anglo-Saxon scholar, Francis Junius, a MS., consisting of a poem, which, both from its subject and style, was supposed by the latter to be no other than the poem of Cædmon above described, and which was accordingly printed by him[2], under the name of that poet, in 1655. On the death of Junius, it passed, with the rest of his collection of MSS., to the Bodleian library, where it is still preserved with the number, (Junius, No. 11.) It is written upon 114 leaves of parchment, measuring $12\frac{1}{2}$ inches by 8, (a full page containing 25 leaves, the first 106 leaves in handsome and uniform Anglo-Saxon characters, the remainder of the MS. being in a somewhat different hand; the different sections or chapters, commencing with large and singularly ornamented initial letters[3], mostly composed of birds or dragons, intertwining together, one of them holding the tail of another in its mouth. The text is profusely ornamented with drawings, as subsequently mentioned in more detail. The publication of Junius was unaccompanied by any translation or by any fac-similes of these drawings; but the whole of the latter were engraved by private subscription about the middle of the last century, and at length published in the 24th volume of the Archæologia; the text itself having been carefully revised by Mr. B. Thorpe[4] was also published at the same time, accompanied by a literal translation,

---

[1] Hickes' Thesaurus, vol. ii.

[2] ' Cædmon's Monachi Paraphrasis poetica Genesios ac præcipuarum sacræ paginæ Historiarum abhinc annos MLXX Anglo-Saxonice conscripta et nunc primum edita a Francisco Junio F. F. Amstelodami, 1655.'

[3] After page 75 the initials are merely plain black capital letters.

[4] ' Cædmon's Metrical Paraphrase of parts of the Holy Scriptures in Anglo-Saxon, with an English Translation, Notes, and a verbal Index.' By Benjamin Thorpe, F.S.A. London, 1832. 8vo.

and preceded by a detailed account of the MS. itself and its supposed author. The Poem opens with the following lines, here copied with a view of contrasting them with the Poem of Cædmon, as given by Bede (and of which Astle has given a fac-simile : tab. xix. 8.) :—

Us iꞅ ꞃihꞇ micel· ðæꞇ ƿe ꞃoðeꞃa ƿeaꞃð· ƿeꞃeða ƿulðoꞃ cininᵹ· ƿoꞃðum heꞃiᵹen· móðum luꝼien· he iꞅ mæᵹna ꞅꞃeð· heaꝼoð ealꞃa· heah-ᵹeꞅceaꝼꞇa· ꝼꞃea ælmihꞇiᵹ· næꞅ him ꝼꞃuma ǽꝼꞃe· óꞃ ᵹeƿoꞃðen· ne nu enðe cýmþ· écean ðꞃihꞇneꞅ· ac he bið á ríce· oꝼeꞃ heoꝼen-ꞅꞇolaꞅ· heaᵹum þꞃýmmum· ꞅoðꝼæꞅꞇ ⁊ ꞅꞃið ꝼeꞃom· ꞅƿeᵹl-bóꞅmaꞅ heolð·

For us it is much right, that we the guardian of the skies, the glory-King of Hosts, with our words praise, in our minds love. He is of power the essence, the head of all exalted creatures, the Lord Almighty. To him has beginning never origin been, nor now cometh end of the eternal Lord, but he is ever powerful over the heavenly thrones. With high majesty, just and most vigorous, he ruled the heavenly concaves.

After this exordium, the poem proceeds with an account of the fall of the rebel angels, and the design of the Creator to replenish the void thus occasioned by a better race, and creation of the world, paraphrased from the first book of Genesis. The pride, rebellion, debates, and punishment of Satan and his companions, are again introduced, " with a resemblance to Milton so remarkable, that much of this portion might be almost literally translated by a cento of verses from that great poet."[1] This is followed by the temptation and disobedience of our first parents, and the judgment pronounced upon them by the Almighty. This part of the poem is stated by Mr. Conybeare to be, in its form and character, remarkably dramatic ; and quite in the style of the " mysteries" of a later period. The histories of Cain and Abel, the Patriarchs both before and after the Flood to the time of Abraham, are almost literally scriptural in their language ; but in the account of the miracles wrought by Moses in Egypt, and the overthrow of Pharaoh's host in the Red Sea, the style again becomes spirited. This is followed by a paraphrase of the first five chapters of the prophet Daniel, and the manuscript terminates by a distinct poem, the subject of which is the triumphal entry of Christ into Hades, familiarly known in the middle ages under the name of the Harrowing of Hell. The return of our Saviour to the earth, his several appearances to his disciples after his resurrection, and his ascension, are all described in this part of the MS.

The MS., in the opinion of the most competent judges, was written about or soon after the year 1000.[2] Junius, from the identity of the subject, at once ascribed this Paraphrase to Cædmon ; but Hickes and Wanley[3] being unable to find the verses of King Alfred in the MS., and from its dialect and style (which the former called Dano-Saxon), considered the work as the later production of a second poet of the same name, whom he designated by the name of Pseudo-Cædmon. Mr. Thorpe, however, considers it to be the production of the Monk of Whitby, allowance being made for the interpolations and corruptions of ignorant transcribers; and he asserts that he has not succeeded in tracing a vestige of the Dano-Saxon dialect throughout the poem. It must be borne in mind, however, that the Dano-Saxon of Hickes and of Thorpe are not analogous. The term was applied by the former to our literature as it existed between the beginning of the 9th to the middle of the 11th century, and as it may be supposed to have been affected by our communion with the Danes. The Junian Paraphrase is, of course, written in the dialect which prevailed during this period.

The fragment given by Bede and King Alfred is, indeed, very short ; but it is to be observed (notwithstanding Mr. Thorpe's assertion of the correspondence in every particular, between the Hymn of Cædmon and the Junian Paraphrase), that neither Bede nor King Alfred say anything of the entire machinery of the fallen

[1] Conybeare's Synopsis of the Poem, contained in " Illustrations of Anglo-Saxon Poetry." London, 1826. The plot of this paraphrastic history in fact so much resembles that of the " Paradise Lost," that " it has obtained for its author the name of the Saxon Milton." (Wright, Biogr. Brit. Liter., p. 198.) When, however, the following circumstances are taken into consideration, I think we are, on the other hand, fully warranted in supposing that this striking resemblance was not altogether accidental, but resulted from Milton having borrowed his plot from the Anglo-Saxon poet. The MS. of Junius was published in 1655. About this period, Milton was engaged upon his History of England previous to the Norman Conquest, such a publication would therefore, doubtless, find its way to him. " Paradise Lost" was published in 1667, but its composition occupied a number of years. (*See* The Life of Milton, by his nephew Edward Philps. Pickering's Edit. of Milton's Poet. Works, 1826, vol. i., p. lxii.) And we learn from Philps, that it was at first intended for a tragedy ; "and in the fourth book of the poem there are six verses which, several years before the poem was begun, were shown to me and some others as designed for the very beginning of the said tragedy." *These verses commence with what stands as the 32nd line of the 4th Book.* Now it will be at once remembered that the first three Books are occupied with the history of the expulsion of the devil and his angels from Heaven, their discussions, &c., and it is precisely this portion of the Anglo-Saxon Paraphrase which is so strikingly similar to the " Paradise Lost." Can it be supposed that Milton was ignorant of the publication of Junius ? And is it not evident that the first three books of the " Paradise Lost" were an after-thought, entirely induced by the plot of the Paraphrase ?

[2] " Sæculo decimo exeunte (ut videtur) scriptus," Wanley, in Hickes' Thes. 2, p. 77. Astle says, " circa A.D. 985."

[3] Hickes' Thesaurus, p. 133, and Wanley 2, p. 77 ; and Hickes' Letter to Bishop Nicolson, quoted by Thorpe (p. ix.)

angels, which forms so spirited and extended a portion of the Junian MS. Respecting these portions of the poem, Sir F. Palgrave[1] observes, that they possess an oriental character, that there was no Latin version of the Bible in which they could be found, and that they may be strongly suspected to be of Rabbinical origin, which it is not impossible to suppose was understood by the Anglo-Saxon author, Joannes Scotus and Bede himself being versed in Hebrew[2].

This portion of the poem, in fact, although "founded on legends of which it is not now easy to trace the origin[3]," might perhaps furnish us with a solution of the question, whether it be the real production of Cædmon, or whether this portion of it at least may not be a later interpolation. We know, in fact, from one of the homilies of Ælfric (published in the fourth Number of the Ælfric Society), that, in the beginning of the eleventh century, even this divine taught the doctrine, that the creation of man was consequent upon the fall of one of the ten races of angels, whose place was to be supplied in the universe by the new inhabitants of a world to be created half way between Paradise and Hell (hence the earth is called mid-earth, miððanȝeapð); and it may perhaps not be impossible that this theology had its origin in the apocryphal book of Enoch[4].

Mr. Conybeare (who adopts the opinion that the verses of King Alfred are verbally those of Cædmon, and that Bede's Latin is also a literal translation of the latter),[5] observes that the exordium of the Junian Paraphrase conveys exactly the same thoughts as the Hymn of Cædmon, clothed in nearly the same expressions; that most of the titles applied to the Deity by Bede's Cædmon frequently occur in the Paraphrase; and that the poetical ornaments are also common to both; yet it must be acknowledged that there exists in these respects so great a degree of uniformity throughout the great mass of Saxon poetry, that the argument cannot be considered as decided. The question, therefore, whether the Bodleian MS. exhibits the genuine remains of the great head of this school, or of some one among his later disciples, must be considered as undecided. It is in this doubt, and for the other reasons above mentioned, that I have preferred speaking of the MS. as the production of an author not proved to have been Bede's Cædmon. It appears that other copies of the Paraphrase must have been made, as the famous Exeter MS. contains the Song of Azariah, evidently extracted from a more correct MS. of the Paraphrase than the Junian copy.

The fac-simile in the accompanying Plate, No. 3, is taken from the commencement of the 22nd Chapter of the MS., and is as follows, being the account of the settling of the waters after the Deluge:—

Þ⁊ ȝemunðe ȝoð· meɲe-liðenðe· ɲiȝoɲa palðenð· ɲunu lamecheɲ· ꝛ ealle þa pócɲe· þe he pɪð pæcɲebeleac· liɲeɲ leoht-ɲɲuma.

THEN remembered God *the* seafaring; *the* Lord of triumph, *the* son of Lamech; and all the living beings which he had enclosed against the water, the author of life's light,—

"in the ship's bosom. Led then the warrior Lord of Hosts, a wind over the wide land; the well-flood began again to lessen. The water ebbed dark under the firmament; the just Creator had from his children the dire stream averted; the bright in course, the rain had stilled. The foamy ship rode a hundred and fifty nights under Heaven since that the nailed timber, vessel most excellent, the flood upraised; until the number of the dire period of days had passed. Then on the mountain sate lofty, with its lading, greatest of ocean houses, the Ark of Noah[6]."

The following notice of the drawings contained in this MS. will complete my account of this interesting production:—The drawings with which the first portion is ornamented are merely outlines in a kind of bistre, slightly shaded with brown. But in the second part they consist of outlines, having the different parts of each subject drawn with a different coloured ink—namely, red, green, and black; whilst the third portion of the MS. (after the 48th leaf) has blank spaces left for drawings, the last of which represents the

---

[1] Archæologia, vol. xxiv., p. 343.

[2] Sir F. Palgrave considers that the name Cædmon itself is of Rabbinical origin, not being Anglo-Saxon, but being, in fact, the initial word of the Book of Genesis in the Chaldee Paraphrase or Targum of Onkelos, and that the name Adam Cadmon, holds a most important station in Cabalistic Theology. As Bede, however, may be supposed to speak of Cædmon almost from personal knowledge, we may perhaps question the propriety of this speculation.

[3] Wright, Biogr. Brit. Lit., p. 198. And see his St. Patrick's Purgatory, an Essay on the Legends of Purgatory, Hell, and Paradise, current during the middle ages. 12mo, 1844.

[4] Quoted in the Epistle of Jude. The partiality of the Anglo-Saxons for the Apocryphal Books of Scripture, may be mentioned to render this supposition probable. The Book of Enoch was known entire till the eighth century, after which only fragments of it were known to be preserved, until Bruce brought three perfect MSS. from Ethiopia. *Vide* the Book of Enoch, by Lawrence, 8vo, Oxford, 1821; and Enfield's Compendium of Brucker's Account of the Cabalistic Philosophy.

[5] Ill. Anglo-Saxon Poetry, p. 7.

[6] Thorpe's Cædmon's Metrical Paraphrase, p. 84.

approach of Abraham to the Holy Land. Only a single figure of God the Father, dispensing the benediction according to the rite of the Roman Church, and represented, according to the most ancient type of Christ, as a young man, and without a beard [1] (on the recto of leaf 11), is finished in thick opaque colours; in this the under robe, which appears on the breast, right-hand, and lower part of the body, is of a dark red-brown colour, relieved with dull yellow lights; the upper robe is dark green, relieved with paler green lights; the hair is dirty red; the band across the head white, edged with red-lead; the outlines of the right-hand are red, and those of the features, feet, and left-hand, dark brown. The book, which is held in the hand, is pale greenish yellow, with the edge of the leaves red, and the flesh is left uncoloured.

The Frontispiece represents the Almighty seated on a cushion, surrounded by Cherubims above the clouds. He is represented as an aged man, with a forked beard and with a cruciferous nimbus round his head [2]. His right-hand is elevated, with the first and second fingers extended, and in his left-hand he holds a kind of baton or roll. The displeasure of the Almighty at the rebel Angels occupies the second Plate [4]; and the fall of the latter, and the binding of Satan in Hell's mouth, are elaborately represented in the third Plate. Here, as well as in many of the subsequent drawings, the artist seems quite to have entered into the supernatural character of the text, and has produced imaginative effects as striking as any of those with which the wonderful talents of John Martin has surprised the modern lovers of art. This is especially the case with the delineation of the up-rearing of the firmament, with the Spirit of God moving over the face of the waters, and in the different representations of Hell. The drawing copied in the woodcut below represents the Patriarch Seth and his Family, and will serve to show the general style of the

drawings, in which we perceive the comparative slenderness of the figures, especially of the legs; the diminutive size of the female's head and feet, and the fluttering drapery, all so characteristic of the later Anglo-Saxon art. This drawing is also interesting, as affording an illustration of the regal habits and thrones and the ordinary Anglo-Saxon seats, as well as of the forms of the shields, and swords of the warriors. The use also of large hanging drapery, suspended between the pillars of the building, is here shown; and the antiquarian architect will not look without interest at the remarkable capitals with

[1] Waagen, Arts and Artists in England, 2, 214.

[2] Christ himself (under the name of Salvator) is also similarly represented (fol. 7), in both these respects, but inclosed in the "vesica piscis," and in the act of benediction, with the first two fingers of the right-hand elevated.

[3] At the bottom of one of the pages is represented a small profile of

a man inclosed in a circular frame, inscribed ælᵹpɪne; and it has been suggested that this Ælfwine may possibly have been the Abbot of Hyde Abbey, near Winchester, for whom the Cotton. MS. Titus, D. 27, (described by Dibdin. Bibl. Decam. 1, p. lv.) was written by the monk Ælsinus.

which the columns at the sides of the drawing are crowned, and which, in the original, support a segmental arch. The branches of the tree, introduced above the head of the female, are interpolated from another drawing of the MS., to show the peculiar style in which they are generally represented in MSS. of this period. In another of the drawings, we find the columns ornamented with interlaced foliage, and the capitals formed of lions' heads, similar to the ornaments which I have copied from the Gospels of Canute. In general the arches are either represented as semicircular or triangular-headed, and the columns themselves mostly plain. Many of the buildings are represented as being several stories high, and the ark appears in the form of a large building of three stories, with short conical pinnacles, surmounted by *weathercocks.*

Sir Francis Palgrave also informs us [1] that Ludovicus Pius, being desirous of furnishing his subjects with a version of the Holy Scriptures, applied to a *Saxon* Bard of great talent and fame, who had been instructed in a dream to render the precepts of the Divine Law into the verse and measure of his native tongue. This translation, now unfortunately lost, was of great beauty, and comprehended the whole of the Bible, interspersed with mystic allusions.[2] Are we not in this statement almost led to conceive that nothing more was intended than that Louis, having heard of the fame of the poetry of Cædmon through Bede's writings, applied to some Saxon scholar of his own day for a copy?

5. ÆLFRIC'S ANGLO-SAXON HEPTATEUCH.

The name of Ælfric, Archbishop of Canterbury (died 1006), is endeared to the inhabitants of this land, not only by the doctrines which he taught, but also by his laborious attempts to disseminate a knowledge of the Christian religion amongst our forefathers, both by a translation of the Sacred Books into the Anglo-Saxon language, and by his collection of Sermons (or Homilies), eighty in number, written in his native tongue, which the Society, lately established, and bearing his own name, have selected as the first subjects of their publications. [3] Of his translations from the Scriptures only two manuscripts are known to be in existence. The first of these is preserved in the Bodleian Library at Oxford (Laud. 509,—E. 19). It is an octavo volume, consisting of 141 leaves of parchment, measuring $8\frac{1}{2}$ by $5\frac{1}{2}$ inches; a full page containing twenty-six lines, and comprises the Heptateuch, or seven first books of the Old Testament. Its capitals are plain, and coloured red, green, or blue, and it is destitute of drawings. At the beginning is a " Catalogus Tractatuum in isto volumine," written in the same hand which occurs in the same manner in so many of the Cottonian MSS. and the autograph of Archbishop Laud appears on the first page. The preface (which has been several times published by Wharton, Thorpe, and others) is dedicated to Æthelwærd, the Ealdorman. The first line of which is copied in my fac-simile No. 1, and is to be read, ÆLFRIC MUNUC GRET ÆÐELⱣÆRD EALDOR-MANN—or, Ælfric, the Monk, greets Æthelwærd, the Alderman[4]. The specimen numbered 2 will show the character of the writing. It is the commencement of the Book of Genesis, and is as follows:—

<table>
<tr><td>INCIPIT LIBER GENESIS ANGLICE.
(ÆLFRIC.)</td><td>HERE BEGINNETH THE BOOK OF GENESIS IN ENGLISH.
(LISLE'S TRANSLATION. MS. Bodl. Laud. 381.)</td></tr>
<tr><td>ON ANGINNE GESCEOP GOD HEOFE-
NAN AND EORÐAN SEO EORÐE
roþlice þær yðel ꞵ æmtiʒ ꞵ
þeorτꞵu þæꞵon oꝼeꞵ þæꞵe
nꞵpelnꞵꞵe bꞵaðnꞵꞵe· ꞵ
ʒoðer ʒaꞵt þær ꞵær ʒeꝼeꞵoð
oꝼeꞵ þæτeꞵu· ʒoð cꞵæþ
þa· ʒepeoꞵðe leohτ· ꞵ
leohτ peaꞵþ ʒepoꞵhτ.[5]</td><td>IN THE BEGINNING GOD CREATED
HEAVEN AND EARTH. THE EARTH
was voide and empty, and
darkes were over the
face of the deep, and
the Spirit of God was carried
over the waters. God said
then Let there be light, and
light was made.</td></tr>
</table>

This manuscript, supposed at the time to be unique, was published, with some other articles, by Thwaites, at Oxford, in 1699.[6]

---

[1] Archæologia, vol. xxiv., p. 341.

[2] " Præfatio in librum antiquum lingua Saxonica conscriptum," published amongst the Epistles of Hincmar, Bishop of Rhemes, (Bibliotheca Patrum, Paris, 1644, vol. xvi., p. 609,) quoted by Sir F. Palgrave.

[3] On the religious doctrines of our forefathers compare Soames' Inquiry into the doctrines of the Anglo-Saxon Church, in eight Sermons, preached before the University of Oxford in 1830, with Lingard's Antiquities of the Anglo-Saxon Church.

[4] The identity of Ælfric the translator, with Ælfric the author of the Homilies, is confirmed by the Homily " On the Old and New Testament," published by L'isle, Oxford, 1623. Reprinted 1678.

[5] It will be seen that the MS. is slightly glossed with Latin, as in the second line the Latin words "erat inanis & vacua," and erant; ferebatur, in the second line, and " facta ÷" (est) in the third line.

[6] " Heptateuchus, Liber Job et Evangelium Nicodemi, Anglo-Saxonice. Historia Judith fragmentum Dano-Saxonice."

The Cottonian Library, however, possesses a noble copy of this translation of the Heptateuch, marked Claudius B. iv.[1] This fine manuscript, which Wanley truly called a " Monumentum pietatis majorum nostrorum sane spectabile," consists of 158 leaves of parchment, measuring 13 inches by 9, and written throughout in strong-set Anglo-Saxon characters, with the initials of the different paragraphs quite plain, about an inch high, and in blue, green, and red colours. It is profusely ornamented with miniatures, many of the pages having two, or even three, paintings, which afford the most valuable materials for the knowledge of the peculiar dresses, &c. of the Anglo-Saxons of the period at which the volume was written.[2] Like many of the MSS. of this period, the paintings towards the end of the volume are more or less unfinished, and enable us to see the entire process of their execution, in which two different modes have been adopted; in the one, the outlines of the entire picture, including the features and folds of the garments, were in the first place carefully drawn with a pen, a different coloured ink having been used in the different parts of the picture, which were afterwards to receive a different local tint. In some parts of the volume these outlines are in green, lilac, red, and blue colours. A thick body of opaque colour was then laid on the different parts, the shades being produced by darker dashes of the different tints, and which are then relieved by white lines. In others, a very slight, and also invisible, outline may be perceived, and the first layers of colour were put in before the coloured outlines were drawn.

The commencement of the Dedication to Æthelwærd is wanting; the Book of Genesis commencing on fol. 1. v. as follows :—

On angýnne geꝛceop gôð heôꝛonan ꞃ eoꝛðan ꞃe eôꝛðe ꞃoðlice pæꞃ iðel ꞃ æmti ꞃ þeoꞃtꞃa pæꞃon oꝛen ðæꞃe nýpelnýꞃꞃe bꞃaðnýꞃꞃe ꞃ ꝣôðeꞃ ꝣåꞃt pæꞃ ꝣeꝛeꞃoð oꝛen pæteꞃu· ꝣoð cꝥ ða ꝣeꝛuꞃðe leôht ꞃ leoht pæaꞃð ꝣeꞃoꞃht,

thus differing slightly from the Bodleian MS. The second leaf (recto) is occupied by a large painting of God, held by Angels in a blue oval shield, with the ends acute (the vesica piscis, as it is termed by antiquaries); and the downfall of the rebel Angels, which are preyed upon by a gigantic red serpent. Then follows the Creation, all the events of which are illustrated; that of the Birth of Eve, who is drawn by God out of a slit in the side of the sleeping Adam, is very singular; as is also the translation of Enoch (fol. xi. verso). The drawing, which I have selected, occurs on the verso of leaf 7. It represents the expulsion from Paradise, and the instruction of our first parents in husbandry. It is executed with much spirit, and affords a specimen of the manner in which trees were generally represented with the branches entwined together.[3] In the drawing of Adam behind the tree, allowance seems to have been made for the intervention of the latter by giving half of Adam's figure on one side, and the other half on the other side of the tree. I have noticed this mode of treatment in other Anglo-Saxon drawings, where an object has been represented as interposed between the figure represented and the spectator. The hair and beard of these figures will be seen to be represented blue, a circumstance of common occurrence in Anglo-Saxon MSS., which led Strutt to suppose that the practice of dyeing the hair was of common occurrence.[4] The forms of the spade and pickaxe will also not be overlooked in this drawing, nor the minute size of the feet of Eve.[5]

Many others of the drawings in this MS. are of great interest, amongst which may be mentioned the first rainbow (fo. 16 v.), the vine-yard and wine-press (fo. 17 r.), the Tower of Babel (fo. 19 r.), the battle of Abraham and the Five Kings to rescue his brother Lot (fo. 24 v.), in which Abraham is represented crowned and clad in the ringed byrn borrowed from the Phrygians,[6] being one of the earliest representations of this kind of armour; God descending from Heaven upon a ladder, supported by angels, and appearing to Abraham (fo. 29 r.); Lot and his wife conducted by Angels, represented in a manner very similar to the drawings in the Duke of Buckingham's Hyde Abbey book (Dibdin, Bibl. Dec. 1, p. 57); the journey of Abraham and interrupted sacrifice of Isaac (fo. 39); the deception of Jacob practised upon his blind father (fol. 43 r.); Jacob's dream (fo. 45 r.); and various figures of the Ark; all merit particular notice, as do many of the drawings in which the architectural character of the Anglo-Saxon erections are interestingly

---

[1] The Cotton. MS., Otho, B. 10, containing a second copy, was burnt in the Cotton. fire.

[2] " Scriptus paullo ante Conquisitionem Angliæ." Wanley, Hickes' Thes. 2, p. 254.

[3] Such a mode of representing trees occurs amongst the sculptures upon the famous Runic font in Bridekirk Church, Derbyshire, engraved in the 14th volume of the Archæologia.

[4] Dress and Habits of the People of England, vol. i., p. 77.

[5] This is so common a mode of representing the feet of females, that I am almost inclined to surmise that their size was intentionally diminished, like that of the feet of Chinese females.

[6] This figure has been copied repeatedly, and introduced into all our works on ancient costume.

pourtrayed.[8] Some of these, together with a figure of Lot seated upon a chair, ornamented with the heads of the lion and eagle, (to which the Anglo-Saxons were so partial,) are represented on the accompanying wood-cut, and need no further notice, than that columns similar to those of fig. *a* occur in some of our oldest

Anglo-Saxon churches, where they have been supposed to be peculiar only to the belfry lights (as in the church of St. Benedict at Cambridge); that capitals, similar to fig. *b*, occur in the ancient Priory Church of St. Bartholomew, near Smithfield. (Vetusta Monumenta, vol. ii. pl. 37.) And that triangular-headed arches like *c*, occur in the portico of Lorsch (A.D. 764,) the old Palace at Westminster, the Church of St. Benedict, at Cambridge, &c. Many of these drawings have been partially engraved by Strutt in his different works (but erroneously attributed to the eighth instead of the eleventh century), and in the Pictorial History of England, vol. i.

This MS. is thickly glossed in every vacant space, even in the open parts of the drawings, with passages from Bede, Josephus, Methodius, &c., as shown in my plate. The specimen No. 5 is the translation of Genesis iv. 9, 10, and is to be read as follows (the Anglo-Saxon being written in ordinary letters in the second line, and a literal English translation being given in the third line) :—

Ða	cpæð	ðnihten	to caine·	hpæn	iſ abel
Tha	cwaeth	drihten	to caine	hwaer	is Abel
Then	quoth	the Lord	to Cain,	where	is Abel

ðin	bnoðon:	ða anðſpanoðe he	ꝝ	cpæth
thin	brothor :	tha andswarode he	&	cwaeth
thy	brother :	then answered he,	and	quoth,

ic	nat.	seȝſt ðu ſceolðe ic minne bnoðon
ic	nat.	segst thu sceolde ic minne brothor
I know not ;		sayst thou should I mine brother

healðon·	ða cpæð ðnihten to caine :	hpaec
healdon·	tha cwaeth drihten to caine :	hwaet
hold ?	then quoth the Lord to Cain :	what

ðyðeſt	ðu·	þineſ bnoðon	bloð	clypað
dydest	thu·	thines brothor	blod	clypath [2]
did'st	thou ?	thy brother's	blood	cryeth

up	co me oſ	eonðan
up	to me of	eorthan
up	to me off	the earth

There is scarcely a word in this Anglo-Saxon passage which is not retained in our modern language.

The specimen No. 6 is part of the heading of the book of Numbers, which is to be read :—' Her ongynð seo boc ðe is genemned on ebreisc Uale imber ðæt is on leden Numerus and on Englisc getel.'—Here beginneth the book which is called in Hebrew Uale imber, that is, in Latin, numerus, and in English getel. The forms of many of the capitals are worthy of notice, as the E N G M L A and U (resembling those in the Bodleian MS.), and the intermixture of a few minuscule letters, with the rustic capitals, as in the word Ðæc in the second line.

In addition to the preceding MSS., the following contain early versions of the books of Moses :—

Public Library, Cambridge, a quarto volume, written on parchment, long after the Conquest, in a Norman-Saxon hand, containing the first twenty-four chapters of Genesis, from Ælfric's version.

Corp. Christ. Coll. Cambridge, S. 18. N. 78. An Extract from Ælfric's version of Genesis (ch. xxxvii. to xlvii.)

The Library of the Dean and Chapter of Lincoln contains some fragments of Ælfric's Heptateuch.

Corp. Christ. Coll. Camb., R. 11. An octavo volume, written on parchment, containing the books of Genesis and Exodus, in very old English rhyme, of which the following is an extract :—

Luuen God and serven him ay,

For he it hem þel gelden may—

And to alle Cristenei men

Boren pais and luue by tþem.

Fader God of alle ðhinge
Almightin Louerd hegest kinge
Thu give me seli timinge
To than men ðis þerdes bigininge
The Lauerd God to purðinge
Queðer so hic rede or singe.

---

[1] A careful comparison of the architectural and other ornaments, represented in Anglo-Saxon MSS., with those of some of our oldest churches, would, I apprehend, satisfactorily prove (notwithstanding the assertion of Mr. Britton (Arch. Antiq. of Normandy, p. iii.) that "no one structure, scarcely any one fragment, in Great Britain, is now in existence, that can be referred, with certainty, to the Saxon era") ; that many erections, fonts, &c. attributed to the Norman period, are, in fact, much earlier than the dates assigned to them. This view of the subject has not hitherto been sufficiently recognised.

[2] Clyped—hence yclept, a word so common in old English.

LXVIII · INFINEMPROHIS QUI
COMMUTABUNTUR DAUID

SALUUMME
FAC DS QM INTROIERUNTAQE
USQUEADANIMAMMEAM INFIXUS
SUM INLIMUM PROFUNDI ET
NON EST SUBSTANTIA···

PSALMIOMNIHODAMINSTITUTIONEMSPITALISDISCIPLINAEHABENT·

TEDEUM LAUDAMUS · TEDOMINUM CONFITEMUR ·
Te aeternum patrem · omnis terre ueneretur ·
Tibi omnes angeli · tibi caeli & uniuersae potestates ·

INCIPIT   ORIGO   PSALMORUM
DAUID FILIUS IESSE CUM ESSET INREGNO SUO IIII ELEGIT QUIPSALMOS FACEREN,

The Psalter of Saint Augustine

THE PSALTER OF ST. AUGUSTINE.

PREVIOUS to entering upon our review of the Anglo-Saxon Psalters, it will be necessary to notice the various ancient versions of the Psalms written in the Latin language, since it happens that (unlike the Anglo-Saxon Books of Moses, and some of the Gospels which were written throughout in our old language alone) all the Anglo-Saxon versions of the Psalms now known to be in existence were made either by interlineations in previously written Latin MSS., or in conjunction with one or other of the Latin versions simultaneously written either in alternate lines or opposite columns.

The following extract from Waterland's Treatise on the Athanasian Creed, comprises a concise account of the early Latin versions of the Psalter :—

" There are four kinds of Latin *Psalters,* which have passed under the names of *Italick, Roman, Gallican,* and *Hebraick.* The *Italick* Latin Psalter is the old translation, such as it was before St. Jerome's time. The *Roman* Psalter is not very different from the old *Italick.* It is nothing else but the old version cursorily and in part corrected by Jerome in the time of Pope Damasus, A.D. 383. It has had the name of *Roman,* because the use of it began the soonest and continued the longest in the Roman offices. It obtained in Gaul nearly as soon as at Rome, but was laid aside in the sixth century, when Gregory of Tours introduced the other Psalter, since called the *Gallican.* The *Gallican* Psalter is Jerome's more correct Latin translation made from Origen's Hexapla, or most correct edition of the Greek Septuagint, filled up where the Greek was supposed faulty from the Hebrew, distinguished with obelisks and asterisks, denoting the common Greek version in those places to be redundant or deficient. This more correct Psalter was drawn up by Jerome in 389, and obtained first in Gaul about 580, or not later than 595, from which circumstance it came to have the name of *Gallican* in contradistinction to the Roman. From Gaul it passed to England before 597, and into Germany, Spain, and other countries. The Popes of Rome, though they themselves used the other Psalter, yet patiently connived at the use of this in the Western Churches, and even in Italy; and sometimes privately authorised the use of it in churches and monasteries, till at length it was publicly authorised in the Council of Trent, and introduced a while after into Rome itself by Pope Pius V. It was admitted into Britain and Ireland before the coming of Augustine, the monk; and prevailed after, except in the Church of Canterbury, which was more immediately under the archbishop's eyes, and more conformable to the Roman offices than other parts of the kingdom. It has been said (Hodius, de Text. Bibl. orig. p. 384), that this very Gallican Psalter is what we still retain in our Liturgy, called the reading Psalms, in contradistinction of the other Psalms in our Bibles of the new translation. But this is not strictly true; for the old translation, though it be taken in a great measure from the Gallican, has yet many corrections from the Hebrew (where they were thought wanting), first by Coverdale, in 1535, and by Coverdale again, 1539, and, last of all, by Tonstall and Heath, in 1541, according to which edition is the Psalter now used in our Liturgy (Durell, Eccles. Anglican. vindic. p. 396). The *Hebraick* Latin Psalter means Jerome's own translation immediately from the Hebrew, made in the year 391. This, though otherwise of great esteem, was never used in the public church offices."

1

THE PSALTER OF ST. AUGUSTINE.

The following specimen from the Quincuplex Psalterium Stephani (1509), being the commencement of the 17th (18th Hebr.) Psalm, will show the style of the variations in these versions :—

GALL.	ROM.	HEBR.	VETUS ITALA.	CONCILIATUM.
Diligam te Dñe, fortitudo mea, dñs firmamentum meum, et refugium meum, et liberator meus, Deus meus, adjutor meus, et sperabo in eum. Protector meus, et cornu salutis meæ, et susceptor meus. Laudans invocabo dominum, et ab inimicis meis salvus ero.	Diligam te dñe, virtus mea, domine firmamentum meum, et refugium meum. Et liberator meus, deus meus, adjutor meus, et sperabo in eum. Protector meus, et cornu salutis meæ, adjutor meus. Laudans invocabo dominum, et ab inimicis meis salvus ero.	Diligam te dñe, fortitudo mea, dñs petra mea, et robur meum, et salvator meus, Deus meus, fortis meus, et sperabo in eo; scutum meum, et cornu salutis meæ, et susceptor meus. Laudatum invocabo dominum, et ab inimicis meis salvus ero.	Diligam te, Dñe, fortitudo mea, Dominus firmamentum meum, et refugium meum, et liberator meus, et sperabo in eum. Protector meus, et cornu salutis meæ, et redemptor meus. Laudans invocabo Dominum, et ab inimicis meis salvus ero.	Diligam te Dñe, fortitudo mea, Dominus firmamentum meum, et refugium meum, et liberator meus. Deus meus, adjutor meus, et sperabo in eum. Protector meus, et cornu salutis meæ, et susceptor meus. Laudans invocabo Dominum, et ab inimicis meis salvus ero.
Circundederunt me dolores mortis, et torrentes iniquitatis conturbaverunt me. Dolores inferni circundederunt me, præoccupaverunt me laquei mortis.	Circundederunt me gemitus mortis, et torrentes iniquitatis conturbaverunt me. Dolores inferni circundederunt me, prævenerunt me laquei mortis.	Circundederunt me funes mortis, et torrentes diaboli terruerunt me. Funes inferni circundederunt me, prævenerunt me laquei mortis.	Circundederunt me dolores mortis, et torrentes iniquitatis conturbaverunt me. Dolores inferni circundederunt me, prævenerunt me laquei mortis.	Circundederunt me dolores mortis, et torrentes iniquitatis conturbaverunt me. Dolores inferni circundederunt me, præoccupaverunt me laquei mortis.

The high degree of veneration with which the Psalter has in all ages been regarded, was doubtless the cause of its incomparable riches having at a very early period been presented to our ancestors in translations of it into their own language. Aldhelm, the Anglo-Saxon poet, who died A.D. 709, and Guthlac, who died A.D. 714, are both affirmed to have translated the Psalms; and William of Malmesbury informs us that King Alfred, at the time of his death, had also commenced an Anglo-Saxon version of the Psalter, which he left unfinished [1]. Unfortunately there is now no means of identifying the various versions which have come down to our times with those made by these authors, neither have we any means of ascertaining by whom these versions were made.

The following is a list of all the Anglo-Saxon Psalters, of which I have been able to find any notice, and which is more complete than any former enumeration :—

1*. The Codex Augustini ; Cott. MS. Vespasian, A 1.

2*. The Codex Vossii, in the Bodleian Library, formerly belonging to Junius.

3*. The Codex Baconii, in the Public Library of Cambridge.

4*. The Codex Lambethanus.

5. The Codex Stowensis, originally belonging to Spelman, who used it in his Edition of the Anglo-Saxon Psalters, and subsequently to Astle, who describes it (Origin of Writing, p. 85,) as the Psalter of King Alfred, without, however, mentioning on what authority this assertion is made, which was the more requisite, as the specimen which he gives of it, (Tab. xix., sp. vi.,) appears rather to be taken from a MS. of the beginning of the 11th century; although Astle states it to have been written between the years 872 and 878. The account which Dr. O'Conor gives of this Psalter (in his Account of the Library at Stowe,) throws no additional light upon the question, but rather the historical statements which he makes render it the more doubtful. (Bibl. Stowensis, vol. ii., p. 28.) The Anglo-Saxon version is almost identical with that in the Cotton. MS. Vitellius E. 18, and especially the Arundel MS. No. 60 [2].

6*. The Codex Parisiensis, formerly belonging to the Duke of Berry.

7. The Codex Arundelianus, No. 60, now in the British Museum.

8*. The Codex Reg., 2 B 5, in the British Museum.

9. The Codex Vitellius, E. 18 of the Cottonian Library.

10*. The Codex Tiberius, C. 6 of the Cottonian Library.

11. The Codex Dunelmensis, containing only the Penitential Psalms.

12. The Codex Salisburiensis, mentioned in the Preface to the 2nd volume of Hickes' Thesaurus, by Wanley, since which time it has remained unnoticed.

13*. The Psalterium Eadwini, in the Library of Trinity College, Cambridge.

Fac-similes of portions of those Psalters marked with the *, will be found in the present and subsequent articles.

In the year 1640, was published " Psalterium Davidis Latino-Saxonicum vetus, a Johanne Spelmanno D. Hen. fil. editum. E vetustissimo exemplari MS. in Bibliotheca ipsius Henrici et cum tribus aliis non multo minus vetustis collatum," 4to, London. And, in 1835, Mr. B. Thorpe published his " Libri Psalmorum versio antiqua Latina, cum Paraphrasi Anglo-Saxonica partim soluta oratione partim metrice composita, nunc primum e Cod. MS., in Bibl. regia Parisiensi adservato." Oxon., 8vo.

---

[1] De Gest. Reg. Angl. p. 44. See the note on the 5th Codex, mentioned below.

[2] It appears most probable that the statement of William of Malmesbury led to the supposition that this MS. contained King Alfred's translation, and this to the idea that it originally belonged to him. Dibdin, O'Conor, &c., call it the most ancient Psalter in the kingdom. It cannot, however, be compared with the Cottonian volume before us. The interest of Dibdin's *imperial* anecdote concerning the volume (Bibl. Dec. 1, p. liv.) is thus destroyed.

THE PSALTER OF ST. AUGUSTINE.

The first of these MSS. consists of 160 leaves of vellum, measuring 9 inches by 7. The body of the manuscript is written with 22 lines of the Latin text of the Psalms in a page, with a more recent interlineary Anglo-Saxon version.

It is described in the first leaf as the 'Psalterium *Romanum* antiquo charactere,' with the observation—'Codex iste scriptus videtur anno 700, a Nativ. Xpi. ; ' and, in Planta's Catalogue of the Cottonian Library, as of the eighth century, and as consisting of the " Psalterium D. Hieronymi *Romanum*." To this manuscript was formerly attached the Charter of King Æthelbald [1] (alluded to in the fourth and fifth pages of the article on the Anglo-Saxon Pentateuch), written in Roman uncials, not very unlike those of the text of the Psalter itself, and dated, A.D. 736.

The first leaf of the Codex in its present state is an interpolated illumination of the twelfth century. Its recto is occupied by a figure of Christ, with the symbols of the four Evangelists, painted on a burnished gold ground, and the verso with a very large and elaborate B (being the initial letter of the first Psalm.)

The second leaf is a sheet of parchment, entirely different from the rest of the volume, being semi-transparent and almost like horn. Its recto is blank, but on the verso is written the commencement of a Latin preface to the Psalms, beginning with the words—

" OMNIS scriptura divinitus inspirata utilis est ad docendū, hac ipsa de causa ab spū scō conscripta," &c. [2]

This is written in thin rustic Roman capitals [3], without any separation between the words, and I have the authority of Sir F. Madden for stating that it is the only specimen existing amongst the MSS. of the British Museum (and probably in the whole kingdom), of this kind of writing, in which are written most of the ancient Latin MSS. (of the fourth, fifth, and sixth centuries) which have come down to us; (such as the Florence and Vatican Virgils, the Paris Prudentius, and the Vatican Terence and Sallust, of all of which fac-similes are given by the Benedictines and Silvestre), and which, in fact, is the kind of writing discovered on the walls of Herculaneum [4].

The third leaf is of the ordinary vellum used throughout the volume; on it is *continued in the same hand,* the remainder of the preface; on the verso the second portion of the preface thus commences (as copied in specimen No. 3, from which it will be seen that this writing very closely resembles that of the Florence Virgil, written in A.D. 498, but differing in the form of the M from every other rustic MS.)

" PSALMI omnimodam institutionem spĩtalis disciplinæ habent, ibi multiplex prophetia, tam de xp̃o quam de ecclesiâ quam de prædicatoribus quam de martyribus, ibi mala declinanda et quæ bona sunt sectanda docetur," &c.

The form of the letters A (destitute of a bar), M, N, T (partaking of a minuscula form), and L, elevated above the line, is to be noticed.

The eight following leaves are occupied, on both sides, by Epistles, and Verses upon the Psalms, by Damasus, Jerome, &c., and other short treatises on the origin, order, interpretation, &c., of the Psalms, including an Exposition of the Alleluia amongst the Hebrews, Chaldæans, Syrians, and Romans.

These are also written in small rustic capitals, but the letters are of a much more elegant form, and the words are, for the most part, separated from each other, with the headings and initials in plain red letters, the former in a rude kind of rustic letter like the text itself, and the latter destitute of any ornament. From one of these, the specimen, No. 5, is taken, which is to be read as follows :—

'Incipit origo Psalmorum. David filius Jesse eum esset in regno suo iiii elegit qui Psalmos facerent— id est Asaph, Eman, Ethan, et Idithun, ergo lxxxyiii dicebant Psalmos et ducenti sub Psalma et cithara percutiebat Abiuth cum David rege,' &c. It is difficult to fix a date to this part of the MS., as this form of rustic capitals remained in partial use until driven out by the modern Gothic ; but the circumstance of entire pages being written in it is of itself an evidence of very great age, and the nearest resemblance to it which I can discover is the specimen given by the Benedictines, from a MS. of St. Augustine, on the City of God, referred by them to the 5th or 6th century [5].

---

[1] See Steph. Monast., App. v., 1. 208.

[3] The first word Omnis is alone written in plain square Roman capitals, larger than the text.

[2] " L'Ecriture capitale rustique paraît venir directement de la plus ancienne des Romains. Cette écriture paraît dans les anciennes inscriptions. Il est vrai qu'on cesse d'assez bonne heure d'écrire des MSS. entiers en cette écriture ; elle était cependant encore souvent employée à cet usage aux V. et VI.ᵉ siècle. On peut disputer si elle le fut au suivans." N. Tr. de Dipl., vol. ii. 505.

[4] See Dissertationes Isagogicæ ad Herculaniensium voluminum explicationem, Pars 1, 1797 ; and Ottley in Archæologia, vol. xxv.

[5] N. Tr. de Dipl. 3 p. 92, pl. 37, V. II. ii.

The form of the letters A, U, M, G, N, and L, is worthy of observation, as well as the conjoined N and T at the end of the line. The letter H is often written like a K.

The twelfth leaf contains the end of the second, and the third and fourth Psalms; the two previous leaves, which evidently contained the first and beginning of the second Psalm, and an illuminated title-page, having been cut out.

The Psalms extend to the 140th leaf.

The text of the Psalms is written in uncial letters, not exceeded in beauty by any known MS. The words are but semi-distinct, and the tails of the letters which reach below the line run into a slender oblique stroke. The letter A varies in its form. The second specimen given by the Benedictines, in their 43rd plate, from the MS. of St. Prosper, in the Bibliothèque du Roi of the sixth century, comes the nearest to our MS. Several others (also in their 44th Plate) of the 7th century, may also be compared with it; as may also the specimens which will be given in this work from the Gospels of St. Augustine, at Oxford and Cambridge; the Charters of Sebbi and Æthelbald, and the Bodleian rule of St. Benedict, also said to have belonged to St. Augustine. The specimen in the accompanying Plate, No. 2, is the commencement of the 68th (69th) Psalm, and is to be read as follows :—

LXVIII. In finem pro his qui commutabuntur David.

Salvum me fac Deus quoniam introierunt aquae usque ad animam meam; infixus sum in limum profundi. et non est substantia [1]."

The following is a copy of the 53rd (54th) Psalm, of the Latin text, which will show the version employed in this MS.

" Ds in nomine tuo salvum me fac et in virtute tua libera me. Ds exaudi orationem meam, auribus percipe verba oris mei. Qūm alieni insurrexerunt in me et fortes quesierunt animam meam et non proposuerunt dm ante conspectum suum. Ecce enim ds adjuvat me et dns susceptor est anime mee. Averte mala inimicis meis et in veritate tuo disperde illos. Voluntarie sacrificabo tibi et confitebor nomini tuo dne qūm bonum est. Qūm ex omni tribulatione eripuisti me et super inimicos meos respexit oculus tuus."

It will be seen that the Latin text is accompanied by an Anglo-Saxon interlineary version, which bears evident proof of being executed long after the MS. itself. But although it is impossible to determine at what period, I presume that it was subsequent to the ninth century.

Mr. Baber (Introduction to the misnamed Wickliffe New Testament) affirms it to be of very high antiquity.

Mr. Wright (Biogr. lit. Brittan. i. 51), assigns the name of the *Age of Glosses* to the earlier part of the ninth century, and regards the frequent occurrence of interlineary Glosses, as a *sure decay of Latin scholarship*. Ought we not rather to consider it as resulting from the practice of reading the scriptures to the people in their native language? and are not this and the other Glosses on the Scriptures rather of the tenth, or beginning of the eleventh, century?

Mr. B. Thorpe states that this version and that of the Gospels of Lindisfarne (Bibl. Cott. Nero D. iv.) are the only relics in existence of the ancient Northumberland dialect. The gloss in specimen No. 2, is as follows :—

Ꝛalne mec ꝺoa ᵹoꝺ, ꝼopꝺon inpoꝺun peꞇen oꝺ ꞃaꝑle mine : ᵹeꝼeꞃꞇnaꝺ ic eam in lam ᵹꞃunꝺeꞃ ꞇ niꞃ ꞃꝑoeꝺ.

The gloss upon the 53rd Psalm is as follows; and is here given in order to allow this version to be contrasted with that contained in the other Psalters:—

Goꝺ in noman ꝺinum halne mec ꝺoa ꞇ in meᵹne ꝺinum ᵹeꝼnea mec : ᵹoꝺ ᵹehen ᵹebeꝺ meinun miꝺ eapum, onꝼoh popꝺ muꝺeꞃ mineꞃ ꝼopꝺon ꝺa ꝼnemꝺan apeoꞃun in mec ꞇ ꝺa ꞃꞇponᵹan ꞃohꞇun ꞃꝑle mine ꞇ no ꝼapeꞃeꞇꞇun ᵹoꝺ biꝼopan ᵹeꞃihꝺe heapa. ᵹehꝺe ꞃoꝺlice ᵹoꝺ ᵹeꝼulꞇumeꝺ mec ꞇ ꝺꞃyh onꝺꞃenᵹa iꞃ ꞃꝑle minꞃe aceꞃ yꝼel ꝼeoꞃꝺum minum ꞇ in ꞃoꝺꝼeꞃꞇniꞃꞃe ꝺinne ꞇoꞃeꞃeᵹꝺ hie ; ꝑilꞃumlice ic onꞃeaᵹ ꝺe ꞇ onꝺeꞇꞇo noman ꝺinum ꝺꞃyhꞇꝼopꝺon ᵹoꝺ he iꞃ ; ꝼopꝺon oꝼ alꝑe ᵹeꞃꝑenceꝺnꞃꞃe ꝺu ᵹencꝑeꝺeꞃ mec ꞇ oꝼeꞃ ꝼeonꝺ mine ᵹelocaꝺe eᵹe ꝺin.

The initial letter of each Psalm is about $1\frac{1}{2}$ inch high, and drawn in the genuine fantastic Anglo-Saxon style; the strokes terminating in the heads of animals with the bodies formed of beautiful interlaced patterns; no two letters being ornamented alike. The initial letters of the Verses are uncials about twice the size of the ordinary text, and alternately coloured red and blue.

---

[1] The vetus and the Gallican versions have the word "intraverunt," and the Hebraick one, " venerunt," instead of " introierunt," and in all the versions in the Psalterium Quincuplex, the word "limo" is used instead of " limum."

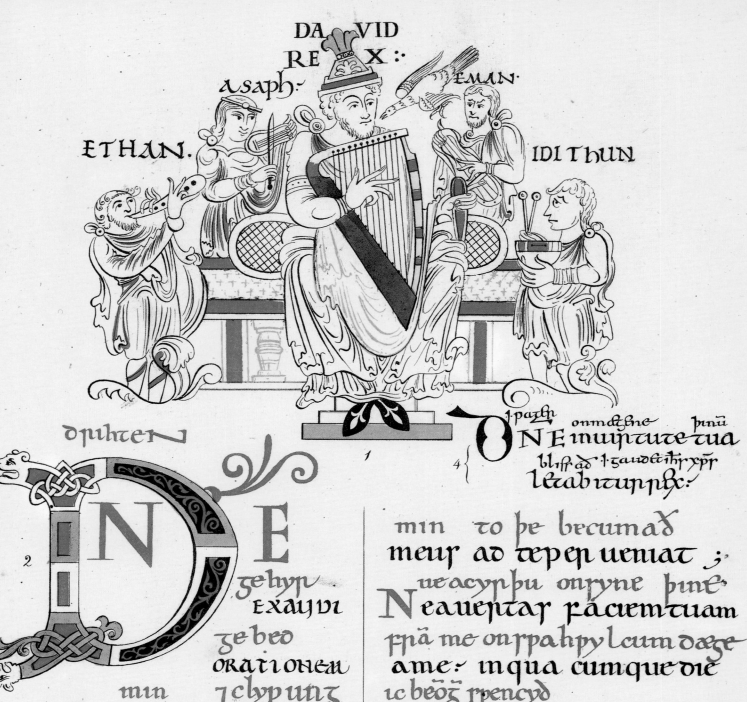

DA VID
RE X :·
Asaph. EMAN.
ETHAN. IDITHVN

ðrihten

N E min to þe becumað
meus ad te pen ueniat ;
ue acyrþu onsyne þine·
N e auertas faciem tuam
fra me on rpahpylcum dæge
ame· in qua cumque die
ic beo ð rpencyd
ðrubulon

gehyr
EXAVDI
ge bed
ORATIONEM
min ⁊ clyp uni g
meam· et clamor

ÐINE inuirtute tua
blirrað ⁊ gaudebit þr xpr
lætabitur þx·

In fine pueno dni ʃd q: locuts ē ðno
urba cantici huus In die qua

ILGAM Te·
ðriht mæʒth min ðriht ʒrumbys
ð ne wistur mea diʒ pyrmamentum
min ⁊ rebelʒh min
meum et refugium meum:
onlerænd min ʒod min pultu min
⁊ lubrlettor mr ðr mr ad lutor mr rprabo In eum

Anglo-Saxon Psalters. Nº 1

ANGLO-SAXON PSALTERS, Nº. 1.

DESCRIPTION OF THE PLATE.

1. Drawing of King David and his attendants ; and
3. Commencement of the 17th Psalm, from the Bodleian Codex Vossianus.

2. Commencement of the 101st Psalm, from the Cambridge Psalter.
4. Commencement of the 20th Psalm, from the Royal MS., 2 B. 5, in the British Museum.

THE three MSS. illustrated in the accompanying Plate agree in having the Latin text of the Psalms written in Anglo-Saxon letters, as well as the gloss in the latter language.

The first of these is a fine MS. of 276 leaves (552 pages) of parchment, measuring 10½ by 6½ inches, with 32 lines in a full page. It was bequeathed by the famous Archbishop Matthew Parker to Sir Nicholas Bacon, and by the latter presented to the University Library of Cambridge, where it is now preserved, with the mark F. f. 1. 23. The Latin text is written in a fine black letter, and the Anglo-Saxon interlineary translation in red letters of the same size and hand; whence it is evident that both are coeval, the date, according to Wanley, being shortly before the Norman Conquest. On the verso of the first leaf occurs the drawing of King David and his attendants, represented in my specimen, No. 1, inclosed within a frame-work pattern, somewhat similar to that of the Canute Gospels, but far less elaborate. In the original, Ethan and Idithun occupy two compartments below the King.

This drawing is highly characteristic of later Anglo-Saxon art, and furnishes specimens of the dresses and some of the musical instruments of our forefathers. The use of music amongst the Anglo-Saxons is fully proved, not only by the many representations of musical instruments in the illuminations, but also by the special treatises of Bede and Alcuin, the former of whom divides his treatise into two parts, Musica Theoretica and Musica Practica,[1] and who expressly mentions the organ, viol, harp, atola, psaltery (very similar to the harp-lute of the present day), drum, cymbals, &c.[2] In the Cotton. MS. Tiberius, C. vi., are also represented various other musical instruments (all engraved by Strutt), under the names of nabulum, pennola, corus, &c., of which the descriptions are very vague. Figures of numerous other early musical instruments are given by Willemin. Trumpets, also, of various kinds, and bells, played upon by the hand, also occur in the Anglo-Saxon MSS. The reader may refer to a short but very incomplete treatise on this subject by F. D. Wackerbarth, A.B., with the title, "Music and the Anglo-Saxons," 8vo, London, 1837; and to the Appendix to Lingard's "Antiquities of the Anglo-Saxon Church."

The Holy Ghost is represented in the form of a dove, flying to the mouth of the Psalmist,—a curious but not uncommon mode of representing sacred inspiration.

On the opposite page is the commencement of the Psalter "Beatus vir," &c., inclosed within an ornamental border, the initial B being in the more ordinary Anglo-Saxon style, and not less than six inches in height.

On the recto of the 167th leaf is a drawing of the Crucifixion in coloured outlines. The figure of Christ in the centre is six inches high, but much too short in proportion to the size of the upper part of the body and lower part of the legs, which are greatly attenuated. The Virgin on the left side is, on the contrary, too tall; she is represented with uplifted hands, and is clothed in fluttering drapery. The figure of St. John, on the other side of the cross, is much better drawn. In two circles above the cross are the busts of two weeping figures, inscribed Sol and Luna, and a hand is stretched forth from the clouds above the head of our Saviour.

On the opposite page is the illuminated commencement of the Psalm "Quid gloriaris," in a plain border, having two small well-drawn miniatures, in circular shields, similar to those represented in the plate of the Canute Gospels, in this work. The initial Q is of large size, and ornamented like the letter D in the accompanying plate. On the 331st page is a drawing of our Saviour's Ascension, the figure of Christ being inclosed within the Vesica Pescis, supported by two angels above and two below, the whole within an ornamental border. On the opposite page is the commencement of the 101st Psalm, copied in my specimen, No. 2, inclosed within a plainer border. It is as follows:—"DNE *EXAUDI ORATIONEM* meam, et clamor meus ad te perveniat. Ne avertas faciem tuam a me in quacumque die tribulor." The Anglo-Saxon gloss being: "Dɲıhτen ȝehyɲ ȝebeð mın ꝺ clypunȝ mın to þe becumað; ne acypþu onɲyne þine ꝼɲa me on ɲpa hɲylcum ꝺæȝe ıc be oȝɲpencyð."

For convenience in the arrangement of my plate, this extract has been placed in two columns, which is not the case in the original.

---

[1] Bedæ op., t. p. 344—351.

[2] Bedæ op., t. viii., p. 900.

On the 381st page is a figure of Christ triumphant, holding a cross in his right hand, and a book, inscribed 'Sup. aspidem et basiliscum ambulabis,' in his left hand, and having a dragon and a lion beneath his feet. The drawing of the Saviour is sadly attenuated, and measures eight inches in height. On the opposite page is the commencement of the Psalm, Dixit insipiens, not ornamented as is usual.

The end of the volume is occupied by the Canticles, Te Deum, Pater Noster, Creed, &c. The initial letter of each Psalm is drawn with great spirit, but with singular and often grotesque ornaments; some are merely foliated, but many consist of dragons, serpents, &c. The human figure is also occasionally introduced; thus a quaint looking head and arm is converted into the letter Q, and two naked men, tied together by the neck, with the arms and legs extended, form a strange-looking M.

The gloss upon the 53d Psalm is as follows:—

Goꝺ on naman þinū halne me ᵹeꝺō ⁊ on mæᵹyne þinum ᵹeꝼꞃeꝺ me : ᵹoꝺ ᵹehyn ᵹebeꝺ min eaꞃum onꝼoh poꞃꝺ muꝺyꞅ minyꞅ ; ꝼoꞃþon þa ꝼꞃemꝺan on aꞃiꞅon on me ⁊ ꞅꞇꞃonᵹe ꞅohꞇon ꞅaple mine ⁊ ne foꞃeꞅeꞇꞇon ᵹoꝺ beꝼoꞃan ᵹeꞅihꝺꞇe hiꞅ : eꝼnenu ꞅoꝺlice ᵹoꝺ ᵹeꝼulꞇumiᵹe me ⁊ ꝺꞃihꞇyn anꝺꝼenᵹe yꞅ ꞅaple minꞃe : acyꞃꞃ yꝼyl ꝼeoꞃꝺa minꞃa ⁊ on ꞅoꝺꝼæꞇnyꞅꞅe þinꞃe ꞇo ꞅꞇꞃeᵹꝺ hi : pyllynlice ic oꝼꝼꞃiᵹe þe ⁊ ic and yꞇꞇe naman þinū ꝺꞃihꞇ ꝼoꞃþon ᵹoꝺ hyꞇ ys : ꝼoꞃþon oꝼ ealꞃe ᵹeꞅꞅenceꝺnyꞅꞅe þu ᵹeneꞃyꝺyꞇ me ⁊ oꝼyꞃ ꝼynꝺ mine ᵹelocoꝺe ieᵹe þin.

The specimen, No. 3, is taken from a fine MS. in the Bodleian Library, numbered Junius 27, having formerly belonged to that celebrated scholar, who received it from Isaac Voss, whence it has been named the Codex Vossianus. It measures 10 inches by 6½, and 1¼ inch in thickness; a full page having 20 lines in Latin, written in beautiful Anglo-Saxon characters, accompanied by an interlineary Anglo-Saxon gloss, written in a small and extremely neat hand, and is supposed by Wanley to have been written about the time of King Athelstan. The volume contains no drawings nor illuminated borders. At the beginning of the volume is the Calendar, which, however, as well as various parts of the MS., has been much defaced by having some of the illuminated capital letters cut out. The strange style of these letters will be best perceived by the specimen in the plate. The initials in the Lambeth Aldhelm, the Bodleian Pseudo-Cædmon, and a fine MS. in the Library of Trinity College, Cambridge, are similarly treated.

The specimen is the commencement of the 17th Psalm, and is to be read:—"In fin*em* puero D*omi*ni D*avi*d *qui* locut*us est* d*omi*no verba cantici hujus in die qua, &c. Diligam te d*omi*ne virtus mea d*ominus* firmamentum meum et refugium meum. Et liberator m*eus* d*eus* m*eus* adjutor m*eus* sperabo in eum:" and the Anglo-Saxon gloss is as follows (the first two words not being glossed):—"ꝺꞃyhꞇ̄ mæᵹen min ꝺꞃyhꞇ̄ ꞇꞃymeniꞅ min ⁊ ᵹebeoꞃᵹ min ⁊ onleꞅenꝺ min, ᵹoꝺ min, ꝼulꞇu min ic ᵹehyhꞇe in hine." This may be compared with the fac-simile of the gloss in the Augustine Psalter, given by Astle, Plate IX.

The gloss on the 53d Psalm is as follows:

D̃s on noman ꝺinu halne me ꝺo ⁊ on mæᵹene ꝺinu alieꞅ me ᵹoꝺ ᵹeheꞃ ᵹebeꝺ min miꝺ eaꞃū onꝼoh poꞃꝺ muꝺeꞅ mineꞅ ꝼoꞃꝺon ꝼꞃemꝺe aꞃiꞅon on me ⁊ ꞅꞇꞃonᵹe ꞅohꞇon ꞅaple mine ⁊ no ꝼoꞃeꞅeꞇꞇon ᵹoꝺ beꝼoꞃan ᵹeꞅihꝺe hiꞃa. ꞅehꝺe ꞅoꝺlice ᵹoꝺ ᵹeꝼultumaꝺ me ⁊ ꝺꞃyhꞇ̄ anꝺꝼenᵹa is ꞅaple minꞃe aceꞃ yꝼel ꝼeonꝺū minū ⁊ soꝺꝼaeꞅꞇneꞅꞅe ꝺinꞃe ꝼoꞃꞅpilꝺ hie : pilꞅumlice ic onꞅecᵹe ꝺe ⁊ ic on ꝺeꞇꞇe noman ꝺinu ꝺꞃyhꞇ̄ ꝼoꞃꝺon ᵹoꝺ he iꞅ ꝼoꞃꝺon oꝼ eallum ᵹeꞅꞅince ꝺu ᵹeneꞃeꝺeꞅ me ⁊ oꝼeꞃ ꝼienꝺ mine ᵹelocoꝺe eaᵹe ꝺin.

The fourth specimen in the Plate is copied from the British Museum MS., Reg. 2 B. 5. It is a small folio volume, containing the Latin Psalter, written in a fine plain Anglo-Saxon hand, with an interlineary Anglo-Saxon Gloss. It is destitute of miniatures, borders, and illuminated letters; the initials measuring about 1 inch in height, except that of the 1st Psalm, which is a large plain roman B.

The specimen given in the Plate is from the commencement of the 20th Psalm:—"Dn̄e in virtute tua letabitur rex;" the Gloss being partly in Latin and partly in Anglo-Saxon:—.⁊. (id est) pater, on mæᵹene þinū bliꞅꞅaꝺ (.⁊. ᵹauꝺeꞇ jh̄s xp̄s).

The Gloss upon the 53d Psalm is as follows:—

ᵹoꝺ on noman þinū halne ꝺo ⁊ on mæᵹene þinū alyꝼe ᵹehyꞃ ᵹebeꝺ min miꝺ eaꞃū onꝼoh poꞃꝺ muþeꞅ mineꞅ ꝼꞃēꝺe on aꞃiꞅon on me ⁊ ꞅꞇꞃanᵹe ꞅohꞇon ꞅaple mine ⁊ na ꝼoꞃeꞅeꞇꞇon ᵹoꝺ beꝼoꞃan ᵹeꞅihꝺe hiꞅ . ꞅoꝺlice ᵹeꝼylꞅꞇeꝺ me anꝺꝼenᵹ iꞅ ꞅaple minꞃe acyꞃ yꝼelu oꝼ ꝼeonꝺū minu ⁊ on ꞅoþꝼæꞅꞇniꞅꞅe þine ꝼoꞃꞅpil hẏ pilꞅumlice ic oꝼꞃiᵹe þe ic anꝺeꞇꞇe naman þinū ꝼoꞃꝺon ᵹoꝺ he iꞅ oꝼ eallu ᵹeꞅpince þū ᵹneꞃeꝺeꞅꞇ mec ⁊ oꝼeꞃ ꝼynꝺ mine ᵹelocoꝺe eaᵹe þin.

Wanley considers that this MS. was written about the time of King Alfred. It was formerly the property of Thomas Cranmer, Archbishop of Canterbury, whose autograph appears on the first page of the Psalms.

Anglo-Saxon Psalters. Nº 2.

ANGLO-SAXON PSALTERS. NO. II.

THE Manuscripts from which the specimens in the accompanying plate have been taken differ from those represented in the preceding plate of Anglo-Saxon Psalters in having the Latin text written entirely in Roman, without any mixture of Anglo-Saxon characters, the headings being written in uncial or rustic Roman capitals.

The first of these specimens is from the Cottonian Psalter, Tiberius, C. 6, which, although much injured by the Cottonian fire, is one of the most important relics of Anglo-Saxon art. It has recently been very carefully repaired and bound, each leaf being mounted on thick paper. It consists of 129 leaves of vellum, measuring 10 inches by 6, a full page comprising 25 lines of the Latin text, with an interlineary Saxon gloss. It is evidently of the latter part of the tenth or beginning of the eleventh century. The ink is particularly black, and the handwriting very elegant. It commences with some tables of the lunar and ecclesiastical computations, enclosed within rounded arches, supported by plain columns with foliated bases and capitals. At the head of one of these pages (fol. 5 b) is represented a party seated at a feast, with servants waiting on their knees, and holding the meat on long spits, from which it is cut by the guests.[1] On fol. 6 v is a singular representation of Life and Death contrasted, the former with a cruciferous nimbus and standing upon the wings of the latter. On the verso of the next leaf commences a series of drawings (eighteen in number) of scriptural subjects, of large size, each design occupying the entire page, one of which, representing the entrance of Christ into Jerusalem, is represented in my plate.

The subjects of these drawings, which are executed with great freedom, are as follows :—

1. The Spirit of God upon the face of the water: a singular and highly imaginative design.

2. David killing the Lion.

3. David killing Saul.

4 & 5. David and Saul.

6. David playing on the harp, with the Holy Ghost, in the form of a dove, seated on the top of the sceptre, and with its neck extending to the mouth of the King.

7. The contest between Christ and Satan in the wilderness.

8. The entry of Christ into Jerusalem.

9. Christ washing the Disciples' feet. An angel from above holds a large napkin over the head of Christ.

10. The betrayal of Christ by Judas. The attitude and astonishment of the former are represented with much effect.

11. Christ bound and brought before Pilate.

12. The Crucifixion.[2]

13. The angel appearing to the three Maries; the Tomb itself, representing a tall building ornamented with several series of arcades, and the figure of the angel being finely delineated.

14. The Harrowing of Hell. Christ represented as treading upon the devils, and drawing the souls out of the infernal regions.

15. The incredulity of Thomas. Except in the figure of Christ being too tall, this is perhaps the most pleasing of the series; the figure of the Apostle is very natural, and the attitude of the Saviour very spirited, being seven inches high.

[1] Copied in Pictorial Hist. of England, I. p. 336.

[2] A reduced figure of one of the soldiers is given in Pictorial Hist. of Engl. I. 332.

1

16. The Ascension : the upper part of the figure of the Saviour hidden by the clouds at the top of the picture.

17. The Descent of the Holy Ghost, represented as a dove, with flames of fire issuing from its mouth, the tail held by a hand in the clouds.

18. The Contest between Michael the Archangel and the Devil. A very spirited design.

These drawings are, perhaps, the most interesting examples of the peculiar style of Anglo-Saxon art of the period which are now in existence. Drawn with a pen, with great freedom, in different-coloured inks, and destitute of any shading, they teach us the ideas of composition entertained by the artists of the day, who, although so unskilful in the higher branches of Art, were, at the close of the tenth century, as at the beginning of the eighth, unrivalled in their ornamental designs, of which the Benedictional of Æthelwold or the Gospels of Canute is a sufficient proof.

The strange want of perspective in the specimen in my plate, the ludicrous manner in which the artist has attempted to delineate the spreading of garments in the path of our Saviour, and the attenuated extremities of the figures, scarcely need comment.

To these succeed several pages of illustrations and descriptions of variously-formed musical instruments including a figure of David playing on the Psaltery[1]; on the verso of the last of which is a miniature of Christ, seated and inclosed within the vesica piscis, with an angel sounding a trumpet on each side, and with the Virgin and two priests standing at the bottom of the drawing. This is highly finished, in thick glazed body-colours, similar to those used in the illuminated initials of the Psalms.

The recto of the 19th leaf is surrounded by an illuminated border, somewhat similar to the style of the Canute Gospels, inclosing the commencement of the Treatise on the Origin of the Psalms, " David filius Jesse cum esset in regno suo," &c., the D being large and finely illuminated.

Then follow various treatises referring to the Psalms, of which the Gallican version is here employed, and which commences on the 31st leaf, the preceding page having a miniature of David playing on the harp, with his four attendants, enclosed within an ornamented border and coloured in the same style as the miniature of Christ in the vesica piscis. In this curious drawing, which has been several times[2] engraved, two of the attendants are represented playing on the horn, a third on the violin, whilst the fourth acts the part of a juggler[3] engaged in throwing up three knives and three balls. As usual, the king is represented of a much larger size than his attendants. The commencement of the 1st Psalm is highly illuminated with a large initial B, copied by Shaw, (who has also given portions of some of the borders from this MS. in his ' Illuminated Ornaments ;') the following words being written in fine Roman capitals, in alternate lines of red, blue, and green ; the whole enclosed within a finely-ornamented border, in the same style as the Canute Gospels, but destitute of gold.

The commencement of the Psalms " Quid gloriaris," and " Dñe exaudi orationem meam," are similarly ornamented, and the initials of about a dozen of the other Psalms are also illuminated in the same singular, but not inelegant style, one of which I have copied in my specimen, No. 1. The initials of the other Psalms are of moderate size, and plain.

Each of these two Psalms (viz. the 52nd and 102nd) is preceded by a page on one of which is drawn a figure of Christ, and on the other a priest richly robed, each standing beneath a rounded arch, and executed in the same style as the drawings at the beginning of the volume.

Each Psalm is preceded by a short prayer, as in the Duke of Buckingham's Psalter, with which this also nearly agrees in the Anglo-Saxon text ; whence I infer, as well as from the style of the illuminated capitals (one of which is given by Astle), that the pretended Psalter of King Alfred is coeval with the one now before us.

All the Psalms after 114 are wanting.

The specimen No. 1 is copied from the commencement of the 38th (39th) Psalm ; the Anglo-Saxon gloss being as follows :—

Ic cpæð ic ᵹehealbe peᵹaᵹ mine þ ic ne aᵹylte on tunᵹa minɲe Ic aɲette muð minū ᵹe heoɲbunᵹa þon ɲe ɲynɲulla onᵹean me.

---

[1] A reduced copy of this drawing is given in the Pictorial Hist. of England, I. 321.

[2] By Strutt and in Pict. Hist. of England, I. 322.

[3] Strutt adduces this drawing and the frontispiece of the Augustine Psalter as affording illustrations of the performances of the Anglo-Saxon Glıᵹman, or Gleeman. It is curious that he should have overlooked another illustration of the Gleeman throwing balls, which is to be found in the Cottonian MS. Claudius, B. iv. fol. 33, verso.

ANGLO-SAXON PSALTERS.

The Anglo-Saxon version of the 53rd Psalm, given in order to allow collation with the other Anglo-Saxon Psalters, is as follows :—

ȝoð on naman þinum halne me ðo ꞇ on mæȝene þin . . . . ȝehyꞃ ȝebeð min mið eaꞃū onꞃoh poꞃð muðeꞃ mineꞃ ꞅoꞃðon ꞅꞃembe aꞃiꞃon piðꞇ onȝean me ꞇ ꞅꞇꞃanȝe ꞃohꞇon ꞃaple mine—na-ꞅoꞃꞃeꞇꞇon ȝoð beꞅoꞃan ȝeꞃihðe hiꞃ—ꞃoðlice ȝeꞅylꞅꞇeþ me ꞇ ðꞃih anðꞃenȝ ꞃaple minꞃe acȳꞃ ẏuelu onꞅeonðū minum on ꞃoþꞅæꞃꞇniꞅꞅe þina þuȝeneꞃeðeꞃꞇ hẏ. þinꞃumlice ic oꞅꞃiȝe þe ꞇ ic anðeꞇꞇe naman þinū ðꞃihꞇene ꞅoꞃðon ȝod he iꞅ. ꞅoꞃþon oꞅ eallum ȝeꞃꞃince þuȝeneꞃeðeꞃꞇ me oꞅeꞃ ꞅȳnð mine eaȝe mine.

The specimen numbered 3 is from a fine MS. in the library of the Archbishop of Canterbury, containing the Gallican version of the Latin Psalter, written apparently about the time of King Edgar, in strong Roman minuscule characters with an interlineary Anglo-Saxon version. It consists of 211 leaves, measuring 8½ by 6½ inches ; a page containing sixteen Latin lines with its corresponding Anglo-Saxon interlineations.

With the exception of the large initial B of the first Psalm (which is of the Roman form, but ornamented at the top and bottom of the first stroke with interlaced patterns, terminating on each side in eagles' heads, and in the open parts with foliated ornaments finely drawn with pink ink and shaded with green), all the capitals throughout the volume are of a character similar to those in the specimen in my plate. The initial letters of the other Psalms are in blue, lilac, red, and green colours, and those of the verses are smaller and in red.

The specimen before us is the commencement of the 109th Psalm, the Anglo-Saxon Gloss being as follows :—" Sæðe ðꞃihꞇen ꞇo ðꞃihꞇne minum ꞃiꞇe æꞇ ꞃꞃȳðꞃū minum oþ þæꞇ ic aꞃeꞇꞇe ꞅeonð þine on ꞅoꞇ ꞃceamele ꞅoꞇa þinꞃa : ȝȳnðe maȝneꞃ þineꞃ aꞃenðeþ ðꞃihꞇen," &c.

It will be seen that some of the words are marked beneath with dots, which, according to Wanley (Hickes' Thes. 2, preface and p. 268), are intended for musical notes, although quite unlike the Gregorian notes. It is also marked with asterisks and obeli, which are wanting in many MSS.

The Anglo-Saxon version of the commencement of the 53rd Psalm is as follows :—

" Eala þu ȝoð on naman þinum ȝehæl me ꞇ on mihꞇe þinꞃe ðem me : ȝeheꞃ min ȝebeð mið eaꞃum undeꞃꞅoh poꞃð muþeꞃ mineꞃ ꞅoꞃþam þe ælꞅꞃemeðe on aꞃiꞃon ꞇo ȝæneꞃ me ꞇ þa ꞅꞇꞃanȝan ꞃohꞇon ꞃaple mine ꞇ hiȝ neꞅoꞃꞃeꞇꞇon ȝoð ꞇoꞅoꞃan anꞃȳne heoꞃa."

Astle has given a fac-simile of the commencement of the 101st Psalm, both from this and the Duke of Buckingham's Psalter, which may be contrasted with my specimen from the Cambridge Psalter in the preceding plate.

At the end of the MS. are the Canticles, Lord's Prayer, Creeds, &c., and two leaves of a composition respecting the female Anglo-Saxon Saints, the latter entirely in Anglo-Saxon.

The specimen No. 4, and the accompanying autograph, is from the Psalter preserved in the Bibliothèque du Roi, at Paris, formerly belonging to Jean, Duke of Berry, third son of King John of France, and presented by him, in 1406, to the Church of Bourges, and which in a manuscript catalogue, composed in the middle of the last century, was thus described :—" Les heures du duc Jean, reliées en long ; à côté du Latin il y a une colonne d'une traduction qu'on croit d'ancien Anglo-Saxon ou d'Hongrois." It is a long and narrow folio, and in the margins are painted many scutcheons of the arms of France and Boulogne. It consists of eighty-six leaves of fine vellum, and comprises the Psalms with a parallel version in Anglo-Saxon, and the usual Canticles.

At the end of the volume is inscribed the autograph of its former royal owner, copied at the foot of my plate. The writing, according to Champollion, is a fine Gallican minuscule mixed with some Anglo-Saxon letters in the translation, and which is supposed, by Silvestre, to be of the 13th century.

The specimen in my plate is copied from Silvestre, and represents the commencement of the 45th Psalm —" Deus noster refugium et justus [virtus]," the Anglo-Saxon text being :—

" Dꞃȳhꞇen ẏꞃ uꞃe ȝebeoꞃh ꞇ uꞃe mæȝen ꞇ uꞃe ꞅulꞇu"—menð.

And the Gloss upon the 53rd Psalm is as follows—as given by Mr. Thorpe, in his volume containing the version in this manuscript, published in 1835 :—

1. On þinum þam haliȝan naman ȝeðo me halne Goð, alȳꞃ me ꞅꞃam laðum þurh þin leoꞅe mæȝen. 2. Goð, min ȝebeð ȝeaꞃuꞃe ȝehyꞃe anð eaꞃum onꞅoh min aȝen poꞃð. 3. Foꞃþam me ꞅꞃembe oꞅꞇ ꞅacne ȝeꞃꞇoðon, ꞃohꞇan mine ꞃaple ꞃꞃiðe ꞃꞇꞃanȝe anð na heom Goð ꞃeꞇꞇon ȝleaꞃne on ȝeꞃyhðe. 4. Eꞃne me þonne Goð ȝleaꞃe ꞅulꞇumeð iꞅ anðꞃenȝa ece Dꞃihꞇen ꞃaple minꞃe

he me ꞃuncan ne ꝥile.   5. Aꝼyꞃ me ꝼæcne yꝼel ꝼeonꝺa minꞃa anꝺ hi ꞃoꝺꝼæꞃꞇ ꞇo ꝥeoꞃꝥ ꞃyꝺꝺan ꝥiꝺe.   6. Ic ꝺe luꞃꞇum lace cꝥeme anꝺ naman þinne neoꝺe ꞃꝥylce ᵹeaꞃa anꝺeꞇꞇe ꝼoꞃꝺon ic hine ᵹooꝺne ꝥat.   7. Foꞃꝥon þu me alyꞃꝺeꞃꞇ liꝼeꞃ Ealꝺoꞃ, oꝼ eaꞃꝼoꝺum eallum ꞃymble ; ealle mine ꝼynꝺ, eaᵹum oꝼeꞃꞃaꝥe.

In addition to the mention of Ervenius and Wolstan, at the end of the article on the Canute Gospels, the following notices of the artists of the period in question have come down to us :—

St. Dunstan himself, amongst his other accomplishments, was both a calligrapher and painter. His own portrait, drawn by himself, kneeling at the feet of Christ, is still extant in the Bodleian Library, at Oxford (MS. N.E.D. 2, 19. Auct. F. 4, 32 [1].) It is likewise recorded of him that he drew a pattern for a sacerdotal vestment, which a religious lady of the 10th century executed in threads of gold [2]. Wanley has preserved the following notice respecting the talents of Dunstan, from a life of him, written by one of his friends, " Hic itaque inter sacra literarum studia ut in omnibus esset idoneus artem scribendi necne citharizandi *pariterque pingendi* peritiam diligenter excoluit atque ut ita dicam omnium rerum utensiliū. vigil inspector fulsit."—(Vide MS. Cott. inscr. Faust B. 13.   Hickes' Thes. 2, p. 63, note *.)

The famous Osmund [3], who was consecrated Bishop of Salisbury, A.D. 1076, did not disdain to spend some part of his time in writing, binding, and illuminating books.—(Henry, Hist. of Great Britain, Vol. VI. p. 226, quoted in Bibl. Decameron, I. p. cxxii.)

The name of the calligrapher by whom the Duke of Devonshire's famous Benedictional was executed also appears in the following lines, written in gold in the volume itself :—

" Atque Patri magno jussit qui scribere librum hunc,
Omnes cernentes biblum hunc semper rogitent hoc,
Post meta carnis valeam celis inherere,
Obnixe hoc rogitat *scriptor supplex Godemann.*"

This Godemann was a monk of the Monastery of Hyde, or New Minster, about the latter part of the 10th century, and the MS. was executed for Ethelwold, who was Bishop of Winchester between 963 and 984, and who appears to have been a munificent patron of art [4]. This monastery appears to have been celebrated for its illuminated MSS. as proved by the *Hyde Abbey Book*, in the library of the Duke of Buckingham, at Stowe, which contains portraits of King Canute and his wife, and other interesting drawings, of one of which, a fac-simile, is given by Dibdin (Bibl. Decameron, I. p. lvii.).   Another interesting little MS., executed at Hyde Abbey in the year 978, is preserved amongst the Cotton. MSS. in the British Museum (Titus, D. 27), in the calendar of which we read the following entry :—' 6 Non Julii Obitus Walfrici—Pictoris.' Dibdin has given an excellent fac-simile of one of the drawings in this MS. (Bibl. Decam. I. lv.)   The name of Ethric also appears with a similar addition, thus proving the esteem in which these artists were held.

---

[1] A fac-simile of this portrait is contained in the Royal MS., 10 A. 13, from which it has been engraved by Strutt in his Dresses and Habits, Vol. I. pl. 50. Hickes engraved the Oxford drawing in his Thesaurus, Vol. I. p. 144.

[2] Pictorial Hist. of Engl. I. p. 320.

[3] Brompton Chron., col. 977.

[4] See Will. of Malmsbury, Hist. of Engl. 1815, 4to, p. 172.

Catt   Rọx   hebr

God   deus

EVS in
nomine. post non
— mundo pdicatu est
in nomine tuo
tuo iudicarim uirtute
qin
qin mun do
saluum me fac: & in
futuro iudicio.   f secerne aziphets.
uirtute tua iudica me
qquia iflore zipheox a te peto.
Deus exaudi oratio —

nno
hinum halue
mine tuosal
me zedo
uum me fac
& murtute
hine defuolse
tua libera
me Deus God
zehin
exaudi
zebed
orat   10 —

et
uino
tuen uum
mine tuosal
salue mei
na me & e
en ta
in forticudme
torce uenge
tua uleiscere
mei Deus Deus
on
exaudi
la mere
orat   10 —

The Psalter of Eadwine.

THE TRIPARTITE AND TRIGLOT PSALTER OF EADWINE.

DESCRIPTION OF THE PLATE.

Illustration of the 63rd (64th) Psalm and Commencement of the 53rd (54th) Psalm.

THE Manuscript from which the illuminations in the accompanying plate have been copied, is preserved in the Library of Trinity College, Cambridge, and it is by the kind permission of the Venerable Archdeacon Thorpe, (President of the Camden Society,) that I am enabled to offer these illustrations of one of the most valuable, as it is one of the most splendid volumes which have come down to us, illustrating, as it does, the state, not only of the fine arts, but also of the languages of our country, at that most interesting period, the middle of the 12th century.

The volume is of a large folio size, consisting of 280 leaves, measuring 18 inches by 13, and containing a Calendar; the tripartite Latin Psalter of the Hebraic, Roman, and Gallican versions—the Gallican holding the chief rank and bearing a Latin gloss—the Roman having an Anglo-Saxon (or rather Norman-Saxon) inter-lineary version, and the Hebraic with an old Norman-French interlineary version.

To each Psalm is prefixed a short Prayer. At the end of the Psalms are the usual Canticles, Te Deum, Creed, &c.

The transition state of the English language during the 12th and first half of the 13th centuries, is of the greatest interest to the philological student; and the true date of so many of the pieces which have been referred to this period being subjects of dispute,[1] it will at once be perceived that the present Manuscript is of high importance, as its date is satisfactorily fixed by the entries in the Calendar, and yet but little use appears to have been hitherto made of this fine volume. It must be borne in mind that Hickes applies to the state of our language subsequent to the Norman Conquest, the term Norman-Saxon, and Dr. Johnson states that " the adulteration of the Saxon tongue by a mixture of the Norman, becomes apparent: yet it is not so much altered by the admixture of new words, which might be imputed to commerce with the Continent, as by changes of its own forms and terminations, for which no reason can be given." It will be seen, however, from the Manuscript before us, that a hundred years' intercourse with the Normans (even in the south of England, as the Manuscript before us was evidently written at Canterbury,) had scarcely effected any alteration in the old Anglo-Saxon tongue;[2] the gloss on the *Roman* version of the 53rd Psalm being as follows:—

" Goð on næmæn þinum hælne me ȝæðo ꞡ on mæȝne þine ȝeꝼꞃiolꝛe me : ȝoð ȝehiꞃ ȝebeð mmæ mið eaꞃum onꝼoh poꞃð muðeꝛ mineꝛ : ꝼoꞃþan ꝼꞃembe on æꞃiꞃon on me ꞡ ꞃꞇꞃanȝe ꞃohꞇen ꞃaꝼle mine ꞡ næ ꝼoꞃe ȝeꝛeꞇꞇon ȝoð beꝼoꞃæn on ꞃine ꞇꞃihðe hiꞃ."

The Norman gloss on the Hebraic version is as follows:—" Deus el tuen num salue mei e en ta force uenge mei Deus oi la meie oreisun ot tes oreilles receit les paroles de ma buche; kar li estrange sesdrecerent encuntre mei e li fort questrent la meie aneme e ne proposerent deu en leur esgardement tutes ures."

The character of the writing of this Manuscript is not less interesting, since it clearly exhibits the first traces of the modern Gothic hand in the angulated tops and obliquely truncate bases of many of the letters.

---

[1] Thus, of the pieces which Warton gave as specimens of the 12th century, " there is not one which may not be safely referred to the 13th century, and by far the greater number to the close of that period."—Hist. of Engl. Poetry (Ed. of 1824), i. 7.

[2] The Arundel MS., No. 57, in the British Museum, dated 1340, written in the dialect of Kent, contains a very interesting proof how long the old Saxon tongue was retained in some parts of the kingdom. The Lord's Prayer being as follows:—" Vader oure þet art in heuenes ẏhalzed biȝ þi name cominde þi riche. ẏworþe þi wil, ase in heune and ine erþe, bread oure eche daẏes ẏef ous todaẏ, and ourlet ous oure ẏeldinges ase and we uorleteþ oure ẏelderes and ne ous led nazt into uondinge ac vri ous uram queade."

The following, although at least 150 years earlier in date, will be seen to be much nearer to the modern English. It was sent by the English

Pope Gregory VIII. (circ. 1187) to King Henry II., and " was used in all the churches of England with universal approbation."

" Ure fader in heuene rich
Thi name be haliið euerliche
Thou bring vs to thi michelblisce
Thi will to wirche thu vs wisse
Als hit is in heavene iðo
Ever in earth ben hit also
That holi bred that lasteth ay
Thou send hit ous this ilke day
Forgiue ous all that we hauith done
Als we forgivet vch other mon
Ne let us falle in no founding
Ak scilde us fro the foule thing
     Amen."

THE TRIPARTITE AND TRIGLOT PSALTER OF EADWINE.

The initial letters of each Psalm are highly illuminated in gold and rich body colours, the style of which will be seen from the specimen before us to differ entirely from the designs of the Anglo-Saxon calligraphers : the initial letter of the first Psalm, B, is six inches high, and most elaborately coloured.

Each Psalm is illustrated by a drawing embodying the subject of the text in a singularly quaint but expressive manner : thus the specimen in the plate illustrates the 63rd (64th Psalm), where David calls upon God to hide him from the wicked, " who whet their tongue like a sword and bend their bows to shoot their arrows, even bitter words."—" But God shall shoot at them with an arrow."

This extensive series of drawings, of which my specimen is one of the least elaborate, is of great interest, from the many representations of the dresses, habits, customs, &c., of our forefathers, which it affords. The drawings are freely sketched with a pen and black ink, and the colours dashed on with good effect of light and shade—red, blue, green, and brown, alone being employed. The first page is entirely occupied by a large drawing, in two compartments, in the upper of which are given two buildings of handsome elevation ; one inscribed " Sancta eccl.," in which the " Beatus Vir " is seated ; whilst in the opposite one, " Superbia " is seated. Between these two buildings is a contest between a man and an angel, the latter endeavouring to draw the mortal to the former building. Beneath is a representation of the infernal regions.

Two of the pages at the end of the volume are entirely occupied by a large bird's-eye view of the Monastery of Christ Church, Canterbury, with all its buildings and grounds. This highly curious plan has been engraved in the Vetusta Monumenta, as well as the full-length portrait of Eadwine himself, more than a foot in height, engaged in writing, holding a metallic calamus in his right hand, and a knife in his left, and surrounded by the following jingling Latin verses :—

SCRIPTOR.

Scriptorum princeps ego nec obitura deinceps,
Laus mea nec fama, qui sim mea littera clama.

LITERA.

Te tua scriptura quem signat picta figura,
Prædicat Eadwinum fama per secula vivum,
Ingenium cuius libri decus indicat huius.

The name of the writer also appears in the following Prayer, after the fashion in ancient Psalters:—

" Omnipotens et misericors Deus clementiam tuam suppliciter deprecor ut me, famulum tuum Eadwinum tibi fideliter servire concedas et perseverentiam bonam et felicem consummationem michi largire digneris et hoc Psalterium, quia in conspectu tuo cantavi ad salutem et ad remedium animæ meæ proficiat sempiternum. Amen."

The date of the volume is ascertained by the following entry in the Calendar :—" XI Kal Maii, obiit pie memorie Anselmus arcp̄," Anselm having died during the reign of King Stephen. In the Calendar, also, are inserted entries concerning other archbishops, as well as the dedication " Ecclesiæ Christi," which evidently alludes to the Church of Christ at Canterbury : indeed, we find in the Cottonian MS. (Galba, E. 4) containing an inventory of the books belonging to the Cathedral of Canterbury, drawn up in the year 1315, several books of a certain Edwin :—" Liber Edwini Anglicé"—" Biblia Edwini"—and " tripartitum Psalterium Edwini," —which was doubtless the volume now before us, as suggested by Wanley (Hickes' Thes. Vol. 2).

Silvestre has given a fac-simile from a tripartite Psalter, preserved in the Bibliothèque Royale de Paris ; which, in the style of its writing and illuminated initials, precisely corresponds with Eadwine's book. It is described by Silvestre as having only the Hebraic Version accompanied by an old French gloss, which is regarded by Champollion as of high importance. Unlike the Cambridge MS., the drawings with which it is ornamented are not contemporary with the text, but were successively executed ; so that there is at least two centuries in the difference of the styles of the first and last miniatures ; all which, moreover, exhibit traces of Italian art.

The Harleian MS., No. 603 (in the British Museum), is a large folio Latin Psalter, written about the time of King Edgar (but some of the leaves restored about the time of the Conqueror), and interesting from its containing a series of sketches, by different hands, very similar to the drawings in the Psalter of Eadwine, which were apparently copied from them. The sketches are drawn with great freedom, with a pen, and comprise a great fund of illustrations of national manners, dress, &c. Unfortunately, the page containing the 63rd Psalm has been cut out, so that we cannot compare the drawing with that in Eadwine's Psalter, but some of the sketches are evidently identical in both MSS. The initial letters are plain. Many of the drawings have been published by Strutt, and in the Pictorial History of England (Vol. 1).

The Gospels of Macregol.

THE GOSPELS OF MAC-REGOL.[1]

DESCRIPTION OF THE PLATE.

Commencement of the Gospel of St. Luke, "Quoniam quidem multi conati sunt," in long angular letters.

The words " euangelii ihū xpi filii dei," (Mark i. 1.) and the letters b h and n in smaller angular letters.

The passage, " Fuit homo misus a Deo cui nomen erat johannis," (John i. 6.) and the name of the scribe, " Mac Regol dipinxit hoc euangelium."

The entries made by the two glossers, Farmen and Owun.

THE Volume of the Gospels from whence the accompanying Plate has been copied is preserved in the Bodleian Library, (D. 24, No. 3946) and both in respect to the style of its writing and illuminations and the interlineary Anglo-Saxon gloss, is justly regarded as one of the most precious of our national monuments. It is of a large quarto size, measuring 14 inches by 11, and consists, in its present state, of 169 leaves, containing the four Gospels in Latin, written and ornamented in the same general style as the Gospels of St. Chad and Lindisfarne. The commencement of the MS. as usual in Irish MSS. of the Gospels not written in the Vulgate version, does not contain the ordinary Canons, Prefaces, &c.;[2] the Gospel of St. Matthew commencing on the first page, and extending to fo. 50 v., at the end of which are written the words (more Hibernico) " Finit Amen Finit Amen Finit."

The first page of this Gospel is written in the large angular letters, except the initial word LIBER; the L and b being very large and rounded, and the i formed into a j extending to the foot of the page, these letters being ornamented in the same manner as the Q in the Plate.[3] At the end of the Gospel is the inscription copied in the plate, made by Farmen, a priest, by whom the gloss on the Gospel of St. Matthew and the commencement of St. Mark had been written. It is to be read:—

"Faṛmen pḃṛ þaṛ boc þuṛ ʒleoṛeƀe dimittet ei dṇṛ omnia peccata ṛua ṛi fieṇi potest apud deum." [4]

On the 51st fo. r. is a rude pen-and-ink drawing of St. Mark, and on the following page another figure of this Evangelist in the true Hibernian style, drawn and painted in the rudest possible manner, and with a very odd winged lion hovering over his head. The Evangelist holds a book with both hands, and is surrounded with a border ornamented with plaited ribbons, lacertine animals and spiral lines.

The opposite page contains the first few words at the beginning of St. Mark's Gospel, highly ornamented; the INI being united together into a large letter precisely as in the Gospels of Lindisfarne, &c. This Gospel extends to fo. 84 r., on which is inscribed "finit euangelium marci: incipit euangelium lucæ," the portrait of St. Luke occupying the following page. The Evangelist is represented seated in a chair, which is surmounted by two eagles' heads; he wears a moderately long forked beard, and holds an open book, inscribed "lucaṛ," with the left hand, resting it on his knees, and is in the act of dipping his pen into the ink-stand, which is supported on a long slender foot-stalk, which fits into a little knob at the side of the chair. A winged calf is represented above the head of the Evangelist. The entire design is quite childish as a work of art, whilst the borders are in the ordinary complicated Irish style.

The commencement of St. Luke's Gospel is written on the following page, being ornamented in the same style as the title-pages of the other Gospels, and of which the accompanying plate offers a copy. It is to be observed, however, that the execution of the ornamental details in this manuscript is by no means so careful or elaborate as in the Book of Kells, or Gospels of Lindisfarne, especially the spiral lines, which are neither so precisely and truly traced, nor the centres of the coil so much diversified. The marginal borders also have been omitted in order to allow fac-similes from other parts of the MS. In some of the compartments of the different borders are introduced grotesque figures of men with their limbs intertwined, as in the drawing of the Virgin and Child, copied in this work from the Book of Kells; and in one of the ornamental pages is introduced the singular figure of a human head copied at the top of my plate.

At the end of the Gospel of St. Luke (fo. 126 r.) is inscribed " Explicit euangelium secundum Lucam Incipit Euangelium secundum Johannem."

The portrait of St. John appears on the following page, drawn in the same style as the other Evangelists,

---

[1] This MS. has also been described under the name of the Codex Rushworthanus, having formerly belonged to a gentleman of the name of Rushworth.

[2] This is an important distinction overlooked by Wanley and others, who question whether former pages of this MS., containing these Canons, &c., have not been abstracted.

[3] The commencement of the historical part of this Gospel does not occupy a separate page, as usual in Irish Codices; but the word xp̄i (autem generatio) occurs in fo. 2 v., written within a square about two inches high.

[4] Several of the contractions in this line are worthy of notice.

1

and holding a long scroll with the left hand and a pen in the right hand. He and St. Mark are represented with very short beards, and St. John appears to have the circular tonsure at the top of the head.

The commencement of St. John's Gospel occurs on the following page; the letters INP being of very large size, and conjoined together as usual.

At the end of the Gospel is written "Finit Amen," with the entry made by Owun, as follows: fol. 168 v. and 169 r. "Ðe mið bruca gebiððe fore opun ðe ðar boc ȝloerbe fæþmen ȝæm preorte æc harapyba hæfenu boc apritne. Bruca mið pilla rymle mið roðum ȝileorfa rib ir eȝh pæm leoforct." [1]

The last page in the volume (fo. 169 v.) is divided into six compartments, in four of which are written the laudatory verses on the four Evangelists, "Matheus instituit virtutum tramite moras, bene vivendi justo dedit ordine leges. Marcus amat terras inter cœluque volare," &c.; and in the two other compartments the scribe Mac-Regol has written, "Mac Regol dipinxit hoc euangelium.∴ Quicumque legerit et intellegerit hanc narrationem orat̄ pro Mac Regiul scriptori," part of which is copied in the plate, together with a number of additional letters to complete the alphabet.

The text of the volume is evidently not a copy of the Vulgate, as described by Astle, but possesses, on the contrary, many readings of the Vetus Itala. The following passages will serve to determine this point :—

Matth. 1—16. Joseph virum mariae de qua natus est jh̄s qui vocatur x̄ps.—V. 2. et aperuit os suum docebat eos dicens Beati pauperes, &c. Beati mites, &c. Beati qui lugent nunc quoniam ipsi consolabuntur. Beati qui esuriunt, &c. 19—1. Et factum est cum consummasset jh̄s sermones istos transtulit se a galilea et venit in fines judae trans jodanem et secutae sunt eum turbae multae et curavit eos ibi. 27—48. ceteri vero dicebant sine videamus an veniat helias et liberat eum alius autem accepta lancia po̅pungit latus ejus et exiit aqua et sanguis.[2] 27—66. Signantes lapidem et discesserunt.

John 1—6. Fuit homo misus a d̄o cui nomen erat johannis[3] hic venit in testimonium ut testimonium perhiberet de lumine erat lux vera quae inluminat omnem hominem venientem in hunc mundum In hoc mundo erat, &c.—xxi. 21. Petrus dicit ihū dn̄e hic autem[4] quid. Dicit ei ih̄s sic eum volo manere donec veniam quid ad te tu me seque exivit ergo sermo iste inter fratres quia discipulus ille non moritur, non dixit ih̄s non moritur sed sic eum volo manere donec venio quid ad te.

The following passages will show the style of the Anglo-Saxon Gloss, which is very valuable, being quite distinct from the Gloss in the Gospels of Lindisfarne.

Matth. v. 3—8. (The 4th and 5th verses being transposed.) Eabiȝ þa þurfende inȝarce forþon heora hir heofunarice —— þa milbe forþon þelne ȝericctaþ eorðu —— .... nu fþon þe hie beoþ afroefnebe —— þa þi hie hynȝnip ꝺ ðyrteþ roð færtnirre fþon þelne fulle þe—orþaþ —— þa milbheorcnirre fþon þe hie milbheorcnirre beȝetaþ —— þa claene heorctan þelne ȝoð ȝrcapað t[5] ȝereoþ.

John xxi. 15—17. cpæð rimon petre ðe hæc. rimon joh lyfarcu mec rriðor ðirrum. cpæð him ȝee ðrih ðu parc þte ic lurabe ðec, cpæð him foeð lombor mine. cpæð him efterrona rimon joh lufarc cu cpæð him ȝee ðrih ðu parc ðæcte ic lufo ðec. cpæð him foeð lombor mine. cpæð him efterrona rimo joh lufar mec; ȝun roþað pær petrur forðon cpæð him ðe ðirba lufarcu mec ꝺ cpæð him ðrih ðu alle parc þte ic lufað ec cpæð hi feoð rcip mine.

Of the origin and age of this volume, it is to be observed that Astle, overlooking the Irish name of the scribe, and confounding the large round Irish hand and the Anglo-Saxon together, under the name of Roman-Saxon writing, asserts this MS. to have been written in England in the latter end of the 7th, and the inter-lineary gloss in the 10th century; and Wanley states that it was the property of Venerable Bede, which "may be the case, as it seems older than the Cotton MS." (Nero, D. 4.) Dr. O'Conor, however, succeeded[6] in detecting in the Irish Annals of the year 820 the decease of a scribe of this name—"Mac Riagoil, nepos Magleni, Scriba et Episcopus Abbas Biror (hodie Birr in Comitatu Regio in Hibernia), periit."[7]

---

[1] Wanley gives the following as the translation of this passage :— "Qui me (sc. Codicem) versaverit oret pro Owuno qui hunc Codicem glossavit, Fermenni Presbyteri Harawudensis gratia, jam tandem Codicem perscripsit, Utere mente simili, vera fide, Pax (sit) cuilibet (sive ubique) charissima."—Hickes' Thesaurus, vol. ii. p. 81.

[2] It is deserving of notice that Owun omitted to gloss this interpolation, thence leading us to infer that his gloss was copied from a previous version made from a MS. not containing this passage.

[3] It will be seen that this passage, as copied in my plate, No. 4, is precisely similar in the character of the letters and orthography to the specimen given by Astle (plate xv. No. 2) from the C.C.C.C. Gospels of St. Luke and John, and which was inscribed by Archbishop Parker, "Hic liber olim missus a Gregorio Papa ad Augustinum Archiep." That the volume may have belonged to St.

Augustine is not impossible, but from an examination of the MS. itself, I can affirm it to be a production of the Irish school of art.

[4] The W-like contraction is here written for the word autem; the orthography is also Hiberno-Latin—as cotidie for quotidie; Moses for Moyses; Centorio for Centurio; luciscit for lucescit; velud for velut, &c.; and the Irish abbreviation h for vero occurs in Matth. v. 16.

[5] The Anglo-Saxon contraction used for vel resembles a t, or rather was a written l with a bar, being the contraction of the Anglo-Saxon word lice, like, alias, and not of the Latin word vel, as supposed by Whittaker.

[6] Script. Vet. Hibern. 1, cxxxi.

[7] Annal. Ult. ann. 821, and Ann. iv. Magistr. ann. 820; and see O'Conor in Annal. Ult. p. 130 et seq. on the Irish scribes.

Anglo-Saxon Gospels.

ANGLO-SAXON GOSPELS.

IN former articles upon the Anglo-Saxon versions of the Scripture, we have seen that the Books of Moses and the Psalter were especially the subjects of translation by our forefathers; indeed, with the exception of the Book of Job, part of the History of Judith, and numerous detached passages which occur in the Anglo-Saxon Homilies, I believe no other entire book of the Old Testament now exists in that language. In like manner, I have been unable to find any notice of Anglo-Saxon versions of other books of the New Testament than the four Gospels. Of these, however, we possess a rich store, of which the following is the list :—

Cottonian Library, Nero, D. 4, being the famous Gospels of Lindisfarne, Durham Book or Gospels of St. Cuthbert (as it has been named), with a Northumbrian Gloss.

* Cottonian Library, Otho, C. 1, written in Anglo-Saxon.
* Royal MSS., I.A. 14, written in the Norman-Saxon dialect.

Bodleian Library, The Northumbrian Gloss in the Gospels of Mac Regol, separately described in this work.

* Bodleian Library, No. 441 (N. E. F. 3, 15), Archbishop Parker's Anglo-Saxon Gospels.
* Bodleian Library, Hatton, No. 38 (65), Gospels written in Norman-Saxon; temp. Henr. II.
* Public Library, Cambridge, Leofric's Anglo-Saxon Gospels, including the Pseudo-Gospel of Nicodemus.
* Corpus Christi Coll. Camb., Ælfric's Autograph Saxon Gospels, collated by Abp. Parker.

The accompanying plate contains fac-similes from six of these MSS., marked above with an asterisk.

Unfortunately we possess no copy of the translation of St. John's Gospels made by the Venerable Bede (Cuthberti Vita Ven. Bedæ), and which was the first portion of the New Testament translated into the Anglo-Saxon dialect. It is probable, however, that literal translations of the lessons selected from the scriptures were read in the daily service of the Anglo-Saxon Church.[1]

The Anglo-Saxon Gospels, with the English version, was published in 1571, by the celebrated Archbishop Matthew Parker, with a Preface written by the Martyrologist, Foxe, dedicated to Queen Elizabeth. The presentation copy, given to the Queen by Foxe himself, is now in the library of the British Museum. Two other editions of the Anglo-Saxon Gospels were published—namely, by W. Lisle, in 1658, at London; and by Thomas Marshall, in 1665, at Dordrecht, together with the Mœsogothic version—for the latter six MSS. were collated—namely, the Oxford, Cambridge, Benet, Hatton, Lindisfarne, and Mac Regol; and Mr. Thorpe has recently published another edition of the Anglo-Saxon Gospels (12mo, London, 1842), using as the basis of his text the Cambridge University Library MS., collated with the C. C. C. MS., and occasionally with the Bodleian, No. 441, and the Cottonian Otho, C 1. I understand it is also his intention to publish in a separate work the Northumbrian version.

The Gospels of Lindisfarne, from its pre-eminent interest as one of the most ancient monuments of literature and the arts in this country, especially merits a detailed description. This noble manuscript, the glory of the Cottonian Library, and the most elaborately ornamented of all the Anglo-Saxon MSS., consists of 258 leaves of thick vellum, measuring 13½ inches by 9½, and contains the four Gospels written in double columns, according to the Latin Vulgate, with an interlineary Anglo-Saxon Gloss, preceded by the preface of

---

[1] This is indeed stated to have been the case by Dr. Lingard (Antiq. Anglo-Saxon Ch., p. 199), who, nevertheless, apologises for the *Latin* service of the Church, on the ground that it would have been "a degradation of the sacrifice to subject it to the caprice and variations of a barbarous idiom," as if the WORD OF GOD could be translated into a tongue too "barbarous" for the human composition of the prayers of the Church of Rome ! But even this slight portion of the service was in after ages denied to the unlearned; and it was not until the reign of King Edward VI., that the injunctions of the Protector and Cranmer required the Epistles and Gospels to be read in English instead of Latin.

1

St. Jerome to Pope Damasus, the Eusebian Canons, arguments of each Gospel and capitula of the Lessons; the whole written in a beautifully clear large rounded hand, and most exquisitely ornamented with drawings, illuminated initials, and tessellated designs; the entire volume being in an extraordinarily perfect state of preservation, although now 1150 years old.

The commencement of the Epistle of St. Jerome, "Novum opus," &c., together with the commencement both of the genealogical ("Liber generationis," &c.), and historical part (Xpi autem generatio, &c.), of St. Matthew's Gospel, and the commencement of each of the three other Gospels, respectively occupies an entire page, written in large curiously formed capital letters; the initial letters of each being of gigantic dimensions, and most elegantly ornamented with an endless variety of patterns, in which the interlaced ribbons, spiral lines, and intertwined lacertine birds and beasts are everywhere introduced, the intervening spaces profusely ornamented with red dots arranged in a great variety of patterns. The page containing the commencement of St. Luke's Gospel has been published by Strutt and Astle, and that of the historical part of St. Matthew by Shaw (Illum. Ornaments). The initial N of the Epistle of St. Jerome has the first stroke elongated down the left margin of the page, and the connecting stroke is composed of two large spiral ornaments. The initial L(iber generationis), is large and of the rounded form; the i formed into a long j, crossing the lower part of the L, and the b also large and of the rounded form (as in the Gospels of the Bibliothèque du Roi, published by Silvestre, &c.); and the initials INI(tium) and IN P(rincipio) of the two other Gospels are conjoined together, as in most of the early Anglo-Saxon and Irish Codices, the first stroke being nearly 11 inches long. The wonderful precision and delicacy of touch exhibited in the ornamental patterns of·which these large initials are composed, has justly attracted the admiration of every writer on the subject [1]. It is difficult to imagine what were the instruments used by the caligrapher, so perfectly regular and free from error is the drawing even in the most complicated parts of the patterns; indeed, from the appearance of the reverse of the leaves, it seems evident that a very hard instrument has been used, and I believe it has even been suggested that it can only have been executed by means of cut tools or blocks.

The other letters in these ornamental pages vary from $\frac{1}{2}$ an inch to $1\frac{1}{2}$ inch in height; they are greatly diversified in their forms, scarcely any two being alike. An extensive series of them is given by Astle, who considers that some are identical with those of the Phœnicians, Pelasgians, Etruscans, Greeks, Romans, and others; "and that this alphabet alone bears strong testimony that the letters used by our Saxon ancestors are derived from the Phœnician, the Etruscan, and the Greek letters *through the medium of the Roman.*[2] "

Many of these letters are evidently, however, the result of the fancy of the caligrapher, whilst others at least clearly appear to have been obtained from other sources than the Roman alphabet. The pure Greek letters found in this and other contemporary MSS. are to be accounted for from the intercourse between the early Irish, Anglo-Saxon, and Greek Christians. The capital M also, singularly formed as it mostly is, of three perpendicular strokes united across the middle with one horizontal bar [3]; or occasionally with two bars [4]; is not to be found in any Roman inscription, so far at least as I have been able to discover; but on the contrary is evidently of Phœnician or Pelasgic origin.

The Eusebian Canons [5] occupy eight leaves, and are inscribed within highly ornamented columns, supporting rounded arches, and which, from the beauty of their execution, are very deserving of being engraved. The first word of the prefaces, arguments, and capitula of each of the Gospels are also written of a comparatively large size, and ornamented like the title-pages [6], but the text of the Gospels is continued throughout, without any illuminated capitals to the several divisions; the first letter of each verse rather larger than the text, and coloured with patches of red, green, &c. The character of the letters of the Latin text is quite similar to, but smaller than, that of the Book of Kells, Gospels of St. Chad, Mac Regol, &c. The d is either uncial or minuscule, the f p q with short tails below the lines; the r, either capital or shaped like **n**, the **s** also either capital, or like **f**, the top elevated above the line. The letters at the end of the lines are often singularly conjoined for want of space.

---

[1] Selden (Præfat. ad Hist. Angl. Script. 1652, p. xxv.); Marshall (Observ. in vers. Sax. Evangel.); Smith (Bibl. Cott. Hist. et Synopsis, p. xxxiii.); Dibdin (Bibl. Decam. i. p. 50); Astle (Orig. of Writing, pl. 14 and 14 a); Strutt, Shaw, Waagen, &c.

[2] Astle, Origin of Writing, p. 97.

[3] See the second plate of the Gospels of Mac Durnan for a specimen. Sometimes, for want of space, the letter was placed on its side—*i. e.*, with one upright and three short transverse bars. I

believe the Roman capital M occurs in none of these ornamental title-pages.

[4] As in the specimens, from the Gospels of St. Chad and Book of Kells, pl. 1.

[5] Dibdin describes these as the Calendar. I believe, however, that it was only at the head of Psalter that the Calendar was inscribed.

[6] The beautiful initial M. copied in my plate, is that of the first word of the Preface to St. Mark's Gospel.

In addition to the illuminated title-pages, each of the five divisions of the volume is preceded by a page completely covered with coloured tessellated patterns of the utmost intricacy, generally disposed so as to form a cruciform design in the centre of the page. This elaborately beautiful feature is entirely peculiar to MSS. executed in Ireland, or by the Irish scholars; and in its neatness, precision, and delicacy far surpasses the productions of contemporary nations on the Continent. A likeness also of each of the Evangelists, accompanied by his respective symbolic animal, occupies a page at the head of the several Gospels, executed in a style of art quite unlike that of the Irish or early Anglo-Saxon school, and bearing evident traces of Byzantine origin, not only in its composition but also in the Greek words inscribed (in Roman capitals) O AGIOS MATTHEUS, instead of the Latin *Sanctus Mattheus*, and which in the picture of St. Mark is written O AGIUS MARCUS, with a Latin termination. " They are, notwithstanding, very different from the contemporary Byzantine and Italian paintings, as well as from those of the monarchy of the Franks of the 8th and 9th centuries; for in all these the character of ancient art, in which the four Evangelists were originally represented, is very clearly retained in the design and treatment; these paintings, on the contrary, have a very barbarous appearance, but are executed in their way with the greatest mechanical skill. Nothing remains of the Byzantine models but the attitudes, the fashion of the dress, and the form of the seats. Instead of the broad antique execution with the pencil in water-colours, in which the shadows, lights, and middle tints were given, all the outlines here are very delicately traced with the pen, and only the local colours put on; so that the shadows are entirely wanting, with the exception of the sockets of the eyes and along the nose. The faces are quite inanimate, like a piece of caligraphy; the folds of the drapery are marked with a very different local colour from that of the drapery itself: thus, for instance, in the green mantle of St. Matthew, they are vermilion. Besides this, there is no meaning except in the principal folds of the garments; in the smaller ones the strokes are quite arbitrary and mechanical—among the colours, which are often laid on very thick, only the red and blue are, properly speaking, opaque, but all the colours are as brilliant as if the paintings had been finished only yesterday. Gold, on the contrary, is used in very small portions."[1] Engravings of these figures of the Evangelists are given in Strutt's Manners and Customs, Vol. I.

The vellum is very thick and smooth, and the colours appear to have been mixed with thick gum, or size, which has not only caused the raised tessellated appearance of the drawings, but has evidently tended to their preservation; the ink, like that of the Irish or Hiberno-Saxon MSS., is very black.

The interlineary gloss is of the highest value, not only as an early specimen of the Northumbrian dialect[2], but from its numerous readings, which vary both from the Greek and Latin texts. This circumstance, as a collateral proof of the independence of the Anglo-Saxon Church, has not, I believe, been hitherto sufficiently investigated.[3] And it is to be hoped that the facts stated in this and other articles of this work, may induce a more extended examination by some competent scholar of this question.

We have seen that in most of its Palæographical characters this MS. perfectly agrees with the finest specimens now extant of early Irish art; and the history of the volume itself enables us fully to understand this circumstance, having been written at Lindisfarne (which was first resorted to by the Irish missionaries in the middle of the 7th century) at the end of the 7th or very beginning of the 8th century. A short Anglo-Saxon note at the end of St. Matthew's Gospel, and a longer entry at the end of the volume, in the same hand-writing as the gloss itself, (together with the account given by Simeon, precentor of Durham at the end of the 11th century) proves that the MS. in question was written by Eadfrith (a monk of Lindisfarne, and who held that see from 698 to 721[4]), in honour of God and Cuthbert (who died in 687): that the illuminations were executed by Œthelwald, who was a contemporary monk with Bishop Eadfrith, and who succeeded him in the bishopric of Lindisfarne, which he held till his decease in 737; that a splendid silver gilt cover, adorned with precious stones, was made for the book by Bilfrith; and that Aldred, a priest by whom the gloss and note were

---

[1] Waagen's Arts and Artists in England, i. 137.

[2] Some difference of opinion has existed as to the date of this gloss. Henshall (Etymol. org. Reasoner), who published the gloss on St. Matthew's Gospel, as compared with the Mœso-gothic version of Ulphilas—pronounced it to be of the 8th century; but Ingram supposes it to be about the middle of the 11th, and the language Dano-Saxon; whilst Wanley (Hickes, Cat. lib. Oct. Sept., p. 252,) considered it as of the time of Alfred; and Horne states, that it was at the earnest persuasion of Bishop Aldhelm (first Bishop of Sherborne) that Eadfrid executed the Anglo-Saxon version. This, however, as we shall subsequently learn, is erroneous.

[3] Semler, Apparatus ad Nov. Test. interpr., pp. 72, 73. Marsh's Michaelis, vol. 2, pp. 158, 637. Horne, Introd. ii. p. 247. Mr. Thorpe incidentally, in a note on Mark xv. 32, mentions that the Saxon version was no doubt translated from one of the older Latin versions.

[4] This Eadfrith is known to have been a friend of the venerable Bede, who dedicated to him his prose Life of St. Cuthbert (which he had written at his request, his veneration for that Saint being further manifested by the dedication to him of the volume before us); and it is more than probable that he is the same as Eadfrid, to whom Aldhelm dedicated one of his letters, and consequently he had visited Ireland, where he had doubtless learned the art of Irish caligraphy exhibited in the present MS.

3

written, added the interlineary Saxon version, with some marginal notes.[1] It does not indeed appear at what date Aldred lived, but he is stated by Astle to have been bishop of Durham from 946 to 968; and Wright (Anglo-Sax. Lit., p. 427) conjectures that it was during the first half of the 10th century that this gloss was written, as the same name is attached to an Anglo-Saxon gloss in the Durham ritual,[2] recently published by the Surtees Society, with a note relating to Bishop Alfsige, who flourished during the latter half of the 10th century. A comparison of the hand-writing of the two glosses would settle the question.

Many marvellous tales were recorded by the Monkish Chroniclers of Durham respecting this precious MS. Amongst others it is asserted, that when the monks of Lindisfarne were flying from thence to avoid the depredations of the Danes, the vessel in which they were embarked was overset, and the volume fell into the sea, but through the merits of St. Cuthbert the tide ebbed much further than usual, and the book was found upon the sands above three miles from the shore without having received injury from the water.

Archbishop Matthew Parker's Gospels, preserved in the Bodleian Library, No. 441, are written in a large upright minuscule character, of an unusual size and clearness, with plain red and green initials. The volume measures 12 inches by 7, with 25 lines in a page. The specimen No. 6 contains the latter part of the first verse of St. John's Gospel—" þ porþ pæʒ miþ ʒoþe ꝺ ʒoþ pæʒ þ porþ." Wanley considers it to have been written before the Norman Conquest.

The Cottonian MS. Otho C. 1, is of a large quarto size, plainly written, but very much injured by the destructive fire whereby so many treasures of that library were destroyed.

Bishop Leofric's Gospels, preserved in the University Library at Cambridge, is a finely-written MS., containing 401 pages, measuring $12\frac{1}{2}$ by $8\frac{1}{2}$ inches, with 26 lines in a page, and with plain red, green, and blue capitals; containing on the first leaf, in Latin and Anglo-Saxon, the donation of the volume by Leofric, Bishop of the church of St. Peter in Exeter (Exancestre), for the use of his successors. The specimen No. 4 contains a copy of the heading and commencement of St. Luke's Gospel. According to Wanley, it was written about the time of the Norman Conquest.

The Gospels of Ælfric are preserved in the Corpus Christi College, Cambridge, written in a moderate-sized plain upright minuscule character, with an ornamented initial letter to the Gospel of St. John, copied in the specimen No. 3 (the commencement of the three other Gospels being wanting). It measures 12 inches by $8\frac{1}{4}$, with 27 lines in a page. A copy of Ælfric's autograph (from the MS. given by Astle) is added in No. 7 [3]. The MS. contains numerous Anglo-Saxon entries, and lists of the popes (beginning with " Pætrus p̄. p̄.," and ending with Nicolas and Alexander); and of the different English archbishops and bishops of the various sees, from which it appears that the volume was written in the eleventh century.

The Royal MS. 1 A. 14, in the British Museum—is written in a moderate-sized minuscule character, inclining to the modern gothic, with the initial letter of each Gospel slightly ornamented in colours; and is considered by Wanley to have been written about the reign of King Henry II. This MS. was originally in the abbey of St. Augustine, of Canterbury, and afterwards belonged to Archbishop Thomas Cranmer. The specimen No. 2 is from this MS., and contains the heading and commencement of St. Luke's Gospel, as follows:— " Nu þe pillaþ heꞃ eoꞃ aꞃeceen. Lucaꝼ boc Ꝺaꝼ halʒan ʒoþꝼꝃelleꞃeꝼ. Foꞃþa̅ þe pꝛcoþlice maneʒa þohce þaꞃe þinʒe paceʒe enþebyꞃþen þe on uꝼ ʒeꝼylþe ꝼinc."

The Hatton Gospels are preserved in the Bodleian Library (No. 38), written in an incipient modern gothic character, considered by Wanley to be of the time of King Henry II., with which period the ornamental initials will well accord. The MS. measures $9\frac{1}{2}$ by $6\frac{1}{2}$ inches, with 25 lines in a page, and has the autograph of " Johēs Parker" at the commencement, written in red chalk, which is also employed throughout in marking the Gospel and chapters. The specimen No. 5 is from this MS., and is the heading and commencement of St. Matthew's Gospel. As a specimen of Norman-Saxon this MS. is of great value.

Astle has given (Pl. 20, No. 9) a fac-simile from a charter of King Henry I. to the cathedral of Canterbury, written in characters very similar to those of the last mentioned MS.

---

[1] All these names occur in the Register of Benefactors to Durham Cathedral, contained in the Cott. MS. Dom. A. 7.

[2] Rituale Ecclesiæ Dunelmensis, 8vo., Lond. 1840. Edited by Stevenson.

[3] The entire note is as follows, and occurs at the end of St. Matthew's Gospel: " Ego Ælfricus scripsi hunc librum in Monasterio Baththonio et dedi Brithwoldo preposito. Qui scripsit vivat in pace in hoc Mundo et in futuro sēlo et qui legit legator in eternum." Astle gives this entry as about the time of King Edward the Con-

fessor, which would not agree with the conjecture that this MS. was written by the great Anglo-Saxon reformer, Archbishop Ælfric. Indeed, I find no account of either his or Alfric Bata's having been engaged in a translation of the Gospels, nor yet of either of them being resident in the Monastery at Bath; yet the circumstance of this translation having been made by an " Ælfricus," will accord with the characters of either of those writers, opposed as they were to the Romish Church of the time. Ælfric died in 1006, and Alfric Bata in 1051, which latter date will accord with Astle's statement.

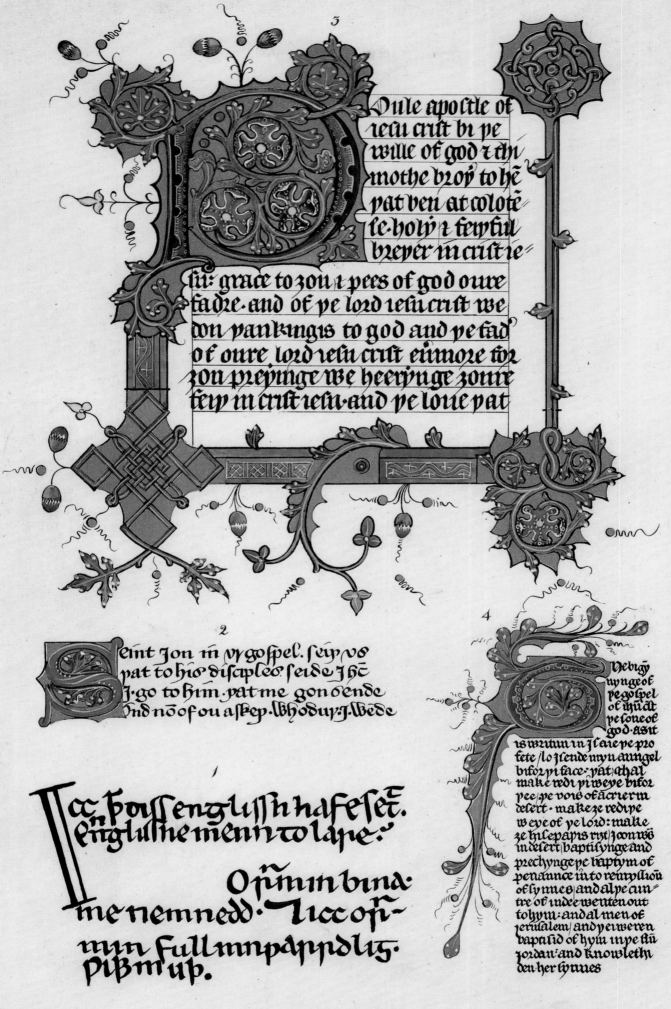

3

Oule apostle of
iesu crist bi þe
wille of god z þin
mothe bzoy to hē
þat ben at coloten
se holy z fertfül
bzeyer in crist ie

sü: grace to ʒou z pees of god oure
fadze. and of þe lozd iesu crist we
don þankingis to god and þe fad
of oure lozd iesu crist eümoze for
ʒou preyinge we heeringe ʒoure
feiþ in crist iesu. and þe loue þat

2

eint Jon in þy gospel. seiþ vs
þat to his disciples seide Jhc
J. go to him. þat me gon sende
ünd no of ou askeþ. Who duy J. We de

Icc þus englissh hafe set.
englisshe menn to lare:

Of him bina
me nemned. Icc of-
min full inpappdliʒ.
þiʒm up.

4

þe bigy
ninge of
þe gospel
of ihesü crist
þe sone of
god. as it
is writun in ʒsaie þe pro
fete / lo ʒsende myn aungel
bifoz þi face: þat schal
make redi þi weye bifoz
þee/þe vois of a crier in
desert · make ʒe rediþe
weye of þe lozd: make
ʒe his paþis riʒt/ Joon wos
in desert baptisynge and
prechynge þe baptym of
penaunce into remyssioü
of synnes · and al þe cun
tre of iudee wenten out
to hym · and al men of
ierusalem / and þei weren
baptisid of hym in þe flu
iozdan · and knowleth
den her synnes

EARLY ENGLISH BIBLICAL MSS.

IN several of the articles on the Anglo-Saxon versions of the Bible, it has been noticed that for a long period after the Conquest the old Saxon tongue remained in use. Hence, it is not surprising that we should meet with so few MSS., written in the early English dialect, previous to the middle of the 14th century. The earliest of the few which have been recorded is a long, narrow MS., (20 inches by 8,) preserved in the Bodleian Library, (Junius, No. 1,) called *Ormulum*, being a paraphrase of the gospel histories, composed by one Orme, or Ormin. By Hickes and Wanley it was considered to be prose, whilst Ellis states that it is really written in verse, of 15 syllables, without rhyme, in imitation of the most common form of the Latin tetrameter iambic The following is a short specimen from the commencement of the paraphrase of the Lord's Prayer:—

Paterr nosterr ꝥatt is ꝥ godess name
Beo Rihht lofedd her & purrþedd
For þhase godess name matt
Rihht lofennn her & purþenn
He þinneþþ spa ꝥ he shall ben.

The writing of this MS. is large and very coarse, as will be seen in our specimen, No. 1, in which the author tells his name, and that he has written his book in " Englissh," that " Englisshemenn " might learn.

Richard Rolle, the hermit of Hampole, who died in 1349, wrote a metrical paraphrase in English upon the Book of Job, the Lord's Prayer, and Psalms, (Bibl. Reg. Mus. Brit. 18 D. 1) ; and the Bodleian Library possesses a huge volume of religious poetry, which is known under the name of Sowlehele (No. 779). It measures not less than 23 inches by 15, and is 5 inches thick, being written with two or three columns in a page, with illuminated capitals, in the style of the 14th century, of which No. 2 is a specimen, which is to be read —

Seint Jon in ur gospel seiþ us
þat to his disciples seide Jhc (Jesus)
I go to him þat me gon sende
And no of ou askeþ whodur I wede (wende)

There is another MS. of the Sowlehele in Corpus Christi College, Cambridge, in which is also a metrical version of the Psalms, executed about the year 1300, (of which there are also copies in the Bodleian and Cottonian Library, Vespasian, D. 7). With the exception of one or two glosses and partial translations of the parts of the Gospels read in the service of the Church, we have no English version of the Bible before the latter part of the 14th century. From a collation made by my friend the late Rev. T. Symonds, I find that the English translation of the Bible, contained in the Bodleian MS., Fairfax, No. 2, considered by Archbishop Usher to have been written at the close of the 13th century, (and of which MSS. are also said to be in Christ Church, and Queen's Colleges, at Oxford,) is of the Wickliffite period, agreeing with the Arundel MS. 108, and the Lambeth MS., Wickliffe, Wicklef, Wecklef, Wycleve, or Wycliffe, as he has been variously named, (assisted by Nicholas Hereford,) having translated the whole Bible, circ. 1380.

Whether the assertion of More, the opponent of Wickliffe, (that his translation was needless, as there was a translation of " the hole byble long before Wickliffe's dayes,") was false, or whether he alluded to the old Norman-Saxon versions, still lingering in the land, we have now no means of determining. As, however, the Church at that period considered the possession of the Scriptures by the laity to be heretical, and as one of Archbishop Arundel's constitutions, passed at the Oxford Convocation in 1408, was directed against Wickliffe by name, and as another prohibited the English translation of the scriptures, we may easily conceive the spirit which would have crushed the wakening energy of the people in matters of religious controversy, by withholding from them not only this " engine of wonderful power," as Wickliffe's version has been styled by a Romish writer. but also the older version of the " hole byble," if, indeed, any such were in existence.

It was Mr. Turner, I believe, in his History of England, ii. p. 561, who first suggested that although Wickliffe's ordinary style was somewhat darkened and confused, and less perspicuous than that of the Hermit of Hampole, yet that, with respect to his version of the scriptures, " the unrivalled combination of force, simplicity, dignity, and feeling in the original, compel his old English, as they seem to compel every other language into which it is translated, to be clear, interesting, and energetic."

This observation was, doubtless, founded upon the version published by Lewis and Baber,* being regarded as that of Wickliffe. In like manner in Bagster's historical account, prefixed to the English Hexapla, the same circumstance is affirmed and ascribed to the Providence of God and the dignity of the Book itself.

It is, however, well known that some few of the early English Biblical MSS. differ so materially from the rest, that we are led to believe that there must have been two distinct translations of scripture (Baber, p. lxix) —and as it has happened that the most perspicuous of these MSS. has been ascribed to Wickliffe, it is not improbable that Archbishop Usher was thence induced to infer that the older and less perspicuous version (agreeing, in fact, with Wickliffe's ordinary style) was older than Wickliffe. Amongst these MSS. (of which copies occur in most of our libraries) are some which are referred to Wickliffe's curate, Purnay, or Purvay, and it is I believe, ascertained that it is the version contained in them that has been published as that of Wickliffe, of whose translation no part has hitherto been published. Well, indeed, might Fabricius long ago exclaim, " Mirum vero est apud Anglos eam [versionem Wiclivitanam] tam diu neglexisse, quum vel linguæ causa ipsis in pretio esse debeat" (Bibl. Lat. Med. et infr. Ætatis, Vol. V., p. 321, 1754). This reproach, however, will, I trust, be speedily removed, as I am informed that Sir Frederick Madden and Mr. Forshall have investigated the subject at great length, and have undertaken the printing of the Old Testament of the true Wickliffe version.

One of the most important MSS. of this period has been lately obtained by the British Museum, having previously belonged to the celebrated biblical scholar, Dr. Adam Clarke. It is in two large folio volumes (a third, containing the first half of the Old Testament being wanting) written in modern Gothic letters, and with illuminated capitals and borders in the style of the latter end of the 14th century (not unlike those in the Liber Regalis of Westminster), and bearing on its first page the Arms of England, asserted by its late owner to be those of Thomas à Woodstock, youngest son of King Edward III., and brother to John of Gaunt, the great patron of Wickliffe. Sir F. Madden, however, considers that they are the arms of the Good Duke Humphrey. This circumstance of royal ownership, and the fact that "the language is older than that in most of the copies which pass under the name of Wicklif,"† seems sufficient to prove it to be the genuine Wickliffe version. It is from this MS. that my specimen No. 3 is copied, being the commencement of St. Paul's Epistle to the Colossians, which is to be read :—" Poule apostle of iesu crist bi þe wille of God & Thimothe broþ to he þat ben at Colotese holy & feiþful breþer in crist iesu grace to ȝou & pees of god our fadre and of þe lord iesu crist we don þankingis to god & þe fad̄ of our lord iesu crist eūmore for ȝou preyinge we heerynge ȝoure feiþ in crist iesu and þe loue þat" &c.

The specimen No. 4 is copied from the pretty little MS. employed as the Wickliffe text in the English Hexapla of Bagster, and which then belonged to his late Royal Highness the Duke of Sussex. The fac-simile is from the commencement of St. Mark's Gospel, and is to be read—" The bigynynge of þe Gospel of īhu c̄st þe sone of god as it is writun in Isaie þe profete lo I sende myn aungel befor þi face, þat shal make redi þi weye befor þee þe vois of a crier in desert make ȝe redi þe weye of þe lord, make ȝe hise paþis riȝt Joon was in desert baptisynge and prechynge þe baptym of penaunce in to remyssion of synnes and al þe cuntree of iudee wenten out to hym and al men of Jerusalem and þei weren baptised of hym in þe flū Jordan and know-lechiden her synnes." ‡

* The New Testament, &c., translated out of the Latin Vulgat by John Wicklif, &c. By John Lewis, Lond. 1731, fol. A second Edition was published in 1810, 4to., edited by the Rev. H. H. Baber, with an introductory historical account of the Saxon and English Versions of the Scriptures previous to the 15th century.

† Catal. of MSS. of Dr. A. Clarke, London, 1835, p. 20, wherein it is stated that it was purchased by him at Dr. Fell's sale, his only opponent being a goldbeater, who bid for it for the purposes of his trade. It cost Dr. A. C. £10, and so overjoyed was he at the purchase, that he bore it off in triumph on his shoulders, notwithstanding its weight.

‡ The Anglo-Saxon letter þ is used in these MSS. for th, instead of the þ. It subsequently degenerated into a y, still used by old-fashioned people for th.

2

ICI FAIT HERODE OCIRRE LES INNOCENS.

ST LI SIRE
AL OMEN SEIG
NUR SE DEVERS
LES COTIES DESTRES
Desque ico pose
les tuens enemis:
escamel de tes piez.

Dieu moult de milliers de chevaliers a cheval z oy leur nobre
vint fois mil. z dix mille z auoient haubers de fer z de iacitte
z de souffre z les testes de chevaulz estoient aussi coe testes de leon.

Beneurez li huem chi nealat el conseil des feluns: & en la ueie des
peccheurs ne stout: & en la chaere de pestilence ne sist. Mais en la
lei de nre seignur la uolunteit de lui: & en la sue lei penserat par iurn
e par nuit. Et iert ensement cume le fust qued e plantet de iuste
les decurs des ewes. chi durrat sun fruit en sun tens.

French Mss.

ANCIENT FRENCH MANUSCRIPTS.

ALTHOUGH it does not appear that any translation of the Scriptures into the French language was made previous to the beginning of the 14th century, (when Jean de Vignay, or de Vignes, translated the Epistles and Gospels read in the service of the Church, at the request of Jane of Burgundy, Queen of Philip of France), versions of detached parts of the Bible exist, of a previous date, in MS., which are consequently regarded as of great value by the French philologists. Nor are they less esteemed by the English antiquary, considering the long and intimate connection between the French and English nations, especially during the period when our language was undergoing its transformation from the old Anglo-Saxon to the modern English, proving as they do (notwithstanding all the pains taken by the Conqueror and his successors to diffuse the Norman-French language in England,[1] and all the intercourse which must necessarily have taken place between the Norman invaders and their descendants, and the natives), how trifling was the influence of the Norman on the English language.

The Psalter seems especially to have been early translated into Norman-French. A fine MS. of the tripartite Latin version of the Psalms (very similar to the Psalter of Eadwine, which also contains a Norman-French version,) exists in the Bibliothèque Royale, one of the versions bearing an ancient French interlineary Gloss.[2] The Cottonian MS. Vitellius, E. 9., also contained an elegantly written Latin-French Psalter of the time of Henry I., but it is much damaged by the Cottonian fire. One of the most valuable MSS. of this portion of the sacred volume is a Latin-French MS., contained in the Cottonian Library, (Nero, C. 4,) from which the fac-similes, No. 1 and 2, in the accompanying plate, have been taken. It is a small folio volume, measuring 13 inches by 9, and consists of 122 leaves of vellum, the first 38 of which contain an extensive series of scriptural drawings, of singular interest, from the numerous representations which they afford of the dresses, manners and style of art of the Anglo-Norman period, many of which have been engraved by Strutt, Shaw, &c. ; a number of them are also given in the Pictorial History of England.[3] The drawing of the Murder of the Innocents, copied in the plate, is one of the most interesting of these designs, in which Herod is represented seated, wearing a golden crown, ornamented with strawberry leaves, a long beard, a long loose tunic, looped on the right shoulder, and having a slit, to allow the arm to pass through, and with the sleeves very wide at the wrist. The two soldiers wear the conical helmet, furnished with the nasal ; ringed hauberks ; one of them also wears the long tunic beneath. One of these warriors has the face shaven, but the other wears long mustachios, one also has the leg bandaged. The executioner will also be seen to be disguised by a mask of a classic character, and the female figure has the gown fitted close to the figure, with the sleeves tight to the wrist, and then suddenly widening and falling almost to the feet, and the couvre chef (kerchief) on the head very long. This drawing is inscribed " Ici fait Herode ocirre les Innocens." In the original drawing the arches are surmounted by the representation of a city strangely out of perspective, and the upper half of the page contains another drawing, representing the Flight into Egypt, (partly copied by Mr. Shaw,) of the same size as the one before us.

---

[1] " It was from England and Normandy that the French received the first works which deserve to be cited in their language."—Abbé de la Rue, in Archæolog. 12, p. 50. The only known Norman French poet previous to the time of the Conqueror, is Thibaut de Vernon, Canon of Rouen, who translated from Latin into French verse the lives of St. Wandril and other saints.—Ellis's Early Engl. Poets, 1, p. 41. The earliest troubadours or Provençal poets, were William of Poictiers, and Raymond of Toulouse, (circ. 1080). —La Combe, Dict. du Vieux Lang. pref.

[2] Messrs. Silvestre and Champollion have given a fac-simile from this MS., speaking of it as of the highest importance.

[3] Vol. i., pp. 277, 279, 280, 284, 286, 327, 344, 636, 637 ; vol. ii., p. 149.

Some of the earlier of these pages have three, and even four, subjects on each, but in the majority there are only two. The genealogy of Christ, fo. 8 r, occupies the entire leaf, the tree forming a highly ornamental design, very similar in its details to the same subject in the Psalter of St. Louis in the Library of the Arsenal.

The Assumption of the Virgin, inscribed "Ici est la symtion de nostre dame," (fo. 28 r,) and the portrait of the Virgin, on the following page, inscribed "Ici est faite reine del Ciel," respectively occupy the entire page, and are far more highly finished than any of the other miniatures, betraying evident traces of Byzantine art; the Saviour himself occupying the centre of the upper part of the latter painting, bearing in his arms the soul of the dead Virgin, swathed like an infant, and the hand of the Creator, in the act of benediction, according to the Romish Church, being extended out of the clouds. The last of these drawings is an extraordinary representation of Hades, the immense jaws of which are secured by a door, of which an angel holds both the knocker and key inserted into the lock.

To this succeeds the Calendar,[1] occupying twelve pages.

Many of these drawings are, as will be observed, illustrations of Gospel subjects, whence it might be inferred that they did not originally belong to the remainder of the MS., but as it was the custom of that period to decorate the Psalter with a general series of Bible pictures, this objection is not well founded. The text of the MS. is written in double columns, the Latin on the left side, and the Norman-French on the right. The latter only has been copied in No. 2, which is to be read "Dist li sire al mien seigneur sede vers les meies destres Desque ieo pose les tuens enemis escamel de tes piez." Psalm 109, v. 1, the first line being in Roman capitals, (except the final uncial E), the three following in debased rustic capitals, and the remainder in an incipient Gothic minuscule, nearly similar to that used in the Psalter of Eadwine. At the end of the Psalter are the usual Canticles, Lord's Prayer[2], Creed, Litany, &c.

The initial letters of the Psalms are for the most part either plain green, red, and blue capitals, or have them ornamented with pen flourishes of different colours; the initial of the first Psalm is, however, large, and ornamented with figures of David, writing the Psalms in the upper division, and playing on a violin in the lower part.

A few of the other chief Psalms are also distinguished by larger initials, as in the specimen No. 2 in the Plate.

The specimen, No. 3, is copied from the first Psalm in Mr. Douce's French Psalter and Canticles of the 13th century, now in the Bodleian Library, which is a neat MS., consisting of 38 leaves, being 12 inches by 8 in size, with 39 lines in a page. With the exception of the pretty initial copied in the plate, the capitals are small and plain red and green letters. The specimen before us is to be read—"Beneurez li huem chi ne alat el conseil des feluns et en la ueie des peccheurs ne stout et en la chaere de pestilence ne sist Mais en la lei de nre Seigneur la voluntet de lui et en la sue lei ppenserat par jurn e par nuit. Et iert ensement cume le fust qued e plantet de uiste les decurs des ewes che dunrat sun frut en sun tens."—Ps. i., 1-3. The following is the 100th Psalm :—

"Cantéz á nóstre segnor túte térre. Seruéz al segnúr en ledéce. Entrez en les guardement de lúi en esléecement Saciez que li sire meesme é ds il meesme fist nus e neient nus meesme Li poples de lui e les oeilles de la sue pasture entrez les portes de lui en confessiun les aitres de lui en loenges regehisseiz a lui Loez le num de lui kar suefs est li sire en parmanableted la misericorde de lui e desq. en generaciun e generaciun la verited de lui."—Comp. Hickes, ii, 168.

Other early French Psalters exist, in Trinity College Library, Cambridge, the Arundel Library, No. 230,[3] (and see No. 248 and several others mentioned in the Preface to the Catalogue of that Library,) also the Harleian MSS., No. 273, (of the 13th century,) 1770, 4070, 4327, and 4508. Also the additional MS., No. 4906, which contains a rhythmical French version of the Psalms.

Samson de Nanteuil translated the Proverbs into French verse, at the instance of Adelaide de Condi, wife of the governor of Horn Castle, in Lincolnshire, in the reign of King Stephen. This version is preserved in the Harleian MS. 4388.

---

[1] The name of Thomas à Becket does not of course occur in the month of December—the volume being of an earlier date.

[2] The Lord's Prayer is printed in Janvier's "Rapport sur l'Académie de Caen," p. 202, from a communication of the Abbé de la Rue.

[3] A specimen of this Psalter may be seen in Don's Icon Libellarum, p. 200.

The Royal MS. 20, B. 5, contains the New Testament in French. But of all the books of this portion of the sacred writings, none appears to have been so greatly in vogue as the Apocalypse, the contents of which well accorded with the propensity of the middle ages for the fantastical, the wonderful, and the strange. From one of these, which belonged to the Duke of Sussex, the specimens Nos. 4 and 5 were copied. This elegant MS. of the 14th century consists of 39 leaves (10½ inches by 7), and contains not fewer than 70 miniatures, chiefly occupying the entire width of the page, and very carefully drawn in a style not destitute of spirit and effect. The specimen No. 5 is to be read—" Et ie ui moult de millrs de chevalrs a cheval & oy leur nobre vint fois mil & dix mille & avoiet haubers[1] de fer & de jacitte & de souffre & les testes de chevauls estoiet aussi coe testes de leon."—Rev. ix., 16, 17. Many of these miniatures have the panelled back group, so common at the period when this MS. was executed.

Three illuminated copies of the Revelation exist in the library of Trinity College, Cambridge, (one of which contains a very exquisite series of drawings[2]). Two are in the Library of Corpus Christi Coll. Cambridge, one in verse, of which the following is a specimen of the commencement :—

> " La vision ke jhu crist
> A son serf moustrer fist
> Ke lost couendra estre feit
> Par son angel signefieit
> A Johan ke de jhu crist
> Porta temonie de ceo qi uit.
> Benoit soit q la uision lit
> E oient les moz de ceste escrit
> E le escripture recendra
> Kar le tens sei aprochera."

Others also exist in the libraries, of the Archbishop of Canterbury at Lambeth Palace, the British Museum, &c.

The Epistle to the Ephesians, and other detached parts of the New Testament, are also preserved amongst the Harleian MSS.

Raoul de Presles, or Praelles, translated the Bible into French as far as the Psalms, by order of Charles V. of France, in the 14th century, a fine copy of which is preserved among the Lansdowne MSS., in the British Museum (No. 1175).[3]

Guiar de Moulins, Canon of St. Pierre d'Aire, between 1291 and 1294, translated the biblical Historia Scholastica of Peter Comestor into French.[4]

The identical copy of Guiar des Moulins' version, found in the tent of John, King of France, after the Battle of Poictiers, and also the copy which belonged to his son, the Duke of Berry, are both in the Library of the British Museum.

[1] In the Laws of William the Conqueror, the hauberk is spelt halbers—" viii. chevalz selez e entrenez, iiii. halbers," &c. In the middle figure of the drawing No. 1, the hauberk is seen to be slit upwards on each side ; it also covers the neck and ears.

[2] Dr. Waagen speaks of this MS. as the richest and most distinguished Apocalypse MS. he had met with, the design, drawing, and treatment of which indicate the first half of the 13th century. The invention is much in the spirit of the text, highly original, fanciful, and spiritedly dramatic. The various dragons and devils, in particular, are everything that can be wished. (Arts and Artists in England, iii., p. 326.)

[3] See also the Harleian MS. 4412.

[4] Several copies of this translation exist in the Bibliothèque Royale at Paris. The Rev. Mr. Tobin also possesses a remarkably fine copy.

A pokalypsis dit ist die offe
barunge ihesu crish. Die
yme goth gegebin hat
offenbar zcu tune sine
knechten die schire ge
sehen sal.

German Apocalypse

J. W.

THE GERMAN APOCALYPSE OF HIS LATE ROYAL HIGHNESS THE DUKE OF SUSSEX.

DESCRIPTION OF THE PLATE.

Commencement of the Apocalypse, with part of the Illumination, illustrating the beginning of the 20th Chapter [1].

THE Manuscript from which the accompanying illustrations have been copied belonged to his late Royal Highness the Duke of Sussex, and comprises an old German version of the Book of Revelation, accompanied by a commentary in the same language. It is ascribed to the fourteenth century by Mr. Pettigrew in his Catalogue of the Manuscripts of his late Royal Highness. It consists of 38 leaves, measuring 14 inches by 10½; with the writing arranged in double columns. According to Dr. Kuper, as we learn from Mr. Pettigrew's work [2], it contains many ancient German Gothic words, especially nouns, which have become obsolete for centuries past. The translation is far from being a literal one, but there are no passages materially differing from the original and modern version. Many errors occur in the interpretation; in some places words being left out, and in others wrong ones introduced, which has probably arisen from the ignorance or carelessness of the Scribe. The glosses are not numerous, but in some places passages from the original text are interwoven with and introduced among the interpretations. The division of the text does not correspond with the modern arrangement into chapters. In the description of the Heavenly Jerusalem there are several material omissions. The last verse of the final chapter is also left out. The MS. appears to be also defective, from what should be ch. xviii. 22, to xix. 13, and from ch. xx. 6, to xxi. 6. The short passage figured in the plate is to be read—

"𝔄𝔭𝔬𝔨𝔞𝔩𝔦𝔭𝔰𝔦𝔰, 𝔡𝔦𝔱 𝔦𝔰𝔱 𝔡𝔦𝔢 𝔬𝔣𝔣𝔢𝔟𝔞𝔯𝔲𝔫𝔤𝔢 𝔧𝔥𝔢𝔰𝔲 𝔠𝔯𝔦𝔰𝔱𝔦. 𝔇𝔦𝔢 𝔭𝔦𝔫𝔢 𝔤𝔬𝔱𝔥 𝔤𝔢𝔤𝔢𝔟𝔢𝔫 𝔥𝔞𝔱 𝔬𝔣𝔣𝔢𝔫𝔟𝔞𝔯 𝔷𝔢𝔲 𝔱𝔲𝔫𝔢 𝔰𝔦𝔫𝔢 𝔨𝔫𝔢𝔠𝔥𝔱𝔢𝔫 𝔡𝔦𝔢 𝔰𝔠𝔥𝔦𝔯𝔢 𝔤𝔢𝔰𝔠𝔥𝔢𝔫 𝔰𝔞𝔩."—i. e.—

" The Apocalypse, that is, the manifestation of Jesus Christ, which God gave unto him, to show unto his servants things which must shortly come to pass."

The MS. contains 14 Illuminations, in gold and colours, each occupying an entire page, and containing many figures illustrative of the text, many of them very grotesque and singular. The one I have selected is drawn with the greatest spirit, representing the Angel binding Satan, in which the attitude of the former (who has been delineated in the ordinary mode of representation of St. Peter), is not devoid of effect. In the original, St. John stands on the right-hand side of the picture, looking up to and with his right hand raised towards the Angel. The figures are drawn with a coarse pen, and the tints shaded off, leaving the lights entirely destitute of colour. The gold is brilliant, and raised on a cretaceous basal layer.

In some of the Illuminations the soldiers are armed with basinets or helmets, fitting close to the head, and with side-pieces extending as low as the shoulders; distinct epaulettes and pointed knee-caps appear, and the shield is small, with the angles rounded off, and a deep notch on one side at the top. The capital letters are in blue and red ink, except the first, which is much larger than the rest, and relieved with gold.

The following passage, being the commencement of the 20th Chapter of the Revelation, and of which the Illumination in the accompanying Plate is an illustration, will serve as a specimen of the text of the volume:—

" 𝔘𝔫𝔡𝔢 𝔦𝔠𝔥 𝔰𝔞𝔠𝔥 𝔢𝔶𝔫𝔢 𝔢𝔫𝔤𝔢𝔩 𝔲𝔦𝔡𝔢𝔯 𝔟𝔞𝔯𝔦 𝔟𝔬𝔫 𝔡𝔢𝔪𝔢 𝔥𝔦𝔪𝔢𝔩𝔢. 𝔡𝔢𝔯 𝔥𝔞𝔱𝔩𝔢 𝔢𝔶𝔫𝔢𝔫 𝔰𝔩𝔲𝔷𝔦𝔩 𝔡𝔢 𝔞𝔟𝔤𝔯𝔲𝔫𝔡𝔦𝔰, 𝔲𝔫𝔡 𝔢𝔶𝔫𝔢 𝔤𝔯𝔬𝔷𝔢 𝔨𝔢𝔱𝔥𝔦𝔫𝔢 𝔦𝔫 𝔰𝔦𝔫𝔢𝔯 𝔥𝔞𝔫𝔱, 𝔲𝔫𝔡 𝔟𝔢𝔤𝔯𝔢𝔦𝔣 𝔡𝔢𝔫 𝔱𝔯𝔞𝔠𝔥𝔦𝔫 𝔡𝔢𝔫 𝔞𝔩𝔡𝔢𝔫 𝔰𝔩𝔞𝔤𝔦 𝔡𝔢𝔯 𝔡𝔞 𝔥𝔢𝔦𝔷𝔦𝔱 𝔡𝔢𝔯 𝔱𝔲𝔣𝔦𝔩 𝔲𝔫𝔡 𝔰𝔞𝔱𝔥𝔞𝔫𝔞𝔰. 𝔲𝔫 𝔞𝔱

---

[1] And I saw an angel come down from heaven, having the key of the bottomless pit, and a great chain in his hand. And he laid hold on the dragon, that old serpent, which is the Devil and Satan, and bound him a thousand years.—Verse 1 & 2. And the Devil was cast into the lake of fire and brimstone, where the beast and the false prophet are.—Verse 10.

[2] Bibliotheca Sussexiana, v. i. p. 242.

in tusint jar. un waif in burnin de fur unde beslos in unð bezcepcht de ubir in ða; her nicht mer uorbas boleite die lute bis ða; irfullit wor ðin tusit jar. unð ðar noch so sal inpunði ioðe sathanas eyne kurte czyt."

I regret that I am unable to give any information as to the author of the version and commentary copied in the MS., or indeed as to any other German version of the sacred Scriptures, previous to the invention of printing, except the following:—

Within little more than a century from the mission of St. Augustine to this country, we find Anglo-Saxon missionaries zealously attempting to disseminate the truths of the Gospel on the banks of the Weser the Rhine, and the Danube. St. Wilfrid in Friesland, Ecgbert in the North of Germany, Willebrod at Utrecht, the brothers Ewald in the territories of the old Saxons, Swidbert in the Mark of Brandenberg, Willehad, the founder of the Cathedral of Bremen, were all Anglo-Saxons; and, to the honour of our country, the title of the Apostle of Germany has been bestowed by posterity upon Winfrid (or St. Boniface, as he was afterwards named), a native of Crediton in Devonshire. By him the monasteries of Fritzlar and Amelburg, and the rich and magnificent Abbey of Fulda[1] were founded, as well as the Convents of Bischofesheim, on the Tuber; Chitzingen or Kissengen, in Franconia; Heidenheim, near the Brentz; and the four episcopal sees at Erford, Buraburg, Aichstad, and Wurtzburg. Hence it is not surprising that we find the genius of the Anglo-Saxon Church re-appearing in Germany, and it is to this that I would attribute the existence in Germany of a very ancient version of the Bible, and other theological works in the old dialect, named the Theotisc; of which, however, we find no notice in the Rev. T. H. Horne's Introduction. I shall have occasion, in another portion of this work, to enter into further particulars respecting these relics of ancient Germany.

Dr. Dibdin describes a fine manuscript, in the Imperial Library of Vienna, in six folio volumes, which contains, on the authority of M. Kopitar, one of the most ancient German versions of the Bible extant, which was written in the fourteenth century for the Emperor Wenceslaus[2]. He also describes a curious history of the Bible, in German verse, written in 1381, contained in the public Library of Stuttgart[3].

The first printed German version of the Bible, translated from the Latin Vulgate, appeared in 1466; but the author is unknown, and it is now extremely rare. A Lower Saxon version, also from the Vulgate, was printed at Lubeck in 1494, of both which works an account will be found in Dibdin's Bibliotheca Spenceriana. The first portion of Luther's versions appeared in 1517[4].

The manuscript before us is written in the character known under the name of Modern Gothic, to distinguish it from the writing of the ancient Goths, of which the Gospels of Ulphilas, still preserved at Upsal, offer a specimen. The modern Gothic was adopted in Germany as early as the ninth or tenth century, according to Astle[5], although it did not prevail in other parts of Europe till the twelfth or thirteenth. It appears to me to have originated[6] at first in a desire to write the minuscule letters without the top and bottom curves (in order, in fact, to keep these small letters distinct from each other); for we find the earliest modern Gothic writing with many of the strokes straight at the bottom, where they are merely obliquely cut off; by degrees, however, the angulated character was more univérsally adopted, the gradations from the old Roman prototypes of the letters being easily traced. In the fourteenth, fifteenth, and sixteenth centuries, we find the modern Gothic letters gradually assuming their most elaborate and perfect form. Such is the style which is often called Old English Text, a very improper denomination, as the character prevailed over most of Europe.

And here I may be allowed to make an observation, which I have nowhere met with, upon the simultaneous development of this character with that peculiar style of architecture which prevailed after the Norman period, and which is, with equal impropriety, known by the name of the Gothic[7].

---

[1] A friend, recently returned from Germany, informs me that a most beautiful statue of St. Boniface has been erected during the present year in the Great Square at Fulda.

[2] Bibl. Tour, iii. p. 290.

[3] Ibid. iii. p. 30.

[4] Horne, Introduction, vol. ii. part 11, pp. 88, 89.

[5] Origin of Writing, p. 147. It is, of course, very difficult to draw the line of distinction between two styles of writing, which so gradually blend together as the Roman minuscule and early modern Gothic; but I think Mr. Astle has at least by two centuries antedated the German origin of the latter, or rather that he has regarded as modern Gothic the writing in MSS. of the ninth or tenth century, which have a far greater resemblance to Caroline or Roman minuscule than to the

real angulated modern Gothic. For instance, the Autograph Evangelistiarium of St. Udalrich of Augsburgh (copied by Sylvestre in his 8th Livraison), written in the 10th century, and the Theotisque Gospels of the Cottonian Library (Calig. A. 7); which last Astle himself copies as the first specimen in his plate of Modern Gothic Writing, are much nearer to Caroline minuscule than to modern Gothic.

[6] The reader who would seek a much more detailed notice of the origin, progress, and decline of modern Gothic writing must consult the 2nd volume of the Nouv. Traité de Dipl. pp. 658—666.

[7] Hence will be seen the impropriety of introducing into modern churches, built in the Norman or early English style, texts of Scripture, written in florid modern Gothic characters. Recent instances of this might, however, be pointed out.

2

The introduction of this term *Gothic*, as applied both to architecture and writing, is alike. As to the former, " it originates with the Italian writers of the fourteenth and fifteenth centuries, who applied the expression of *La maniera Gotica*, in contempt[1] to all the works of art of the middle ages. From these writers it was borrowed by Sir Christopher Wren, the first English writer who has applied it to English architecture[2]." " It has been well conjectured," observes another author[3], " by several eminent antiquarians, that it (the term Gothic) was applied solely for the purpose of casting an opprobrious epithet on it, at the period of introducing the Greek or Roman style into this country ; and where the ancient religion was to be exploded, so also was the ancient style of its sacred edifices."

" Whether they," (the writers upon architecture of the seventeenth century, who used the term Gothic), " had then a retrospect to those particular times, when the Goths ruled in the empire, or only used it as a term of reproach to stigmatise the productions of ignorant and barbarous times, is not certain[4]."

As applied to writing, the Benedictines state that the term Gothic, " ne lui fut point donnée ni dès le tems de sa naissance, ni lors même qu'il exerçoit une tyrannie absolue, sur presque toutes les écritures de l'Europe. On croyoit alors voir des agrémens et des beautés qu'on n'apercevoit plus dans la noble simplicité des caractères antiques. Mais à proportion que le goût de la belle littérature reprit ses anciens droits, on se passionna pour les vraies lettres *latines*, et l'on traita de *gothiques* celles qui s'en étoient écartées. Sous la plume des premiers restaurateurs des belles lettres, les caractères qu'ils trouvèrent en usage furent déclarés gothiques. Et *comme ils ne pouvoient les attribuer aux anciens Romains, ils les mirent sur le compte des Goths qui avoient renversé leur empire[5]*."

The impropriety of the term *Gothic* has accordingly led to the suggestion of others. By some the term Saracenic, Pointed, Norman, and English have been severally employed to distinguish the architecture of the fourteenth and fifteenth centuries, whilst others have styled them Monkish[6], just as the modern Gothic characters have been named " Monacales[7]," by some French writers, and " Monkish English," by Astle[8].

How far the two arts of Gothic architecture and modern Gothic writing may have exerted an influence upon each other, is, perhaps, unnecessary to inquire ; but the fate of both has been identical.

Respecting the former, Sir Christopher Wren observes, that, " about 200 years ago, when ingenious men began to reform the Roman language to the purity which they assigned and fixed to the time of Augustus and that century, the architects also, ashamed of the modern barbarity of building, began to examine carefully the ruins of old Rome and Italy, to search into the orders and proportions, and to establish them by inviolable rules.[9]" And a more recent author observes, " Imagination seems, after its establishment, to have been tortured to invent new combinations of ornaments and tracery. It overstepped at length the true bounds of architecture, and was abandoned in the sixteenth century for the introduction and restoration of Roman, or more properly speaking, Italian architecture[10]."

In like manner, of manuscripts written in modern Gothic characters, the Benedictine authors of the incomparable Nouveau Traité de Diplomatique, thus express themselves[11] :—

" La plupart de ceux de XIVe et XVe siècles sont misérables. L'écriture en est serrée, compliquée, hérissée d'angles, de pans, de pointes et de crochets, non moins ridicules qu'inutiles[12]. La cessation presque totale des études et des copistes, dans les monastères où l'on n'entendoit rien aux questions embarrassées et aux vaines subtilités, que les scholastiques avoient mises à la mode ; les abréviations arbitraires et inintelligibles de ceux-ci, l'invention du papier de chiffe au XIIIe siècle, le mauvais goût qui régnoit alors, tout cela a été cause qu'il ne nous reste de ces tems barbares qu'une multitude de MSS. horriblement laids——La difficulté de lire et de peindre le gothique fut une des causes de l'ignorance prodigieuse de la noblesse de ces tems-là, où les plus grands seigneurs pour la plupart ne savoient ni lire ni écrire ;" whilst of the variations adopted in this style of writing, it is affirmed by the Benedictines, that they " vont toujours de mal en pis *jusqu'à ce que le renou-*

---

[1] Ought we not rather to say, in ignorance of the real history, both of the Goths themselves and of early Architecture.

[2] Archæologia, vol. xii.

[3] Essays on Gothic Architecture, p. viii.

[4] Bentham, Hist. Cathedr. Church of Ely, Sect. v.

[5] N. Tr. de Dipl. ii. 659. [6] Evelyn's Account of Architectures.

[7] " Parce que les moines en ont fait un fréquent usage. Mais n'employèrent-ils pas encore plus souvent les beaux caractères ; surtout jusqu'au commencement du XIIIe siècle ?" demand the Benedictines, N. Tr. De Depl. iii. 203.

[8] Origin of Writing, pp. 148, 149.

[9] Wren's Parentalia, p. 306.

[10] Brande's Dictionary of Science, p. 79.

[11] Vol. iii. p. 394.

[12] Abbot Godefroy de Bessel of Godwic describes it as " Ingens litterarum sibi connexarum involutarumque Chaos."

vellement de lettres ait reveillé le goût des beaux caractères;" that is, as they are described in another place by the same writers, the " beaux et anciens caractères romains, renouvellés d'abord en Italie puis en France, ensuite dans les autres royaumes, où l'écriture latine avoit cours[1]." " En Italie dès l'an 1430 le bon goût des anciens siècles romains s'étoit renouvellé par rapport à l'écriture, comme par rapport aux beaux arts[2]." Whilst, however, this style has been rejected by most of the countries of Europe, it is remarkable that it is still retained in Germany, where, as we have seen, it (as well as the Gothic style of architecture[3]) first flourished ; in which country not only are modern works in the native language, printed in these characters, but a cursive Gothic, perfectly illegible to the rest of Europe, is ordinarily employed in correspondence, the writers considering it almost as unconstitutional to use other characters as to speak another language, and regarding the former as truly national as the latter.

It is evidently on this account that the term German Text has been applied to this kind of writing. Its origin, however, in that country is far more recent than the German language ; and, indeed, the claim of the Germans to it is denied by the Benedictines, who assert that if the Germans have remained attached to it " plus long-tems que presque toutes les nations d'Europe ; il ne seroit pas difficile de prouver, que loin d'en être les auteurs, ils s'en préservoient encore, ou que du moins ils n'en étoient pas totalement infectés, tandis qu'il dominoit paisiblement chez leurs voisins. Il ne seroit donc pas juste de leur imputer en particulier *une écriture odieuse,* qui leur fut long tems commune avec tant d'autres peuples[4]."

I have dwelt upon the preceding parallel with the view of showing what have been the opinions of men fully qualified to judge on such subjects, and of raising a warning voice (slight though it may be), against the revival, in the construction and adornment of modern temples devoted to the service of the Protestant Church of this country, of those Gothicisms which prevailed during the most extended reign of, and which are so appropriate to and symbolical of, the rites of the Roman Catholic religion ; but which, at the same time, are so entirely opposed to the genius of Protestantism. Almost prophetically indeed spake the Benedictines, when they exclaimed, " Heureux si nous ne voyons pas un jour les restes du Gothique, qui la déshonorent, reprendre le dessus et causer une révolution dont nous croyons apercevoir les préludes[5] ! "

---

[1] N. Tr. de Dipl. ii. p. 664.
[2] Biblioth. Univers. de la Polygr. Espanol. Prolog. fol. xiv.
[3] " It appears incontrovertible that the Germans were the first to carry this style of architecture to its highest perfection."—BRANDE's Dict. p. 79.
[4] N. Tr. de Dipl. ii. p. 533.
[5] N. Tr. de Dipl. ii. 534.

P.S. Since the above was written, I have discovered that the parallel between Gothic architecture and writing had been slightly alluded to by the Marquis Maffei[1], who states that the changes adopted in the former were effected on the same principles as those which were produced in the latter; in fact, he even asserts that Gothic writing rather gave the tone to architecture than took it from it. The Benedictines also seem to have had the same parallel in view when they state of modern Gothic writing that " au XIVe siècle ses excès, pour ne pas dire ses extravagances, furent portés à leur comble *en écriture comme en architecture[2].*"

---

[1] Verona Illustrata, col. 355.
[2] N. Tr. de Dipl. ii. 531.

Icelandic, Hungarian & Bohemian Mss

MŒSOGOTHIC, ICELANDIC, HUNGARIAN, AND BOHEMIAN MSS.

MŒSOGOTHIC MANUSCRIPTS.

THE epithet Mœsogothic has been applied to that particular national species of writing employed by the Gothic tribes, who were established in Mœsia and Wallachia (having been conquered by the Huns) in the 4th century, under the Emperor Valens. Amongst these hordes, as we learn from Socrates, a Greek ecclesiastical writer of the 5th century, and other Byzantine authors, Ulphilas, who assisted at the Council of Constantinople in 359, and had been carried away by them from Cappadocia, was elected bishop, and translated the Bible into the language of his conquerors, inventing also for them (as generally affirmed) a new alphabet (founded indeed upon that of the Greeks), and which has thence been called the alphabet of Ulphilas.[1] Ascholius, Bishop of Thessalonica, towards the middle of the 3rd century, and Audius, a Greek priest, also assisted in spreading Christianity among the Goths. The former is extolled by Basil the Great, and the latter by Epiphanius.[2]

Of this version of the Bible there were considered to exist, until very recently, only two fragments, namely, the Codex Argenteus, and the Codex Carolinus, the latter in the library of Brunswick Wolfenbuttel. The former of these MSS., written on violet-coloured vellum, in gold and silver letters, contains a considerable portion (more than 160 leaves) of the four Gospels, written in large uncial letters, very similar in general appearance to the most ancient and finest Greek MSS. It was first discovered in the Abbey of Werden, near Dusseldorf, in Westphalia, and, after several migrations, is now preserved in the library of Upsal. The cover of the volume is of embossed silver, and, from the character of the writing, it has been supposed by some

---

[1] The invention of the Gothic alphabet by Ulphilas is denied by some writers (Hickes, Astle, &c.). Hickes also positively disallows the Upsal MS. to be written in the translation of Ulphilas, asserting it to have been made by some Teuton or German, as old, or even older than Ulphilas.

[2] Mason's Hist. Anc. Germ., Vol. 1, 383, and 2, p. 412.

critics to have been printed with some kind of moveable type; but this opinion, it seems, is now fully disproved.[1]

The text of this MS. was first published by the celebrated Junius, in 1665, at Dordrecht; again by Stiernhelm, at Stockholm, in 1671, and thirdly, with great additions and corrections, (including a revision of the entire MS. by Benzel, Archbishop of Upsal), by E. Lye, at Oxford, in 1750. Ihre published two small essays upon the subject, entitled Ulphilas Illustratus, in 1752 and 1755; Hickes published a fac-simile in his Thesaurus, vol. i., p. 8; and the Gospel of St. Matthew was also published by Henshall in 1807.

The woodcut at the head of this article will give an idea of the characters of the text of the Codex Argenteus. The three upper lines represent the 24th verse of the 11th chapter of St. Matthew's Gospel.

[Swe] THAUH CWITHA IZIUS THATEI AIRTHAI SAUDAMGE SUTIZO WAIRTHITH IN DAGA STAUOS THAT THUS[2]:— (TRULY I SAY TO YOU THAT FOR THE EARTH OF SODOM BETTER IT SHALL BE IN THE DAY OF JUDGMENT THAN FOR YOU).

The words cwitha, (for *quoth*,) airthai, (earth,) daga, (day,) barn, (bairn, a child,) &c., in this MS., prove the near affinity of its language to the ancient Theotisc and Anglo-Saxon. Indeed, Procopius, in the 6th century, and, still more positively, Walafrid Strabo, in the 9th, assert that the Goths, who dwelt in the provinces of Greece when converted to Christianity, used the Theotisc language, and had the Scriptures translated into their own language, of which copies were still in existence; which seems sufficiently to disprove Hickes's objection above referred to.

The fourth line is the alphabet copied from this MS., arranged as follows:—A, B, G, (or GH,) D, E, F, J, (G or Y,) H, I, K, L, M, N, O, P, Q, (Quh or Wh,) R, S, T, T-H, U, C-W, (C-U, and sometimes C in the middle of words,) W, (and upsilon,) C-H, (or X or K-H,) and Z.

With very few exceptions, these letters accord with those of the Greek, the few additional ones being requisite for the expression of sounds in the Mœsogothic language, of which there are no Greek analogues.

The u has the form of ɴ minuscule; the th is evidently the Greek φ; the ʀ is like κ; the cw like ʋ; and the ᴊ like an ill-formed ɢ.

The ornamental arcades, in the woodcut, contain the references to the parallel passages in the different Gospels, arranged thus—St. Matthew, St. John, St. Luke, and St. Mark; whose names are inscribed (but abbreviated) in golden letters, beneath the four widest arches at the foot of each page: the specimen before us indicating that

$$\left.\begin{array}{c} \text{MTH} \\ 109 \\ 110 \end{array}\right\} \quad \text{corresponds with} \quad \left\{\begin{array}{c} \text{Luk} \\ 112 \,; \end{array}\right.$$

there being no parallel passage in Sts. John and Mark. The numbers are those of the sections, the division into chapters and verses not having been made at the time when this MS. was written.

In 1756 Knittel discovered, in a Codex rescriptus belonging to the library of the Duke of Brunswick, at Wolfenbuttel, some fragments of St. Paul's Epistle to the Romans, of the same version as the preceding. These he published in 1762, which were reprinted in 1763, with notes, at Upsal, by Ihre, whose dissertations, with additions, were republished at Berlin in 1773, and a subsequent treatise on the subject of these Ulphilas MSS., by Fulda, Reinwald and Zahn, at Weissenfels, in 1805.

These two MSS. were indeed the only known proofs even of the existence of the Mœsogothic language and characters, until the celebrated Cardinal Angelo Maï, in 1817, discovered five additional Mœsogothic MSS. in the Ambrosian Library of Milan, and subsequently another in the Vatican, MS. No. 5750. These MSS. were palimpsests, the original text having been nearly erased, and the vellum re-employed for later Latin compositions. By the care of Monseigneur Maï, assisted by M. Castillionei, these invaluable fragments have been restored.

The first of the Ambrosian palimpsest MSS. (S. 36) contains 204 pages of vellum, and the Gothic writing comprises most of St. Paul's Epistles, and a fragment of the Gothic Calendar; the second (S. 45) contains 156 pages, and consists of another copy of a great part of the Pauline Epistles; the third (G. 82) contains fragments of the Books of Kings, Ezra and Nehemiah, being the only parts of the Old Testament known to be in existence; the fourth (I. 61) consists of a single leaf, apparently of the Codex Argenteus, being some of the

[1] N. Tr. de Dipl. IV., pref. p. V., and following: Coxe's Travels in Russia, &c.: Dr. E. D. Clarke's Travels, Vol. VI.
[2] The fac-simile published by Horne, (Introd. 2, 241,) and affirmed by him to be the most correct then known to be extant, represents all the words as written apart from each other, and the letters as much more slender than in Ihre's fac-similes.

wanting chapters of St. Matthew; and the fifth (G, 147) consists of a Mœsogothic Homily, rich in Biblical quotations.

These fragments, as well as the Codex Argenteus, are referred by Maï and Castillionei [1] to the 6th century, when the Goths invaded Italy.

A fac-simile of the Vatican MS. is given by Silvestre.

ICELANDIC MANUSCRIPTS.

The history of the Church of Ireland informs us, that missionaries from that country visited Iceland at an early period [2]. Subsequently, in 861, it was discovered by the Northmen; who altered its previously aristocratic government into a republic. With this change, a change probably took place in the language of the country, which thenceforth became one of the numerous branches of the ancient Teutonic root of that portion of the Scandinavian genus termed Normanno-Gothic. How far the employment of Runic letters had been general, is not easy to determine; but with the introduction of Christianity, the Roman alphabet was also introduced; but it became slightly modified in some of its elements, in order to suit it for the expression of native sounds foreign to the Roman language. We find, in fact, even in the short extract in our plate, letters perfectly similar to those introduced by the Anglo-Saxons into the alphabet, which have engaged our attention in former pages of this work; namely, the real Runic letters wen (ρ=w), thorn (þ=th), and that (ð=that); and these we find in use up to the period when the MS. before us was written, which was most probably towards the end of the fifteenth century, if not still more recent. This MS. is preserved amongst the Additional MSS. in the British Museum, No. 503. It is a missal, of a small folio size, written on paper, with large rudish-painted capitals and musical notes. The three lines at the head of the plate are part of " Gudspiallid Skaifar Sanctus Johanis," commencing, " I than tyma Jesus sagde til sina lærisueina, &c.; [3]" followed by the rubric, " A Himta Sunnu Dag skal fyrst syngia Veni Sancte Spiritus;" the hymn itself (Veni Sancte Spiritus, mentes tuorum visita, &c.), commencing, " Kom thu gode heilage ande fyllupp hiorttu thina," &c., closely resembling the German and Anglo-Saxon, and forming part of the service for Whit Sunday. The whole of the Breviary is thus translated into the native tongue; and remembering the ancient fame of the Scalds, and the existence of literature in Iceland from a very early period, it is interesting to see that music and poetry were still cherished. The MS. is written in a slightly angulated modern Gothic character, and the capitals are ornamented in the style of the twelfth century—probably copied from some European MS. of that date.

Dr. Henderson, in his Historical View of the Translation and different Editions of the Icelandic Scriptures, contained in his " Journal of a Residence in Iceland during 1814, 1815 " (Edinb. 1818, 8vo; vol. ii., pp. 249, 306), has shown that during the sixteenth century several translations of the Bible and Gospels were made under the patronage of the reigning kings, Christian III. and Frederic II. [4]

The British Museum is rich in Icelandic MSS., but the one before us is the only theological one in the national collection.

HUNGARIAN MANUSCRIPTS.

The Onigours and Madjars, originally natives of Tartary, established themselves, about the end of the ninth century, in ancient Pannonia and Dacia, bringing with them their language, which is arranged by philologists in the Ouralian or Finnish family. The Duke of Geisa was the first to demand to be baptised, and his son Stephen rendered the institution general throughout his country, of which he was elected King, and his regal authority confirmed by Pope Silvester II. Here, as elsewhere, the Latin language consequently became the vehicle of all documents of State and Religion, and hence there are but very few existing ancient documents written in the native tongue. Indeed, it was not until the last century that the Emperor Francis I. authorised the use of the mother-tongue in all State documents. Still, however, the introduction of the Christian religion rendered necessary a knowledge of the sacred Scriptures; and we accordingly find that the

[1] Ulphilæ partium ineditarum in Ambrosianis palimpsestis ab Ang. Maio repert. Mediol. 1819, 4to; and Ulphilæ Gothica Versio Epist. D. Pauli ad Corinthos II., ed. C. O. Castillionæus. Mediol. 1829, 4to.

[2] Cons. Lanigan, Eccl. Hist. of Ireland, iii., p. 220; Johannæus, Hist. Eccles. Island. Havn. 4to, 1772; O'Conor, Epist. Nuncup., pp.

26, 28; Johnstone's Antiq. Celto-Scand., pp. 19, 20, 157; Thorkelin's Fragments, pref., p. 10.

[3] Which is to be translated "At that time Jesus said to his disciples—"

[4] See also Le Long Bibl. Sacra, cap. 12, § 1; and Epist. de Bibl. Elianis, ann. 1604, Norimberg.

only three manuscripts in this language, discovered by M. Silvestre in the libraries of Pesth, Vienna, and Munich, are theological. One of these, in the Royal Library of Vienna (No. 3458, R. 81), contains an Hungarian version of the Bible, written in the fourteenth century (from which the fac-simile in our plate No. 2 has been copied), in a modern Gothic cursive character, as Champollion well remarks, " dans son état le plus tourmenté et le plus éloigné des belles formes latines ; " the figure of the Trumpeter added to one of the initial letters, giving " un peu de grotesque à toutes ces difformités." The text is from the Book of Judges, the proper names Israel, Juda, Jeroboam, Ozyas, and Joab, having the initial letter daubed with red paint. The initial D is copied from a series of capitals from this MS., given by Silvestre. Another of M. Silvestre's fac-similes is from an Evangeliarium, written in the year 1466, in Moldavia; Louis I., King of Hungary, having united that country to his own about that period. The ornamental details of this MS., which is written upon paper, are entirely destitute of good taste, as may be perceived in the small portion copied at the right-hand side of our plate. M. Silvestre's third fac-simile is from a MS. in the National Museum of Pesth, containing a series of sermons, " Super sepulchrum ; " but I do not find any description of this plate given in the text. The fac-simile is destitute of ornament, with small plain red capitals ; and it is indicated on the plate as being of the twelfth century.

BOHEMIAN MANUSCRIPTS.

About the middle of the fourth century Bohemia (so named from the Boii, a Celtic nation who had long previously established themselves there) enjoyed a settled and quiet government under its own duke ; but about the middle of the sixth century it was conquered by Sclavonians from the shores of the Black Sea, whose names Czechowe and Tschechen are still employed by the modern Bohemians as their own name. By Charlemagne the country was again put under tribute, although its government was not altered until the eleventh century, when it was raised to the rank of a kingdom. The Czechish or Bohemian language was the first of the Sclavonic idioms which was cultivated scientifically. It is spoken, with slight variations, in Bohemia, Moravia, Silesia, part of Hungary, and Sclavonia ; it affords, nevertheless, no written documents of remote antiquity, although it is certain that the language of the period previous to the introduction of Christianity was similar to the present, from the names of gods, rulers, cities, rivers, &c.

The Christian religion penetrated about the middle of the ninth century into Bohemia, under Duke Boriwog, when the inhabitants received the Græco-Sclavonian ritual, the Cyrillo-Sclavonian characters being employed ; but when the Latin Church supplanted the Greek (the prevailing religion at the present time being the Roman Catholic), the Latin alphabet also came into use, and as the Latins endeavoured to annihilate all the writings of the old ritual [1], and the Czechish language was in many cases obliged to give way to the Latin, Bohemian literature suffered incalculable injury. Hence, from the earlier centuries, we possess but a few insignificant relics in the characters above mentioned. Indeed, we find no specimen of Bohemian MSS. in M. Silvestre's great work. In the tenth century the Bohemians had a school at Kudet, in which they learnt Latin. Their most ancient relic is the hymn (Hospodine Pomiluyny) of Bishop Adalbert, which is sung to the present time by the natives, and even by the Russians and Poles, and which is considered by some to be of still greater antiquity. A few sheets and strips of parchment were discovered by Hanka, the keeper of the Bohemian National Museum, in a room in a church in Koniginhof, apparently written at the end of the thirteenth century, containing some fragments of a series of national songs without rhyme, and which Goethe considered worthy of particular attention ; a Bohemian Psalter and a legend in rhyme on the twelve Apostles (the latter a fragment only, at Vienna) ; a fragment of a History of the Passion of the Saviour ; the hymn Swaty Waclawe and some poems have also been preserved of the fourteenth century, during which period the University of Prague was founded.

The first Bohemian translation of the Bible was made and published at Prague in 1488, from the Latin Vulgate ; another was made towards the end of the sixteenth century, for the use of the Protestants in Bohemia. The Bodleian Library possesses a beautiful MS. of the New Testament, written in 1518 upon paper, which has supplied our fac-simile No. 3. The text is written in a strong but wretched modern Gothic character ; the initials and marginal ornaments are, however, executed with great elegance, resembling those introduced into the early printed German Bibles of Fust and Schoeffer.

---

[1] Thousands of MSS. were also destroyed in the seventeenth century by the monks, then newly introduced into Bohemia.

Alanzelo de lagiexia de claodia scriui ꞇ ui comenza la septima epľa/c/dixe
alanguolo q̃sto che segue ꞇ Questo dixe la uerita de testimonio fidele c/uero.

el pouolo de israel

maria sorore
de moyses e de
Aaron :~

iosue

Lonono comandamento. No desiderare la chasa del to proximo ne debi desiderare alguna altra soa cossa immobele
Lo decimo comandamento. No desiderare la moyere del to proximo/e no desiderare
elso seruo/la soa/ancilla/la soa piegora/el so bo/et elso aseno. E no desiderare alguna
cossa che sea del to proximo.

Italian MSS. of the 14th. Century.

ITALIAN MANUSCRIPTS OF HIS LATE ROYAL HIGHNESS THE DUKE OF SUSSEX.

EXPLANATION OF THE PLATE.

The upper portion is an extract from the Apocalypse, Chap. iii. v. 7. Et al'angelo, &c. The drawings represent the sister of Moses and the women of Israel rejoicing at the overthrow of Pharaoh ; and one of the captive kings brought before Joshua. The text in the lower part of the Plate, is the tenth Commandment divided into two ; the first and second Commandments being united together as usual in the writings of the Roman Catholic Church.

THE manuscript from which the lower subjects in the accompanying plate is taken, contains a series of drawings of the historical events recorded in the Old Testament, beginning with the Israelites in bondage in Egypt, and terminating at the 519th miniature, with the Burial of Joseph ; each drawing being accompanied by descriptive text in old Italian, written at the top and bottom, and in the middle of the page. They are drawn upon 85 leaves, of vellum, 13 inches by 9½, each page having generally four miniatures, each measuring 4 inches by 3¾ ; some, however, occupy half the page, and there are five which severally take up the entire page ; to many of the figures the names are attached. These miniatures are freely drawn with a pen, and the colours washed in with considerable vigour. " In the type, as well as in the whole cast, there appears a strong influence of the school of Giotto, in the manner, however, in which it appeared about the year 1400 [1]." This is probably nearly the correct date of the volume, for whilst the late Mr. Ottley, as I learn from Mr. Pettigrew, was of opinion that the miniatures are not later than 1360 or 1370, Sir S. R. Meyrick referred them to 1420. In many of the subjects, we perceive a recurrence to a peculiar classical style, as for instance in the figure of the sister of Moses. copied in my plate, as also in the fourth and eighteenth subjects ; the first of which represents a marriage ceremony. In many places we see God the Father speaking out of a cloud, just as he is represented in the old Mosaics of Italy. Elsewhere, he appears as a middle-aged man, with a short beard and moustaches, his hair parted over the forehead, and with the fore-finger of his left hand extended. The following subjects are also treated in a manner worthy of notice :—

The plagues of Frogs, Flies, Lice, and Grasshoppers are very curious, whilst the overthrow of the Egyptians in the Red Sea, with the Israelites on the shore, is quite primitive in its style ; the sea being a great green patch, occupying half the picture. (No 68.)

Aaron standing beneath a beautiful arch, is interesting, from his being crowned with a *triple* diadem. (No. 126.)

Moses and the Heads of the Twelve Tribes ; and the Oxen drawing Wagons, (No. 169) ; as well as the Israelites viewing the Promised Land, (four turreted castles, surrounded by moats !) No. 219 ; respectively occupy half a page.

Moses and his Army clad in Armour, entering into Esebon over the moat, is very spiritedly drawn, (No. 262.)

Others are equally interesting as affording delineations of the dresses, manners, and armour of the Italians at the close of the fourteenth century ; such are especially No. 307 ; a party seated at table, beneath a trellis of vines ; and various groups of citizens, females, and warriors, from which I have selected the two in the accompanying Plate.

The first of these (No. 69), is thus described :—

" Como Maria Prophetissa sorore de Moyses e de Aaron, sonava per alegreça un timpano, e si ondaua cantando spiritualmente devanco da tute le femene del pouolo de Israel laldando dio che li aveva libera de le man del re pharaon e che lo aveva mega in lo mare rosso pharaon cum tuto el so exercito."

In this spirited group, we see the general features of Italian citizens of the middle ages ; the hinder figures are especially characteristic ; the old nobleman, with the hooded nun, portly abbot, and bearded monk, can all

---

[1] Waagen. Art and Artists in England, II. p. 37.

be at once fixed upon; whilst the figures of the sister of Moses, the mother and baby, and the half-grown girl, are even classically designed.

The other miniature (No. 428), inscribed:—

"Como el Re de la Cita de hay vene a presenta liga e prexo devanco a Josue,"

and shows us the form of the armour in use among the Italians at the period of the execution of the volume; in which respect, as we learn from Sir S. R. Meyrick's notes communicated to Mr. Pettigrew, the present MS. is especially valuable to the Archæologist.

The following observations by this first-rate authority upon everything connected with ancient armour, will be considered interesting. They are incorporated by Mr. Pettigrew, in his description of the volume:—

When it is remembered that the MS. is Italian, and that the fashions, generally speaking, arose in Italy, and travelled through Germany and France to England, it may, perhaps, be allowed to be twenty-five years older than Lydgate's Life of St. Edmund, in the Harleian Collection (No. 2278). Many fashions prevalent in the time of Richard II. and Henry IV., as the Capuchon à la queue, the escalopped sleeves, &c., besides the form of the armour, are here delineated; but others are introduced which were not known in England until the middle or latter end of the fifteenth century.

The total absence of the vizored salade, which, though of German origin, was worn by the military of Europe throughout the reign of Henry VI., chiefly guided Sir S. R. Meyrick in his decision as to the date of this MS. In some of the figures the ventail is attached to the basinet, but the figures do not wear the knight's military belt of the reign of Henry VI. Others have basinets without the ventail, and sometimes they are ornamented with feathers. The infantry are armed with the ordinary salade, and with a glaive, and trumpets like those of the time of Edward III., but they are used with hoods and pendant sleeves, as in the time of Henry IV. The Turks (for the enemies of the Israelites are so represented) are armed with bows and arrows, and sometimes with scimetars and straight swords. The MS. also affords the earliest instance of lamboys made of steel, instead of cloth, as they may be actually seen in the Tower of London. In the illuminations of Louis XII., given by Montfaucon (Mon. Fr. &c.), the same occurs; but the rest of the armour in this MS. is of the date of 1420, whereas, in the instances quoted, the square toes, &c., are of the close of the fifteenth, or beginning of the sixteenth century. We have thus here an authority for the invention 80 or 90, if not more than 100, years earlier than previously known. The lamboys are open in front, for convenience in riding, as in Henry the Seventh's armour. The jupon is laced all the way down in front, or at the side, as in many monumental effigies of the time of Edward III., and in the jupon of the Black Prince, still preserved a Canterbury. Joshua wears epaulettes corresponding with the lamboys, and bears a mace. In some the armour is worn without the sollarets, and consequently exposes the black shoes. The basinets, in some, have coverings for the cheeks, which look as if suggested by some ancient Greek helmet. The dagger and sword, in some, are worn low down; and the ordinary salade, or helmet, is in some pointed at the top. Oval shields, and a buckler, a pointed shield with the cushion placed longwise instead of across, kite-shaped and oblong pavois, gis-arms, pole-axes, and martels-de-fer, appear in various of the drawings.

The architecture in several of the drawings, especially No. 291, corroborates the date assigned to this MS., although in No. 4 it appears of the Norman character.

The upper portion of the plate represents an elegant initial E, illuminated in the style which was very prevalent in Italy in the fifteenth century, and which is taken from a folio volume of an exposition of the Apocalypse, by Nicolao de Lyra. The capitals are very variously ornamented, and the text is written in a small kind of Roman-Gothic character. The specimen is to be read—"Et al angelo de la grexia de claodia scrivi. Qui comenza la septima epistola(e) dixe al angielo questo che segue. Questo dixe la veritade de testimonio fidele e vero."—Revel. iii. v. 7.

At the end of the volume is written—"Explicit la vulgar exposition sopra l'apocalipsi de sco Johane applō evangelista ōpilada et ordinada p̄ frate frederigo da Vinecia del ordine di p'dichatori magro de la sancta theologia.

"Questi glose over exposition sono de magrc Nicolo da Lira del ordine de frati minori e de li altri comendatori ch'ano comendato sopra lapochalipsi."

Another note states it to have been copied "p̄ me Bardo di Mazi da bressa," to the honour of the most high God and the most holy St. John; and that "Āno dni ōpleta fuit hoc opus existēteï pictura civitatis Urbini anno 1456, Diei 8 Octobris."

2   THE END.